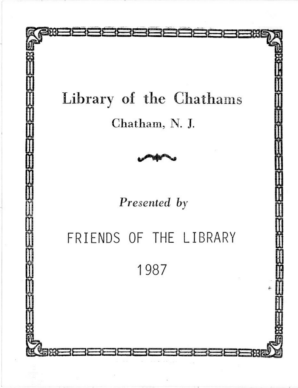

ARE WE TO BE A NATION?

PUBLISHED IN COOPERATION WITH THE NEW YORK PUBLIC LIBRARY

ARE WE TO BE A NATION?

The Making of the Constitution

RICHARD B. BERNSTEIN *with Kym S. Rice*

HARVARD UNIVERSITY PRESS

CAMBRIDGE, MASSACHUSETTS, AND LONDON, ENGLAND

Copyright © 1987 by The New York Public Library
Printed in the United States of America
10 9 8 7 6 5 4 3 2

This book is printed on acid-free paper, and its binding materials
have been chosen for strength and durability.

Set in Linotron Baskerville and designed by Marianne Perlak

Library of Congress Cataloging-in-Publication Data
Bernstein, Richard B., 1956–
    Are we to be a nation?

    Bibliography: p.
    Includes index.
        1. United States. Constitutional Convention (1787)
    2. United States—Constitutional history. I. Rice, Kym S.
    II. Title.
    KF4520.B47   1987   342.73'029   86-19590
    ISBN 0-674-04475-4 (alk. paper) 347.30229
    ISBN 0-674-04476-2 (pbk. : alk. paper)

This book is for my parents, Fred and Marilyn Bernstein

CONTENTS

FOREWORD

W<small>HEN IN</small> May 1784 John Adams warned that "Our Country" was "not yet out of danger," he was, in uncharacteristic fashion, understating the perils confronting the people of the United States. Possessed of a vast expanse of territory by virtue of the victorious peace of 1783 with Great Britain, the people of the thirteen states had no assurance that they could keep their hard-won independence, create a sense of national identity as Americans, reinvigorate a seriously weakened postwar economy, and promote a durable union.

It is these grand themes that Richard B. Bernstein addresses. Political and cultural leaders of a nationalist bent recognized the need to "Americanize" the national culture and endow the central government with energy. Others, less cosmopolitan in outlook but equally concerned about perpetuating the spirit and goals of the American Revolution, were fearful that a leviathan state would undermine republican virtue, weaken the individual states, and endanger personal liberties.

Thus the framing of the Constitution of the United States two centuries ago posed a profound political and intellectual challenge, to which a group of exceptionally gifted statesmen responded. Bookish and scholarly but not reclusive, they were articulate activists who drew on contemporary experience, political theory, and history, both ancient and modern, to create a charter "for posterity" that has functioned longer than any other written constitution of the modern world.

Are We to Be a Nation? accords us a view of the emergence of nationhood, one possessing both great breadth and unusual depth. In analyzing the range of intellectual sources upon which the Founding Fathers drew, Richard Bernstein has drawn heavily on the rich resources of The New York Public Library, which, in preparing its bicentennial exhibition of the framing and ratification of the Constitution, has assembled not only its own exceptional treasures in Americana but also many uniquely representative manuscripts, books, pamphlets, and illustrative materials from other libraries and archival sources worldwide. Bernstein elaborates the significance of the framers' intellectual milieu. Many were classicists, steeped in Cicero, Vergil, Horace, Suetonius, and Seneca and familiar with the notable figures of ancient history extolled by Plutarch. They knew their Machiavelli, Harrington and Locke, Montesquieu, the English radical literature emanating from the days of Cromwell, and the Scottish philosophers, like Hume and Robertson. They wrote their public letters and pamphlets with the literary models of Addison and Steele in mind. Because most of them had been trained in the law, they were familiar with Coke and Blackstone, as well as with international jurists of the stature of Grotius, Pufendorf, and Vattel. As a result, the delegates at the Convention could discourse learnedly about the structure of confederacies and republics, both ancient and modern, their strengths and their weaknesses, and their dissimilarities to the union that was now being forged. But Richard Bernstein shows that the framers of the Constitution were also remarkably innovative; though respectful of European theorists, they drew heavily on the American experience with colonial charters, plans of union, state constitutions, and the Articles of Confederation. Gifted and informed men such as Franklin, Jefferson, and John Adams ably defended their deviations from what some European *philosophes* regarded as proper models for the new republic, and Bernstein discusses perceptively the ensuing polemical exchange between the Old and New Worlds.

Drawing upon the writings of James Madison and his Anti-Federal counterparts and on the latest scholarship, Richard Bernstein reveals a burgeoning sense of national crisis spurred by economic distress, diplomatic futility, and events such as the Annapolis Convention and Shays's Rebellion. He provides fresh perspectives on the Federal Convention, the battle over ratification, and the establishment of the national government and incisively analyzes the triumphant achievements of the initial years of the Washington administration—the drafting of the Bill of Rights, the Judiciary Act, and Hamilton's financial program. The result is an account of the Constitution and its unique features that invites us not only to celebrate the charter's bicentennial, but also to cerebrate it—to remember that constitutional issues were as controversial at the document's inception as they are today.

Richard B. Morris
Gouverneur Morris Professor of History Emeritus
Columbia University

PREFACE

THE BICENTENNIAL of the Constitution of the United States is an appropriate time for us to remember that American history has never taken place in a vacuum. Rather, it is part of the history of what Michael Kraus has called the "Atlantic civilization," with a lively and fruitful exchange of people, ideas, trade, culture, and even hostility across the seas. The "great confluence" of ideas and historical and political experience that Americans and Europeans debated and celebrated in the 1770s and 1780s is unparalleled in scope, richness, and vigor.

In addition to this rich heritage, *Are We to Be a Nation?* explores the history of the United States under the Articles of Confederation, the obscure and unjustly neglected first charter of government of the new nation; the major diplomatic triumphs of the struggling young republic and the ceaseless activities of its remarkable diplomatic corps—Benjamin Franklin and Thomas Jefferson in France, John Adams in England and the Netherlands, and John Jay, first in Spain and then as the Confederation's secretary for foreign affairs—and the political experimentation by the citizens of the newly independent states. As they debated and tested new constitutional devices designed to secure liberty and promote republican government, Americans also rewrote their laws to eliminate outmoded vestiges of the old common law and to cope with new problems, especially those posed by Americans who either refused to withdraw their allegiance to Great Britain or sought to steer a middle course in the revolutionary turmoil.

In the debates over the flaws of the Articles of Confederation, the calling of several conventions (culminating in the Federal Convention of 1787) to reform the federal government, and the struggle for ratification of the Constitution, we witness the birth and growth of a *national* political community. We see how the drama and passions stimulated by the ratification controversy generated a remarkable political discourse between supporters and opponents of the new charter. In particular, *The Federalist*—that invaluable American contribution to political philosophy—emerges as an unexpected gift to their countrymen from Alexander Hamilton, James Madison, and John Jay.

As the Constitution, now the oldest continuing charter of government in the world, enters its third century, we should seize upon the Bicentennial not merely as an occasion for patriotic self-congratulation but also as an opportunity to reflect on our responsibilities as citizens. In this era, when so many have been disillusioned by the political process, we must recall the remarkable examples of the men who in 1787 faced political obstacles seemingly even more daunting than those we face today, yet who overcame these obstacles by high policy and practical political infighting to create "a more perfect union." They debated the most basic of questions posed by the American experiment—"Are we to be a nation?"—and displayed their faith and courage in their willingness to answer "Yes." The question they asked then confronts us still, and their example inspires us to reaffirm their answer.

WE ARE GRATEFUL to The Bank of New York and The John Ben Snow Memorial Trust for their generous support of this publication and the related exhibition, to the National Endowment for the Humanities, without whose aid the exhibition would not have been possible, and to the American Library Association for helping to disseminate and extend the scholarly content of the exhibition to a national audience. We especially thank the Association's Executive Director, Thomas Galvin, and its Associate Executive Director for Communications, Peggy Barber. We gratefully thank all the other people and institutions whose contributions made this book and the Bicentennial Project possible.

Vartan Gregorian
President and Chief Executive Officer
The New York Public Library

ARE WE TO BE A NATION?

1

PROLOGUE:
THE STATE OF THE UNION
IN THE 1780s

THE CONSTITUTION of the United States was the product of a revolution in political thought at least as important and far-reaching as the winning of American independence from Great Britain. The battles of this revolution were contests of speeches, pamphlets, and votes—not of shot and shell; its battlegrounds were constitutional conventions and legislative sessions—not redoubts or besieged cities; and its relics and monuments are instruments and institutions of government—not tattered flags or rusting weapons. The American experiments in self-government in the Revolutionary era were a critical part of our attempts to define our identity as a nation, and the making of the federal Constitution was the culmination of the intellectual ferment and political experimentation in the new republic.

BY MAY OF 1787, the month that saw the opening of the Federal Convention, the United States of America had been an independent nation for just over a decade and a nation at peace for less than five years. Yet, as successor to the colonial system known as British North America, the United States also embodied one hundred seventy years of continuous British presence in the New World. The thirteen American states may have seemed rustic and provincial to the citizens of London, Paris, Madrid, or Vienna. Nonetheless, they had mastered the art of politics, had evolved a thriving and complex society, and were in the process of formulating a national social, economic, and cultural identity.

By far the most astonishing aspect of the United States was its size. From north to south the new nation spanned about twelve hundred miles, and from the Atlantic coast to the Mississippi River approximately six hundred. Any of the thirteen American states was at least as large as a medium-sized European nation, and England itself could have just about fit within the state of New York. The United States seemed blessed almost beyond imagining with natural resources and especially with room for growth. Even if the American population doubled every twenty years, as Benjamin Franklin predicted in 1751, there still seemed room enough in the new republic for "the thousandth and thousandth generation," as Thomas Jefferson confidently asserted in 1801.[1]

Figure 1.1
Artist unknown. *View upon the Road from New-Windsor, towards Morris Town Jersey.* Line engraving, 1789.

Although the United States was the largest nation in the Western world except Russia, its population was comparatively sparse. Fewer than four million inhabitants occupied the populated strip extending about two hundred miles inward from the Atlantic coast (Figure 1.1). Beyond this frontier lay the territory acquired from Great Britain after the Revolution; this area was largely the domain of Indian tribes, with a scattering of American and British military posts. The British maintained a military presence in this territory despite the stipulation in the Treaty of Paris of 1783 that these forts were to be evacuated; they argued that they were entitled to keep their forts until the Americans fulfilled their obligation under the treaty to pay debts owed to British creditors.

The Americans were for the most part a nation of farmers, although a few farseeing writers such as Tench Coxe predicted a glorious future for the United States as a manufacturing and commercial nation.[2] Even the tenth of the population who practiced the professions—lawyers, doctors, and the clergy—never fully abandoned agriculture as a source of income or provisions. Agriculture's economic centrality made it central also to the political and social thinking of most Americans.[3] Of the seven of every ten Americans who earned their livelihood by working on small farms, three were laborers on farms owned by others, whereas four owned the land they tilled. Most of these farms consisted of about ninety-six to one hundred sixty acres, but only a few acres were in active cultivation; the rest were used for pasture for livestock or for growing timber or were left fallow. Even so, these farms required the full commitment of a farmer and his wife, their children, and hired help—or, in the South, the labor of a few slaves—and as a result most Americans rarely saw anyone outside their own household on a day-to-day basis. They did travel on occasion, usually to the nearest town to buy provisions that they could not grow or produce themselves, to sell their cash crops, and to find out the latest news. If they were members of a church, they might also make the effort to attend religious services, although by the late eighteenth century church membership and attendance were on the decline. The lives of most Americans in this era were closely tied to the rhythms of the agricultural economy, with its cycles of plantings and harvests (Figure 1.2). Their existence was a hard one, with few amenities or opportunities for entertainment, but their standard of living was high—in many ways the highest in the Western world.[4]

Most Americans did not take an active part in the political life of the new republic, contenting themselves with voting if they met the requirements established by state constitutions and laws. All the states maintained some form of property test for voting and still higher property qualifications for holding elective office.[5] These requirements grew out of a few basic assumptions about political life that dominated the thinking of the eighteenth century: first, one ought to have a stake in society and be able to prove it before one could have a voice in directing that society's affairs; second, only truly independent voters, whose independence could be proved by their ability to satisfy the property test, were desirable participants in political life. Just how many Americans did meet these property tests for voting in this period is a matter of vigorous historical dispute, though it now seems that the property tests were far easier to satisfy than was previously believed. Of the fraction of the total population who could play a role in the political process, however, few aspired to hold office. The society that had evolved since the first British settlements at Jamestown in 1607 was governed by unspoken assumptions and principles bound up in the shorthand term *deference*. There were basically two kinds of Americans: gentlemen, who did not need to worry about earning a livelihood and thus were well suited to hold office and shape policy; and everyone else, usually grouped as "the common sort." For the most part, the common sort did not challenge the assumption that the elite were entitled to dominate the political system, but the deferential society of colonial America was buffeted and weakened by the doctrines let loose by the Revolution, and as a result the distinction between gentlemen and the common sort began to erode in the 1770s and 1780s.[6]

This distinction was not a rigidly defined class barrier of the type found in Europe; in Denmark, for example, there existed a nine-class system in which it was a crime for members of the upper three classes to interact with members of the lower six.[7] It was possible for the tenth son of a Boston tallow chandler, a runaway apprentice, to come to Philadelphia virtually penniless and eventually become wealthy, respected, and powerful—this was

Figure 1.2
James Peake after Paul Sandby
after Governor Thomas Pownall.
*A Design to represent the beginning
and completion of an American
Settlement or Farm.* Line engraving, 1768.

the achievement of the great Dr. Franklin, who became a symbol of the possibilities of America to his admiring compatriots. Similarly, a brilliant illegitimate child could find backing to be educated at King's College (now Columbia University) and become a pillar of the New York legal profession as well as one of the ablest and most respected proponents of a stronger national government—such was the climb of Alexander Hamilton, who nonetheless strove to obscure the circumstances of his early life. The idea of the self-made man was thus an early development in American thought, though it was still the exception rather than the rule.[8]

In addition, the elite of American society were themselves heterogeneous, divided by occupation, education, religion, and geography. New England divines, merchants, and lawyers found it difficult to establish common ground with southern planters, and vice versa. The cleavages and divergences between the various states and regions that made up the United States were among the most daunting obstacles to forging a union of the American states.

Whatever the structure of American politics and the fluid and evanescent quality of the distinctions between the elite and the common sort, several key groups were excluded by common consent even from the common sort and thus had no direct role in shaping American politics—Indians, blacks, women, and the desperately poor or debtor class.

Of these groups, the Indians loomed largest in the minds of most Americans.[9] From the outset, native Americans had viewed the Europeans' colonization of North America with puzzlement and suspicion. They had at first sought to help the struggling settlements but soon realized that their differing views on the concept of land ownership and exploitation of natural resources made such cooperation impossible. Some tribes maintained friendly or "arm's-length" relations with the colonial governments and later with the states and the Confederation; others withdrew from contact or sought to drive the new settlers out of North America by waging war. During the colonial wars of the seventeenth and eighteenth centuries, the British and French forged alliances with various Indian tribes, and the outcomes of those conflicts spelled extinction for tribes unfortunate enough to be allies of the losing imperial power; similar alliances were made during the Revolution, with similar consequences. By the mid-1780s, most Americans had at least heard rumors of the "savagery" or "barbarism" of the Indians' methods of warfare, if they had not actually witnessed it; consequently, in frontier settlements in the West and South, fear of Indian attacks prompted settlers to support a strong general government that could field and support an army to repel such attacks and preserve their security.

In Virginia, in the same year that witnessed the founding of the Virginia House of Burgesses, a ship bearing twenty "Nigars" docked in Jamestown harbor. These first black residents of British North America were indentured servants, who had committed themselves to work for a term of years as deferred payment for their passage to Virginia. Within a generation, however, the white settlers had laid the foundations for the system of chattel slavery.[10] By 1787, the black population of the United States numbered some 650,000, most of whom were slaves. Slavery existed in nearly every state, though many northern states were either contemplating or moving toward abolition of the institution.[11] Most slaveholders lived in the southern states, where the cultivation of labor-intensive crops such as tobacco, rice, and indigo made dependence on slave labor necessary. Large slaveholding estates, however, were the exception rather than the rule. Most slaveholders owned fewer than five slaves; few operated on the scale of Virginia's George Mason, who owned as many as ninety slaves to till his seventy-five-thousand-acre plantation, Gunston Hall. These slaves were deemed to be property, pure and simple,[12] though their lives were not as harsh as those of their descendants in the next century, the age of King Cotton.

Nonetheless, the institution of chattel slavery was a blight on the new republic, distorting and crippling opportunities for the comparatively few free blacks in the North and condemning hundreds of thousands of men, women, and children to lives of unremitting toil and degradation. Furthermore, the issue of slavery threatened the political stability of the United States.[13] In the 1770s and 1780s, distinguished northerners such as Benjamin Franklin, Benjamin Rush, and John Jay founded or joined manumission societies and campaigned for the abolition of slavery. Enlightened southerners such as Washington, Jefferson, Mason, and Madison hoped that slavery somehow would eventually wither away, though they took few steps themselves to help bring this about. Other southerners, such as the Rutledges and Pinckneys of South Carolina, defended the institution as a necessary part of the plantation economy and the southern way of life, and even as a positive good for the slaves themselves. Slavery thus had the potential to cause irreparable cleavage in the American political community, and most politicians of the period regarded it as a problem to be handled with extreme care—if indeed at all.

The role of women in American society in the Revolutionary era is one of the major new fields of historical inquiry.[14] Recent scholarship has illuminated not only this specific subject but also the general character of the Revolution. Most women in this period found themselves consigned largely to the private realm of home, family, and childbearing and -rearing. Some women, such as the Baltimore printer Mary K. Goddard or the historian, poet, dramatist, and polemicist Mercy Otis Warren of Boston, were able to lead their own lives and take at least some part in the public controversies of the day. Nonetheless, the prevailing legal and political assumptions of colonial America persisted into the Revolutionary period. Although academies for young women brought literacy and learning to some, it was a matter of controversy whether women should be educated at all, on the rationale that education would only tend to make them dissatisfied with their place in society. Married women were still subject to the common-law doctrine of coverture, under which a married couple was considered as one person—the husband; married women thus had no claim to property during the existence of their marriage. As Linda K. Kerber has pointed out, thanks to the old political assumptions linking property with political rights and participation, the conventional wisdom concluded that married women had no capacity to play a role in political affairs. Nonetheless, the Revolution had profound consequences for the role of women in politics and society. The various economic boycotts of British goods in the pre-Revolutionary period depended for their effectiveness on the cooperation of women (Figure 1.3), and gradually, painfully, a theory of patriotism applicable to women began to coalesce. Women also came to play critical roles in the fighting of the Revolution itself—not as combatants, but in the equally crucial role of providing logistical support for the Continental Army, such as food, cleaning, nursing, clothing, and even intelligence work. The doctrine of coverture also raised issues of loyalty and patriotism when the new states and the Revolutionary government came to consider the plight of wives of Loyalists: were they bound to their husbands' choices of allegiance under law, unable legally to make political choices on their own, or did they have independent political capacity?

Choices such as these required women in the Revolutionary era to rethink the old view that they were exclusively creatures of the private sphere and must leave the public sphere of politics, diplomacy, and war to men. Indeed, the wives of a few key Revolutionary leaders showed themselves equal to many of their husbands and male kinsmen in their grasp of

political realities and ideas, shrewd sense for valid and erroneous political news, and daringness and originality of political thought.[15] And yet the Revolution did not lead to a comparable transformation of women's political rights and responsibilities in the new republic. Although the symbolism of America and of liberty was primarily female—we need only look at the many political cartoons of the period depicting America as a halfclad Indian maiden or as the reincarnation of the Greek goddess Athene—the women of the new nation were not permitted to enter fully into the political life of the new republic. Rather, the dominant ideology of the period, with its roots in republican political theory and classical history, recognized women as embodiments of the ideal of "republican motherhood," namely, that women could best serve the republic by acting as good wives and mothers and transmitting the values of republicanism and the American polity to their children, who, depending on their sex, would either continue this tradition by passing these values to the next generation or would grow up to become good citizens.

The least obvious group of Americans excluded from political decision-making in this period was not the women of the new nation, nor the free

Figure 1.4
Artist unknown. A bankruptcy
scene. Mezzotint, ca. 1750–1800.
In this British caricature a
family's belongings are repos-
sessed by the authorities to pay
their debts.

and slave blacks, nor the Indians, but those who were too poor to have a
legitimate voice in politics—in a popular phrase of the time, the "desperate
debtors."[16] Many people, male and female, came to the British colonies and
later to the United States as indentured servants, to pay for their passage
from Europe. Indentured servants were not treated as property in theory
or in practice, and they also knew that they were bound only for a finite
period; in all other respects, however, they were virtually indistinguishable
from chattel slaves.[17]

Those who were not bound for service were not immune from economic
collapse. Because there was very little specie, or hard cash, in the United

States in this period, the dominant medium of exchange was the note. The person making the note would promise to pay a specified sum at a specified date in exchange for goods or services to be provided by the person to whom he gave the note. The recipients of these notes then endorsed them over to other persons in payment for other goods and services; thus the economic life of the period ran on these written statements of credit and debt. The hope of the maker of a note was that, by the time the note became due or was presented to him for payment, he would have accumulated enough hard currency or other notes to be able to satisfy the obligation. Unfortunately, thanks to the uncertainties of agriculture and of commerce, many Americans' notes came back to them at times when they could not satisfy the demands.

The problem of debt affected Americans at every level of society (Figure 1.4).[18] Many wealthy planters actually had to carry mountainous loads of debt, which on occasion brought them crashing down to ruin; so Thomas Jefferson discovered in the last years of his life, when the creditors of Wilson Cary Nicholas, for whom he had cosigned a note, came to Jefferson to satisfy the note when Nicholas defaulted. Associate Justice James Wilson of the Supreme Court died, senselessly raving, in a small inn in North Carolina, pursued by creditors after his huge and impracticable financial speculations disintegrated, leaving him and his family destitute. But the problem of debt struck most often and most cruelly at the small farmers and tradesmen; for every failure of a Jefferson or a Wilson, there were hundreds if not thousands of failures of much smaller scale, though equally catastrophic for the debtors involved. In some states, those who owed debts sought to induce the state governments to cause inflation by printing new issues of paper money; by flooding the money supply with depreciated currency, they reasoned, they could pay off their debts more quickly and exorcise the twin specters of litigation and debtor's prison. This pattern of inflationary politics appeared most frequently in Rhode Island, giving the tiny state an almost unshakable reputation for turbulence, faithlessness, and radicalism. This fear of Rhode Island's and other states' actions to cause inflation, to impede out-of-state and British creditors from collecting debts, and otherwise to vitiate or destroy the value of debts owed by their citizens was a major stimulus to the efforts to strengthen the general government of the United States.

American society in the 1770s and 1780s was thus a rich mosaic of groups, interests, and social strata, and it seems almost incredible that such a crazy-quilt collection of people could coalesce into a nation. Nonetheless, the American people were able to forge a national identity and sense of purpose that strengthened as the century drew to a close. This emergent nationalism was the product of several factors.[19] For one thing, the Americans all spoke a common language, though there were regional variations in dialect and an occasional pocket of people like the Dutch-speaking patroons of the upper Hudson River valley in New York. For another, despite the sectarian differences between Congregationalists and Baptists, between Anglicans and Presbyterians, most Americans in this period shared the common religious heritage of Protestant Christianity—although, again, there were scattered pockets of Catholics in Maryland and other middle Atlantic states and a handful of Jews in New York, Rhode Island, and Philadelphia.[20] Despite local loyalties, many Americans who pursued a college education crossed state lines to do so; southerners occasionally attended Harvard, Yale, or Princeton, and northerners enrolled in the new university in Philadelphia.[21] Similarly, learned societies sprang up in the new republic and attracted members from all over America; the American Philosophical Society of Philadelphia and the American Academy of Boston are but two examples.[22]

Ultimately, however, what united the Americans, whether members of the elite or the common sort or even those ordinarily excluded from politics, was the experience of the Revolution itself.[23] The Revolution compelled citizens of different states to consider the possibility that they were more than New Yorkers or Pennsylvanians or Georgians. The idea gradually emerged that there might be a national interest and common good transcending state and local loyalties and interests. Especially for those who served in the Confederation Congress or the Continental Army, the idea of an American nation took on a reality and an immediacy that eventually translated themselves into political action. Because the Revolution essentially focused on issues of political theory and questions of governmental structure and powers, the idea of national identity was intimately bound up with conceptions of politics. And the reverse was true, as well: once they were willing to conceive of the United States of America as a nation rather than as a collection of autonomous states, the Americans were ready to risk new political experiments to construct a national government.

2

A NEW GOVERNMENT
FOR A NEW NATION

THE AMERICAN REVOLUTION is the key to understanding the making
of the Constitution and the creation of the American republic. The
American colonists' opposition to what they saw as the British government's
arbitrary and tyrannical assertions of power crystallized the political wisdom
and experience accumulated over nearly two centuries. Their understand-
ings of constitutionalism and politics, their habits of thought and expecta-
tions of what government was and should be, may have begun as elements
of their case against British colonial policy, but these ideas soon took on a
life of their own and shaped Americans' reactions to the problems of government in the 1770s and 1780s.

Other than formulating the American challenge to British policy, the
greatest obstacle facing the leaders of the Revolution was to persuade all
thirteen colonies to work together, to present a united front against Britain.
This problem was nothing new to Americans; several times during the
colonial period, either on their own or at the insistence of the mother
country, they had proposed or taken part in experiments with the idea of
intercolonial union. Few of these proposals had succeeded; and the few that
proved feasible were responses to an imminent external threat—that of
French invasion or Indian raids or both. For most of the pre-Revolutionary
period the colonists were only too happy to go their separate ways, relying
on Britain to coordinate the colonies' actions when coordination and centralization were necessary. Britain also provided a focus for the loyalties and
identities of thirteen diverse and distinct societies. Not until the British
themselves became the external threat did the Americans assume the burden
of learning to act in concert. The American Revolutionary movement developed a set of shadow institutions that became the seeds of the governments adopted at the state and national levels once independence was
declared.

Two sets of ideas, values, and beliefs shaped the creation of the Articles
of Confederation, the first constitution of the United States. The first originated in the lingering interstate rivalries, misunderstandings, and distrust
that had impeded all earlier attempts to forge a continental union. The
Continental Congresses and the necessities of the Revolution dispelled only
a little of this localism. The Articles created a loosely organized league of

largely autonomous member states retaining sovereignty over their citizens; Congress was given a meager, grudging measure of authority with virtually no enforcement powers. But the decision to create so weak and incomplete a federal government was not solely or even principally the result of interstate rivalries. It was just as much the result of the ideas of the Revolution—specifically, the principle that only a government as close to the people as possible could legitimately exercise the authority to tax the people and to make laws restricting their behavior.

The government created by the Articles deserves credit for several notable achievements critical to the success of the Revolution. Nonetheless, immediately after the Articles were adopted, questions arose whether the government they created was energetic enough to hold the nation together. Indeed, the achievements of the Confederation government at home and abroad simultaneously produced the conditions giving rise to these questions and pointed the way toward the answers the Americans ultimately developed.

Creating the Confederation

The thirteen colonies began at different times, in different ways, and for different reasons.[1] And yet the idea of American union predated the idea of American independence by more than a century.[2]

The first flowering of the idea came in 1643. Representatives of the colonies of Massachusetts Bay, Plymouth, New Haven, and Connecticut sought to form a confederation in order both to defend themselves against the French and hostile Indian tribes and to create a forum for resolving intercolonial disputes. Rhode Island and Maine were excluded from this rudimentary league. Massachusetts had long claimed Maine as part of its own territory and soon made its claim good by annexation. When the fledgling colony of Rhode Island sought to join the Confederation in 1664, the other colonies rejected the proposal, distrusting the Rhode Islanders' radical religious and political ideas. The United Colonies of New England, also known as the New England Confederation, had no constitutional sanction in the charters of its member colonies; rather, it was a joint advisory council, composed of two members from each participating colony, requiring a vote of six out of the eight commissioners for any action. Until 1664, the Confederation held annual meetings, but in that year Connecticut annexed New Haven, and thereafter the commissioners met only irregularly. The Confederation was revived to coordinate New England's role in King Philip's War but lapsed into disuse after that conflict ended in British and colonial victory. When the colony of Massachusetts lost its charter in 1684, as a result of disputes with the British government, the New England Confederation dissolved.

In 1686 the British government created its own version of the Confederation, but this union was to be established and dominated by and answerable to Whitehall. The Dominion of New England fused all the New England colonies, New York, and New Jersey into one unit to be ruled by a royal governor and his appointed council. The governor, Edmund Andros, ruled without a legislature, promulgating laws after they were approved by a majority of the councillors. The colonists resented the Dominion and its supplanting of their colonial legislatures, even though Andros effectively resisted the menace of the French and Indians. In 1689, as a result of the Glorious Revolution, which toppled the Stuart monarchy in England, the Americans also revolted, bringing down the Dominion government and temporarily jailing its officers. Later that year, King William and Queen Mary permitted the colonies to resume their former status, and the British government thus abandoned the Dominion experiment.

The colonists extolled the Confederation's accomplishments in centralizing and directing colonial defense but denounced the Dominion's abrogation of colonial self-government. These two experiments and the colonists' assessment of them shaped all later attempts to form an intercolonial union. Proposals frequently surfaced to recreate or update the Confederation, but it was not until 1754 that the most deliberate and carefully conceived attempt to forge an intercolonial union took place.

Once again, the spark for this effort was fear of war with the French and their Indian allies. In 1753 and 1754 on the Pennsylvania frontier there were several skirmishes between French forces moving south from Quebec and a detachment of Virginia militia under the command of twenty-two-year-old Major George Washington. Washington had been ordered by Virginia's energetic lieutenant governor, Robert Dinwiddie, to investigate reports of French incursions into British North America. At the same time, British officials in London and in the colonies worried that relations with key Indian allies were deteriorating, thanks in large part to disagreements among the colonies. Consequently, Governor William Shirley of Massachusetts and Acting Governor James Delancey of New York persuaded the British Lords of Trade to issue a call for a conference to meet in Albany in June 1754 to conduct joint negotiations with the Six Nations, also known as the Iroquois Confederation, and to discuss other measures for coordinating the colonies' defense.

Invitations went to nine colonies: Massachusetts, New Hampshire, New York, New Jersey, Pennsylvania (which also governed what is now Delaware), Maryland, Virginia, Rhode Island, and Connecticut (the last two were invited by Shirley and Delancey): North Carolina, South Carolina, and Georgia probably were not included because they were too far from the probable theaters of war. New Jersey declined the invitation, despite the expostulations of its governor, on the grounds of expense; Virginia also declined, citing another conference with Indian representatives scheduled for almost the same time, but its real reason, like that of New Jersey, was the issue of expense. The colonies that accepted the invitation appointed men experienced in intercolonial and Indian affairs. Several commissioners at the Albany Congress later played major parts on both sides in the Revolution—

among them Thomas Hutchinson of Massachusetts, Stephen Hopkins of Rhode Island, and Benjamin Franklin of Pennsylvania.

The delegates had varying instructions from their colonies—a problem that would bedevil all later intercolonial and interstate conferences until after ratification of the Constitution. Only Massachusetts authorized its delegates to go beyond the matters of Indian affairs and intercolonial defensive arrangements; Governor Shirley directed them to enter "into articles of Union and Confederation with the aforesaid Governments for the general Defence of his Majesty's Subjects and Interests in North America as well in time of Peace as of War."[3] Nonetheless, several of the delegates had already given serious thought to the problem of forging a union of the British colonies in North America. As early as 1751, Franklin had sketched a plan for uniting the colonies for common defense. In 1754, in response to news of the skirmishes in Pennsylvania, Franklin published an article in the *Pennsylvania Gazette* calling for a colonial defensive union, and added to it the first political cartoon ever published in North America—the famous "Join or Die" drawing of a snake chopped into several pieces.[4] He also drafted an expanded version of his 1751 plan, modestly titled "Short Hints," and sent it to several distinguished colonial politicians for their comments. Their favorable reactions prompted him to bring the plan with him to Albany, tinkering with it on the way, and he was ready to propose it formally at the Albany Congress.[5]

The Albany Congress achieved the goals for which it had been summoned. It prepared a plan for pooling colonial resources in anticipation of the impending war, and laid the groundwork for a coherent and unified system of regulating colonial relations with the Indians. The aspects of the Albany Congress that served as an instructive precedent during the Revolution and have fascinated later historians were its discussions and proposals for achieving an intercolonial union.

The Albany Congress appointed a committee, including Franklin, to prepare a memorandum setting forth the outlines and terms of a proposed union. The committee report, surviving only in a transcript prepared by Meshech Weare, a New Hampshire delegate to the congress (Figure 2.1), drew extensively on Franklin's "Short Hints," even for its title—"Short Hints towards a Scheme for a General Union of the British Colonies on the Continent."[6] The first paragraph of the report acknowledged the difficulties of constructing a plan of American union in terms characteristic of all later attempts:

> In Such a Scheme the Just Prerogative of the Crown must be preserved or it will not be Approved and Confirmed in England. The Just liberties of the People must be Secured or the Several Colonies will Disapprove of it and Oppose it. Yet Some Prerogative may be abated to Extend Dominion and Increase Subjects and Some Liberty to Obtain Safety.[7]

The plan proposed by the committee would preserve the individual colonial charters as instruments of government but would erect a new structure of government above them. Its Grand Council would be composed of at least two members from each colony chosen by the colonial assemblies for a term of three years. There would also be a president general appointed by the crown and paid by the British government, which would have the power to approve or veto acts of the Grand Council and the duty to carry them out. The authority of the council and of the president general would extend to Indian affairs, the purchase and settlement of lands not comprised within any extant colony, and the common defense. Each colony would contribute to the financing of this level of government in accordance with an agreed-upon quota. The system would be established by a temporary act of Parliament.

After some discussion of the report, the congress appointed Franklin to prepare a plan of union based on it; his plan, approved by the congress on 10 July 1754, followed the general outlines of the committee report but was more specific about colonial representation on the council, finance, procedures for filling vacancies in the office of president general, and other matters. After adopting the plan the Albany Congress dissolved, sending it and another document, a "Representation" of the state of the British colonies drafted by Thomas Hutchinson, to the colonial assemblies for their consideration.[8]

The Albany Plan of Union was the most detailed proposal to create a union among the American colonies ever attempted. It contemplated a government with the authority to operate directly on the citizens of the several colonies and with unchallenged authority in the matters assigned to it by the plan. Indeed, the plan's provisions checked the powers of the British government over the colonies as much as it did the powers of the colonies over the matters committed to the proposed union's authority. Many scholars regard this document as the ancestor of both the American idea of federalism and the British Commonwealth.

The Albany Plan of Union was received coldly by the colonial legislatures and sank in a swirling confusion of objections. Some colonial politicians denounced it as an attack on the authority and prerogative of the king; others claimed that it would undermine the colonial charters. Essentially, the Albany Plan failed because its supporters could not overcome the hostility of the colonists to any form of government that threatened to remove the determination of policy from colonial assemblies directly responsible to the people.

Even Governor Shirley of Massachusetts, one of the originators of the Albany Congress, disliked the plan. In his view, it catered too much to popular or democratic sentiments. In a correspondence with Franklin in late 1754, Shirley floated his own ill-fated ideas for an intercolonial union— a council composed of the governors of the colonies, with jurisdiction and authority similar to that contemplated in the Albany Plan. Franklin answered that, although such a government might work, it would be unpopular because it provided no role in decision-making for the people or their elected representatives. Shirley modified his plan to take account of Franklin's objections but could find no support for his proposal either in the colonies or in London.[9]

The next attempts to bring about an American union had no official blessing from the British government or the governors of the American colonies. The committees and congresses that we now revere as stages in the movement for independence—the Stamp Act Congress, the committees of public safety and correspondence, and the First and Second Continental Congresses—were all informal bodies, created either by their members or by unauthorized actions of the colonial legislatures. And yet their importance cannot be overstated, for they represent the Americans' first tentative gropings toward the creation of an American government and political community.

These committees and congresses grew out of the worsening crisis in colonial relations with Great Britain following the end of the French and Indian War in 1763 and caused by British attempts to force the colonists to assume part of the costs of that war. Everyone is familiar with the story of the colonists' challenges to these measures as violations of the principle of "no taxation without representation."[10] The important factor in terms of the emergence of an American nation is that the controversy with Britain undermined the colonists' traditional reliance on the mother country as a focus for shared allegiance and a source of coordination of intercolonial affairs. As a result, the colonists were compelled to fall back on their own resources to organize and coordinate political action in response to each discrete development in the controversy.

Neither the Stamp Act Congress nor the First Continental Congress led to formal plans for union. These bodies were called together to express colonial opposition to specific parliamentary measures and to articulate their case based on the constitutional rights of Englishmen, not of Americans. The Stamp Act Congress, which met in New York City in late 1765, coordinated a strategy of declarations of principle and appeals to Parliament, complementing the demonstrations and acts of ritualized mob violence that characterized popular resistance to the Stamp Act.[11] By 1774, when the First Continental Congress met in Philadelphia, relations with Great Britain had grown worse, and the range of measures available to the colonists to resist British authority had broadened correspondingly.

The major action of the First Continental Congress was the adoption of a plan to boycott British goods. Circulated throughout the colonies, the Association of 1774 was enforced by an informal network of committees, based on the committees of correspondence organized to maintain lines of communication among the colonies and to spread political news throughout America. The First Continental Congress demonstrated to colonists disposed to resist British measures that there were alternative sources of authority, chains of command and communication, and mechanisms of enforcement. It also illustrated the potential of the resistance movement to develop a full-fledged structure of opposition and even of government, should the need present itself. The failure of the conservative opposition in the First Continental Congress was just as significant. Its alternative to the Association of 1774, the work of James Galloway of Pennsylvania, was a plan of intercolonial union even more advanced than the Albany Plan, calling for the creation of an American Parliament that would have primary legislative authority over the colonies; the two Parliaments, British and American, would be able to veto each other's enactments dealing with American affairs.[12]

Unfortunately for those who hoped that the controversy between Great Britain and the American colonies could be resolved, the appeals of the

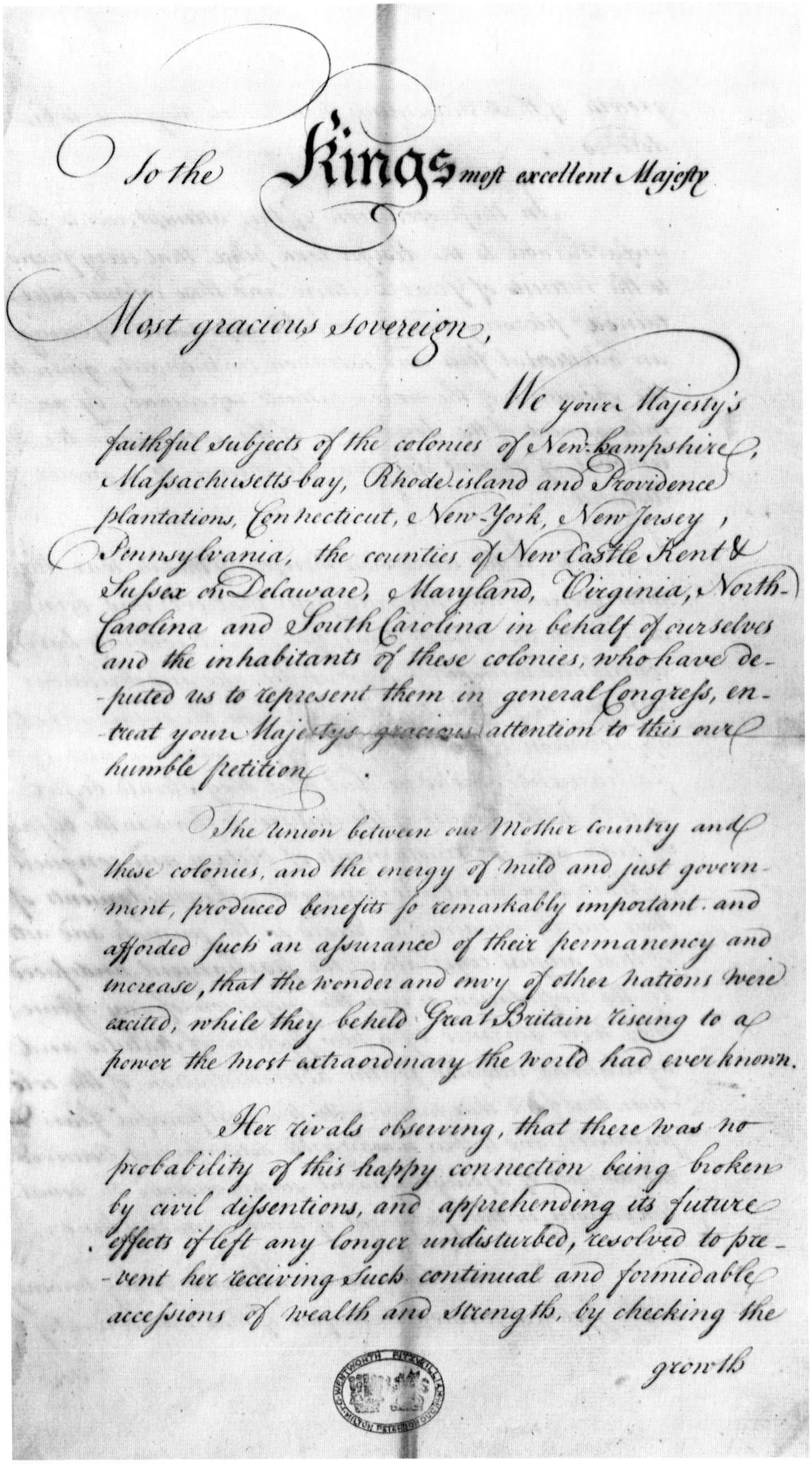

Figure 2.2
[John Dickinson.] Olive Branch
Petition. 5 July 1775.

To the **Kings** most excellent Majesty

Most gracious Sovereign,

We your Majesty's faithful subjects of the colonies of New-hampshire, Massachusetts-bay, Rhode-island and Providence plantations, Connecticut, New-York, New-Jersey, Pennsylvania, the counties of New Castle Kent & Sussex on Delaware, Maryland, Virginia, North-Carolina and South Carolina in behalf of ourselves and the inhabitants of these colonies, who have deputed us to represent them in general Congress, entreat your Majesty's gracious attention to this our humble petition.

The union between our Mother country and these colonies, and the energy of mild and just government, produced benefits so remarkably important, and afforded such an assurance of their permanency and increase, that the wonder and envy of other nations were excited, while they beheld Great Britain rising to a power the most extraordinary the world had ever known.

Her rivals observing, that there was no probability of this happy connection being broken by civil dissentions, and apprehending its future effects if left any longer undisturbed, resolved to prevent her receiving such continual and formidable accessions of wealth and strength, by checking the

growth

First Continental Congress to Parliament fell on deaf ears, and the boycotts, though effectively curtailing British trade with America, had little effect on the political beliefs of the merchants at whom it was aimed. By the time the Second Continental Congress met in Philadelphia in May 1775, British soldiers and Massachusetts militia had already clashed at Lexington and Concord, and as far as the king and his government were concerned, the colonies were in an open state of rebellion.

The Second Continental Congress made one last attempt to appeal for a peaceful end to the crisis. On 8 July 1775, the Congress adopted a document generally known as the Olive Branch Petition (Figure 2.2). In firm but deferential language addressed to George III, it celebrated the rise of the British colonial empire in North America and the joint effort by Great Britain and the colonies to defeat the attempts of Britain's enemies to damage this valuable relationship. And yet the greatest danger to the British colonies in North America came not from Britain's enemies but from Britain itself:

> [The Americans] were alarmed by a new system of statutes and regulations adopted for the administration of the colonies, that filled their minds with the most painful fears & jealousies; and to their inexpressible astonishment, perceived the dangers of the foreign quarrel quickly succeeded by domestick dangers, in their judgment of a more dreadful kind.
>
> Nor were their anxieties alleviated by any tendency in this system to promote the welfare of their Mother country; For 'tho its effects were more immediately felt by them, yet its influence appeared to be injurious to the commerce and prosperity of Great Britain.[13]

Acknowledging that contending armies were already in the field, the petition described the war that had already begun as "a controversy so peculiarly abhorrent to the affections of your still faithful colonists," but insisted that the ministers of the British government had effectively "compelled us to arm in our own defence." After extensive protestations of the colonists' attachment to the king and confidence in his judgment, the petition concluded:

> We therefore beseech your Majesty, that your royal authority and influence may be graciously interposed to procure us relief from our afflicting fears and jealousies occasioned by the System before mentioned, and to settle peace thro' every part of your dominions, with all humility submitting to your Majesty's wise consideration, whether it may not be expedient for facilitating these important purposes, that your Majesty be pleased to direct some mode by which the united applications of your faithful colonists to the throne in pursuance of their common counsels may be improved into a happy and permanent reconciliation; and that in the mean time, measures be taken for preventing the further destruction of the lives of your Majesty's subjects; and that such Statutes

as more immediately distress any of your Majesty's colonies be repealed. For by such arrangements as your Majesty's wisdom can form, for collecting the united Sense of your American people, we are convinced, your Majesty would receive such satisfactory proofs of the disposition of the colonists towards their sovereign and the parent State, that the wished for opportunity would soon be restored to them, of evincing the sincerity of their professions by every testimony of devotion becoming the most dutiful subjects and the most affectionate colonists.[14]

The petition was the work of John Dickinson of Pennsylvania, whose pamphlets criticizing British policy in the 1760s and early 1770s had done so much to fortify colonial opposition to that policy. By this time, however, Dickinson was the leader of the moderate or conservative forces in the Second Continental Congress, resisting efforts to declare American independence. The Olive Branch Petition was the moderates' last appeal to the king and his ministers to reconsider the consequences of British colonial policy. Radical delegates such as John and Samuel Adams of Massachusetts and Patrick Henry of Virginia supported the petition, believing that its failure, which they confidently and correctly expected, would galvanize even moderate delegates into support of independence. As it was, Dickinson's draft was adopted after an even more dutiful and conciliatory address, prepared by John Jay of New York, was rejected; Jay's version asked for more limited relief than Dickinson's version did and also foreclosed American options—such as independence—that Dickinson's version kept open or sidestepped.[15] George III refused to receive the Olive Branch Petition; Arthur Lee and Richard Penn, the American delegates appointed to present it to him, reported: "We . . . were told, that as his Majesty did not receive it on the Throne, no Answer would be given,"[16] This response was an effective rejection of any attempt to resolve the colonial crisis by methods short of force of arms.

The failure of the Olive Branch Petition was as much the result of sheer bad luck as of Britain's intransigence. John Adams, a signer of the petition, had written a private letter criticizing the petition's backers for their timidity and denouncing Dickinson as a "certain great Fortune and piddling Genius, whose fame has been trumpeted so loudly, [for] giv[ing] a silly Cast to our Doings." This letter suddenly appeared in Loyalist newspapers throughout America and found its way to London at almost the same time that Penn and Lee arrived to present the petition. The letter had been captured by the British navy at a ferry crossing in Rhode Island. Whatever its origins, the theft and publication of Adams's letter helped to doom the petition and thus to ensure the Congress's decision to declare American independence.[17]

Within a year of the Olive Branch Petition and despite persistent opposition from moderate delegates led by Dickinson, Congress had taken or authorized measures that would inevitably lead to a break with the mother country. It had fielded the Continental Army and named George Washington, a Virginia delegate to Congress, as the army's commander-in-chief

Figure 2.3
Charles Willson Peale. *His Excellency George Washington Esquire, Commander in Chief of the Federal Army.* Mezzotint, 1780. Peale's skillfully engraved portrait of George Washington on the battlefield at Princeton remains among the finest early images of the commander-in-chief.

(Figure 2.3).[18] It had also adopted a resolution in May 1776 calling on the colonies to prepare new constitutions of government to replace their former royal charters.[19] Finally, in June, Richard Henry Lee of Virginia moved on behalf of this largest and most powerful of the colonies "that these Colonies are, and of right ought to be, free and independent States." Lee's resolution also sought the appointment of American emissaries to conclude foreign alliances and the adoption of a plan of confederation of the independent states. After weeks of debate and the appointment of two committees—one to draft a statement of reasons for the declaration of American independence and the other to prepare a plan of confederation—Congress voted on 2 July to adopt Lee's resolution (Figure 2.4).

The Declaration of Independence was not the instrument but the justification of Congress's vote for independence.[20] It may well be the most

brilliantly successful polemic in American history. Its purpose was to present the Americans' case against Great Britain and for independence to three distinct audiences: the American people themselves; the people and government of Great Britain; and the major European powers, at least one of which might be disposed to enter into an American alliance. The famous preamble set forth the basic principles of an emerging American political ideology. The body of the Declaration, which most contemporaries considered to be the document's most important part,[21] set forth a series of charges against George III drawn from the history of the Anglo-American crisis to establish that the king had failed to meet his obligation to uphold the English constitution as it applied to the Americans. Until this last stage of the crisis, the American opponents of British policy had directed their constitutional arguments against Parliament and the king's ministers, in the hope that the king would intervene to uphold the colonists' rights against parliamentary infringement. The king's refusal to exercise this constitutional responsibility catapulted him into the unenviable role of the Declaration's principal villain. Thomas Jefferson, the principal author of the Declaration (Figure 2.5),

Figure 2.4
Attributed to Edward Savage after Robert Edge Pine. Congress Voting Independence. Stipple engraving, ca. 1798 (plate). Although this engraving was begun at least thirty years after the Declaration of Independence was approved, the rendering of the Assembly Room in the State House is considered accurate. The plate from which this impression was made was given to the Massachusetts Historical Society in 1859.

Figure 2.5
Thomas Jefferson. Declaration of Independence. Fair copy, ca. 1790.

A Declaration by the Representatives of the UNITED STATES OF
AMERICA in General Congress assembled.

When in the course of human events it becomes necessary for one people to
dissolve the political bands which have connected them with another, and to assume
among the powers of the earth the separate and equal station to which the laws of na-
-ture & of nature's god entitle them, a decent respect to the opinions of mankind re-
-quires that they should declare the causes which impel them to the separation.

We hold these truths to be self-evident; that all men are created equal; that
they are endowed by their Creator with inherent & inalienable rights; that among
these are life, liberty, & the pursuit of happiness; that to secure these rights, governments are instituted among men, deriving their just powers from the consent of the
governed; that whenever any form of government becomes destructive of these ends,
it is the right of the people to alter or to abolish it, and to institute new government,
laying it's foundation on such principles & organising it's powers in such form as to
them shall seem most likely to effect their safety & happiness. prudence indeed will
dictate that governments long established should not be changed for light & transient
causes. and accordingly all experience hath shewn that mankind are more disposed to
suffer while evils are sufferable, ——————, themselves by abolishing the forms
they are accustomed. but when a long train of abuses & usurpations, begun at a distin-
-quished period, & pursuing invariably the same object, evinces a design to reduce them
under absolute despotism, it is their right, it is their duty, to throw off such government
& to provide new guards for their future security. such has been the patient sufferance
of these colonies; & such is now the necessity which constrains them to expunge their
former systems of government. the history of the present king of Great Britain, is a
history of unremitting injuries & usurpations, among which appears no solitary fact
to contradict the uniform tenor of the rest; but all have in direct object the esta-
-blishment of an absolute tyranny over these states. to prove this, let facts be sub-
-mitted to a candid world, for the truth of which we pledge a faith yet unsullied by falsehood.
He has refused his assent to laws the most wholesome & necessary for the public good:
he has forbidden his governors to pass laws of immediate & pressing importance, un-
-less suspended in their operation till his assent should be obtained; & when so
suspended, he has neglected utterly to attend to them:
he has refused to pass other laws for the accommodation of large districts of people, unless
those people would relinquish the right of representation in the legislature,
a right inestimable to them & formidable to tyrants only:

phrased the specifications of the charges against George III so that each item had solid, recognizable roots in English constitutional history. Moreover, Jefferson nationalized the case against George III; the Declaration speaks throughout of *American* rights and injuries, not of those of any particular colony. Like Franklin's "Join or Die" editorial and cartoon of 1754, the Declaration was a powerful brief in favor of American nationhood.

The delegates to the Second Continental Congress realized that a decision to declare independence would create a political vacuum. Congress could act as an ad hoc government in the short term, but it was necessary to create an institution or structure of government to fill that vacuum. Indeed, the opponents of immediate independence urged that Congress formulate a plan of confederation or union to serve as a foundation for a united front, either to oppose British usurpations within the framework of the empire or to effectuate a later campaign for independence. Supporters of independence conceded the need for a plan of confederation; thus the second part of Richard Henry Lee's famous motion of 7 June 1776 urged that "a plan of confederation be prepared and transmitted to the respective Colonies for their consideration and approbation." The thirteen-member committee appointed by Congress to act on this part of Lee's motion presented a draft of "Articles of Confederation and Perpetual Union" prepared by John Dickinson, who had refused to sign the Declaration of Independence but had acquiesced in the decision for independence. After nearly a year of vigorous debate behind closed doors, in 1777 Congress sent the Articles (Figure 2.6) to the state legislatures in a form considerably weaker than the Dickinson draft. It was another four years before Maryland became the thirteenth state to ratify the Articles and thus put them into effect.[22]

The central institution of the Confederation government was the Confederation Congress (Figure 2.7). Based on the Second Continental Congress, the Confederation Congress was a unicameral deliberative body in which each state had one vote regardless of its wealth, population, or importance or the size of its delegation. The Articles left it to the states to determine how their delegates would be chosen, and most states selected their delegates by action of their legislatures.

The Confederation Congress stood alone at the top of the federal pyramid. The Articles did not provide for a coordinate executive or judicial branch; the "President of the United States in Congress Assembled" was merely the presiding officer of Congress, without any independent executive powers.[23] The ninth article did provide for a mechanism for hearing disputes between states,[24] but this was the extent of the Confederation's judicial powers. Congress by resolution created a Court of Appeals in Cases of Capture for hearing admiralty and prize appeals—that is, cases involving shipping and captured ships on the high seas. Although attempts to give this court more secure authorization failed, the body persisted until 1787.[25] Similarly, Congress could and did create executive positions to deal with war, foreign affairs, and finance.[26] They were a necessity because Congress was not in continuous session. The Articles created an executive committee

Figure 2.6
Articles of Confederation and Perpetual Union between the States of New-Hampshire, Massachusetts-Bay, Rhode-Island . . . (Lancaster [Pa.]: Francis Bailey, 1777).

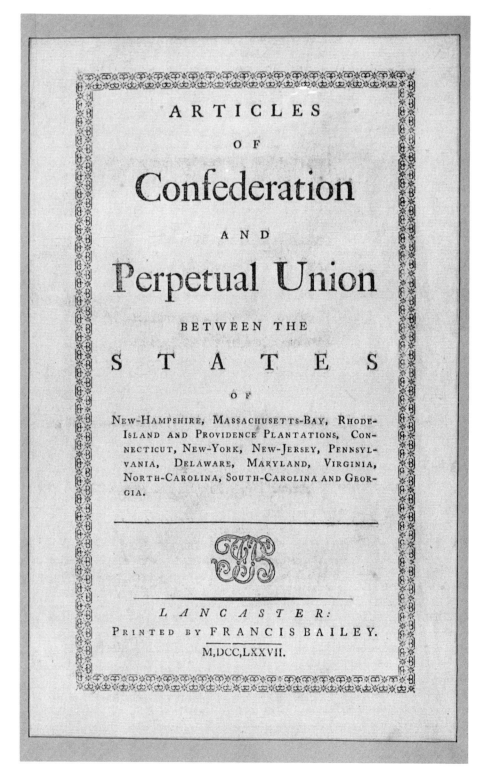

Figure 2.6
Articles of Confederation and Perpetual Union between the States of New-Hampshire, Massachusetts-Bay, Rhode-Island . . . (Lancaster [Pa.]: Francis Bailey, 1777).

Figure 2.7
James Trenchard after Charles
Willson Peale. *A N.W. View of the
State House in Philadelphia.* Line
engraving, 1787. Except for some
wartime interruption, the
Confederation Congress met in
the State House on Chestnut
Street regularly between 1777
and 1783. Based on a 1778 drawing by Peale, this engraving was
originally issued to coincide with
the Federal Convention.

called the Committee of the States, composed of one member from each
state, to oversee the affairs of the Confederation between sessions of Congress. The executive officers of the departments usually reported to the
Committee of the States.

The issues that complicated and protracted the framing and adoption
of the Articles were the mode of representation in the Confederation Congress, the division of powers and responsibilities between the Confederation
and the state governments, and the resolution of several states' conflicting
claims to western lands.[27] Each of these issues requires separate attention.

Beginning with the First Continental Congress, the colonies had grudg-
ingly accepted the mode of equal representation, with each colony receiving
one vote regardless of its size, wealth, or power, and this arrangement
persisted into the Second Continental Congress and finally was lodged in
the Articles of Confederation, though not without repeated controversy at
each stage of the process. Delegates from large states such as Pennsylvania
and Virginia protested what they regarded as an inequitable system of
representation, but never managed to secure the adoption of a proportional
system of representation. Aside from the small states' adamant opposition
to proportional representation, large-state delegates could not agree on the
basis of a proportional system; southern large-state delegates favored basing
representation on the number of a state's inhabitants, free and slave, or the

value of its property, whereas northern large-state delegates favored basing representation on the number of a state's free inhabitants. The problem was reversed in the deliberations concerning the states' responsibility to finance the Confederation government: northern delegates supported using property as the way to measure a state's contribution, whereas southern delegates stressed the number of free inhabitants. The question of financing was resolved by the adoption of a formula in Article 8 determining the amounts of the states' financial contributions to the Confederation by reference to "the value of all land within each State, granted to or surveyed for any person." The Confederation Congress was left free to determine the exact mode of valuation for land and for buildings or other "improvements" on it. The states were assigned the responsibility for levying and collecting taxes to make up their contributions to the Confederation.

As for the question of dividing up the powers of government, or sovereignty, between the Confederation and the state governments, the draftsmen of the Articles still believed in the classical political dictum that sovereignty was indivisible, and they determined that it would rest with the state governments. These decisions are embodied in the first three Articles:

> ARTICLE 1. The stile of this confederacy shall be "The United States of America."
>
> ARTICLE 2. Each State retains its sovereignty, freedom and independence, and every power, jurisdiction, and right, which is not by this confederation expressly delegated to the United States, in Congress assembled.
>
> ARTICLE 3. The said states hereby severally enter into a firm league of friendship with each other for their common defence, the security of their liberties and their mutual and general welfare; binding themselves to assist each other against all force offered to, or attacks made upon them, or any of them, on account of religion, sovereignty, trade, or any other pretence whatever.

Nonetheless, under Article 9 Congress had sole authority over matters of war, peace, and foreign policy, and Article 6 barred the states from acting on these matters. A review of these provisions of the Articles confirms the conclusion of Alfred Kelly, Winfred Harbison, and Herman Belz: "In a legal and constitutional sense . . . the Confederation did not possess a republican form of government—that is, a government based on the people as constituent power and organized and conducted according to the principles of republican constitutionalism. The Articles were concerned with relations among states rather than with the proper balance between power and liberty in the constitutional system."[28]

The last article had a flaw that eventually destroyed the Articles of Confederation as an effective system of government. Under Article 13, unanimous action by all thirteen states was required to adopt the Articles and to amend them thereafter. Thus any one state could block an amendment desired by all twelve of its sister states. This obstacle was apparent from the outset, threatening the adoption of the Articles as the government of the United States. Until it was overcome, the Continental Congress continued as the de facto government of the United States, waiting hopefully for the day when it could at last do business as an authorized government.

The problem arose from the question of the proper disposition of the western lands of the United States. When the colonies were created in the seventeenth and early eighteenth centuries, some of them received royal charters providing no western or southern boundary but instead giving them the real-estate equivalent of a blank check. These open-boundary charters, designed to encourage settlement of the territory in question, created disputes between colonies—and, later, states—whose open-ended grants overlapped and, even more important, between colonies or states with and those without such grants. The open-ended grants provided an enviable windfall for those fortunate states, which sold large parcels of these lands as a profitable source of revenue. The states without such grants demanded at first that this vast, rich territory be apportioned equally among the thirteen states. Later Maryland, the last holdout of the "landless" states, demanded that the fortunate states cede their claims entirely to the United States. Most of the landholding states resisted this proposal, but eventually, when they realized that Maryland was adamant, they gave up their claims to the disputed territories.[29] On 1 March 1781 Maryland finally ratified the Articles of Confederation, putting them into effect as the official instrument of government for the United States (Figure 2.8).

Achievements at Home and Abroad

Although it took four years for all thirteen states to ratify the Articles of Confederation, by 1781 the Articles effectively transformed the Continental Congress from a *de facto* to a *de jure* government. Thus the Confederation deserves credit for the accomplishments of the Continental Congress occurring before the formal ratification.[30]

The Confederation's most important accomplishment was the winning of American independence. This achievement required the invention of governmental machinery of several different types.

First, the Continental Congress and the Confederation had put together an army that, ill equipped and ill manned as it was, managed to defy the might of the British Empire. Under the command of General Washington, who had scrupulously resigned as a delegate to Congress in order to assume the post of commander-in-chief, the Continental Army of necessity developed guerrilla warfare into a high art, inflicting frustrating defeats on British forces (Figure 2.9). The hit-and-run tactics of the Continental Army kept a final victory out of the grasp of the British during the first years of

Figure 2.8
"According to the order of the Day . . . " Copy in the hand of John Adams, 1 March 1781. This extract from the minutes of the Continental Congress prepared by Charles Thomson, secretary of the Continental and Confederation Congresses from 1775 to 1789, certified that Maryland delegates John Hanson and Daniel Carroll ratified the Articles of Confederation for their state, "by which Act the Confederation of the United States of America was compleated."

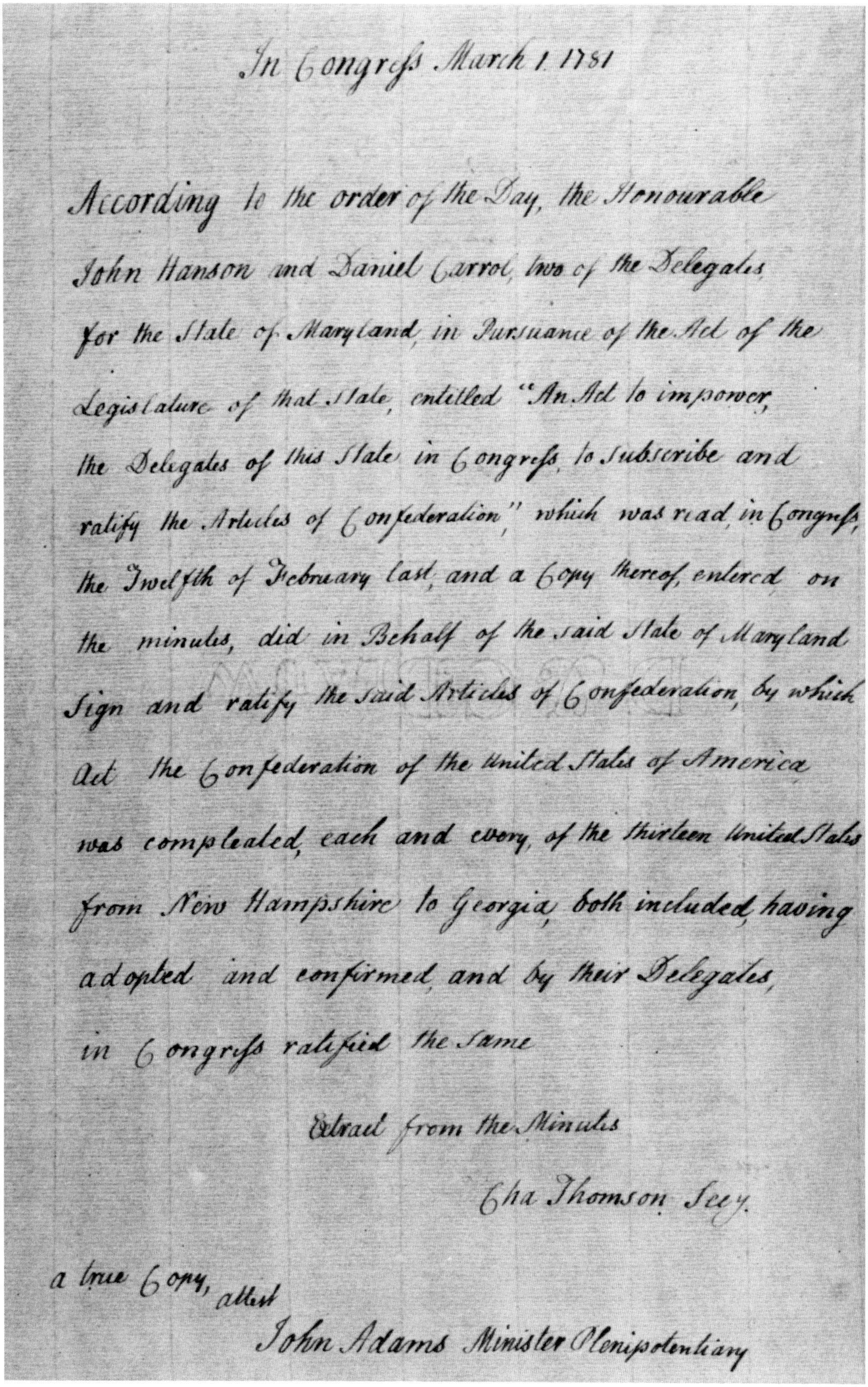

In Congress March 1. 1781

According to the order of the Day, the Honourable John Hanson and Daniel Carrol, two of the Delegates for the State of Maryland, in Pursuance of the Act of the Legislature of that State, entitled "An Act to impower the Delegates of this State in Congress, to subscribe and ratify the Articles of Confederation," which was read in Congress, the Twelfth of February last, and a Copy thereof, entered on the minutes, did in Behalf of the said State of Maryland Sign and ratify the said Articles of Confederation, by which Act the Confederation of the United States of America was compleated, each and every, of the thirteen United States from New Hampshire to Georgia, both included, having adopted and confirmed, and by their Delegates, in Congress ratified the same

Extract from the Minutes

Cha Thomson Secy.

a true Copy, attest

John Adams Minister Plenipotentiary

Figure 2.9
Nicolas Ponce. *Précis du Traité de Paix* . . . Etching, ca. 1784. In this French print ten small vignettes of Revolutionary naval battles surround the figure of Peace. Included in the group is the famous 1779 engagement between the *Bonhomme Richard*, under the command of John Paul Jones, and the *Serapis*. The illustration appeared in *Recueil d'estampes Représéntant les Différents Evénemens de la Guerre* . . . (Paris, ca. 1784).

the Revolution; the Franco-American alliance of 1778 provided the necessary assistance to guarantee British defeat, which occurred for all practical purposes at Yorktown in 1781.[31]

The Continental Army was itself a powerful nationalizing force. But the new army was also a source of worry for the Confederation (Figure 2.10). In the spring of 1783, in the most serious challenge to civil supremacy in our history, a group of disgruntled officers tired of waiting for Congress to take action to grant them pensions and proposed a coup d'état against Congress. George Washington learned of this plot from his aide Alexander Hamilton, who hinted that Washington might want to assume the leadership of the movement. Still smarting from the Conway Cabal, which had attempted to replace him with General Horatio Gates, Washington determined instead to head off the conspirators, who were planning to gather in Newburgh, New York, and in a pungent letter denounced their plans:

> And let me conjure you, in the name of our common Country, as you value your own sacred honor, as you respect the rights of humanity,

Figure 2.10
Letter from General Nathanael Greene to Governor John Rutledge, Head Quarters, 21 January 1782. Although Congress had empowered South Carolina and Georgia to organize black regiments when the British invaded the South in 1778 and 1779, the southern states strongly resisted any moves to arm blacks. Greene, the commander of the Southern Army, favored the idea. Here he urged Rutledge, the governor of South Carolina, to take action "for the more effective protection and security of this country."

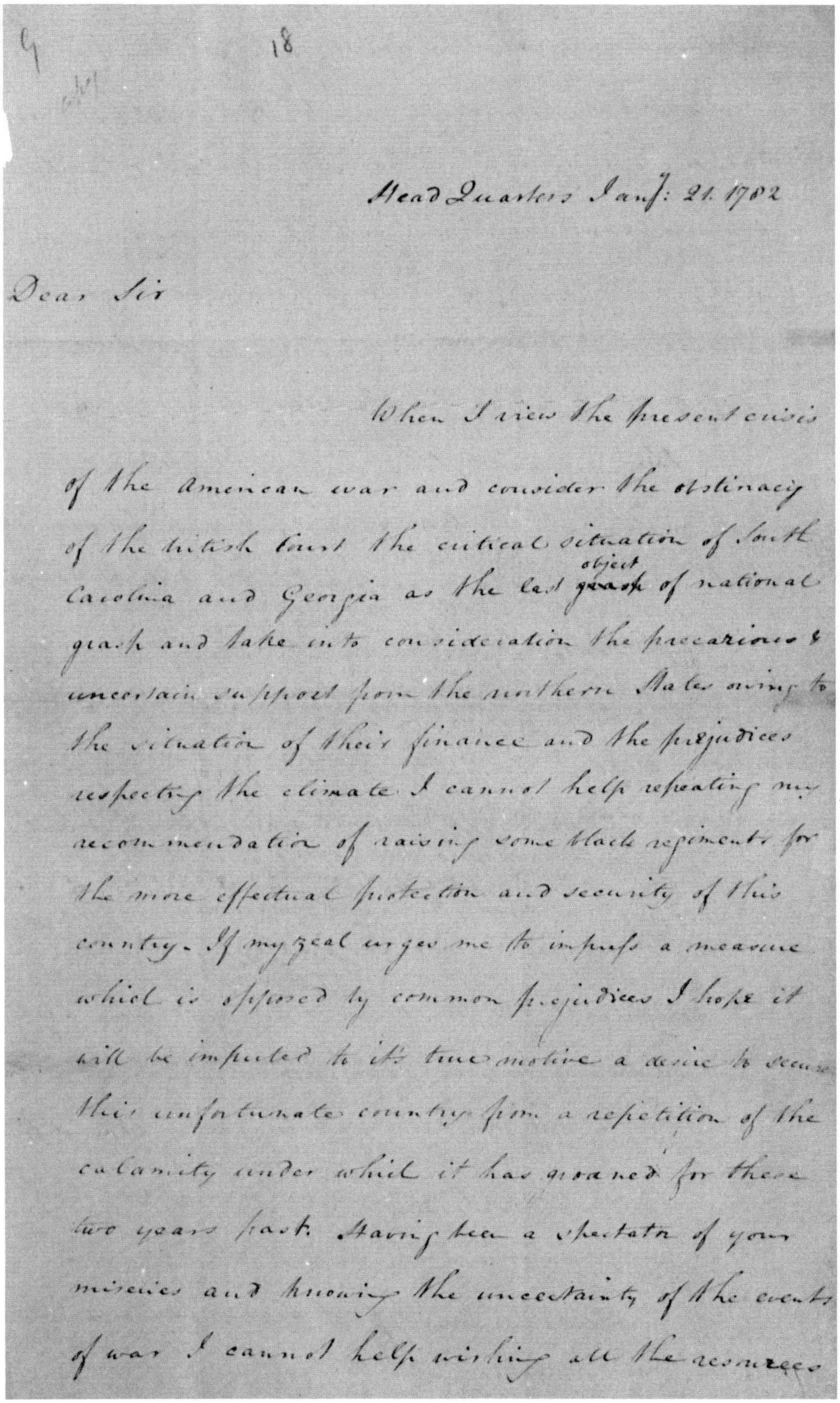

Passy Decr 7. 1778

My dear Sir

On the 21 May, I wrote you a very long Letter, on the Subject of

foreign Affairs in general, and particularly in this Country: on the 28 July, I wrote you another lengthy Letter, on the 7 August I wrote you again in answer to yours of 21 June, which is all I have ever recd from you on the 27 November I wrote you again. I hope some of these have reached you, but so many Vessells have been taken that I fear some have miscarried.

I wish I could unbosom myself to you without Reserve, concerning the State of Affairs here, but you know the danger. The two Passions of Ambition and Avarice, which have been the Bane of Society and the Curse of human kind, in all ages and Countries, are not without their Influence upon our Affairs here, but I fancy the last of the two has done the most Mischief. Where the Carcass is there the Crows will assemble, and you and I have had too much Experience of the Greediness with which the Loaves and Fishes were aimed at under the old Government and with which the Continental Treasury has been sought for under the new, to expect that the Coffers of the American Banker here, would not make some Mens Mouths water. This appetite for the Banker's Treasure, I take to have been the Source of most of the altercations and Dissentions here

Your old Friend is a Man of Honour and Integrity, altho to be very proud, and very impatient, he cannot, easily at all Times any more than your humble Servant govern his Temper, and he has some Notions of Elegance Rank and Dignity that may be carried rather too far. He has been of opinion that the public Money has been too freely issued here, and has often opposed. The other you know personally, and that he loves his Easy [scated] to offend, and seldom gives any opinion until obliged to do it. I know also and it is necessary you should be informed, that he is overwhelmed with a Correspondence from all Quarters, most of them upon trifling subjects, and in a more trifling style; with unmeaning Visits from Multitudes of People, chiefly from the Vanity of having it to Say that they have Seen him. There is another Thing which I am obliged to mention, there are so many private Families, Ladies and Gentlemen that he visits So often, and they are so fond of him that he cannot well avoid it, and So much [better] course with Academicians, that all these Things together keep his Mind in such a constant State of Dissipation, that if he is left alone here, the public Business will suffer in a degree beyond Description, provided our Affairs are continued upon the present footing and as you regard the Military and National character of America, to express your utmost horror and detestation of the Man who wishes, under any specious pretences, to overturn the liberties of our Country, and who wickedly attempts to open the flood Gates of Civil discord, and deluge our rising Empire in Blood.[32]

Washington also assured his men that Congress would indeed grant them pensions commensurate with their service and contributions to the republic, and Congress did adopt a plan under which officers would receive full salary for five years after the disbanding of the army. The conspiracy's failure helped to ensure the supremacy of the civil over the military power, a key element of the Americans' case against George III in the Declaration of Independence.

Even after the thwarting of the Newburgh Conspiracy and the end of the war, most Americans distrusted the influence of the army on politics. After the Revolution, officers of the army formed a patriotic and benevolent society called the Order of the Cincinnati, membership in which would be hereditary. Aedenas Burke, a noted South Carolina jurist and politician, published a scathing pamphlet denouncing the society as the seed of an aristocracy planning to subvert the people's liberties. The outcry prompted by Burke's pamphlet—and, once again, the influence of George Washington as the Order's first president general—persuaded the society to drop its rule establishing hereditary membership, but Americans' fears of a military aristocracy were slow to dissipate.

Just as important an agency of government and nationalizing force as the Continental Army was the American diplomatic corps.[33] Beginning with the decision for independence, Congress had dispatched some of its ablest members to Europe to secure alliances and financial assistance. The activities of Benjamin Franklin at the French court, where he used his European reputation as a scientist, homespun philosopher, and sage to win the hearts and minds of the Paris intelligentsia, won him a friendly though skeptical hearing from the French government; the American victory at Saratoga in 1777, however, made the Americans' campaign for independence legitimate and plausible, and in 1778 the French agreed to enter into "treaties of amity and commerce, and of alliance eventful and defensive."

The efforts of the American diplomats in France provoked intense political disagreements at home, however, with factions arising in Congress either favoring a closer relationship with the French government or distrusting French motives and plans. These contending factions found advocates among the American diplomats in Europe. John Adams, who clashed repeatedly with Franklin and with French diplomats, complained bitterly to his cousin Samuel Adams and anyone else who would listen about the intrigues of the French court (Figure 2.11). He had far better success with the Netherlands, however, winning Dutch recognition of American independence in 1782 and thereafter securing loans from the bankers of Amsterdam to finance the Confederation government. Meanwhile, John Jay

Figure 2.11
Letter from John Adams to Samuel Adams, Passy, 7 December 1778. Adams described his fellow plenipotentiary Benjamin Franklin as "a Man of Honour and Integrity, altho to be very frank and very impartial, he cannot, easily at all Times any more than your humble Servant govern his Temper, and he has Some Notions of Elegance Rank and Dignity that may be carried rather too far."

experienced great frustration in dealing with the Spanish court; his attempts to secure an alliance with Spain ended in disarray, and he gladly left Madrid, only to be assigned with Franklin, Adams, and Henry Laurens of South Carolina to represent the infant republic in the peace negotiations that succeeded the combined Franco-American defeat of Lord Cornwallis's army at Yorktown in 1781. Laurens was captured en route to the negotiations and spent the balance of the war as a distinguished though involuntary guest of His Majesty's Government in the Tower of London.

Although Laurens's colleagues kept him informed of the progress of the peace negotiations, the main burden fell on Franklin, Adams, and Jay (Plate I). The American negotiators chose to chart their own course in these negotiations, with the goal of vindicating American claims to nationhood and independence. Besides, the French and their allies, the Spanish, had their own agendas and objectives both in their war with Britain and in the peace negotiations.[34] Several times the Spanish were on the point of leaving the war, and on more than one occasion the French sent confidential emissaries to Lord North, the British prime minister, seeking to conclude a separate peace. In addition, other European nations, notably Austria and Russia, were experimenting with the possibility of stepping into the struggle as neutral mediators; their proposals would have frozen the dispute between Britain and the Americans short of a formal recognition of independence. The French attempts to circumvent the Franco-American alliance and the complex, backdoor maneuverings of the great European powers provided ample justification for the American diplomats' decision to pursue their own nation's interests—and especially Jay's insistence that the independence of the United States be recognized by all other parties before a peace could be concluded (Figure 2.12).

The Treaty of Paris of 1783 was the high point of diplomatic achievement under the Confederation (Figures 2.13, 2.14). The critical article from the point of view of the Americans provided that "His Britannic Majesty acknowledges the said United States . . . to be free sovereign & Independent States; that he treats with them as such, and for himself his Heirs & Successors, relinquishes all Claims to the Government Propriety & Territorial Rights of the same & every Part thereof."

The Treaty of Paris doubled the size of the United States (Figure 2.15). It also barred any obstacle to the collection of debts owed by citizens of the United States to British subjects, and vice versa, overruling statutes enacted as part of the states' punitive measures against those citizens who had opposed independence and had thus become enemies of the Revolution.[35]

Although the Articles of Confederation provided for the creation of only one institution of government, they did not restrict Congress from establishing additional machinery of government to carry out its policies.[36] The Continental Congress at first experimented with the use of standing committees to conduct the new government's administrative business. This method did not work well, because delegates were forced to serve on committees in addition to representing their states in Congress, and soon Con-

Figure 2.12
Authentic Copies of the Preliminary Articles of Peace . . . (London: J. Debrett, 1783).

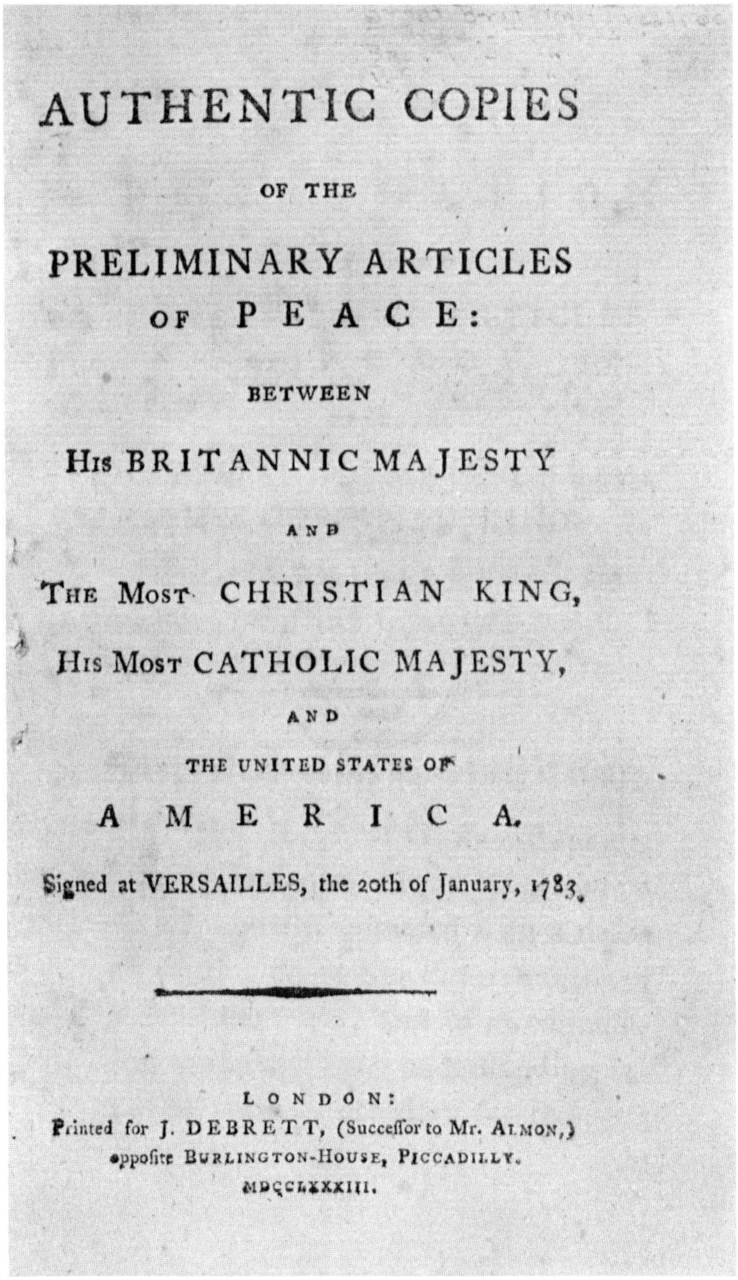

AUTHENTIC COPIES

OF THE

PRELIMINARY ARTICLES
OF PEACE:

BETWEEN

HIS BRITANNIC MAJESTY

AND

THE MOST CHRISTIAN KING,
HIS MOST CATHOLIC MAJESTY,

AND

THE UNITED STATES OF
AMERICA.

Signed at VERSAILLES, the 20th of January, 1783.

LONDON:
Printed for J. DEBRETT, (Succeſſor to Mr. ALMON,)
oppoſite BURLINGTON-HOUSE, PICCADILLY.
MDCCLXXXIII.

gress was forced to experiment with the creation of executive departments to be headed by a single officer. Congress eventually created departments to deal with war, foreign affairs, the post office, and that controversial entity, finance.[37]

After experimenting unsatisfactorily with a three-member Treasury Board, Congress created the office of superintendent of finance in 1781 and appointed Robert Morris of Pennsylvania (Plate II) to fill the job. Morris, who earned the nickname "the Financier of the Revolution," was probably the richest man in the United States. A bold and daring speculator in land

In the image (text visible within the illustration): ENGLAND'S SUN SETTING · PEACE — PEACE — PEACE · AMERICA · ATLANTIC

Figure 2.13
M. Smith. *The Blessings of Peace.*
Etching and engraving, 1783.
While the king confers with his
ministers on one side of the
Atlantic, Franklin crowns the
Indian princess "America," who
sits with her hands suggestively
resting on the knees of the kings
of France and Spain.

and commerical investments, Morris was the focus of hostile suspicion. Repeatedly his enemies leveled charges against his public and business acumen and honesty, but Morris fought such charges with grim determination whether they were true or not. During his tenure as superintendent of finance, Morris bore primary responsibility for overseeing the economic affairs of the Confederation government, including the payment of its debts, the issuance of currency and securities, and the payment and regulation of pensions and government contracts. As part of his nationalist policies, Morris encouraged the foundation of banks, his greatest triumph being the establishment of the Bank of North America in 1782. This bank and others, notably the Bank of New York (founded by Alexander Hamilton and other notable commercial figures in 1784), helped to stabilize and strengthen the commercial system of the new nation. Nonetheless, the charges of corruption, favoritism, and mismanagement against Morris piled up; in October

Figure 2.14
George III. *A Proclamation . . .*
Broadside (New York: James
Rivington, 1783).

BY THE KING.

A PROCLAMATION,

Declaring the Ceſſation of Arms, as well by Sea as Land, agreed upon between His Majeſty, the Moſt Chriſtian King, the King of *Spain*, the States General of the *United Provinces*, and the United States of *America*, and enjoining the Obſervance thereof.

GEORGE R.

WHEREAS Proviſional Articles were ſigned at *Paris*, on the Thirtieth Day of *November* laſt, between Our Commiſſioner for treating of Peace with the Commiſſioners of the United States of *America*, and the Commiſſioners of the ſaid States, to be inſerted in and to conſtitute the Treaty of Peace propoſed to be concluded between Us and the ſaid United States, when Terms of Peace ſhould be agreed upon between Us and His Moſt Chriſtian Majeſty: And whereas Preliminaries for reſtoring Peace between Us and His Moſt Chriſtian Majeſty, were ſigned at *Verſailles* on the Twentieth Day of *January* laſt, by the Miniſters of Us and the Moſt Chriſtian King. And whereas Preliminaries for reſtoring Peace between Us and the King of *Spain*, were alſo ſigned at *Verſailles*, on the Twentieth Day of *January* laſt, between the Miniſters of Us and the King of *Spain*: And whereas, for putting an End to the Calamity of War as ſoon and as far as may be poſſible, it hath been agreed between Us, His Moſt Chriſtian Majeſty, the King of *Spain*, the States-General of the *United Provinces*, and the United States of *America*, as follows; that is to ſay,

THAT ſuch Veſſels and Effects as ſhould be taken in the *Channel* and in the *North Seas*, after the Space of Twelve Days, to be computed from the Ratification of the ſaid Preliminary Articles, ſhould be reſtored on all Sides; That the Term ſhould be One Month from the *Channel* and the *North Seas* as far as the *Canary Iſlands* incluſively, whether in the Ocean or in the *Mediterranean*: Two Months from the ſaid *Canary Iſlands* as far as the Equinoctial Line or Equator; and laſtly, Five Months in all other Parts of the World, without any Exception, or any other more particular Deſcription of Time or Place.

AND whereas the Ratifications of the ſaid Preliminary Articles between Us and the Moſt Chriſtian King, in due Form, were exchanged by the Miniſters of Us and of the Moſt Chriſtian King, on the Third Day of this inſtant *February*; and the Ratifications of the ſaid Preliminary Articles between Us and the King of *Spain*, were exchanged between the Miniſters of Us and of the King of *Spain*, on the Ninth Day of this inſtant *February*; from which Days reſpectively the ſeveral Terms above-mentioned, of Twelve Days, of One Month, of Two Months, and of Five Months, are to be computed: And whereas it is Our Royal Will and Pleaſure that the Ceſſation of Hoſtilities between Us and the States General of the *United Provinces*, and the United States of *America*, ſhould be agreeable to the Epochs fixed between Us and the Moſt Chriſtian King:

WE have thought fit, by and with the Advice of Our Privy Council, to notify the ſame to all Our loving Subjects; and We do declare, that Our Royal Will and Pleaſure is, and we do hereby ſtrictly charge and command all Our Officers, both at Sea and Land, and all other Our Subjects whatſoever, to forbear all Acts of Hoſtility, either by Sea or Land, againſt His Moſt Chriſtian Majeſty, the King of *Spain*, the States General of the *United Provinces*, and the United States of *America*, their Vaſſals or Subjects, from and after the reſpective Times above-mentioned, and under the Penalty of incurring Our higheſt Diſpleaſure.

Given at Our Court at St. James's, *the Fourteenth Day of* February, *in the Twenty-third Year of Our Reign, and in the Year of Our Lord One Thouſand, Seven Hundred and Eighty-three.*

GOD ſave the KING.

LONDON: Printed by CHARLES EYRE and WILLIAM STRAHAN, Printers to the KING's Moſt Excellent Majeſty. 1783.

NEW-YORK: Re-printed by JAMES RIVINGTON, Printer to the KING's Moſt Excellent Majeſty. 1783.

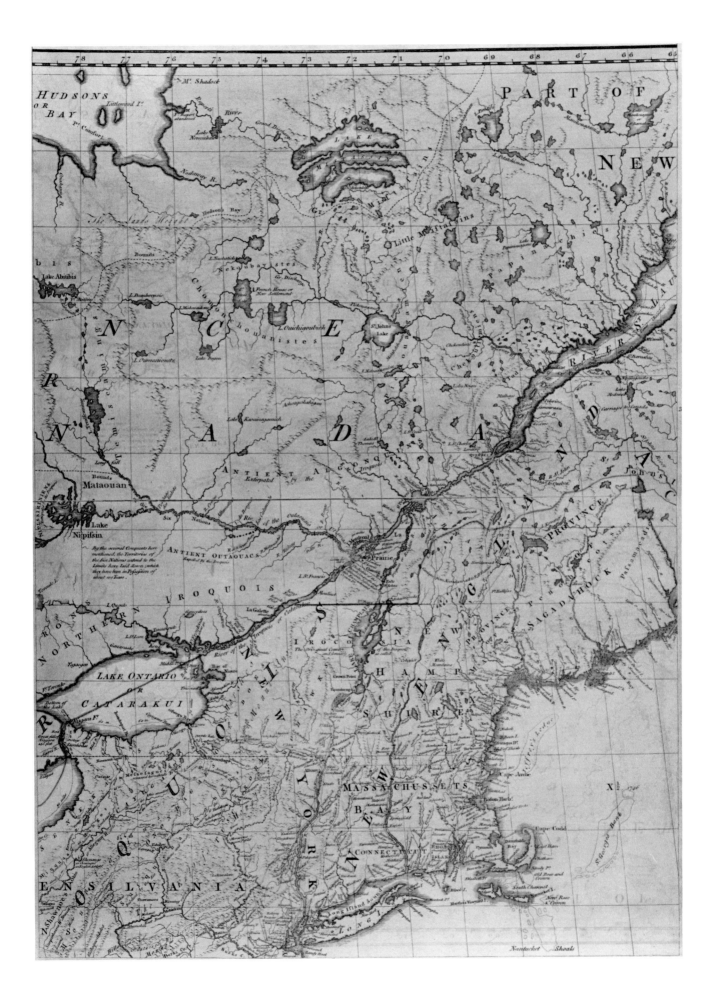

1783 the Massachusetts legislature demanded the abolition of his post and its replacement by a revived Treasury Board, arguing: "History invariably evinces, that the public revenue naturally begets influence to the person to whom the disposal of it is committed; and it must be our wisdom to diminish that bane of all free governments, by placing it in such a manner as to have the least possible effect."[38]

This attack came at the height of a controversy between Morris and his opponents over the issue of securing for Congress the power to raise revenue independent of its requisitions from the states. Seeking to force his opponents' hands, Morris announced his resignation in March 1783, bewailing the nation's failure to accomplish "the last essential work of our glorious revolution" by finding dependable sources of revenue to dispose of the nation's debts. This resignation did not abate the opposition to Morris; rather, his enemies increased the level and virulence of their attacks on him. Despite Morris's resignation, he stayed in office until long after his friends and foes alike decided that his influence was gone, stepping down on 1 November 1784. Soon after Morris's departure for private life, his opponents succeeded in abolishing the office of superintendent of finance, replacing it with a three-member Treasury Board that overhauled the financial records of the Confederation and struggled bravely with the ever-increasing mountain of debt.

The most successful department of the Confederation government was the Department of Foreign Affairs. After a hesitant start in 1782, the department languished until John Jay (Plate III) was elected secretary for foreign affairs in 1784. An experienced diplomat, Jay systematized the department and won authority to conduct all correspondence relating to foreign policy. His greatest achievement as secretary for foreign affairs was to preserve continuity in the critical area of America's relations with Europe. Although he was often the center of controversy—most notably in 1784, when he was denounced for attempting to cede American navigation rights to the Mississippi in exchange for trade privileges benefiting the maritime states[39]—he remained at his post for the duration of the Confederation, stepping down in 1789 to become the nation's first chief justice under the Constitution.[40]

The western lands ceded to the United States by Great Britain under the Treaty of Paris of 1783 posed the single greatest opportunity and constellation of problems facing the nation under the Articles. The Confederation government's resolution of these issues—including controversies over land speculation, existing states' efforts to quell "separatist" movements in territories allegedly within their sovereignty, and disputes over revenue—was its most far-reaching accomplishment.[41]

After the "landed" states ceded their western territories to the United States, the Confederation faced the problem of what to do with these territories. Virginia had attached conditions to its 1781 cession, the most important of which struck at the heart of the numerous land-speculation companies that were busily carving up the new territories, and the land

Figure 2.15
Thomas Kitchen after John Mitchell. *A Map of the British and French Dominions of North America* (detail). Colored engraving, 1755. Mitchell's map was the most accurate of its day and remained the standard map of the continent for four decades. In 1783 both the British and American peace delegations relied on it in their negotiations over the territorial boundaries of the United States.

speculators mounted an energetic campaign to defend their interests. In addition, some of the many settlers flocking to the western territories dreamed of carving out new states. The existing states reacted in various ways to these movements. North Carolina fought a protracted and ultimately successful battle to squelch the "State of Franklin" (now part of Kentucky and Tennessee), whereas Virginia sought to encourage but also to control the settlement and political organization of "the district of Kentucky." Other problems of this sort included New York's bitter efforts to subdue the defiant people of Vermont, who had declared themselves an independent republic in 1777, and the difficulties posed for Massachusetts by the separatist movement in Maine. Congress hoped to avoid similar difficulties by framing a plan for governing the western territories.

After a contest over the conditions it had imposed on its cession, Virginia in December 1783 reconfirmed the cession without the earlier conditions but specified that

> the territory so ceded shall be laid out and formed into States, containing a suitable extent of territory, not less than one hundred nor more than one hundred fifty miles square, or as near thereto as circumstances will admit; and the States so formed shall be distinct republican States, and admitted members of the Federal Union, having the same rights of sovereignty, freedom, and independence as the other States.[42]

This provision of the 1783 Virginia cession embodied the intent of Congress as well, and with its adoption and acceptance by Congress the Confederation was free to establish a basis for governing these territories.

The Confederation's Ordinance of 1784 was largely the work of Thomas Jefferson, who believed that the western territories should not be exploited for the benefit of the existing states. In this view he differed from many of his colleagues, who looked upon the western settlers as little better than bandits or criminals. Nonetheless, Jefferson won adoption of his plan of government for the new territory (Figure 2.16). He sought to lay out ten states of roughly equal dimensions, thereby hoping to avoid the contests between large and small states that had plagued the Continental and Confederation Congresses and that would persist until after the adoption of the Constitution. Settlers in these new districts were to establish temporary governments, based on the existing state constitutions and laws of their choice; when the population of the district reached twenty thousand, the settlers were to call a constitutional convention to prepare a frame of government for the new state and elect a delegate to Congress. The last step of Jefferson's plan—the admission of the new state as a coequal, permanent member of the Union—would take effect when the nascent state's population equaled the number of free inhabitants of the least populous state. The conditions of statehood were that the new state agree never to leave the Union, to subject itself to the authority of the United States, to maintain a republican form of government, and to ban slavery after 1800.[43]

Figure 2.16
The Committee to whom was recommitted the Report of a Plan for a temporary Government of the Western Territory . . . Broadside (Annapolis: John Dunlap, 1784). In the margins of this copy of the ordinance, Thomas Jefferson noted changes made during the debate over its passage. With apparent satisfaction he wrote at the bottom: "Apr 23. 1784. Passed in Congress by the votes of ten states out of eleven present."

The COMMITTEE to whom was recommitted the Report of a PLAN for a temporary Government of the WESTERN TER-RITORY, have agreed to the following RESOLUTIONS.

RESOLVED,

THAT so much of the territory ceded, or to be ceded by individual states, to the United States, as is already purchased or shall be purchased of the Indian inhabitants, and offered for sale by Congress, shall be divided into distinct states, in the following manner, as nearly as such cessions will admit; that is to say, by parallels of latitude, so that each state shall comprehend from ~~south to~~ north *to South* two degrees of latitude, beginning to count from the completion of ~~thirty-one~~ degrees north of the equator; and by meridians of longitude, one of which shall pass through the lowest point of the rapids of Ohio, and the other through the western cape of the mouth of the Great Kanhaway. But the territory eastward ~~of this last meridian, between~~ the Ohio, lake Erie, and Pennsylvania, shall be one state, whatsoever may be its comprehension of latitude. That which may lie beyond the completion of the 45th degree, between the said meridians, shall make part of the state adjoining it on the south, and that part of the Ohio which is between the same meridians, coinciding nearly with the parallel of 39° shall be substituted so far in lieu of that parallel as a boundary line.

That the settlers on any territory so purchased and offered for sale, shall, either on their own petition, or on the order of Congress, receive authority from them, with appointments of time and place, for their free males of full age, within the limits of their state, to meet together for the purpose of establishing a temporary government, to adopt the constitution and laws of any one of the original states; so that such laws nevertheless shall be subject to alteration by their ordinary legislature; and to erect, subject to a like alteration, counties ~~or~~ townships for the election of members for their legislature.

That ~~such temporary government shall only continue in force in any state, until it~~ *when any such state* shall have acquired twenty thousand free inhabitants; ~~when~~ giving due proof thereof to Congress, they shall receive from them authority, with appointments of time and place to ~~call~~ a convention of representatives to establish a permanent constitution and government for themselves.

Provided that both the temporary and permanent governments be established on these principles as their basis. 1. That they shall for ever remain a part of this confederacy of the United States of America. 2. That ~~in their persons, property and territory~~ they shall be subject ~~to the government of the United States in Congress assembled, and~~ to the articles of confederation in all those cases in which the original states shall be so subject. 4. That they shall be subject to pay a part of the federal debts contracted or to be contracted, to be apportioned on them by Congress, according to the same common rule and measure, by which apportionments thereof shall be made on the other states. 7. That their respective governments shall be ~~in~~ republican ~~forms, and shall admit no person to be a citizen who holds any hereditary title.~~ 5. That ~~after the year 1800 of the christian æra, there shall be neither slavery nor involuntary servitude in any of the said states, otherwise than in punishment of crimes, whereof the party shall have been duly convicted to have been personally guilty.~~

That whensoever any of the said states shall have, of free inhabitants, as many as shall then be in any one the least numerous of the thirteen original states, such states shall be admitted by it's delegates into the Congress of the United States, on an equal footing with the said original states; Provided ~~nine states agree to~~ such admission, according to the reservation of the eleventh of the articles of confederation. And in order to adopt the said articles of confederation, to the state of Congress, when its numbers shall be thus encreased, it shall be proposed to the legislatures of the states originally parties thereto, to require the assent of two-thirds of the United States in Congress assembled, in all those cases wherein by the said articles, the assent of nine states is now required; which being agreed to by them, shall be binding on the new states. Until such admission by their delegates into Congress, any of the said states, after the establishment of their temporary government, shall have authority to keep a ~~sitting~~ member in Congress, with a right of debating, but not of voting.

That the preceding articles shall be formed into a charter of compact, shall be duly executed by the president of the United States in Congress assembled, under his hand and the seal of the United States, shall be promulgated, and shall stand as fundamental constitutions between the thirteen original states, and each of the several states now newly described, unalterable, but by the joint consent of the United States in Congress assembled, and of the particular state within which such alteration is proposed to be made.

A second ordinance, adopted the next year, extended the principles of the Ordinance of 1784. Under this ordinance, originally drafted by Jefferson, the territories were to be divided into townships six miles square, each one of which would be divided in turn into thirty-six districts. District 16 would be set aside for a public school (this provision was later modified to include a requirement of religious instruction), and four other districts would be reserved for the United States, which would also receive one-third of the gold, silver, or copper of the township.[44]

Finally, the Northwest Ordinance of 1787, adopted for the governance of the territory north of the Ohio River, modified the territorial system designed by the first two ordinances but preserved many of the essential principles of congressional policy for the territories. Specifically, the Northwest Ordinance repeated the guarantee that the territory would be formed into new states having republican governments on equal footing with the original thirteen states; it also strengthened the antislavery provisions of the Ordinance of 1784, banning slavery outright.

The greatest contribution of these ordinances was their rejection of colonialism, that is, the distinction between a mother country and its colonies. Instead they determined that such territories would be incorporated into the United States, that their settlers would thus have the same rights as citizens of the original thirteen states, and that the distinction between original and new states would become nothing more than a matter of historical curiosity. This insistence of political equality is perhaps the noblest monument to the Articles of Confederation and the government it created.[45]

Finally, the Confederation fostered a group of younger politicians—including James Madison, John Jay, Alexander Hamilton, and Charles Pinckney—who amassed their principal experience of government at the national rather than the state level. They put together an informal network of correspondence reminiscent of the committees of correspondence of the early days of the Revolution to compare notes on national problems and proposed remedies. Moreover, these figures began to develop a vision of national politics, discerning problems that transcended state boundaries and formulating solutions that required a vigorous and effective national government to implement them. This unanticipated consequence of the political system created by the Articles of Confederation proved to be one of its most important legacies to the American people, for when in the middle and late 1780s the Confederation government began to falter, this informal "reform caucus" was able to step into the breach and lead a campaign to remedy the "vices of the political system of the United States."[46]

3

AN AGE OF EXPERIMENTS
IN GOVERNMENT

EVEN BEFORE THEY DECLARED their independence from Great Britain, the Americans set out to frame new forms of government for themselves, in order to protect their liberties and to preserve peace and domestic tranquility. These political experiments gave rise to many of the most important devices and practices of American constitutionalism—among them the idea of a written constitution, doctrines of separation of powers, the declaration of rights, and the constitutional and ratifying conventions.

The Revolution also wrought a significant change in the ways Americans thought about law, the legal system, and lawyers. Reformers in several states attempted to reform the common law and to expand the sphere of legislation—law created by conscious act of the legislature as opposed to the slow accretion of custom and practice. They sought to do away with antiquated doctrines that were vestiges of feudal or colonial times, to encourage transfers of property, and to mitigate the severity of the criminal law. The Revolutionary generation's concerns with law and legality also accelerated the transformation of the American legal profession from a vaguely suspect "order" of men preying upon their fellow citizens into a respectable and learned calling.

Not all Americans supported the Revolution; many either maintained their allegiance to the British crown or tried to avoid choosing between the crown and the Revolution. The new state governments and the Continental and Confederation Congresses thus had to deal with new and perplexing questions of citizenship, loyalty, and treason. They adopted national and state loyalty oaths and imposed harsh penalties on those who refused to take such oaths as well as on active opponents of the Revolution. The Loyalist problem survived the Revolution; the Treaty of Paris of 1783 required the removal of legal and practical obstacles to attempts by Loyalists to recover their own property and by British creditors to recover debts owed to them by American citizens. These lawsuits gave rise to doctrines of judicial review that later became an integral part of American constitutional law, and the Americans' experience during the Revolution with treason and confiscation statutes directed against the Loyalists shaped the Federal Convention's decision to write into the Constitution a precise definition of treason and the legitimate standard of proof of that crime—the only crime so treated by the delegates to the Convention.

An Epoch of Constitution-Making

In the decade following the Stamp Act Congress of 1765, Americans who opposed British colonial policy pieced together a network of committees of correspondence and public safety. Resistance began with these local committees, which then named provincial congresses, which in turn chose delegates to the First and Second Continental Congresses. By 1775, there existed alternative structures of government ready to fill the vacuum that would be created by the abrogation of British colonial rule. The process of building revolutionary "shadow governments" was well under way more than a year before the Continental Congress actually declared American independence.[1]

Months before the break with Britain became a legal reality as well as a practical necessity, the Americans realized the need for new, legitimate sources of governmental authority to replace those soon to be toppled or swept aside by the Revolution. Because there was as yet no constitutional or legal sanction for an American union—the Continental Congresses being extralegal if not illegal organizations—and because most American political figures still considered their primary constituencies to be the individual colonies, this concern with establishing legitimate government focused on the individual colonies.

In late 1775 and early 1776, the provincial congresses of Massachusetts, New Hampshire, South Carolina, and Virginia asked the Continental Congress for advice on what to do about the unsettled condition of government caused by the outbreak of war with Britain. Congress agreed that there was a crisis of authority, but recommended only the convening of popular assemblies to set up interim measures for exercising governmental authority to last until the establishment of a reconciliation with Great Britain.

In the debates on these requests, John Adams and like-minded colleagues urged that Congress act more decisively on them by recommending the establishment of alternative structures of authority as early as possible before any final break with Britain. Conservatives such as John Dickinson of Pennsylvania and James Duane and John Jay of New York argued in opposition that adopting new forms of government would be tantamount to declaring independence and would prevent reconciliation with the mother country.

It was not until 10 May 1776 that the Continental Congress finally adopted the following resolution (Figure 3.1), together with a preamble added on 15 May:

> Resolved, That it be recommended to the respective Assemblies and Conventions of the United Colonies, where no Government sufficient to the exigencies of their affairs has been hitherto established, to adopt such government as shall in the opinion of the Representatives of the People best conduce to the happiness and safety of their Constituents in particular, and America in general.[2]

Figure 3.1
In Congress, May 15, 1776. Broadside (Philadelphia: John Dunlap,
1776).

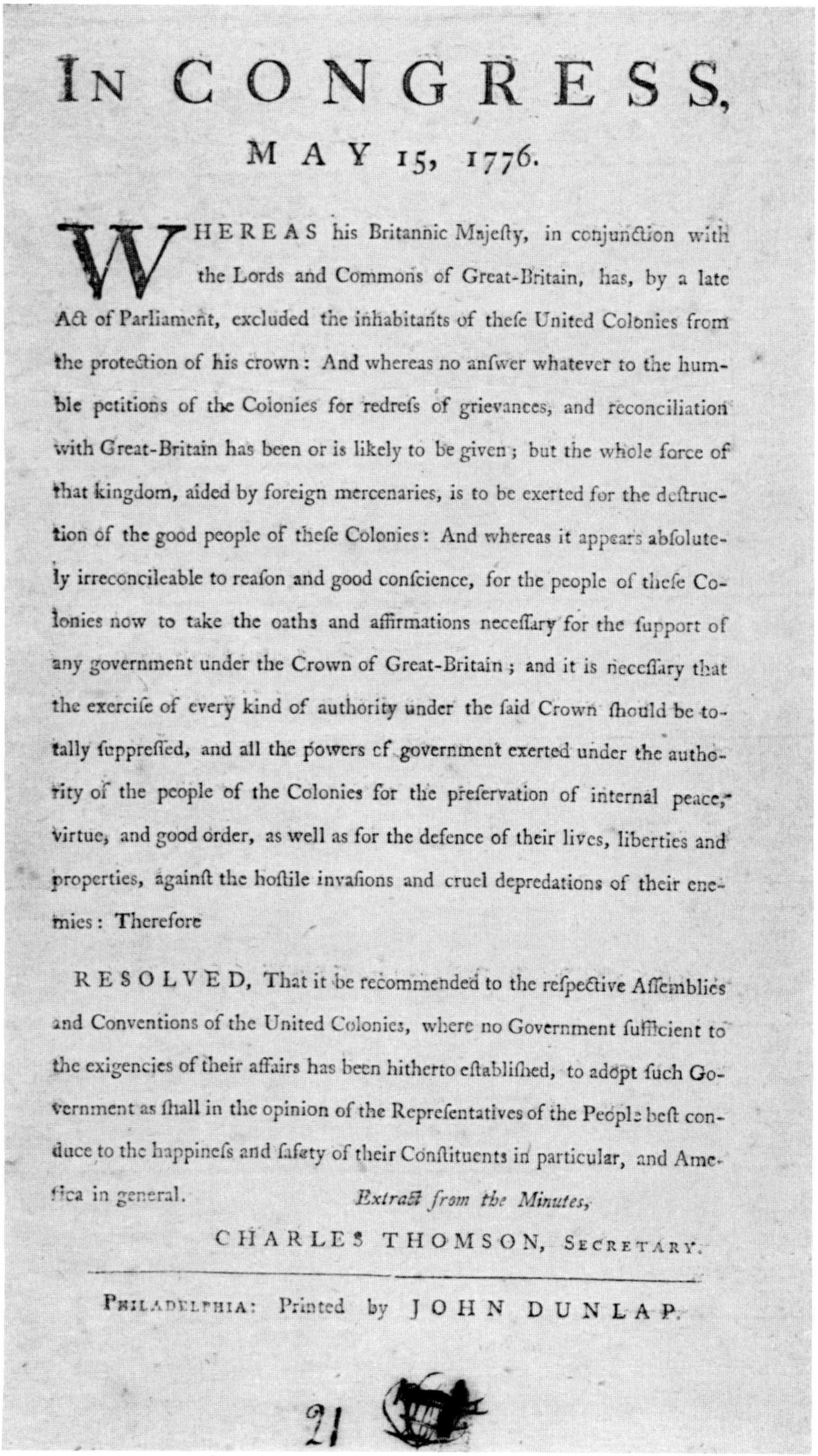

IN CONGRESS,
MAY 15, 1776.

WHEREAS his Britannic Majesty, in conjunction with the Lords and Commons of Great-Britain, has, by a late Act of Parliament, excluded the inhabitants of these United Colonies from the protection of his crown: And whereas no answer whatever to the humble petitions of the Colonies for redress of grievances, and reconciliation with Great-Britain has been or is likely to be given; but the whole force of that kingdom, aided by foreign mercenaries, is to be exerted for the destruction of the good people of these Colonies: And whereas it appears absolutely irreconcileable to reason and good conscience, for the people of these Colonies now to take the oaths and affirmations necessary for the support of any government under the Crown of Great-Britain; and it is necessary that the exercise of every kind of authority under the said Crown should be totally suppressed, and all the powers of government exerted under the authority of the people of the Colonies for the preservation of internal peace, virtue, and good order, as well as for the defence of their lives, liberties and properties, against the hostile invasions and cruel depredations of their enemies: Therefore

RESOLVED, That it be recommended to the respective Assemblies and Conventions of the United Colonies, where no Government sufficient to the exigencies of their affairs has been hitherto established, to adopt such Government as shall in the opinion of the Representatives of the People best conduce to the happiness and safety of their Constituents in particular, and America in general. *Extract from the Minutes,*

CHARLES THOMSON, SECRETARY.

PHILADELPHIA: Printed by JOHN DUNLAP.

21

& for new-modelling the form of Government and for
lishing the Fundamental principles thereof in future.

Whereas George   Guelf king of Great Britain
and Ireland and Elector of Hanover, heretofore entrusted with the exercise
of the kingly office in this government hath endeavored to pervert the same
into a detestable and insupportable tyranny;
by putting his negative on laws the most wholesome & necessary for ye public good;
by denying to his governors permission to pass laws of immediate & pressing impor
-tance, unless suspended in their operation for his assent, and, when so
suspended, neglecting to attend to them for many years;
by refusing to pass certain other laws, unless the persons to be benefited by them
   would relinquish the inestimable right of representation in the legislature
by dissolving legislative assemblies repeatedly and continually for opposing with
   manly firmness his invasions on the rights of the people;
when dissolved, by refusing to call others for a long space of time, thereby leaving
   the political system without any legislative head;
by endeavoring to prevent the population of our country, & for that purpose ob-
   ___ the laws for the naturalization of foreigners & raising the condition
   ___ iations of lands;
   ___ in times of peace, standing armies & ships of war;
   ___ to render the military independent of & superior to the civil power;
by combining with others to subject us to a foreign jurisdiction, giving his as-
   -sent to their pretended acts of legislation
for quartering large bodies of troops among us;
for cutting off our trade with all parts of the world;
for imposing taxes on us without our consent;
for depriving us of the benefits of trial by jury;
for transporting us beyond seas to be tried for pretended offences; and
for suspending our own legislatures & declaring themselves invested with
   power to legislate for us in all cases whatsoever;
by plundering our seas, ravaging our coasts, burning our towns and destro
   -ing the lives of our people;
by inciting insurrections of our fellow subjects with the allurements of forfeiture & confiscation,
by prompting our negroes to rise in arms among us; those very negroes whom
   by his inhuman use of his negative he hath
   ___ refused us permission to exclude by law
by endeavoring to bring on the inhabitants of our frontiers the merciless Indian sa
   -vages, whose known rule of warfare is an undistinguished destruction of
   all ages, sexes, & conditions of existence;

The preamble, drafted by John Adams, cited as justification for this resolution the British statute declaring the colonies to be in a state of rebellion and authorizing military operations to crush that rebellion. The preamble also declared:

> it appears absolutely irreconcilable to reason and good conscience for the people of these Colonies now to take the oaths and affirmations necessary for the support of any government under the Crown of Great-Britain; and it is necessary that every kind of authority under the said Crown should be totally suppressed, and all the powers of government exerted, under the authority of the people of the Colonies for the preservation of internal peace, virtue, and good order, as well as for the defence of their lives, liberties, and properties against the hostile invasions and cruel depredations of their enemies.

Adams's preamble evaded the issue of whether establishing new constitutions would constitute a declaration of independence and placed the onus of the step on the British. In effect, British measures "exclud[ing] the inhabitants of these United Colonies from the Protection of [the] Crown" had compelled the colonists to throw off the authority of the crown. Adams and his contemporaries considered this resolution to be the effective instrument of American independence.[3]

Although the resolution did not direct the states to adopt republican governments, the delegates assumed, and most American thought, that the Revolution was a struggle for republican government. But Congress chose not to prescribe a particular form of republican government or model constitution for all the colonies. The delegates agreed that the people of each colony should adopt a form of government best suited to their needs, local conditions, and ideas of what a government should be. The Americans believed—as did most educated and politically active men of their time—that there was an intimate connection between a people's values and habits, on the one hand, and their institutions of government and systems of law, on the other.[4]

Congress's decision not to prescribe a model constitution for the colonies did not prevent individual delegates from writing constitutions or making recommendations. For example, in May and June 1776 Thomas Jefferson drafted a constitution for Virginia (Figure 3.2), only to discover that the Virginia Convention of 1776 had anticipated him; however, the convention grafted Jefferson's preamble, with its vigorous denunciation of George III (later incorporated into the Declaration of Independence), onto its own version. Constitution-making engrossed delegates to Congress and their colleagues back home. As John Adams wrote in his 1776 essay *Thoughts on Government*: "You and I, my dear Friend, have been sent into life, at a time when the greatest law-givers of antiquity would have wished to have lived. How few of the human race have ever enjoyed an opportunity of making an election of government more than of air, soil, or climate, for themselves or their children."[5] Some delegates to the Continental Congress

Figure 3.2
Thomas Jefferson. Proposed constitution for Virginia. Third draft, before 13 June 1776.

began to complain about the lack of attention to the exigencies of the Revolution, resulting from their fellow delegates' obsession with constitution-making.

The Americans' emphasis on written constitutions was rooted in American colonial history and the circumstances of the Revolution. The term *constitution* in English usage denoted the whole complex of laws, common-law rules, customs, usages, and traditions that shape the political relations, rights, and responsibilities of the polity and its members. As part of the founding of colonies in North America, the crown granted—or the colonists wrote—colonial charters setting forth the guidelines under which political power would be exercised; these new societies were at the same time extensions of England and distinct political communities with their own concerns and unique local conditions. Disputes between the colonists and representatives of the crown over the extent of crown authority and colonial self-government often focused on these written instruments of government and were still fresh in American memories at the outbreak of the constitutional crisis of the mid-1760s. With the drift toward independence, the Americans again recognized the need to specify the basis for their new, independent political organizations in written instruments of government. This perceived necessity accorded with their sense that principles of government were immutable laws of nature, and thus had to be fixed in writing in a form distinct from and superior to mere statutes; by contrast, the unwritten English constitution, subject to the shifts and convulsions of ordinary politics, was not a sufficient bulwark against oppression.[6]

Of all the advice and suggestions produced for writing constitutions in the early years of the Revolution, perhaps the most important and influential was John Adams's *Thoughts on Government*.[7] Adams had long been fascinated by the intricacies of constitutional issues and had acquired a reputation for his extensive study of the subject. In November 1775 Richard Henry Lee of Virginia asked Adams for his thoughts on the structures of government that the Americans should adopt if a break with Great Britain should occur, and Adams gave him a brief sketch of what a new constitution should contain. In March 1776 two North Carolina delegates to Congress, John Penn and William Hooper, approached Adams for advice when they received instruction to return home to help draft that state's constitution. Adams described his response in a letter to his friend James Warren:

> The Time was very Short. However the Gentleman thinking it an opportunity, providentially thrown in his Way, of communicating Some Hints upon a subject, which seems not to have been sufficiently considered in the southern Colonies, and so of turning the Thought of Gentlemen that Way, concluded to borrow a little Time from his sleep and accordingly wrote with his own Hand, a Sketch, which he copied, giving the original to Mr. Hooper and the copy to Mr. Penn, which they carried with them to Carolina.[8]

Adams's "Sketch" attracted more attention than he expected. George Wythe of Virginia caught sight of either Penn's or Hooper's copy, and Adams obligingly wrote out another version at his request. Then Jonathan Dickinson Sergeant of New Jersey asked for a copy. Adams prepared a revised and expanded version (now lost) for Sargeant. When Richard Henry Lee, who had received the earliest articulation of Adams's thinking, asked for a copy of his March 1776 letter, Adams borrowed back Wythe's copy and authorized Lee to arrange for its publication as an anonymous pamphlet, perhaps to stimulate his fellow delegates' consideration of the resolution they finally passed the next month.[9] *Thoughts on Government: Applicable to the Present State of the American Colonies. In a Letter from a Gentleman to his Friend* appeared in Philadelphia in late April of 1776 and was published several months later in Boston (Figure 3.3).[10]

Adams declared that his "Design [in *Thoughts on Government*] is to mark out a Path, and putt Men upon thinking."[11] In part he wrote his pamphlet in opposition to Thomas Paine's *Common Sense*, published in January 1776. Paine's first order of business was to invoke the republican sentiments of the American colonists to encourage resistance to British authority, but he also sketched his idea of the proper mode of government to replace the British colonial system. Paine suggested the creation of unicameral legislatures for each of the colonies, to be subordinate to a unicameral continental congress. Neither level of government would have an independent executive. Paine discarded separation and balance of powers as important principles of republican government; he believed that the legislature, representing the whole people, should exercise all functions of government. Because there was no need to check the voice of the people by creating a second or upper house, Paine said, legislatures should be unicameral.

Adams and other moderate Revolutionary leaders valued *Common Sense* for its vigorous arguments against British rule, but they disliked Paine's radical plan for organizing governments. In contrast to Paine, Adams maintained that the new governments should preserve the best of the Anglo-American traditions of government—especially the idea of separation of powers. *Thoughts on Government* thus represents the moderate brand of Revolutionary constitutionalism.[12]

Like Paine, Adams scoffed at Alexander Pope's lines in *An Essay on Man*: "For forms of government let fools contest, / That which is best administered is best,"[13] declaring:

> Nothing can be more fallacious than this: But poets read history to collect flowers not fruits—they attend to fanciful images, not the effects of social institutions. Nothing is more certain from the history of nations, and the nature of man, than that some forms of government are better fitted for being well administered than others.[14]

Adams argued that only a republic could achieve the proper end of government—the promotion of human happiness, which he equated with virtue, the guiding principle of a republic. But determining the best *form* of a republic is just as important as choosing to create a republic in the first place. Adams thus rejected Paine's reliance on a one-house legislature as the sole institution of government in a republic. Noting many faults of constructing a republican government consisting of a single assembly, Adams cited three as particular threats to republicanism:

> 1. A single Assembly is liable to all the vices, follies and frailties of an individual. Subject to fits of humour, starts of passion, flights of enthusiasm, partialities of prejudice, and consequently productive of hasty

results and absurd judgments: And all these errors ought to be corrected and defects supplied by some controuling power . . .

4. A Representative Assembly, altho' extremely well qualified, and absolutely necessary as a branch of the legislature, is unfit to exercise the executive power, for want of two essential properties, secrecy and dispatch.

5. A Representative Assembly is still less qualified for the judicial power; because it is too numerous, too slow, and too little skilled in the laws.[15]

Adams declared that, for the same reasons, it was unsound to lodge only the power of legislation in a unicameral assembly, for the conflicts between a unitary executive and a unicameral legislature would destroy a republic. The judiciary could not act as a referee between the executive and legislature, because it was under the control of the legislature. Thus, a second house of the legislature was needed to act as mediator between the executive and the lower house in the process of legislation.

Adams suggested establishing a Representative Assembly, which would elect a Council (his term for the upper house, derived from the colonial charters' structure of governor, council, and assembly); both houses would then elect a governor. The governor would be armed with an absolute veto over legislation and would have the power to appoint "Judges, Justices and all other officers, civil and military" with the consent of the Council. To preserve their independence, judges would have tenure for life during good behavior, breaches of which would be punished by impeachment and removal from office. Adams recommended that the governor and all members of both houses of the legislature be elected annually; this limitation "will teach them the great political virtues of humility, patience, and moderation, without which every man in power becomes a ravenous beast of prey."[16] Finally, Adams proposed areas in which the new government should legislate —including public education, the militia, and sumptuary laws (such laws, first enacted in ancient Rome, were designed to tax what we would call conspicuous consumption to guard against the diseases of luxury and corruption, as well as to generate revenue for the government).

Adams reminded his readers that they should not hesitate to rework their new constitutions should actual practice reveal defects in the design; he suggested such reforms as replacing annual elections with longer terms of office, electing the governor and Council by popular vote, and giving both houses of the legislature a say in appointing judges and other officers of government. Nonetheless, he predicted that the government whose outlines he set forth in *Thoughts on Government* would confirm the people in their attachment to republican government and improve them in their daily lives as well:

A Constitution, founded on these principles, introduces knowledge among the People, and inspires them with a conscious dignity, becoming Freemen. A general emulation takes place, which causes good humour, sociability, good manners, and good morals to be generated. That elevation of sentiment, inspired by such a government, makes the common people brave and enterprizing. That ambition which is inspired by it makes them sober, industrious, and frugal. You will find among them some elegance, perhaps, but more solidity; a little pleasure, but a great deal of business—some politeness, but more civility. If you compare such a country with the regions of domination, whether Monarchical or Aristocratical, you will fancy yourself in Arcadia or Elisium.[17]

It is difficult to estimate the influence that *Thoughts on Government* had on the first state constitutions. Adams had intended his pamphlet to spur constitution-making in the southern states in the direction of republicanism, in the hope that they would adopt governments as democratic as those of New England. But *Thoughts on Government* found readers beyond Adams's intended southern audience. Most of the state constitutions framed after Adams wrote were consistent with his prescription, and his friends and colleagues in Virginia, North Carolina, New Jersey, and New York assured him that they had made good use of his advice.[18] The constitutions of all these states established executives headed by a single governor and bicameral legislatures, although most of these governors were weak and dependent on the legislature; Adams's belief in an independent executive as an essential element of republican checks and balances ran counter to the prevailing American distrust of executive power.

The first state constitutions were not submitted to the voters for their approval. Usually a provincial congress or convention, elected by the citizens who had allied themselves with the Revolution, assumed the power and responsibility of drafting a constitution *and* of conducting the day-to-day business of organizing resistance to the British and running the government. Occasionally, as in Delaware, the convention would assume only the "constituent power" of promulgating a constitution and disclaim the legislative power. Once the constitution was drafted—most often in a few days, by a committee of three to fourteen members—the convention would announce its adoption, after which it would either dissolve itself or, more typically, reconstitute itself as the new legislature under the constitution. The constitutions included indictments of George III and the British government in their preambles to explain and justify the state conventions' assertion of the constituent power.[19]

Some state constitutions rejected Adams's recommendation for a bicameral legislature and independent unitary executive. The most controversial of these was the Pennsylvania constitution of 1776 (Figure 3.4). The drafting of this document bitterly divided the Pennsylvanians for several months while a faction led by moderates and conservatives such as John Dickinson and James Wilson but also including such liberals as Benjamin Rush led a dogged resistance. Dickinson, Wilson, Rush, and their allies gave up their fight against the new constitution only when it became clear that the controversy was impeding American resistance to the British.

Figure 3.4
The Constitution of the Common-
wealth of Pennsylvania . . . (Philadelphia: John Dunlap, 1776).

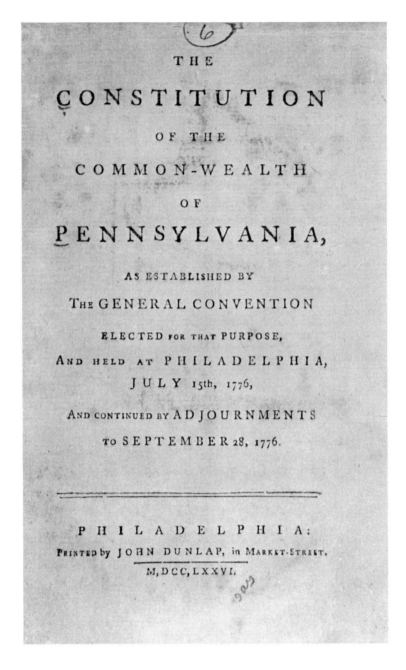

The Pennsylvania constitution concentrated all powers of government in the hands of a popularly elected, unicameral General Assembly; the members of the General Assembly elected a twelve-member Supreme Executive Council whose president was the functional equivalent of the chairman of the board of directors of a modern business corporation. The other peculiar feature of the Pennsylvania constitution was its amending procedure. Every seven years, each city and county would send two representatives to a twenty-four member Council of Censors, derived from a similar institution in the government of the classical Roman Republic; the censors would then conduct an investigation into the workings of the constitution

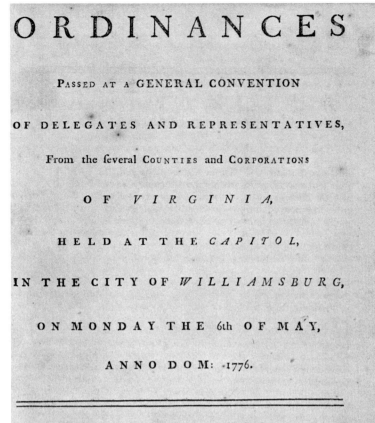

ORDINANCES

PASSED AT A GENERAL CONVENTION

OF DELEGATES AND REPRESENTATIVES,

From the several COUNTIES and CORPORATIONS

OF VIRGINIA,

HELD AT THE CAPITOL,

IN THE CITY OF WILLIAMSBURG,

ON MONDAY THE 6th OF MAY,

ANNO DOM: 1776.

WILLIAMSBURG:
PRINTED BY ALEXANDER PURDIE,
PRINTER TO THE COMMONWEALTH.

Figure 3.5
Ordinances Passed at a General Convention . . . (Williamsburg: Alexander Purdie, 1776). This copy of the Virginia constitution of 1776 originally belonged to Thomas Jefferson.

and, if at least sixteen censors agreed, could require the calling of a constitutional convention within two years.[20]

The Pennsylvania constitution was the focus of partisan politics in that state for fourteen years. Those who supported it styled themselves Constitutionalists; its critics took the name Republicans. The bitter split between Constitutionalists and Republicans at times became violent. On 4 October 1779 a proconstitution mob laid siege to the home of James Wilson, one of Philadelphia's leading attorneys and a tough-minded Republican. Wilson had defended his friend Robert Morris in prosecutions for violating the state's system of price controls. Forewarned, Wilson and thirty like-minded lawyers and merchants armed themselves, barricaded themselves in the house, and held the besieging mob at bay until President Joseph Reed of the Supreme Executive Council and a detachment of the City Horse arrived to quell the riot.[21] Pennsylvania's factional divisions persisted into the 1790s; they shaped the battle over ratification of the federal Constitution in 1787, raged during the replacement of the 1776 constitution with a more conservative, bicameral, checked-and-balanced constitution in 1790, and flared again in the Whiskey Rebellion of 1794.[22]

In drafting their new constitution, the Virginians did not reject separation of powers and embrace majoritarianism as the Pennsylvanians had done. Just how rigid and conservative the Virginia constitution of 1776 (Figure 3.5) was is a matter of historical debate. Dumas Malone, the leading biographer of Thomas Jefferson, declared that this charter "in reality [established] an aristocratic republic, bottomed on inheritance," thanks to its system of property qualifications for voting and officeholding, but other scholars have maintained that these requirements were looser and easier to satisfy than the conventional wisdom suggests.[23] In his draft constitution, Jefferson did not do away with property qualifications, but liberalized them to such an extent that they effectively were abolished. Like the Pennsylvania constitution, the Virginia constitution expressed its drafters' aversion to executive power (Figure 3.6). It did provide for a governor, but he was to be chosen by the legislature and under its sway in nearly all respects, as Jefferson found when he became Virginia's second governor during the state's darkest days in the Revolution.[24] Several years later, in *Notes on the State of Virginia*, Jefferson reprinted his own draft constitution in an appendix and set forth detailed criticism of the state's charter, emphasizing its contradictions of the principle of separation of powers:

> All the powers of government, legislative, executive, and judiciary, result to the legislative body. The concentrating these in the same hands is precisely the definition of despotic government. It will be no alleviation that these powers will be exercised by a plurality of hands, and not by a single one. 173 despots will surely be as oppressive as one. . . . As little will it avail us that they are chosen by ourselves. An *elective despotism* was not the government we fought for; but one which should not only be founded on free principles, but in which the powers of government

Figure 3.6
Artist unknown. Public buildings of Williamsburg. Engraving, ca. 1740 (modern restrike). Virginia's General Assembly met in the brick capitol, shown as number 4 in this panorama, until 1780. The copper plate from which the engraving was made was found in the Bodleian Library at Oxford and is now in the collections of Colonial Williamsburg. Some sources attribute the work to the Philadelphia naturalist John Bartram, who visited Virginia in 1738.

should be so divided and balanced among several bodies of magistracy, as that no one could transcend their legal limits, without being effectively checked and restrained by the others.[25]

The most admired and imitated feature of Virginia's constitution was its Declaration of Rights. This document was the work of George Mason[26] (Plate IV)—although the young James Madison made several suggestions that strengthened the provision protecting religious freedom.[27] It enumerated the basic rights of human beings, and stated the fundamental principles of republican government as understood by the Revolutionary generation. As the Marquis de Lafayette observed in his *Mémoires*, "The era of the American Revolution, which one can regard as the beginning of a new social order for the entire world, is, properly speaking, the era of declarations of rights."[28]

The New York constitution of 1777, the third of the major state constitutions of the period, was drafted by a fourteen-member committee of the state's Convention of Representatives.[29] Chaired by Abraham Yates, Jr., an upstate politician and member of the powerful coalition of the Yates, Lansing, and Gansevoort families, the committee included some of the ablest lawyers and politicians in the state—among them John Jay, Gouverneur Morris, Robert R. Livingston, Robert Yates (the chairman's nephew), and James Duane. Scant evidence of the work of this committee survives (Figure 3.7), but it is agreed that John Jay was the constitution's principal author, and that Morris and Livingston and Robert Yates played major roles in committee discussions and in debate in the full convention, which on 20 April 1777 adopted the constitution.

John Adams called the New York constitution (Figure 3.8) "by far the best Constitution that had yet been adopted."[30] It established a popularly elected, bicameral legislature and a single governor, also to be elected by the voters; the New York constitution was the first to create a popularly elected executive. The governor was granted significant executive powers, including a veto power shared with the chancellor and judges of the state supreme court in a Council of Revision. The constitution also set forth an elaborate mechanism for impeachment trials in which the judiciary played a major part. Thus the New York constitution devoted the most extensive attention and granted the most power to the judiciary of any of the state constitutions. Overall, it was the most carefully constructed system of checks and balances and separation of powers yet adopted in the United States.

Constitution-making on the state level reached its most mature level of development in Massachusetts, where the people wrangled over the proper mechanism and procedures for framing a new form of government for nearly five years. The result, the Massachusetts constitution of 1780, was the best of the state constitutions and the fullest working out of the theoretical issues of Revolutionary constitutionalism.[31]

In Massachusetts, the vacuum of authority created by the suspension of the colonial government was filled at first by the provincial legislature,

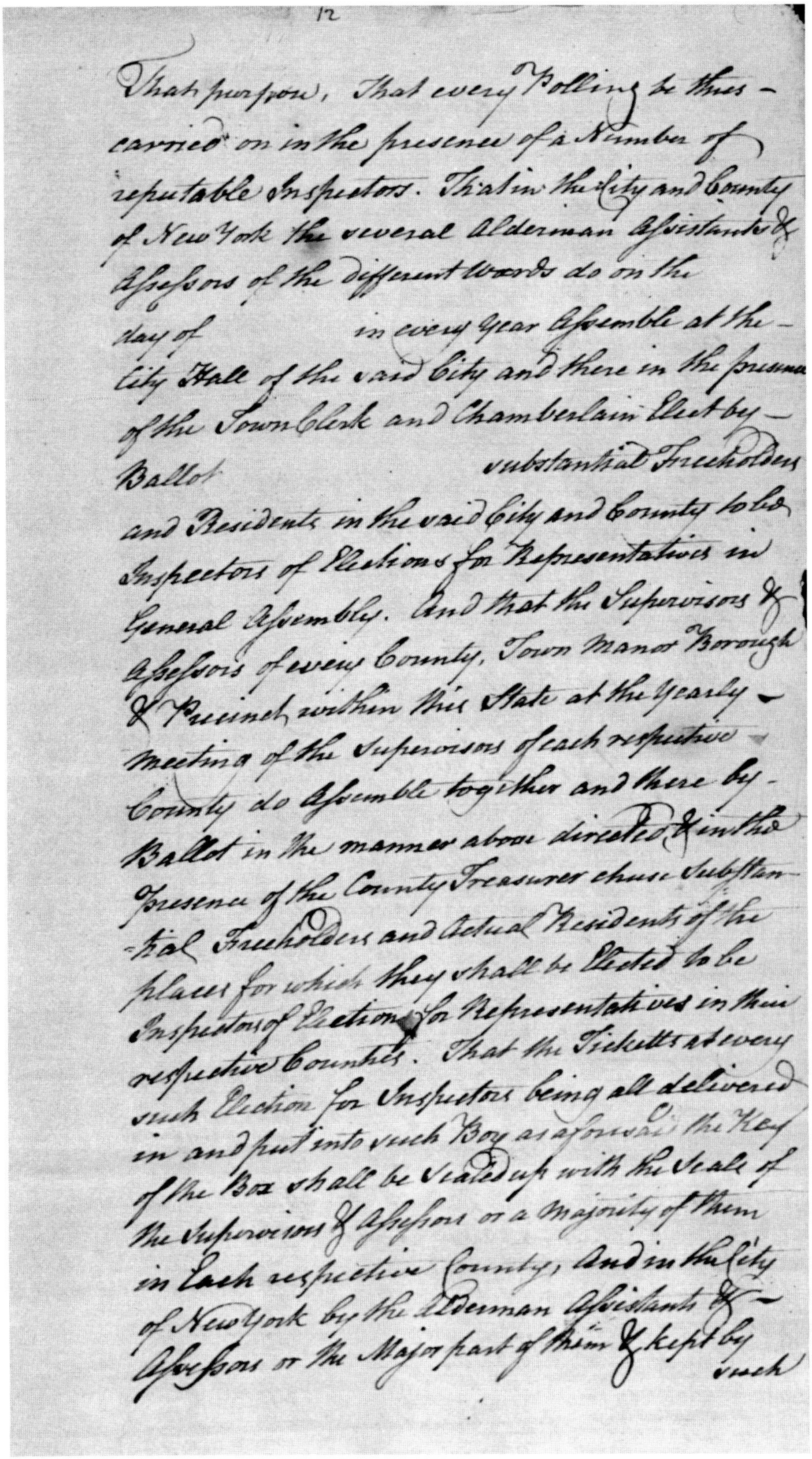
12

That purpose, That every Polling be thus -
carried on in the presence of a Number of
reputable Inspectors. That in the City and County
of New York the several Alderman Assistants &
Assessors of the different Wards do on the
day of in every Year Assemble at the -
City Hall of the said City and there in the presence
of the Town Clerk and Chamberlain Elect by -
Ballot substantial Freeholders
and Residents in the said City and County to be
Inspectors of Elections for Representatives in
General Assembly. And that the Supervisors &
Assessors of every County, Town Manor Borough
& Precinct within this State at the Yearly -
meeting of the Supervisors of each respective -
County do Assemble together and there by -
Ballot in the manner above directed & in the
presence of the County Treasurer chuse Substan-
-tial Freeholders and Actual Residents of the
places for which they shall be Elected to be
Inspectors of Elections for Representatives in their
respective Counties. That the Tickets at every
such Election for Inspectors being all delivered
in and put into such Box as aforesaid the Key
of the Box shall be Sealed up with the Seals of
the Supervisors & Assessors or a Majority of them
in Each respective County, And in the City
of New York by the Alderman Assistants & -
Assessors or the Major part of them & kept by
such

Figure 3.7
Abraham Yates. Minutes of the New York Constitutional Convention. Draft (fragment), 1777.

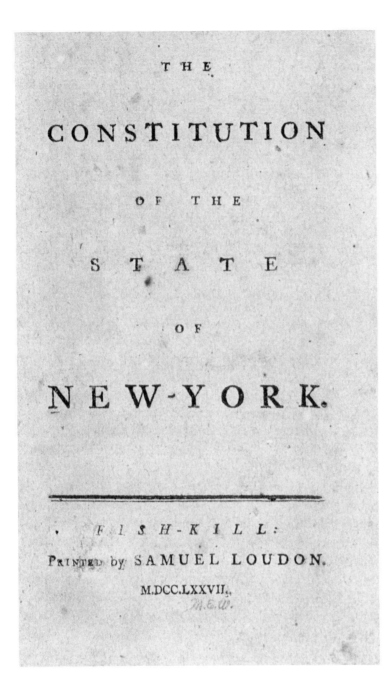

Figure 3.8
The Constitution of the State of New-York (Fishkill: Samuel Loudon, 1777).

or General Court, reconstituted as a provisional government under the Charter of 1691 as modified for the emergency. However, town meetings and county conventions petitioned the General Court for a permanent instead of a provisional constitution. In the fall of 1776 the towns rejected the General Court's proposal that the towns authorize it to write a new constitution; the resolutions of Concord, Lexington, and Pittsfield on this proposal added important new ideas to the controversy. Concord demanded the election of a constitutional convention to write a new constitution, pointing out that "a Constitution [made and] alterable by the Supreme Legislature is no Security at all to the Subject against any Encroachment of the Governing part on any or on all of their Rights & privileges."[32] Lexington and Pittsfield suggested (in the words of the Lexington resolution) that the constitution, once drafted, be submitted to "the Inhabitants, as Towns, or Societies, to express their Approval, or the Contrary."[33] Instead of following Concord's suggestion, the General Court resolved on 4 April 1777 that, at the next election for the legislature, the voters would choose their representatives with the knowledge that these men would be authorized to write a constitution. The resolution also adopted the suggestion of the Lexington and Pittsfield resolutions; it provided that the constitution written by the General Court armed with this constituent power would be submitted to the town meetings, and that every male inhabitant who was free and at least twenty-one years old could vote to accept or reject the constitution.

In early 1778, the General Court announced a constitution providing for a two-house legislature and a popularly elected governor who would be a member of the upper house but would have no veto power over legislation. The constitution lacked a bill of rights and a preamble setting forth the theoretical justification for a constitution, and it contained a provision barring "negroes, Indians, and mulattoes" from the franchise. For the first time in American history, a constitution was put to the test of the votes of all adult male citizens of the political community. The proposed constitution was defeated by a vote of more than four to one—9,972 to 2,083, with 129 town meetings failing to provide any returns at all. The returns from the town meetings cited among the reasons for rejection the absence of a bill of rights, the restrictions on the franchise, and the complex and unfair apportionment of seats in the General Court. Another, equally powerful argument invoked in many of the returns was the impropriety of assigning the drafting of a constitution to the legislature rather than to a specially chosen convention. Foremost among the statements of the town meetings was the "Essex Result," a pamphlet expressing the views of the Essex County convention and written by Theophilus Parsons, a young lawyer from Newburyport. John Adams noted that the reasoning of the "Essex Result" was close to that of *Thoughts on Government*, and was put out that the pamphlet did not acknowledge its debt to the earlier work.[34]

The demand for a convention continued after the failure of the constitution of 1778. Focused in Berkshire County and other parts of western Massachusetts, the Constitutionalist movement—not to be confused with the Pennsylvania Constitutionalists—insisted that the courts could not open until they had legitimate, constitutional authority. Despite their opponents' claims that they merely wanted to keep the courts closed to avoid suits for debt, these Constitutionalists acted for principled as well as economic reasons. A convention of towns in Hampshire County demanded the calling of a new convention on 30 March 1779:

> We are of Opinion that by Delaying and Putting off the Forming of a Bill of Rights and a free Constitution for this State, we are Deprived of a Great Blessing viz Civil Government and Good wholsom Laws—

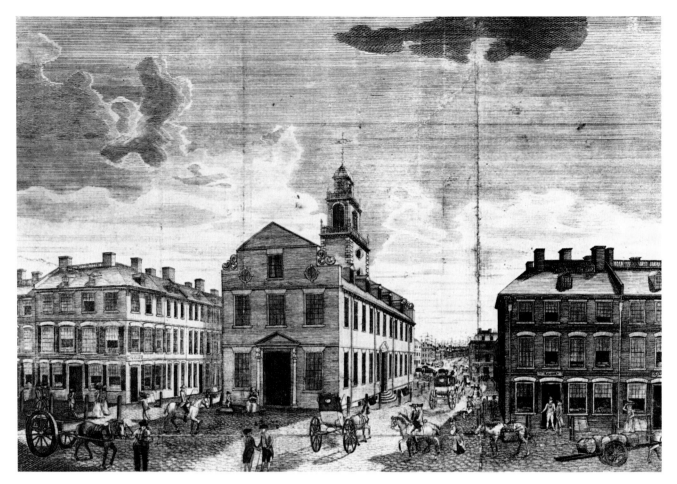

Figure 3.9
Samuel Hill. *A S.W. View of the State House, in Boston.* Etching, July 1793. The Massachusetts State House was built in 1747 and for fifty years housed the provincial and town governments, the courts, and the Merchants' Exchange. Hill's engraving appeared in his *Massachusetts Magazine.*

Founded thereon, whereby the Virtuous may be Protected in their Liberty and Property, and Transgressors Brought to proper Punishment.[35]

The month before, the General Court had given in to the demands for action and resolved that the town meetings should be polled for their views on the calling of a constitutional convention. Presented with a vote of better than two to one in favor, the legislature issued a call in June 1779 for elections to a convention; all freemen over twenty-one years of age could participate in this election and in the vote on the constitution itself. The returns from the towns, voting on the constitution article by article, would be submitted to a final session of the convention, which would determine whether the constitution had been adopted by the necessary two-thirds vote.

During the first week of September 1779, the first session of the convention met in Cambridge. The convention appointed a drafting committee of thirty members, which in turn named a subcommittee of three members— John Adams, Samuel Adams, and James Bowdoin. The subcommittee assigned John Adams the task of writing the constitution, and Adams rose to the challenge, producing what one historian has described as "the most eloquent of all American constitutions."[36] The convention reassembled on 28 October and met until 17 November, when it adjourned yet again, scheduling its next session for 5 Junuary 1780 in Boston (Figure 3.9). The convention did not resume full sessions until 27 February, and continued its work for only a few days, adjourning again on 2 March after submitting the constitution to the towns. On 7 June, the convention held its last session to count the returns of the votes taken at the town meetings. For nearly two weeks the delegates wrestled with the confusing job of tallying the votes on each article; Samuel Eliot Morison has suggested that the convention juggled the vote returns in order to arrive at the conclusion that the constitution had in fact been adopted by the needed two-thirds of the votes.[37] On 16 June 1780, the convention declared the new constitution adopted and announced that it would go into effect on 25 October 1780.

Unlike the failed constitution of 1778 and most of the earlier state constitutions, the Massachusetts constitution of 1780 (Figure 3.10) embodied a full, coherent system of ideas about government, the people, and the individual citizen. Its preamble set forth the view that the constitution represented a "social compact" entered into for the benefit and protection of the people and requiring the solemnity and certainty of a written constitution. The constitution itself had two parts, a Declaration of Rights in thirty articles and a Frame of Government. Most of the provisions of the Declaration of Rights, even those that on their face invoked individual rights, stated principles of government that were essential building block of Revolutionary constitutionalism. The most famous provision of the Declaration of Rights was Article XXX:

> In the government of this Commonwealth, the legislative department shall never exercise the executive and judicial powers, or either of them: The executive shall never exercise the legislative and judicial powers, or either of them: The judicial shall never exercise the legislative and executive powers, or either of them: to the end it may be a government of laws and not of men.

This classic statement of the doctrine of separation of powers captures the essence of the Frame of Government. It created a popularly elected, bicameral General Court containing a Senate and House of Representatives, an independent and popularly elected governor and lieutenant governor, and a Council drawn from the Senate and elected by the General Court to advise the governor and assume executive responsibilities should both the governor and lieutenant governor be outside the state. The governor had the power to veto legislation, but two-thirds of both houses of the General Court could override his veto. A divergence from Adams's preference for an absolute executive veto, this provision was influenced by New York's constitution. The structure of the judiciary was not specified; by implication, the constitution preserved the judicial system that had evolved since colonial times, though leaving the legislature free to alter that system if necessary.

A

CONSTITUTION

or

FRAME of GOVERNMENT;

Agreed upon by the DELEGATES of the People of the State of
MASSACHUSETTS-BAY,

IN

CONVENTION;

Begun and held at *Cambridge* on the First of *September*, 1779;

AND

Continued by Adjournments to the Second of *March*, 1780;

To be submitted to the Revision of their Constituents, in Order
to the compleating of the same, in Conformity to their Amendments, at a Session to be held for that Purpose, on the First
Wednesday in *June* next ensuing.

―――――――――――――――――――――

BOSTON: STATE of MASSACHUSETTS-BAY,

Printed by BENJAMIN EDES & SONS, in State-Street,
M,DCC,LXXX;

Chapter V of the Frame of Government was the only state constitutional provision to address the subject of governmental responsibility for education. Section I transformed Harvard College into a university and reorganized and systematized the state's supervisory authority, leaving the government free to change Harvard's structure for its future benefit "and the interest of the republic of letters." Section II commanded all state and local officeholders "to cherish the interests of literature and the sciences, and all seminaries of them" because of the importance of diffusing "[w]isdom, and knowledge, as well as virtue . . . generally among the body of the people . . . and . . . spreading the opportunities and advantages of education in the various parts of the country, and among the different orders of the people . . ."

John Adams could attend only the convention's first session; just after he finished his draft of the constitution, he had to leave for Paris to take up his duties as the first American envoy to negotiate a treaty of peace with Great Britain. Nonetheless, his handiwork was much on his mind, especially as his frustration at having nothing to do and his feelings of humiliation at the hands of the French increased. On 23 February 1780, he penned a wistful letter to Samuel Adams:

> I hope you will be so good as to inform me of what passes, particularly what progress the Convention makes in the Constitution. I assure you it is more comfortable making Constitutions in the dead of Winter at Cambridge or Boston, than Sailing in a leaky Ship, or climbing on foot or upon Mules over the Mountains of Gallicia and the Pyrenees.[38]

Adams had good reason to look back with fondness upon the convention, for it gave him the chance to present his idea of a perfect commonwealth, suited to the special needs, customs, and habits of his native state and its people. He drew equally upon his constitutional theory and his practical political experience. Relishing the role of framer, in the constitution's preamble Adams even described God as "the Great Legislator of the Universe." In September, when Samuel Adams informed him of the adoption of the constitution, he could barely contain his pride despite his Puritan upbringing.[39] His pride and anxiety for the constitution were still lively even two years later, when he was immersed in the negotiation of treaties of friendship and commerce with the Netherlands:

> Pray, how does your Constitution work? How does the privy Council play its Part? Are there no Inconveniences found in it?—it is the Part which I haven been most anxious about least it should become unpopular and Gentlemen should be averse to Serve in it.—This Form of Government has a very high reputation in Europe, and I wish it may be as well approved in Practice as it is in Theory.[40]

Most Americans shared John Adams's pride in their new constitutions. Soon collected and published in omnibus volumes, the documents were widely read and extensively discussed on both sides of the Atlantic. Two in particular—those of New York and Massachusetts—influenced the framing of the federal Constitution in 1787.[41] These constitutions were authoritative proof that the Americans were making the most sweeping and creative contributions of their time to what John Adams called "the divine science" of politics.[42]

Revising the Laws

The Revolution also induced the Americans to review their systems of statutory and common law, though not with the same venturesome spirit that inspired the drafting of their new state constitutions. Nonetheless, the era of the American Revolution was of critical importance for the law and for the emerging legal profession.

The most ambitious effort to force the law to take account of the Revolution took place in Viriginia.[43] Late in 1776, the General Assembly appointed a five-member Council of Revisors—George Wythe, Edmund Pendleton, George Mason, Thomas Jefferson, and Thomas Ludlow Lee— to review the entire body of statutory and common law then in force in Virginia and prepare a new code of laws for the state. After some initial discussion, both Mason and Lee resigned from the committee, declaring that they were unqualified for the work because they were not lawyers.

Of the three lawyers who remained, Edmund Pendleton and George Wythe, lifelong political and professional rivals, were the titans of the Virginia bar. Pendleton was the perennial Speaker of the Virginia House of Burgesses and its successor, the House of Delegates, and the most respected and successful lawyer in the state. He became the nominal chairman of the Council of Revisors.[44]

Wythe (Figure 3.11) was the leading law teacher in Virginia, numbering Thomas Jefferson among his prize students, and the founder of the first law school in America. An ardent and shrewd champion of independence, he had served as a Virginia delegate to the Second Continental Congress after ten years in the House of Burgesses. Called home to take up his appointment as a member of the Council of Revisors, he wrote to Pendleton accepting his appointment in terms exemplifying his assiduously cultivated Roman temperament and sense of public obligation: "It is the part of my countrymen to say when I shall return to assist in revising the laws; it is mine to obey."[45]

Thomas Jefferson (Plate V), the youngest member of the council and the author of the legislation that established it, had made a name for himself as an eloquent draftsman, a tireless and accomplished legislator, and a shrewd lawyer. He had sparked controversy with his first legislative proposal: a bill doing away with entailed estates—a common-law doctrine under which a grantor might convey real property to a grantee and his lineal descendants *only*, with the rights to the property reverting to the grantor

Figure 3.11
Artist unknown. Portrait of
George Wythe. Pencil and ink
on paper, 25 April 1791.

and his lineal descendants if the grantee or any of his descendants attempted to transfer the property to someone not related to or descended from the grantor. The doctrine of entail had contributed to the rise of great family estates, making it impossible for Virginians of modest means to acquire land. Jefferson's bill produced far-reaching social and economic changes by making it easier for landowners to sell their property.[46] Jefferson's reason for proposing the creation of the Council of Revisors was, as he explained it,

> to accommodate [the common law] to our new principles and circumstances; [and] to take up the whole body of statutes and Virginia laws, to leave out everything obsolete or improper, insert what was wanting, and reduce the whole within as moderate a compass as it would bear, and to the plain language of common sense, divested of the verbiage, the barbarous tautologies and redundancies which render the British statutes unintelligible.[47]

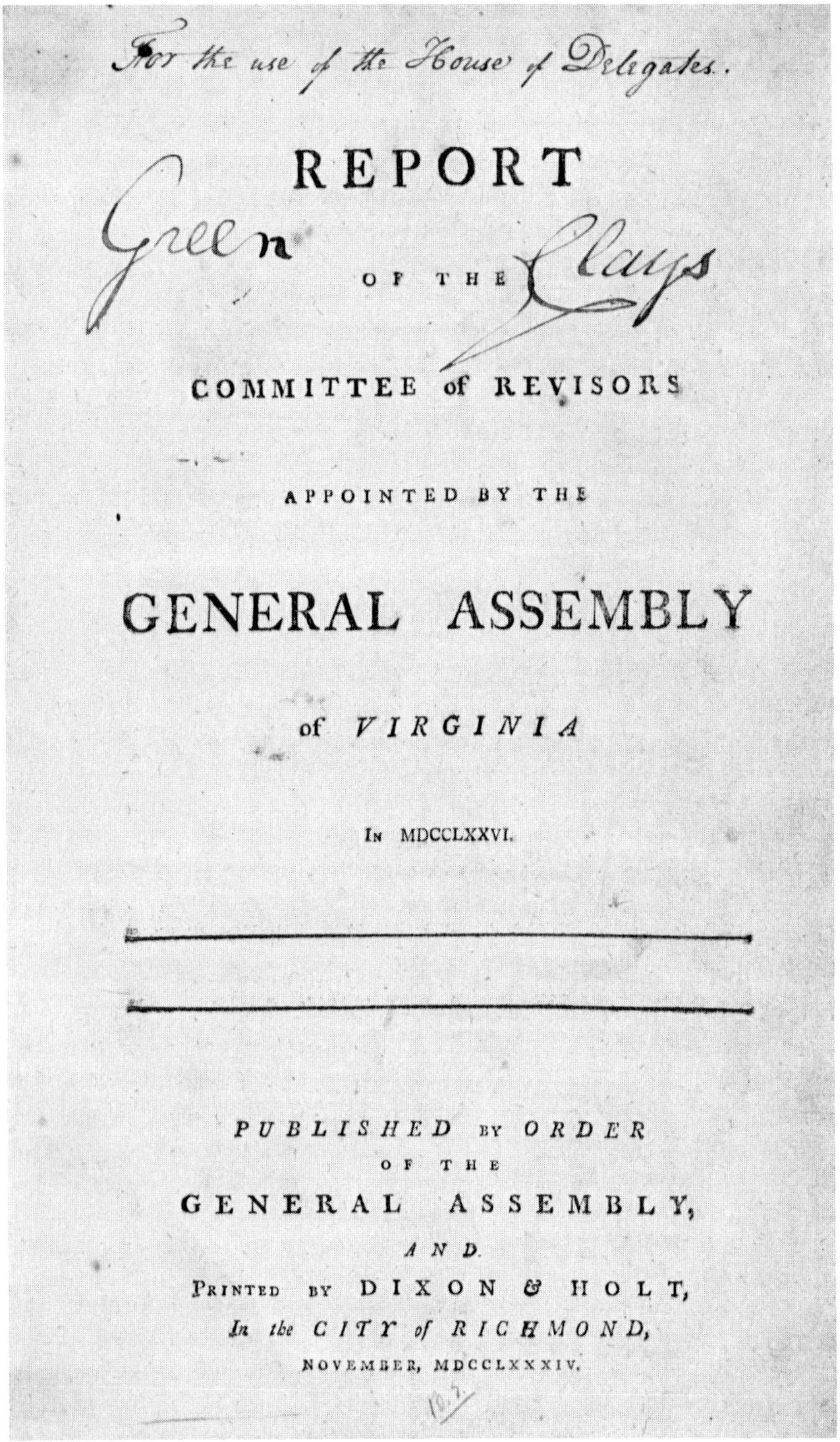

For the use of the House of Delegates.

REPORT

Green

OF THE *Clays*

COMMITTEE of REVISORS

APPOINTED BY THE

GENERAL ASSEMBLY

of *VIRGINIA*

IN MDCCLXXVI.

PUBLISHED BY ORDER

OF THE

GENERAL ASSEMBLY,

AND

PRINTED BY DIXON & HOLT,

In the CITY of RICHMOND,

NOVEMBER, MDCCLXXXIV.

In a preliminary meeting in early 1777, Pendleton, Jefferson, and Wythe divided up the entire body of Virginia law. Jefferson was assigned the common law, to the extent that it was to be altered, and all statutes to the legal beginning of the colony of Virginia; Pendleton had responsibility for the statutes enacted by Virginia; and Wythe drew the English statutes enacted after the establishment of Virginia. Pendleton did not understand that he was to revise as well as edit the statutes for which he was responsible, and Jefferson and Wythe were thus obliged to rework Pendleton's drafts to bring them into conformity with their own efforts.

In 1779, Jefferson and Wythe presented the council's efforts to the Virginia General Assembly in the form of 126 proposed statutes (Figure 3.12). A few of these measures, pertaining to immediate needs of the state, were enacted at once, but most of the report was allowed to lie untouched for five years. In 1784, James Madison managed to get it printed as an official document of the General Assembly and assumed the responsibility of acting as manager for the legislative package, reporting the success of each measure to Jefferson, who by this time was American minister in France. The last of the council's proposals did not become law until the 1790s.[48]

Jefferson took the laboring oar in the work of the Committee on Revision. In his *Autobiography* he singled out four statutes from the fifty-one he had drafted "as forming a system by which every fibre would be eradicated of ancient or future aristocracy; and a foundation laid for a government truly republican."[49] These were his bill abolishing entail; his bill abolishing primogeniture—a common-law doctrine providing that, if a man dies without having made a will, his eldest son inherits his entire estate; his Statute for Religious Freedom; and his "Bill for the More General Diffusion of Knowledge." This last measure was not enacted until the 1790s, and even then only in a stunted version that did not encompass his plans for a comprehensive system of public general education.[50] Other important measures were his "Bill for Proportioning Crimes and Punishments," showing the influence of the Italian *philosophe* Cesare di Beccaria's *Treatise on Crimes and Punishments* (1769), which was rejected by the legislature "because it mitigated penalties in advance of general public opinion;"[51] and his general revision of the laws governing slavery.

The most controversial bill that Jefferson drafted for the Committee of Revisors was his Statute for Religious Freedom.[52] This measure was ignored at first by the Virginia legislature, thanks to the commitment of many of its members to the preservation of the Anglican Church. Patrick Henry was the leading proponent of the established church in the General Assembly; James Madison, Jefferson's friend and protégé, emerged as the champion of disestablishment. Madison won the support of Virginia's Baptist community, which, both for doctrinal reasons and as a despised religious minority, opposed the continuation of Virginia's religious establishment. In 1784 Henry proposed a bill to support teachers of the Christian religion from tax revenues, and offered to include the Presbyterian denomination as a major beneficiary of the bill. This tactic, designed to split the Presbyterian-Baptist alliance opposing the religious establishment, worked at first. But early in 1785 Madison penned an anonymous "Memorial and Remonstrance against Religious Assessments" that was circulated throughout the state, thanks to the efforts of George Mason and other like-minded politicians. Madison's "Memorial and Remonstrance," an eloquent statement of the arguments for complete separation of church and state, joined other petitions in stiffening the resolve of the Baptist community and persuaded the Presbyterians to withdraw their support from the assessments bill. This aroused public sentiment led to the defeat of Henry's bill in the General Assembly in 1786, after which Madison, as legislative floor-manager for the statutes that Jefferson had drafted in the late 1770s, brought forward the Statute for Religious Freedom and steered it through the legislature to enactment.

The Statute for Religious Freedom, which Jefferson counted as one of the greatest accomplishments of his life, and the battle surrounding its adoption have become centerpieces of the modern controversy over separation of church and state, but most students of the disestablishment battle in Virginia have not considered it in its historical context.[53]

Protestant Christianity was an integral part of the lives of the Americans of the eighteenth century; there were scattered, tiny groups of Jews in urban centers such as New York City and Newport, and Catholic congregations in Baltimore, Philadelphia, and New York City, but these groups made up less than five percent of the American population. The Protestant majority believed that church and state should operate together to preserve the morality of the community. Religion and morality were matters of public as much as private concern; government stood as the secular guarantor of the value system of religion, and religion supported government's claim to the allegiance and support of the citizenry. Before the Revolution, the people of every colony from New Hampshire to Georgia presumed that government could encourage or even mandate religious observance and conduct, but not every colony possessed an "establishment of religion." Even those colonies possessing establishments represented a range of institutional arrangements; indeed, a major political controversy in New York before the Revolution focused on whether the colonial government had established the Church of England. An "establishment of religion" often meant something more than government endorsement of a single, preferred denomination, thanks to the remarkable proliferation of Protestant denominations throughout the colonies. Although some colonies—notably Virginia—gave pride of place to the Church of England, most that had religious establishments had "multiple" establishments—systems whereby two or more Protestant denominations received government endorsement and financial support through taxation of the citizenry and apportionment of the revenues thus collected.

The Revolution touched off profound changes in the relationship between church and state in American life. Although the connection between support of the British and Anglicanism is a matter of historical dispute, the Revolution toppled the already shaky Anglican establishments in New York and North Carolina, and seriously weakened the one in Virginia. In writing state constitutions and declarations of rights, the Americans had to face the consequences of constitutional provisions endorsing the principle of religious toleration. *Toleration,* a term put forth by the English philosopher John Locke, implies that a majority permits a minority to maintain itself and its errant ways despite the majority's power and right to compel the minority to conform. Liberal thinkers such as Thomas Jefferson and James Madison disliked the idea of toleration, preferring instead to recognize the idea of religious freedom as protected by the separation of church and state; thus, the twenty-five-year-old Madison suggested a rewriting of George Mason's draft of the Virginia Declaration of Rights that transformed its provision on religion from a statement of toleration to an endorsement of religious liberty.[54] In his Statute for Religious Freedom, Jefferson declared that religion was a matter between an individual and his or her Creator, and that, because government was powerless to compel belief, it could not and should not compel behavior inconsistent with an individual's religious beliefs, such as paying taxes to support a religious denomination with which he disagreed.

Madison added an important dimension to Jefferson's arguments, which were based on individual freedom and the dangers of an established church using government to tyrannize dissenters. Reviving a doctrine originally put forth by Roger Williams, the founder of Rhode Island, Madison contended that separation of church and state was also needed to protect religion from government. An alliance between church and state would permit the state to shape religious doctrine and practice and thus to corrupt religion under the guise of encouraging it. Neither Jefferson nor Madison believed that government support of religion was necessary to protect and encourage religion; both men maintained that religion and government occupied distinct spheres of human endeavor, and should not trespass on each other's legitimate domain.

Jefferson and Madison represented the leading edge of American thought on the relations between church and state. Most Americans believed that religion could not maintain itself without some form of government endorsement and support to encourage public morality and preserve the virtue of the citizenry, which was a needed precondition for republican government. Thus, several state constitutions required candidates for public office to be Christians or at least to believe in God. Nonetheless, a survey of the several state religious establishments during and after the Revolution indicates that single establishments were replaced either by multiple establishments or by disestablishment and that multiple establishments were discarded in favor of separation of church and state.[55] Although this process was not systematic or uniform, it represents the beginning of tendencies that dominated the religious history of the United States in the nineteenth and twentieth centuries.[56]

Only in Virginia did legal reformers attempt so ambitious and comprehensive a revision of the laws. However, recent research suggests that, as William E. Nelson has shown for Massachusetts, "[a]lthough little legal change occurred during the war itself, the attempts of the revolutionary generation to explain and justify the war and its political results set loose new intellectual and social currents which ultimately transformed the legal and social structure of the new state."[57] These changes in rules governing economic transactions and social behavior took decades to work themselves out, however, and may have been stimulated as much by the fiscal policies and economic upturn of the 1790s as by the changes in legal and political thinking occasioned by the Revolution.[58]

The American Revolution has been described as a "lawyer's revolution" because of the significant number of attorneys among its leaders and the centrality of legal and constitutional issues in Revolutionary political thought.[59] Yet many of the most eminent colonial attorneys tended to oppose the Revolution, and most were forced to flee the United States at the war's end;[60] in addition, most prominent lawyers who supported the Revolution gave up private practice for service in the Confederation and state governments. Nonetheless, the Revolution helped to augment the importance and influence of the legal profession, which had already begun to develop a vigorous and confident professional identity in the mid-eighteenth century.[61] The accomplishments of the emerging American bar in the years immediately preceding the Revolution included the establishment of professional associations and promulgation and enforcement of standards of admission and practice; the formalization and systematization of legal education by law teachers such as George Wythe and Judge Tapping Reeve of Litchfield, Connecticut;[62] and the publication of legal treatises, compilations of statutes, and collections of American colonial and state judicial decisions. A well-subscribed edition of Sir William Blackstone's *Commentaries on English Law* was published in Philadelphia in the early 1770s. Thomas Jefferson compiled colonial Virginia cases from the 1730s and 1740s; his notes are often the only surviving records for the cases they describe. In 1788 and 1789 the Philadelphia publisher Mathew Carey corresponded with John Dickinson, seeking to obtain copies of unpublished cases decided before the Revolution; Dickinson obliged Carey with some materials but warned him that he should obtain permission from Edward Shippen, who had compiled the cases, before publishing them.[63] Zephaniah Swift published the first of his many noteworthy legal works, *A System of the Laws of Connecticut,* in 1795; this book was a harbinger of the many distinguished legal treatises of the early nineteenth century.[64]

Despite the services rendered to the Revolution by John Adams, Jefferson, Jay, and Wythe, many ordinary Americans felt free to doubt the utility and desirability of the common law and those who made their living by it (Figure 3.13). In western Massachusetts, farmers plagued by debt

Figure 3.13
William Hogarth. *Hudibras and the Lawyer.* Engraving, 1726. For much of the eighteenth century the legal profession was held in low esteem. This plate is from Hogarth's first series of satirical engravings, which illustrated Samuel Butler's poem *Hudibras.*

maintained that their problems flowed from the lawyers' and the legal system's bias in favor of creditors. In 1786, writing under the pseudonym "Honestus," Benjamin Austin attacked the legal profession in a series of newspaper essays that later appeared in a pamphlet titled *Observations on the Pernicious Practice of the Law* (Figure 3.14).[65] Austin disclaimed any intention of rejecting laws themselves. Instead, he claimed that the domination of dispute resolution by lawyers, the complex, antiquated, and overburdened court system, and the intricate requirements of common-law pleading and procedure combined to render the operation of the law oppressive, mysterious, and costly to the ordinary litigant:

> Laws are necessary for the safety and good order of society, and consequently the execution of them is of great importance to be attended to. When, therefore, *finesse* and gross impositions are practised, and under sanction of the law, every principle of equity and justice is destroyed, the persons concerned in such pernicious measures ought to be brought forward, and their conduct arraigned before the impartial tribunal of the people.

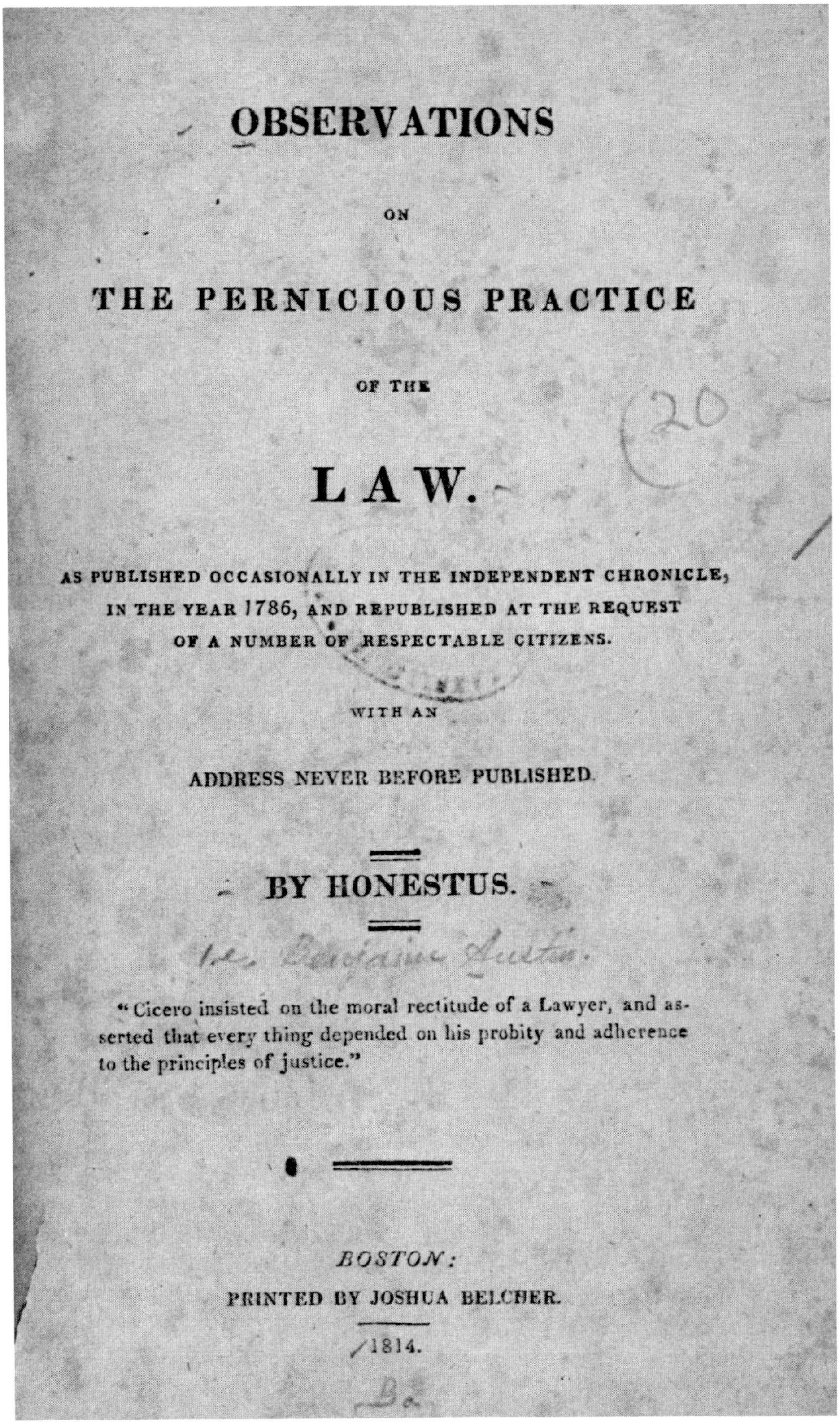

OBSERVATIONS

ON

THE PERNICIOUS PRACTICE

OF THE

LAW.

AS PUBLISHED OCCASIONALLY IN THE INDEPENDENT CHRONICLE, IN THE YEAR 1786, AND REPUBLISHED AT THE REQUEST OF A NUMBER OF RESPECTABLE CITIZENS.

WITH AN

ADDRESS NEVER BEFORE PUBLISHED.

BY HONESTUS.

i.e. Benjamin Austin.

"Cicero insisted on the moral rectitude of a Lawyer, and asserted that every thing depended on his probity and adherence to the principles of justice."

BOSTON:

PRINTED BY JOSHUA BELCHER.

1814.

Figure 3.14
[Benjamin Austin.] *Observations on the Pernicious Practice of the Law . . . by Honestus* (Boston: Joshua Belcher, 1814).

The study and practice of the law are doubtless an honourable employ; and when a man acts becoming the dignity of the profession, he ought to be esteemed by every member in the community. But when any number of men under sanction of this character are endeavouring to perplex and embarrass every judicial proceeding, who are rendering intricate even the most simple principles of law, who are involving individuals, applying for advice, in the most distressing difficulties, who are practising the greatest art in order to delay every process, who are taking the advantage of every accidental circumstance which an unprincipled person might have, by the lenity and indulgence of an honest creditor, who stand ready to strike up a bargain, (after rendering the property in a precarious state,) to throw an honest man out of three quarters of his property. When such men pretend to cloak themselves under the sacredness of law, it is full time the people should inquire, "by what authority they do these things."[66]

To Austin the remedy seemed clear—bar members of the legal profession from the courts and from the legislature and permit litigants to plead their own causes before impartial referees or arbitrators.[67]

Austin's polemic against the legal profession grew out of the same frustrations and difficulties that culminated in Shays's Rebellion later that year. Both the rebellion and Austin's campaign failed, overwhelmed by superior military and intellectual force. And, although the gradual abolition of common-law pleading and forced restructuring of the overburdened court system produced a transformation of the legal system, the society at large had also changed, in ways that would strengthen the authority and legitimacy of the American bar.

The Experience of the Loyalists

In his old age, John Adams estimated that at the beginning of the Revolution one-third of the American people supported Independence, one-third opposed it, and one-third tried to avoid having to make the choice at all. Historians have challenged his numerical estimates, but Adams's point about the division of opinion in the American colonies remains sound. Those who maintained their loyalty to the British crown were known as Loyalists or, derisively, as Tories; eventually both labels were attached to fence-sitting Americans as well as to American allies of the British army. Both groups posed legal, political, and intellectual problems for the new political communities that replaced the colonial system.

The Revolution was partly a civil war, with neighbors fighting on opposite sides. The Revolutionary governments responded to these problems of divided loyalty, developing procedures and mechanisms to punish Loyalists for their refusal to join the Revolution and to persuade or compel would-be neutrals to declare their allegiance to the Revolution.

The Continental Congresses and the states sought to redefine the crime of treason—a necessity when independence shifted Americans' allegiance from the British crown to the governments set up by the Continental and provincial congresses. The first step was the promulgation of loyalty oaths and declarations on national and state levels. For those who refused to take these oaths, the states prescribed harsh penalties. Such individuals had to pay fines and lost the right to vote and other legal rights and privileges. Still other laws authorized the states to confiscate the property of Loyalists—and, later, the property of nonswearing fence-sitters. The states also banished Loyalists behind the British lines and in some cases threatened to impose the death penalty on any banished Loyalist who dared to return home.[68]

The states set up special agencies of government to deal with the Loyalist problem and the administrative difficulties posed by the acquisition and disposition of confiscated estates—a major source of revenue to finance the governments and the war against the British. The most famous and active of these was New York's Committee for Detecting and Defeating Conspiracies. This committee did not act with uniform severity, however. William Smith, an eminent New York jurist and historian, had close ties to both sides during the early years of the Revolution; at one point, while under house arrest for refusal to swear the state's loyalty oath, he consulted regularly with the drafting committee of the New York convention on the preparation of the New York constitution of 1777. Once banished behind British lines, he became chief justice of the courts maintained in New York City, from which post he informed Governor George Clinton that Ethan Allen, the leader of patriot forces in Vermont, was trying to work out a deal with the British whereby they would recognize Vermont's separation from New York in exchange for Allen's switching sides. Eventually Smith left the place of his birth to assume a royal appointment as chief justice of Canada. Smith's distinguished career and powerful connections helped to protect him from the worst rigors of New York's campaign against the Loyalists.[69]

The most bitter and durable divisions occasioned by Loyalism took place in New York. New York City, captured by the British in the fall of 1776, became the primary base of the British army and navy during the Revolution and the principal place of refuge for banished Loyalists. The state was rent in two not only by the battles between the British and American armies but also by the political and violent clashes between New York patriots and Loyalists. New York's legislature enacted the greatest number and variety of anti-Loyalist statutes, and anti-Loyalist feelings persisted in the state for years after the end of the war.[70]

The Loyalist issue was an important element of the peace negotiations that produced the Treaty of Paris of 1783.[71] The diplomats sparred back and forth, with the British insisting that the Americans were obligated to compensate the Loyalist refugees for their confiscated property and the Americans threatening in turn to demand compensation for patriots' property that had been destroyed by British and Loyalist forces. The negotiations produced compromise provisions in the final treaty that pleased no one but

Figure 3.15

Artist unknown. *SHELB-NS SACRI-FICE or the recommended Loyalists, a faithful representation of a Tragedy shortly to be performed on the Continent of America. Invented by Cruelty. Engraved by Dishonor.* Line engraving, 1783. In this British cartoon, America (personified by the Indian warriors) slaughters the unprotected Loyalists while the unpopular prime minister, Lord Shelburne, looks on.

without which a treaty would have been unattainable. Under Article 4, both sides agreed not to impose barriers to creditors' lawsuits to recover "the full Value of all bona fide Debts heretofore contracted." Article 5 committed the Confederation Congress to recommend that the states repeal all anti-Loyalist statutes and take measures to return all confiscated estates and property, and declared the parties' agreement that those seeking to assert "their just Rights" to confiscated property "shall meet with no lawful Impediment" to their efforts. Article 6 committed the United States and the individual states to halt enforcement of existing anti-Loyalist measures and refrain from adopting new ones.

Diehard British sentiment was enraged by Foreign Minister Lord Shelburne's apparent willingness to abandon the American empire and to ignore the Loyalist exiles' pleas for justice (Figure 3.15). The more than 7,000 Loyalists who had fled to Great Britain were disillusioned and embittered by their treatment in the mother country. Dr. Peter Oliver commented angrily in 1784, "What are all the promises of protection and retribution? but to mortify, insult, and disappoint."[72] Led by William Franklin, the illegitimate son of Benjamin Franklin and the former royal governor of New Jersey, they campaigned vigorously but without success against the treaty. In 1783 a group of these expatriates formed an organization to promote their interests and to petition Parliament for financial compensation (Figure

3.16). In response to this controversy, the British government established a Loyalist Claims Commission in July 1783. Continuing its work until 1790, the commission investigated 4,118 Loyalist claims, helped Loyalist and British creditors to bring suit against American debtors, and eventually paid compensation awards of £3,292,452. The records of the commission are a valuable compilation of data for historians seeking to reconstruct Loyalism as a political and social movement.

After the announcement of the Preliminary Articles of Peace, some Loyalist exiles sought to return home and resume the lives they had led before the Revolution, but they usually met with hostility and even mob violence, despite their reliance on the protection of the treaty. In consequence many Loyalists abandoned for the time their hopes of returning home. On 24 November 1783, the day the British finally removed their armies from New York City (a date celebrated as Evacuation Day), thousands of refugee American Loyalists accompanied them. Writing to his son in late July, as the last refugees were gathering in New York, Elbridge Gerry declared, "The Refugees are mostly embarked from this Place, & some say their Number will not be less (including Women & Children) than twenty thousand, which far exceeds my former Ideas of the Matter." These refugees journeyed either to Nova Scotia and other parts of Canada or to England, if they had resources and friends in the mother country who were willing to assist them in making new lives for themselves. New York and a few other states continued to act against Loyalists in violation of the treaty, enacting statutes creating labyrinthine procedures to review applications of would-be returners. Not until the late 1780s did anti-Loyalist feeling abate enough to permit those Loyalists who still wanted to return home to do so.[73]

One lawsuit arising under New York's postwar anti-Loyalist statutes sparked a notable controversy over the validity of such laws under the Treaty of Paris of 1783 and the law of nations. At issue was the Trespass Act of 1783, under which owners of property that had at some point been behind British lines could recover damages for trespass from persons who had occupied that property without permission of the actual owner; the statute barred defendants from relying on British military authorities' permission for the trespass. Elizabeth Rutgers, the owner of a brewery in New York City, had fled the city—and the brewery—when the British army conquered New York City in September 1776. The army ran the brewery for two years and then licensed it to a partnership, one of whose members was Joshua Waddington, a British merchant. When the British evacuated New York City at the end of the war, Waddington remained, although he had given up the brewery in March. Mrs. Rutgers returned, learned that Waddington had used her brewery and was still in the city, and sued him under the Trespass Act for the rental value of the property from September 1776 through March 1783.

Waddington retained Alexander Hamilton, Brockholst Livingston, and Morgan Lewis to defend him in the suit brought by Mrs. Rutgers's lawyers, Attorney General Egbert Benson, Robert Troup, John Lawrence, and Wil-

Figure 3.16
Board of Agents for American Loyalists. *The Summary Case of the American Loyalists* (1785). This document, one of the efforts of the intense lobbying campaign of the Loyalist exiles in Great Britain for compensation for their lost property in America, was published in 1785 as a direct appeal to Parliament.

THE

SUMMARY CASE

OF THE

AMERICAN LOYALISTS.

HIS Majesty's faithful American subjects, who have sacrificed every thing to their attachment to Great Britain, were called forth to support the cause of their king and the laws of their country, by every motive which can actuate the hearts of zealous citizens, and by those assurances of protection, and even of recompence, which are held the most sacred among mankind. *Their induce-ments.*

What the inducements were, under which they acted, will appear from the laws and papers of authority that are now respectfully submitted to the consideration of those, the peculiar province of whom it is to judge of their force, and to give efficacy to the inference, which it is the chief purpose of this Case to draw from them.

The statute of 11 Henry VII. ch. 1. declared, " That, by the common law of England, the subjects are bound, by their duty of allegiance, to serve their prince against every rebellion, power, or might ; and that, whatsoever may happen in the fortune of war against the mind of the prince, it is against all law and good conscience, that such subjects, attending upon such service, should suffer for doing their duty of allegiance." *From Statute.*

" Here," says the celebrated Mr. Justice Forster, " is a clear parliamentary declaration, that, by the ancient constitution of England, founded on principles of reason, equity, and good conscience, the allegiance of the subject is due to the king for the time being, and to him alone. This putteth the duty of the subject upon a rational and safe bottom ; he knoweth that allegiance and protection are reciprocal duties ; he hopeth for protection from the crown, and he payeth his allegiance to it in the person of him whom he seeth in the peaceable possession of it. He entereth not into the question of title ; he hath neither leisure nor abilities, *nor is he at liberty to enter into that question :* but he seeth the fountain, whence the blessings of government flow to him, and there he payeth his allegiance ; and this excellent law hath secured him against all after-reckonings on that account." [Crown-Law, 8vo. edit. p. 399.] *From the Com-mon-Law.*

At the commencement of the late revolt in 1774, the secretary of state wrote to the American governors, exhorting them *to offer every encouragement to those colonists, who appeared in principle adverse to the proceedings of the mal-contents ;* thereby adding, to the declarations of the law, the encouragement of positive promise. [For that Letter, see Parliamentary-Register, 1775, vol. I. p. 186.] *From the Secre-tary of State's promise.*

It was in pursuance of the laws before-mentioned, that the king issued a proclamation in August, 1775, declaring, " That all the subjects of this realm, and of the dominions to the same belonging, are bound by law to be aiding in the suppressing of such rebellion ; commanding all loyal subjects to use their utmost endeavours to withstand such rebellion in the Colonies ; and giving assurances, *that none ought to doubt the protection which the law will afford to their loyalty and zeal.*" [This proclamation appeared in the London Gazette of the 24th of August, 1775.] *From the royal proclamation.*

The royal commissioners, Lord and General Howe, issued a similar proclamation in June, 1776, *under the express authority of the act of parliament,* 16 George III. ch. 5. declaring, among other assurances, " That due consideration shall be had to the meritorious services of all persons who shall assist in restoring the public tranquillity, and that every suitable encouragement shall be given to those who shall promote the re-establishment of legal government." [See Annual Register, 1776.] *From the royal Commissioners assurances.*

The proceedings of parliament, at the repeal of the Stamp-act, being intended as a monitory example for the future, gave encouragement to the Loyalists, equal at least to the foregoing assurances. In February, 1766, the secretary of state proposed a resolve, which was warmly seconded by Mr. Pitt himself, who soon became Lord Chatham, " *That the king's subjects, residing in the Colonies, who have manifested a desire to comply with, or to assist in carrying into execution, the Stamp-act, or any other act of parliament, have acted as dutiful and loyal subjects, and are intitled to the favour and protection of this house.*" [See Com. Journ. 30 vol. p. 603.] *From the par-liamentary re-solves.*

Hence

liam Wilcox. Hamilton took the case to demonstrate his opposition to anti-Loyalist statutes, which he feared would permanently damage the United States by driving valuable citizens into exile. When the case came before the Mayor's Court of New York City in August 1784, Hamilton chose not to dispute the facts alleged by the plaintiff. Instead he maintained, first, that the British order licensing the brewery to Waddington was consistent with international law, and particularly with the rules of war; second, he argued that the Trespass Act was null and void under the peace treaty. In response Benson argued that New York, as a sovereign entity in its own right, was not bound by a treaty entered into by the United States. Benson also maintained that, because the British had waged an unjust war against the United States, neither they nor those acting under British authority, such as the defendant, could claim the protection of the law of nations and the laws of war.

Writing for the court, Mayor James Duane ruled that the law of nations did permit Waddington to occupy Mrs. Rutgers's brewery under the license granted by the British commander-in-chief but not under the license granted by the British commissary-general, who did not have the authority to issue such licenses under the laws of war. Second, Duane ruled that the peace treaty should not be interpreted as conferring rights greater than those recognized by the law of nations. Third, the Trespass Act did not repeal or abrogate the law of nations but should be applied in a manner consistent with those doctrines. By so reading the statute, Duane and his colleagues avoided any conflict between it and the law of nations and were able to avoid the constitutional question of which should prevail. Governor Clinton and his allies, the authors of the Trespass Act, were outraged that the court did not enforce it strictly against Waddington, and the state legislature censured the Mayor's Court for its refusal to enforce the letter of the law.[74]

Hamilton decided that he had to defend his partial victory in *Rutgers v. Waddington* and the integrity of the Mayor's Court in the court of public opinion. He dashed off two eloquent newspaper essays—later collected as a pamphlet (Figure 3.17)—under the pseudonym Phocion, which he took from Plutarch's account of the Athenian general of unquestioned patriotism who urged that banished political adversaries be brought home and treated with forgiveness and generosity. In these essays he maintained that considerations of prudence and justice alike mandated magnanimity toward the Loyalists, and pointed out that the Americans' treatment of the Loyalists might well determine the world's opinion of the success or failure of the Revolution:

> The world has its eye upon America. The noble struggle we have made in the cause of liberty, has occasioned a kind of revolution in human sentiment. The influence of our example has penetrated the gloomy regions of despotism, and has pointed the way to inquiries, which may shake it to its deepest foundation. Men begin to ask every where, who

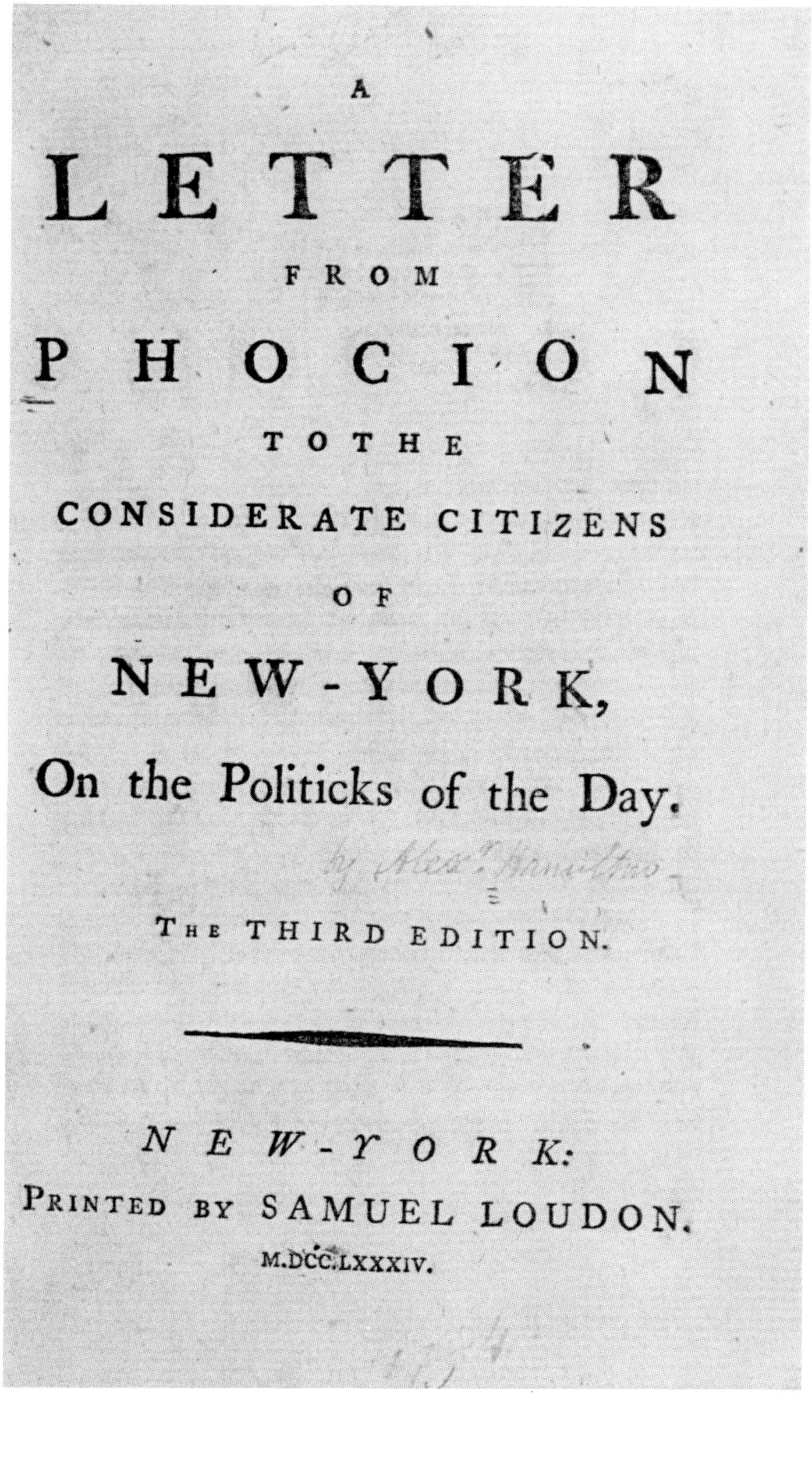

A

LETTER

FROM

PHOCION

TO THE

CONSIDERATE CITIZENS

OF

NEW-YORK,

On the Politicks of the Day.

by Alex. Hamilton

THE THIRD EDITION.

———————

NEW-YORK:

PRINTED BY SAMUEL LOUDON.

M.DCC.LXXXIV.

is this tyrant, that dares to build his greatness on our misery and degradation? What commission has he to sacrifice millions to the wanton appetites of himself and the few minions that surround his throne?

To ripen inquiry into action, it remains for us to justify the revolution by its fruits.

If the consequences prove, that we really have asserted the cause of human happiness, what may not be expected from so illustrious an example? In a greater or less degree, the world will bless and imitate!

But if experience, in this instance, verifies the lesson long taught by the enemies of liberty; that the bulk of mankind are not fit to govern themselves, that they must have a master, and were only made for the rein and the spur: We shall then see the final triumph of despotism over liberty . . . With the greatest advantages for promoting it, that ever a people had, we shall have betrayed the cause of human nature.[75]

Hamilton was not alone in his consciousness of the lessons of the Loyalist controversy for American politics. The animosities generated by Loyalism preoccupied many leading American politicians throughout the 1780s and finally prompted the delegates to the Federal Convention to include a narrow definition of the crime of treason and a demanding standard of proof for the crime—both based on the English Statute of Edward III—as Article III, Section 3 of the federal Constitution. These provisions of the Constitution may be seen as the Loyalists' parting legacy to their countrymen.

4

THE CONFEDERATION
IN QUANDARY

WRITING TO SAMUEL ADAMS from The Hague in May 1784, John
Adams warned that, even though the Revolution was over and the
Treaty of Paris was now in effect, problems for the new nation remained:

> Our Country, My Friend, is not yet out of Danger. There are great
> Difficulties in our Constitution and Situation to reconcile Government,
> Finance, Commerce, and foreign affairs, with our Liberties.—The Pros-
> pect before Us is joyfull, but there are Intricacies in it, which will perplex
> the wisest Heads and wound the most honest hearts and disturb the
> coolest and firmest Tempers.[1]

Adams's forebodings are an accurate summary of the history of the United
States under the Articles of Confederation in war and in peace. During the
Revolution itself, the Continental Congress managed to hold the Union
together and carry on the struggle for independence through the dedication
and determination of a handful of its delegates and the officers of its
executive departments. At that time, the British effort to subdue the rebel-
lious American states provided a needed backstop for the efforts of the
revolutionary government. Once the war ended and the British withdrew
their forces, however, the Americans seemed almost to lose interest in their
common government, concentrating instead on politics at the state level and
on pursuing their own interests.[2]

The Revolution itself had had the primary goal of establishing self-
government for the people of the United States; a corollary aim was to
lodge sovereignty, or ultimate political authority, in institutions as close to
the people and their local conditions as possible, in order to preserve republican government and ensure its responsiveness to the people's needs.
Thus the Articles of Confederation provided that the state governments
were to retain their sovereignty, except for that portion specifically delegated
to the Confederation Congress. These principles of Revolutionary constitutionalism exerted a powerful influence on the majority of Americans and,
in consequence, on most American politicians. The insistence on preserving
the sovereignty of the states had three drawbacks, however. First, the grudg-

ing grant of sovereignty to the Confederation did not include an independent source of revenue, leaving the Confederation at the mercy of the state governments for needed operating funds. Second, clashes between the states over boundaries, claims to western lands, and the regulation of interstate trade clogged the channels of politics and exacerbated state rivalries and tensions. Third, the state governments' jealousy of their own sovereignty often blocked efforts to secure any additional powers for the Confederation, including a source of revenue under its own control.

The difficulties and frustrations plaguing the Confederation and ensnarling American politics alarmed key political leaders in every state. They worried that a too-strong attachment to some of the principles of the Revolution might tear apart the nation whose independence the war had been fought to protect. Moreover, by thus fatally injuring the only nation in the Western world explicitly founded to preserve ideas of liberty and self-government, the defects of the Confederation could destroy the essence of the Revolution. These men also believed that domestic turmoil—the rage for paper money as a panacea for debt that convulsed Rhode Island and threatened to infect other states as well, Shays's Rebellion in Massachusetts and similar insurrections in New Hampshire and the "independent republic" of Vermont, the general resistance to the requirement of the Treaty of Paris to remove legal obstacles to the efforts of British and Loyalist creditors to recover the moneys owed them—posed just as great a threat to the promise of the Revolution, for all that the proponents of paper-money schemes and the "desperate debtors" of New England claimed that their oppressive creditors were the enemies of the Revolution.

Men such as James Madison, George Washington, John Jay, Charles Pinckney, and Alexander Hamilton began to compare notes on the troubles facing the United States and to form interstate networks of correspondence, replicating the growth of opposition to British colonial policy two decades earlier. These leaders—who included many of the most popular and respected men in the United States—shared a common experience of government at the level of the Confederation rather than at the level of the states; this shared experience encompassed service in the Continental and Confederation Congresses, the Continental Army, and the diplomatic corps and participation in the infant national economy. Well organized, well financed (often out of their own pockets), and sounding a message of urgency, they succeeded in reshaping the national political agenda to focus on the issue of granting more powers to the Confederation. Their efforts led to a series of interstate conferences that spread the message concerning the need for sweeping constitutional and political reforms. At last they won from the Confederation Congress an ambiguous mandate that they were to try to effectuate at a general convention scheduled to meet in Philadelphia in May 1787. Preparing for this meeting, James Madison began to sketch the elements of a new theory of politics and a new system of political institutions to reflect his understanding of the wellsprings of political action. For Madison, the impending Federal Convention was an unmatched intellectual opportunity, but he also shared with his allies the view that they were trying to save the Revolution from itself.[3]

"The Imbecility of Our Government"

The nature and extent of the Confederation's predicament in the mid-1780s are debatable. Although the American economy endured a major depression in 1785–86, that setback was brief, and the overall economic picture seems to have improved in 1786–87. Further, the winning of independence prompted in most Americans a feeling of excitement and confidence, a desire to experiment and to launch new ventures, and a hope that the United States could show the decadent nations of Europe the blessings and possibilities of self-government.[4] And yet the American political system in this period did face grave problems, even though they may not have directly affected the lives of most ordinary Americans.[5] Those who paid close attention to the workings of American politics saw much to alarm them in the existing state of American affairs.

Foreign relations provided a host of disquieting signs of the dangerous weakness of the Confederation. Great Britain still did not fully accept the independence of her former colonies, and the British kept up a multifaceted campaign of harassment and pressure against the Americans. Citing the American states' refusal to comply with the provision of the Treaty of Paris requiring the removal of legal barriers to Loyalists' and British creditors' attempts to recover property and debts due them, the British refused to comply with the treaty's provision requiring them to evacuate their forts in the Great Lakes region. Great Britain retained these forts for military and commercial reasons as well—primarily to cut off American access to the Great Lakes. They also explored other ways of restricting opportunities for American trade. The principal theorist of British measures to block commercial outlets for the American economy was Lord Sheffield, whose *Observations on the Commerce of the American States* first appeared in 1783. Sheffield argued that the American colonies had always been more trouble to the mother country than they were worth, and that independence would enable Britain to reclaim its rightful share of the "carrying trade"—that is, shipping. Inspired by Sheffield's reasoning, the British government issued Orders in Council barring American shipping from the Canadian and West Indian trades and scrapped Lord Shelburne's planned commercial treaty with the United States, which would have accorded American vessels the same privileges with regard to customs regulation that British shipping enjoyed. The crown struck another blow at the American economy by banning the export of machine tools to the United States—a measure aimed directly at the fledgling American manufacturing interests. Even more disturbing to the Americans were indications, hints, and rumors that the British and Loyalists were plotting ceaselessly against American liberty and independence, that armed bands of Loyalists supplied by the British were encamped on the Canadian border waiting for the opportunity to invade, and that the British were working with the dreaded Barbary pirates to destroy American shipping in the Mediterranean and to hold American sailors hostage until they should once more declare their allegiance to the crown.[6]

Britain was not the only foreign nation posing a threat to the United States. The Spanish government had entered the war against Great Britain solely for its own advantage and viewed the new republic with suspicion and disfavor, especially as American expansion south and west might interfere with Spanish holdings in North America. The Spanish sought to restrain this expansion by closing the Mississippi to American shipping where both banks of the river were under Spanish control. This restriction effectively barred Americans from the entire lower Mississippi, including the port of New Orleans. Both the Spanish closing of the Mississippi and the British actions restricting American access to the Great Lakes were designed to erode western settlers' commitment to the United States. Although these actions outraged the Americans, Spanish military and naval power made it all but impossible for them to defend their rights to the Mississippi.

The Mississippi question became perhaps the most sensitive foreign policy issue of the mid-1780s. American diplomatic attempts to reach a mutually satisfactory compromise began in early 1785, when Secretary for Foreign Affairs John Jay opened negotiations with the Spanish envoy, Don Diego de Gardoqui. The Jay-Gardoqui talks got nowhere, however. Gardoqui soon made it clear to Jay that the Spanish might tolerate American access to the Mississippi but would never recognize any American *rights* to that waterway. Gardoqui did offer a package of concessions affecting other Spanish and American interests—including a proposed commercial treaty, a conditional offer of support for American efforts to persuade Britain to surrender its Great Lakes forts, and an offer of aid in combatting the depredations of the Barbary pirates—which seemed to Jay to be the best of a bad bargain. Realizing that his attempts to win concessions on the Mississippi issue were futile, and eager to win a commercial treaty embodying Gardoqui's other proposed terms, Jay recommended to Congress that he be allowed to abandon American claims to rights of access to the Mississippi, reasoning that in future the American population in the West would grow so large that the Spanish would be forced to yield to reality. But when Jay made his case before Congress, sectional tensions flared, and delegates from the five southern states refused to permit any concessions of American rights of access. Although Congress voted to permit Jay to make the concessions he proposed, the five southern states demonstrated that they had the power and the intention to prevent any Spanish treaty from getting the two-thirds vote in Congress needed for ratification. Southern delegates, including James Madison and James Monroe, feared northern willingness to sell out the South and West for northern commercial advantage, and Monroe unfairly maligned Jay as a conscious agent of a northern conspiracy against the South. The Jay-Gardoqui talks dragged on through 1786 and 1787, ending inconclusively as Congress slipped into limbo. Resolution of the Mississippi question did not come until the 1790s.[7]

Even France, the foremost ally of the United States during the Revolution, seemed now to be hostile. The French supported the Spanish in the Mississippi controversy, limited American trade with French possessions in the Caribbean, and generally gave the impression that French friendship had been solely a matter of short-term advantage in European power politics, ending with the Treaty of Paris. Indeed, even the system of French consulates maintained throughout the new republic—the most elaborate diplomatic establishment in the United States—looked more and more to the nervous Americans like a network of intelligence-gathering stations and bases for French espionage and covert operations in the United States.[8]

By 1787 the Americans realized that, in the theater of power politics, considerations of morality and principle and protestations of friendship were no more than tactical devices used to secure and promote national interests. In this cold, hostile arena the United States had almost no reliable friends. Furthermore, the debts owed by the new nation and its people to its allies and to the Loyalists and the British were potential sources of weakness; the creditor nations could use these obligations as means to wrest humiliating concessions—even of territory—from the Americans.[9] The likelihood that foreign powers would seek to exploit sources of disunion among the states, and the undermining of American efforts to present a united face to the world by such internecine rivalries and tensions, alarmed John Jay and other continentally-oriented politicians such as Madison, Washington, and Hamilton.[10] Late in November of 1785 Washington observed to Madison:

> We are either a United people, or we are not. If the former, let us, in all matters of general concern act as a nation, which have national objects to promote, and a national character to support. If we are not, let us no longer act a farce by pretending to it. For whilst we are playing a d[ou]ble game, or playing a game between the two we shall never be consistent or respectable—but *may* become the dupes of some powers and, most *assuredly*, the contempt of all.[11]

When Jay and his sympathizers shifted their gaze to the domestic scene, the prospect was just as alarming. The Confederation Congress gave repeated proofs that it was too weak to manage its affairs. Even in so basic a matter as summoning a quorum of states, delegates had frequent reason to complain to their state governments about the general lack of interest in Confederation business. For example, Rufus King reported on 21 November 1785: "We have only five states represented. Pennsylvania & Connecticut are expected—when they are here we can form a House."[12] This lack of interest is attributable to several factors—among them the greater fascination and more immediate importance of state politics to all but a handful of delegates, the inability of many delegates to regard problems affecting other states as worthy of consideration, and the frustration that many delegates felt when problems affecting their own states were not treated with equal urgency by delegates from other states.

The Vermont controversy is a good example of how these tendencies helped to weaken the Confederation. The controversy between the conflicting claims of New York and New Hampshire to these territories had plagued colonial politicians for decades, and a British ruling in 1764 awarding jurisdiction over the territory to settlers with grants issued by New York did not abate the New Hampshire grantees' insistence on their claims. In 1777 residents of the territory, led by Ethan Allen, declared their independence from New York and New Hampshire, dubbing themselves the "independent republic of Vermont" and writing their own constitution. Governor George Clinton of New York viewed independent Vermont as a personal affront and besieged the New York delegates to the Continental and Confederation Congresses with complaints about congressional inaction and demands that the other states support New York's efforts to reassert its sovereignty over Vermont. Clinton redoubled his energies when he learned that Ethan Allen was negotiating with the British to abandon Vermont's claims to independence if the British would recognize its separate status—evidence of which he sought time and time again to have presented to Congress. Congress agreed that an involuntary dismemberment of one of the American states could not be tolerated, but it took no active steps to quell the Republic of Vermont. Just how ineffective New York's complaints were is illustrated by a 1780 letter from Daniel of St. Thomas Jenifer, a Maryland delegate to Congress, to Governor Thomas Sim Lee:

> I need not have Posted to Phila. in the haste I did, as the Crisis relating to Vermont was the occasion of the Summons. The New York Delegates are impatient to subdue the people settled on the New Hampshire Grants, who claim a Jurisdiction of their own; but I hope and trust, that Congress will have more wisdom than to take final Order in this Business, before our independence is established; we have business enough on our hands without carving out more at this time.[13]

When the Vermonters realized that they could expect no useful help from Congress, they pursued an aggressive policy of independence and aggrandizement, annexing towns from New Hampshire and even fighting a brief "border war" with New York in December 1781. In addition, their negotiations with the British commander of Quebec led to a cessation of all hostilities on their northern border in the hope that Britain would accept Vermont as a colony independent from New York and New Hampshire. When it got wind of these talks Congress offered Vermont statehood, and Vermont obligingly suspended the negotiations with the British, but Congress did not follow through on this offer; the American victory at Yorktown, a sign that the war was all but over, caused the British to lose all interest in talks with the Vermonters. Vermont existed in a jurisdictional limbo for the rest of the decade, with New York agitating for help in suppressing the upstart "republic," New Hampshire and Massachusetts remaining cool to the cause of Vermont but resisting New York's claims to the territory, and the other states preoccupied with other matters.

Vermont was the most extreme case of a problem besetting several of the states—how to deal with attempts by settlers of areas only arguably under a given state's jurisdiction to break off and form their own state.[14] These aspiring entities claimed that the overthrow of British authority had created a state of nature entitling them to establish whatever government best protected their interests. The existing states replied that the Revolution had not plunged America into a state of nature and that they were the sole legitimate heirs of British authority; this argument left them in the unenviable position of making the same arguments against the would-be states that the British had made against them.

The conflicting state claims to western lands also disturbed the harmony of interstate relations. Disputes such as that between Connecticut and Pennsylvania over the Wyoming Valley, a rich territory claimed by both states and ultimately awarded to Pennsylvania, tied up the time of delegates to Congress who, under Article 9, were obliged to serve on panels to arbitrate conflicting state claims. These controversies had significance beyond the conflicts over rival claims of sovereignty. Land was the most durable and reliable measure of wealth and power in eighteenth-century America, both for individuals and for the states. A state's territory was a potentially valuable source of revenue that could keep taxes down and, after sale to farmers and settlers, contribute still further to the state's economic growth. Thus border disputes and efforts to establish claims to unsettled territories or to subdue secessionist movements became as important as modern controversies among the arid western states over water rights.

Congress managed to resolve many of the boundary disputes through the appointment of panels of arbitration under Article 9. Ultimately, however, few of the secession disputes were resolved in this way. Because the Confederation was impotent, resolution of these disputes depended on the power of each state to suppress its own secessionist movement. North Carolina was able to subdue the "State of Franklin"; Virginia tolerated but curbed the attempts of the residents of Kentucky to form a new state; New York could not reassert control over Vermont and in 1791 had to acquiesce in the admission of Vermont to the Union as the first new state. New Yorkers remained disgruntled by the Confederation's inability to aid in their campaign against Vermont, and this resentment spilled over into other areas of New York's dealings with the Confederation.[15]

Remembering that the dispute with Great Britain arose from British assertions of authority to control American trade, the drafters of the Articles of Confederation chose not to grant the Confederation an independent, supreme power to regulate commerce or the power to finance itself by levying taxes or imposts on interstate or foreign trade. Congress issued requisitions to the states, based on formulas tied to their population, territory, and other measures of wealth. The revenue raised by this method was barely adequate to the Confederation's needs, even if the states had complied with them. Unfortunately, many states did not send the required funds to Congress, and first Robert Morris, the superintendent of finance, and later the Treasury Board created in 1784 had to write dunning letters (Figure 4.1) to get recalcitrant state governments to yield up their share of the burden of maintaining the Confederation.[16] The paper money of the Confederation (Figure 4.2) increasingly fell prey to the inflation that plagued the Confederation and state governments alike, giving rise to the cliché "Not worth a Continental."

The states' occasional refusals to comply with congressional requisitions reflected more than laziness or shirking. Some states, such as New York, sought to use their unpaid requisitions to force the Confederation to act on matters of central importance to themselves (as the New Yorkers did with regard to the Vermont controversy). Interstate rivalries also provoked occasional trade wars in which each state slapped tariffs, imposts, and customs inspections on commerce crossing its borders from neighboring states. Threats of trade wars became weapons of last resort in interstate disputes. In February 1784, for example, in an attempt to resolve a boundary dispute with New York that had previously been settled by a committee of the Confederation Congress as provided in the Articles, the Supreme Executive Council of Pennsylvania sent James Wilson to conduct investigations and researches into New York's archives. The council's letter introducing Wilson to Governor George Clinton, written by John Dickinson, is a typical blend of eighteenth-century courtesy and veiled threats:

> It becomes our duty to be prepared in the best manner we can, for opposing attempts that threaten the honor, the peace, and the wellfare of Pennsylvania . . .
>
> Another point of importance is suggested to us by a consideration of our mutual interests, & we shall freely mention it, because we repose a very high & particular confidence in the rectitude, prudence and liberality of the Councils by which the conduct of our sister State of New York will be governed.
>
> It is to be apprehended, that if a spirit of jealousy is suffered to arise between the two States, their measures may be reciprocally injurious. Our judgment and inclination point out to us a system totally different. It is our warmest wish, and shall be our diligent endeavor, that they may ever cordially harmonize in their commercial regulations.[17]

Rival systems of state economic regulation, prompted either by interstate rivalry or by a desire to protect local industries, threatened to cripple interstate commerce. Committees of merchants in the large cities organized

Figure 4.1
Circular letter from Robert Morris to Governor George Clinton, Philadelphia, 16 July 1781. Morris reminded each of the state governors "of the Impracticability of Carrying on the War Unless the States will cheerfully furnish the means."

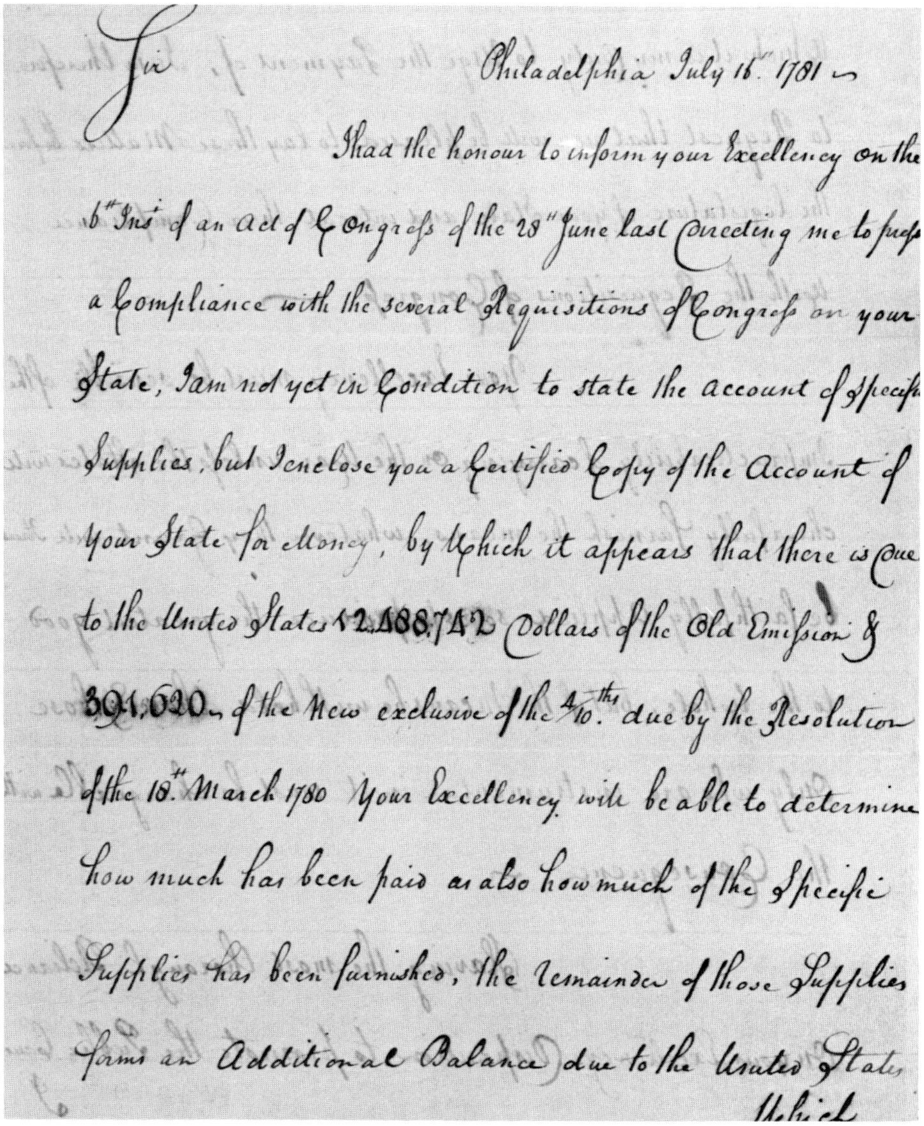

Sir

Philadelphia July 16th. 1781 —

I had the honour to inform your Excellency on the 6th Inst of an Act of Congress of the 28th June last directing me to press a Compliance with the several Requisitions of Congress on your State; I am not yet in Condition to state the account of Specific Supplies, but I enclose you a Certified Copy of the Account of your State for Money, by which it appears that there is Due to the United States 12,488,742 Dollars of the Old Emission & 391,620 of the New exclusive of the 4/10ths due by the Resolution of the 18th March 1780 Your Excellency will be able to determine how much has been paid as also how much of the Specific Supplies has been furnished, the Remainder of those Supplies forms an Additional Balance due to the United States Which

Figure 4.2
United States fifty-dollar certificate. Engraving, 26 September 1778.

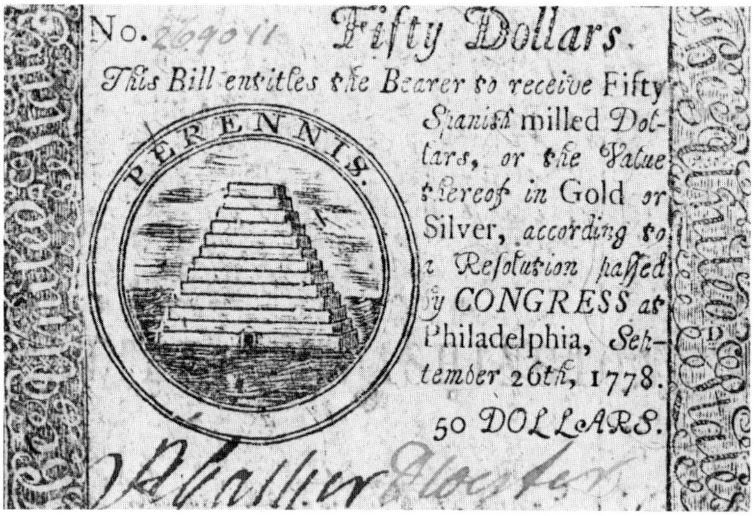

and corresponded with each other, commiserating over the difficulties of dealing with more than a dozen separate systems of customs regulation and working for the adoption of a uniform one, to be administered by the Confederation Congress. In 1785 the Committee of Merchants of Philadelphia described to its Boston counterpart the difficulty of securing such a uniform system:

> however necessary or desirable this might be, a great difficulty lies in the way: the defect in the constitutional power of Congress made the harder to supply from the jealousy of some of the States of the authority of that body. This overcome, another would arise, that of accommodating the generality of the system to the particular circumstances of the states, without some regard to which it would inevitably fail . . .
>
> The Committee have been attentive to this very important subject, and during the last session of Assembly a resolution was passed at our instance, requesting Congress to devise a system of commercial powers for itself to be recommended to the concurrence of the States—and it is not improbable, if Congress should think fit to act upon it, but that in this instance a regard to *national interest* may get the better of that jealous spirit which on other occasions has hitherto defeated the wisest plan for redeeming our *national credit & character*. A copy of our memorial & of the resolution passed in consequence are here transmit.
>
> Should such a general system formed in Congress from its own lights, or assisted by the ideas of a mercantile convention, be rejected when offered to the States, or from the natural difficulties attending it, not perfected in any reasonable time, it is the opinion of the committee that the States ought each then to resort to its own powers; but this necessity must be greatly deprecated, as nothing would give a more violent shock to the first principles of our Union, than such independent acts in a matter of such common interest and concern.[18]

The merchants' hopes for an amendment giving Congress the power to regulate interstate commerce echoed a theme in the history of the Articles of Confederation going back to its adoption in 1781. Alexander Hamilton and other nationalist delegates to Congress tried repeatedly to amend the Articles to grant Congress the power to levy and collect an impost, both to systematize regulation of trade and to provide Congress with an independent source of revenue. States with ports or cities that were major channels for interstate and foreign commerce resisted these attempts out of reluctance to share this lucrative source of revenue even with the Confederation as a whole. Nonetheless, in 1781 and 1783 twelve of the thirteen states agreed to such proposals. These amendments failed because Rhode Island (joined in 1781 by Virginia, which rescinded its acceptance) blocked both proposed amendments as assaults on the sovereignty of the states, even though the 1783 proposal was a scaled-down version of the 1781 proposal with a twenty-five-year time limit. Paradoxically, the leader of the delegates in Congress favoring an independent source of revenue, Alexander Hamilton, opposed the 1783 impost because Congress had so limited it in deference to state sovereignty. Rhode Island's refusal to accept the imposts of 1781 and 1783 earned it the distrust of the other twelve states, confirming in their eyes its reputation for instability and irresponsibility.[19]

Still another source of concern for those who believed that the Confederation was dangerously weak was the condition of state politics in the 1780s. Cropping up in each state but most frequently and dramatically in New England, movements to ameliorate or even abolish the hardships of debt alarmed moderate and conservative Americans, who valued the sanctity of property, contract, and law. These experiments took two forms: artificial inflation through issues of paper money, which reduced the value of debts and thus made it easier to repay them; and closing the courts, intended to prevent creditors from enforcing their claims against debtors. Rhode Island provides the most famous example of the use of inflation as a remedy for debt; the most important example of attempts to close the courts was Shays's Rebellion.

Rhode Island's frequent issues of paper money appalled commercial and professional men in other states; they regarded these measures as examples of the dangerous lengths to which democratic government could go if not properly checked.[20] In Rhode Island's contentious politics, two factions divided by their approaches to the debt issue won and fell from power like alternating ends of a seesaw. In 1786 the radical faction enacted two "tender statutes" requiring creditors of Rhode Island debtors to accept Rhode Island's inflated paper currency as the sole legal tender in payment of such debts. Should a creditor refuse a debtor's attempt to pay his debt in this virtually worthless currency, the debtor could deposit the sum of his debt with accrued interest with the local court or sheriff, who then swore out a writ to the creditor to inform him that this sum was on deposit in his name; the creditor had either to accept the deposited money or lose the entire value of his debt. The second of these laws also imposed criminal penalties for refusals to accept the paper money as legitimate currency in payment of debts or other obligations and established streamlined judicial processes, including a suspension of the jury-trial requirement, that commercial interests immediately attacked as violations of the traditional right of trial by jury.

In the midst of this controversy John Weeden, a Newport butcher, refused the attempt of John Trevett, a Newport cabinetmaker, to pay a debt with Rhode Island paper currency. Trevett thereupon sued Weeden, and the modest debt brought the controversy yet a stage further. Weeden was prosecuted under the second tender statute and was tried without a jury. Two of the state's leading attorneys, Henry Marchant and James Mitchell Varnum, appeared for Weeden. Varnum and Marchant sought to persuade the court that both new statutes were unconstitutional and that the court had the power to overturn unconstitutional legislation. Several factors—the virtually supreme position of the Rhode Island General Assembly in the state's political system, the lack of a bill of rights in the revamped Rhode Island charter of 1663, and the lack of precedent in the state for judicial review of legislation—combined to work against this daring gamble. Perhaps the greatest obstacle to the success of the defense offered by Varnum and Marchant was the structure of the court system; judges were appointed for one-year terms and could be removed at the pleasure of the legislature, which served as the state's appellate court of last resort.

Nonetheless the court did accept Varnum's and Marchant's arguments and threw out the attempted prosecution of Weeden on the grounds that the new laws unconstitutionally deprived defendants of the benefit of trial by jury. The General Assembly exploded in outrage, denouncing the unanimous decision of the participating judges (Chief Justice Paul Mumford chose not to participate—most likely to save his job), and demanded that all five judges appear before the General Assembly to explain and defend their conduct. Only three of the judges accepted this challenge, defending their decision in *Trevett v. Weeden*. The legislature rejected their arguments and removed them from office even before they had had a chance to speak, whereupon they filed a memorial with the legislature demanding due process of law as a precondition of their removal from office. Defended by Varnum and the state's attorney general, William Channing, the judges won a temporary reprieve, as the legislators realized that they could replace the judges in a few months when their terms expired by operation of law. The legislature contented itself with denouncing the judges who had voted against the measure and reasserting its possession of full legislative and judicial authority. The controversy arising from *Trevett v. Weeden* and the paper-money laws led to their repeal in 1789.

In other New England states, where political factions seeking relief from the hardships of debt could not secure the adoption of laws like Rhode Island's paper-money laws, debtors felt compelled to take more extreme measures against the efforts of creditors to collect the sums owed them. In Massachusetts, New Hampshire, and Vermont, embattled farmers decided to take the law into their own hands and out of the hands of the creditors and their agents, the lawyers.

The most famous and important debtors' insurrection was Shays's Rebellion.[21] The root of the rebellion was the American economy's lack of hard money, or specie, and the prevailing use of notes as a substitute currency. British postwar economic restrictions included a requirement that all payments from American merchants be in specie; thus trans-Atlantic commercial concerns had to demand specie payments from their customers, the inland small merchants. These in turn required their customers, mostly small farmers, tradespeople, and "mechanics," to pay for all future purchases in hard money and to make good on notes and outstanding bills. The farmers were accustomed to paying such debts in crops or other bartered goods and services. Suddenly they found themselves having to cope with new rules and requirements that were almost entirely outside their experience. This cycle of demands for specie and demands for payment of debts forced creditors to resort to the extreme remedy of foreclosing on farmers' land and personal property to recover the value of the debts owed them. Suits for debt in the period between August 1784 and August 1786 rose nearly three hundred percent over comparable suits between August 1770 and August 1772 in several counties of western Massachusetts.[22] The farmers were infuriated by the creditors' attempts to enforce their legal rights—especially at a time when dramatic increases in the levels of state taxes placed heavy burdens upon them. Gradually the small farmers of New England came to feel trapped by their economic plight and tried to make their dilemma clear to the commercial interests, the prime movers behind the proliferating suits for debt in the Massachusetts courts.

Farmers agitated for measures to moderate the harsh workings of the law on collection of debt, both by peaceful means of petitions and memorials to the legislature and the courts and by more aggressive, ritualized demonstrations reminiscent of the "rituals of revolution" practiced during the years leading up to the battle of Lexington.[23] These methods did not work, however, nor did the farmers' demands for a further emission of paper money and a tender statute—the Rhode Island expedients. The farmers of western Massachusetts decided that peaceful protests were not enough; rather, they would have to act against "the present gross mismanagement of our rulers," who had rejected "with supreme contempt our respectful petitions" and had denounced the farmers as "traitors, incendiaries, [and] vile creatures."[24] In September 1786 farmers in New Hampshire surrounded the state house and took the governor and legislature prisoners for five hours. In several counties in western Massachusetts, farmers calling themselves Regulators (from a term denoting the use of armed protest to achieve reform) closed the courts, demanding that the state legislature respond to their pleas for amelioration of the debt laws. Outbreaks also occurred in Windsor and Rutland counties in Vermont and New Haven County in Connecticut. With a brief interlude to permit fall harvests, the Regulation movement grew and spread until, by one estimate, nine thousand men— one-fourth of the potential armed force of New England—were up in arms against established authorities.[25]

Daniel Shays (Figure 4.3), a farmer and former captain in the Continental Army from Pelham, Massachusetts, was the nominal leader of the rebellion, but in truth he was just a symbol of the rebellion, having himself been prosecuted more than once for debt. He, Job Shattuck, and other veterans of the Revolutionary War were the Regulators' military leadership. They justified their movement by denouncing their creditors, the New England merchants and commercial speculators, as an emerging aristocracy bent on subjugating the people and depriving them of their liberties.[26]

In response to the initial successes of the rebels, the authorities of Massachusetts determined that a swift and strong military response was

Figure 4.3
Artist unknown. *Gen. Daniel Shays, Col. Job Shattuck.* Woodcut, 1787. The only contemporary portrait of Shays and his associate Shattuck was published on the cover of *Bickerstaff's Boston Almanack* for 1787 (3rd edition).

needed. In a long, remarkable letter—part intelligence report, part strategic proposal—written late in December 1786, Levi Lincoln, a prominent Massachusetts attorney, described the situation in western Massachusetts to Governor James Bowdoin and recommended the raising of a massive army drawn almost exclusively from the eastern part of the state—especially as militiamen in Worcester County had refused to turn out to oppose the Shaysites. Lincoln's letter proposed an elaborate series of marches and countermarches for the militia throughout western Massachusetts—even as far north as Rutland, Vermont—intended to impress the residents of the region with the might of the government:

> The marching thro the Country in different routs, at different periods, and to different posts, will be attended with many advantages. People are generally influenced by their senses. A formidable power displayed to view in a variety of places at the same time will infuse our friends with confidence & spirit, and our enemies with terror and confusion. The former will cheerfully aid, I had almost said mechanically aid, that Govt. which they not only *believe* is *able* but *see* are actually determined to protect them. The latter will either abscond, or tremblingly await, in silence and secresy their own wretched fait, and that of their fellows. Add to this, the troops will be better accommodated on their march, and at their posts, the inhabitants less burdened, Supplies more easily procured, and less consumed.[27]

The legislatures of Massachusetts and New Hampshire quickly enacted laws imposing harsh penalties on any present or former officer or enlisted member of the militia who took part in the rebellion, and in January 1787 Governor Bowdoin ordered the assembling of a force of 4,400 men under the command of General Benjamin Lincoln, brother of Levi Lincoln, a noted general in the Continental Army, and a wealthy merchant in his own right. This force was financed by loans subscribed by many of the wealthiest merchants in the eastern part of the state; if necessary it could call on the aid of a detachment of 1,340 soldiers from the Continental Army, made available by Secretary of War Henry Knox, another Massachusetts general of the Continental Army and a close friend and political ally of Governor Bowdoin and General Lincoln. This force was financed by a $530,000 requisition sought by Congress from the states—ostensibly for use to finance the army's campaigns against the hostile Indian tribes on the western frontier.[28]

The raising of Lincoln's army helped to radicalize the farmers who had taken part in or supported the Regulation movement, and they soon transformed it into an outright rebellion, or armed rising against lawful authority. They changed their tactics from preventing sessions of the debtor courts to launching guerrilla raids against prominent merchants, lawyers, and officeholders; these tactics were intended to dramatize their newfound determination to overthrow what they saw as the oppressive government of the state. The climactic battle came on 25 January 1787, when hastily organized Shaysite regiments clashed with Massachusetts militia guarding the federal arsenal at Springfield; four Shaysites were killed and twenty wounded. The farmers' failure to take the arsenal marked the turning point of the rebellion. On 4 February 1787, marching under the cover of a heavy snowstorm, General Lincoln's army surprised a smaller Shaysite force at Petersham and dispersed it without any casualties on either side. The leaders of the rebellion crossed over to Vermont and New York, taking shelter for a few weeks. An attempt to reenter the state and terrorize the conservatives of Berkshire County ended in a debacle. On 27 February 1787 the forces clashed again at Sheffield, leaving more than thirty Shaysites dead or wounded; government casualties included three killed and dozens wounded.

By mid-June the rebellion had ground to a halt. Despite their successes in the winter elections, which unseated many legislators who had opposed measures to mitigate the harshness of Massachusetts' laws governing debt, the new General Court continued to pass anti-Shaysite measures and to support the government's military operations against the rebellion. Even the replacement of Bowdoin as governor by John Hancock, long thought to be a democrat and a friend of the farmers, offered cold comfort, for Hancock supported vigorous measures to quell the rebellion. In addition, neighboring states—except, again, Rhode Island[29]—sided with the Massachusetts government in taking steps against the rebellion, offering rewards for the capture of Shays and other leaders of the movement (Figure 4.4). Even the British army in Canada, which in February 1787 had flirted with the idea of giving aid to the Shaysites to promote disorder in Massachusetts,

By his EXCELLENCY
George Clinton, Esq.

Governor of the STATE of NEW-YORK, General and Commander in Chief of all the Militia, and Admiral of the Navy of the same.

A Proclamation.

HEREAS His Excellency JAMES BOWDOIN, Esq; Governor of the Commonwealth of Massachusetts, did issue his proclamation, bearing date the ninth day of this instant month of February, setting forth, that the General Court of the said Commonwealth had, on the fourth day of the said month declared, that a horrid and unnatural rebellion had been openly and traiterously, raised and levied against the said Commonwealth, with design to subvert and overthrow the constitution and form of government thereof, and further setting forth, that it appeared that Daniel Shays, of Pelham, and Luke Day, of West Springfield, in the county of Hampshire; Adam Wheeler, of Hubbardston, in the county of Worcester, and Eli Parsons, of Adams, in the county of Berkshire, within the said Commonwealth, had been principals in, and abettors and supporters of the said unnatural, unprovoked, and wicked rebellion against the dignity, authority and government of the said commonwealth: The said proclamation was therefore at the desire of the said General Court, issued for discovering and apprehending the said several offenders above named, so that they might be rendered to justice; and it was thereby declared, that the persons who should apprehend them, should be entitled to receive out of the public treasury for that service, a reward of one hundred and fifty pounds for the said Daniel Shays, one hundred pounds each for the said Luke Day, Adam Wheeler, and Eli Parsons;—and his said Excellency the Governor of the said Commonwealth hath, in conformity to the articles of confederation and perpetual union between the United States, demanded of me, that the said offenders above named, if they shall have fled to this State, be delivered up and removed to the said Commonwealth: And whereas the Senate and Assembly of this State, in order more fully to evince the sense of the government of this State, have requested and to give assurances that the several rewards above mentioned, will be paid out of the treasury of this State, to any person or persons who shall apprehend the said offenders above named respectively, and deliver them into the custody of any of the Sheriffs within this State. I have therefore issued this proclamation, hereby requiring all Sheriffs and other officers, and ministers of justice within their respective bailiwicks and jurisdictions, and all other the citizens of this State, to take and apprehend the said Daniel Shays, Luke Day, Adam Wheeler and Eli Parsons, if they shall be found within this State, and convey to one of the gaols within this State, and deliver them to the keeper of such gaol, who is hereby required to receive them, and to keep them in safe and close custody in such gaol, until they the said several offenders above named shall be removed to the said Commonwealth of Massachusetts, or until they shall severally, by due course of law, be delivered from the gaol to which they shall be respectively committed: And I do hereby offer and assure to the person or persons, who shall, within this State, apprehend the said Daniel Shays, Luke Day, Adam Wheeler and Eli Parsons, severally, and deliver them into the custody of any of the Sheriffs thereof, the respective rewards above mentioned, to be paid out of the treasury of this State: And I do hereby enjoin and require the citizens of this State not to supply with provisions, arms or military stores, nor to afford any other aid whatsoever to any person or persons who shall be found in arms against the said Commonwealth, as they will answer the same at their peril.

Given under my hand and the Privy Seal, at the city of New-York, this 24th day of February, in the eleventh year of the Independence of the said State, 1787.
GEO. CLINTON.

NEW-YORK: Printed by S. and J. LOUDON, Printers to the STATE.

had backed off. An economic upturn in the spring of 1787 helped ease the difficulties of Massachusetts farmers, as did the legislature's efforts to ameliorate the state's debt laws. Finally, realizing that they had virtually no friends anywhere in the region, many of the leaders of the rebellion fled to unsettled northern and western lands; Shays himself settled in Vermont, where he remained, unmolested, to the end of his life.[30]

The rebellion in Massachusetts shocked government leaders throughout the nation and briefly displaced Rhode Island's tactics as the leader of the "parade of horribles" catalogued by critics of the Articles of Confederation. If Massachusetts, the second oldest political community in the United States and the one with perhaps the best and most moderate constitution, could be convulsed by rebellion, what did this insurrection portend for the nation as a whole? The uprisings in New Hampshire and Vermont, though less dramatic and sweeping than Shays's Rebellion, also contributed to a general sense of instability and crisis requiring swift action. Even Massachusetts politicians who had previously opposed attempts to revise the Articles of Confederation changed their minds in the wake of the Shaysite insurrection, and the rebellion lingered on as a reliable propaganda device for the proponents of the Constitution.[31]

The Rise of a Reform Movement

By 1787 the problems of trade regulation, revenue, interstate rivalry, and domestic instability had tangled themselves into a Gordian knot. The efforts of American politicians to untie this knot forced some of the boldest of them to envision a new political system for the United States.

What has since been recognized as the first stage in this movement began as a local dispute between Virginia and Maryland over navigation rights to the Potomac and Pocomoke rivers.[32] In March 1784 James Madison approached Thomas Jefferson and proposed the appointment of delegates from the two states to work out an amicable compromise of their states' competing claims. Jefferson agreed, and soon both states' legislatures acted, appointing a total of seven commissioners. Maryland selected Daniel of St. Thomas Jenifer, Thomas Stone, and Samuel Chase; Virginia appointed George Mason, Edmund Randolph, Archibald Henderson, and Madison himself.

Somehow, however, Governor Patrick Henry and his aides managed to fumble the business so badly that none of the four Virginia commissioners was informed of his appointment or of the place and time of the conference. Thus the Maryland commissioners arrived in Alexandria, Virginia, on 21 March 1785 but none of their Virginia counterparts was present to welcome them. Henderson lived in Alexandria, so the Maryland negotiators found him, informed him of his appointment, and urged that he get in touch with his fellow commissioners to inform them of the business at hand and urge them to come to Alexandria as soon as possible. Henderson sent word to

Mason, who decided that the conference should begin speedily, even though neither Madison nor Randolph was present (they did not get news of the conference until it was too late for them to attend). Mason and Henderson decided to overlook the provision of the Virginia resolution authorizing any *three* of the four commissioners to enter into negotiations with the Maryland commissioners.

Meanwhile George Washington had got wind of the problems that threatened to derail the conference, and invited the commissioners of both states to stay with him at Mount Vernon (Plate VI), where they could transact their business. The Mount Vernon Conference began on 25 March 1785 and continued for three days. Washington took no formal part in the conference, although he was keenly interested in the outcome, having become involved in a massive engineering project to connect the Potomac, Shenandoah, and Ohio river valleys by a system of locks and canals. Washington had lobbied the Virginia legislature in support of this plan and had been appointed—with Thomas Blackburn and General Horatio Gates—as a Virginia commissioner to meet with Maryland commissioners to work out agreements on the responsibilities for constructing these canals.[33] Thanks to Washington's hospitality and expert knowledge of the rivers of the Potomac region, the commissioners meeting at Mount Vernon soon concluded their labors in what Madison described to Jefferson as "the most amicable spirit."[34]

The Mount Vernon Compact dealt not only with problems of tidewater navigation but also with a wide range of issues of navigation and commerce. It settled many disputed questions of overlapping customs duties and regulations, established a unified system of regulations for vessels docking in both states, established that the Potomac would be "a common High Way" to all citizens of the United States, and provided for common fishing rights, for the establishment of lighthouses, beacons, and buoys, for the prohibition of piracy, and many other matters. Further, the commissioners made a series of recommendations governing the respective values of the two states' currencies and foreign currencies, a uniform system of dealing with protested bills of exchange (presaging the various uniform commercial laws of the twentieth century), and uniformity and equality in the customs duties charged by each state. It was thus the most sweeping agreement dealing with interstate matters entered into since the ratification of the Articles of Confederation.[35]

Madison was delighted with the Mount Vernon Compact and acted as its floor-manager in the Virginia General Assembly, which quickly ratified it, as did the Maryland legislature, which also proposed that Delaware be brought into the agreement. In addition, the commissioners gathered at Mount Vernon had written to the president of the Supreme Executive Council of Pennsylvania informing him of their work and inviting that state to join the continuing plans for expanding the navigation of the Potomac. Madison had hoped that the Virginia legislature would agree to submit the compact to the Confederation Congress for its approval, in conformity with

Figure 4.5
Samuel Smith after Thomas Leitch. *A View of Charles-Town, the Capital of South Carolina.* Etching and engraving, 1776. The largest city in the South, Charleston was the capital of South Carolina until the end of the eighteenth century, and home to the state's most powerful political family, the Pinckneys.

Article 6 of the Articles of Confederation, but the legislature turned the proposal down. Instead John Tyler, father of the tenth president, proposed a resolution calling upon the legislatures of the other states to build on the example of the Mount Vernon Conference:

> *Resolved,* that Edmund Randolph, James Madison, jun., Walter Jones, Saint George Tucker, and Meriwether Smith, Esquires, be appointed commissioners, who, or any three of whom, shall meet such commissioners as may be appointed by the other States in the Union, at a time and place to be agreed on, to take into consideration the trade of the United States; to examine the relative situations and trade of the said States; to consider how far a uniform system in their commercial regulations may be necessary to their common interest and their permanent harmony; and to report to the several States, such an act relative to this great object, as, when unanimously ratified by them, will enable the United States in Congress, effectually to provide for the same.[36]

The conference was quickly scheduled to meet in Annapolis, Maryland, on 11 September 1786.

At roughly the same time that Maryland and Virginia were considering the Mount Vernon Compact, the Committee of Merchants of Boston had proposed a resolution, which the General Court adopted, that the Massachusetts delegates in Congress should apply to the Confederation Congress to call a general convention to revise the Articles of Confederation. In their reply Elbridge Gerry, Rufus King, and Samuel Holton declined to obey the legislature's request, explaining that they feared that such proposals would lead to "baleful aristocracies" that might overturn the republican governments of the Confederation and the states:

> Many are of Opinions, the States have not yet had Experience Sufficiently to determine the Extent of power vested in Congress by the Confederation; viz., therefore that every Measure at this Time, proposing an Alteration, is premature . . . We are for increasing the power of Congress as far as it will promote the happiness of the people, but at the same time are clearly of opinion that every measure should be avoided which would strengthen the hands of the enemies to a free government. And that an administration of the present Confederation with all its inconveniences, is preferable to the risk of general dissensions and animosities which may approach to anarchy and prepare the way to a ruinous system of government.[37]

In writing this letter Gerry, King, and Holten were harking back to the traditions of Revolutionary constitutionalism embodied in the Articles, but events were moving more quickly than they realized.

In the summer of 1786, a committee led by Charles Pinckney of South Carolina (Figure 4.5) proposed seven amendments to the Articles of Confederation. These resolutions provided, among other things, for exclusive congressional authority over foreign and interstate commerce; limited congressional power to compel delinquent states to comply with congressional requisitions; the creation of a seven-member court to hear cases against federal officials and appeals from state courts on questions of foreign relations, international law, or congressional regulations concerning commerce and revenue; a reduction of the number of states needed to ratify amendments pertaining to revenue, from thirteen to eleven; and a modification of the requirement of seven states for a quorum. These amendments got nowhere, although they were published in the newspapers and sent to the states; in essence, as Jack Rakove has pointed out, they would have enabled the Confederation Congress to perform its assigned tasks under the Articles rather than transforming it into a real, sovereign government.[38]

Madison had been cool to the idea of another interstate convention, preferring an amendment to the Articles expanding congressional authority over commerce. He was convinced that the only result of a general commercial convention would be an increase in sectional jealousies, which had broken out most recently in the controversy over the Mississippi. He supported Tyler's motion despite his conviction that it would miscarry; with his customary thoroughness, he prepared a memorandum detailing his re-

Figure 4.6
Bénoit Louis Prévost after Pierre
Eugène Du Simitière. Portrait of
John Dickinson. Engraving, 1781.
This portrait of Dickinson
appeared in *Collection des Géné-
raux, Ministres, et Magistrats que se
sont rendu célèbres dans la révolution
. . .* (Paris, 1781).

Figure 4.7
John Vanderlyn after Gilbert
Stuart. Portrait of Egbert
Benson. Oil on canvas, 1794–95.

searches on the structures and weaknesses of ancient and modern confederacies.[39] This memorandum, drawn from a remarkable array of historical sources, eventually found its way into *Federalist* Nos. 18–20.

The Annapolis Convention was far from the success that the Mount Vernon Conference had been.[40] Writing to his brother Ambrose a few days before the Convention began, Madison prophesied its failure: "I came to this place a day or two ago, where I found two Commsrs. only. A few more have since come in, but the prospect of a sufficient no. to make the Meeting respectable is not flattering."[41] His doubts are borne out by a review of the decisions of the several states with respect to the convention. Correspondence among advocates of a stronger general government passed back and forth in the spring and summer of 1786; for example, Jabez Bowen of Rhode Island wrote to President John Sullivan of New Hampshire in August:

> Since answering your Letter to me I am informed that the State of New hampshire have not appointed any Commisioners to meet at Anapolis, to agree on some Commercial Regulations to be adopted by all the United States. I think this is an Offer that we of New England ought not to let pass unnoticed by any means. if we can secure the Carrying Trade of the Southern States, there will be . . . incouragement for the Building of Vessells in the Northern States &c. &c.

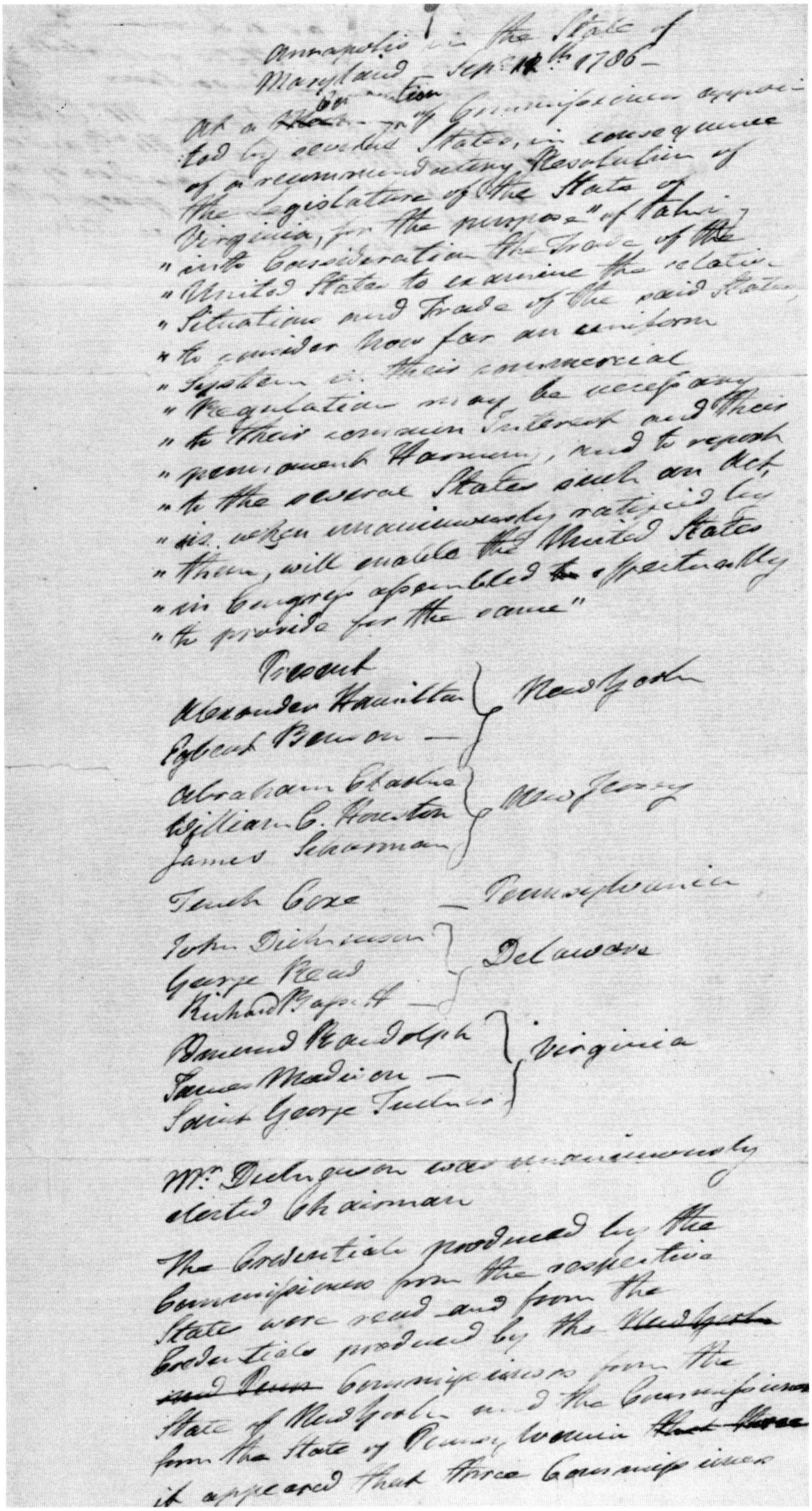

Annapolis in the State of
Maryland Sepr. 11th 1786 —

At a ~~Meeting~~ Convention of Commissioners appointed by several States, in consequence of a recommendatory Resolution of the Legislature of the State of Virginia, for the purpose "of taking into Consideration the Trade of the "United States to examine the relative "Situation and Trade of the said States, "to consider how far an uniform "System in their commercial "Regulation may be necessary "to their common Interest and their "permanent Harmony, and to report "to the several States such an Act, "as, when unanimously ratified by "them, will enable the United States "in Congress assembled ~~to~~ effectually "to provide for the same"

Present

Alexander Hamilton } New York
Egbert Benson —

Abraham Clarke } New Jersey
William C. Houston
James Schureman

Tench Coxe — Pennsylvania

John Dickinson } Delaware
George Read
Richard Bassett —

Edmund Randolph } Virginia
James Madison —
Saint George Tucker

Mr. Dickinson was unanimously elected Chairman

The Credentials produced by the Commissioners from the respective State were read and from the Credentials produced by the ~~New York and Penns~~ Commissioners from the State of New York and the Commissioners from the State of Pennsy. Vania ~~that three~~ it appeared that three Commissioners

Figure 4.8
[Egbert Benson.] Minutes of the proceedings of the Annapolis Convention. Draft, 11 September 1786.

Figure 4.9
John Trumbull. Portrait of Alexander Hamilton. Oil on canvas,
ca. 1804–1808. Trumbull first
painted Hamilton in 1792 at the
request of John Jay. Six replicas
of that portrait are known; this
one dates from after Hamilton's
death.

If your Assembly does not meet soon should Quere whether an Appointment made by the Executive Councill would not be verry necessary.[42]

Unfortunately, neither New Hampshire nor Rhode Island was represented at Annapolis. Only five states' delegates had arrived in time for the meeting. The Maryland legislature, plagued by factional strife, had refused Virginia's invitation; thus the convention would be meeting without the host state's delegates. Three other states—Connecticut, South Carolina, and Georgia—also chose not to send delegates, and the delegates of Massachusetts, New Hampshire, Rhode Island, and North Carolina arrived too late to take part.

Twelve delegates representing New York, New Jersey, Pennsylvania, Delaware, and Virginia met in Annapolis (Plate VII), probably in Mann's Tavern, a short walk from the state house. They unanimously elected John Dickinson (Figure 4.6)—now a resident of Delaware and the senior delegate in years and service—chairman of the convention. They chose as secretary Egbert Benson of New York (Figure 4.7), who kept the only records of the

To the Honorable the Legislatures of Virginia, Delaware Pennsylvania, — New Jersey, and New York.

The Commissioners from the said States respectively to Assembled at Annapolis humbly beg leave to report,

That pursuant to their several appointments, they met at Annapolis in the State of Maryland on the Eleventh day of September Instant, and having proceeded to a Communication of their powers, they found that the States of New York, Pennsylvania and Virginia had in Substance and nearly in the same terms authorised their respective Commissioners "to meet such Commissioners "as were or might be, appointed by the other States in the Union "at such time and place as should be agreed upon by the said "Commissioners to take into Consideration the trade and Commerce "of the United States, to consider how far an uniform System of "their Commercial Intercourse and Regulations might be "necessary to their Common Interest and permanent harmony "and to report to the several States, such an Act relative to this "great Object as when unanimously ratified by them, would "enable the United States in Congress assembled effectually "to provide for the same."

That the State of Delaware had given similar powers to their Commissioners, with this difference only, that the Act to be framed in Virtue of these powers is required to be reported "to the united States in Congress assembled, to be agreed to by "them, and confirmed by the Legislatures of every State."

That the State of New Jersey had enlarged the Object of their appointment, empowering their Commissioners "to con- "-sider how far an uniform System of their Commercial "Regulations and other important matters, might be necessary "to the common Interest and permanent harmony of the several "States" and to report such an Act on the Subject as when "ratified by them would enable the united States in Congress "assembled effectually to provide for the exigencies of the union"

That appointments of Commissioners have also been made by the States of New Hampshire, Massachusetts, Rhode Island and North Carolina, none of whom however have attended; but that no information has been received by your Commissioners of any appointment having been made by the States of Connecticut, Maryland South Carolina or Georgia.

proceedings (Figure 4.8). The delegates compared their instructions and realized that, whereas four of the five states represented had confined their delegates' attention to matters of commercial regulation,

> the State of New Jersey had enlarged the object of their appointment, empowering their Commissioners, "to consider how far an uniform system in their commercial regulations and *other important matters*, might be necessary to the common interest and permanent harmony of the several States," and to report such an Act on the subject, as when ratified by them "would enable the United States in Congress assembled, effectually to provide for the exigencies of the Union."[43]

After three days of discussion, the delegates took the lead offered in the New Jersey instructions and agreed to prepare an address to the legislatures of their respective states and to send copies of this address to the other eight states as well "from motives of respect." This address, the work of Alexander Hamilton (Figure 4.9), the leading spirit of the convention, with some assistance from James Madison, explained that the commissioners decided not to proceed with the business entrusted to them because of the lack of a sufficient number of states. Hamilton's report (Figure 4.10) continued:

> Deeply impressed however with the magnitude and importance of the object confided to them on this occasion, your Commissioners cannot forbear to indulge an expression of their earnest and unanimous wish, that speedy measures may be taken, to effect a general meeting, of the States, in a future Convention, for the same, and such other purposes, as the situation of public affairs, may be found to require. . . .
>
> Under this impression, Your Commissioners, with the most respectful deference, beg leave to suggest their unanimous conviction, that it may essentially tend to advance the interests of the union, if the States, by whom they have been respectively delegated, would themselves concur, and use their endeavours to procure the concurrence of the other States, in the appointment of Commissioners, to meet at Philadelphia on the second Monday of May next, to take into consideration the situation of the United States, to devise such further provisions as shall appear to them necessary to render the constitution of the Foederal Government adequate to the exigencies of the Union.[44]

Figure 4.10
[Alexander Hamilton for the Annapolis Convention.] "Address to the legislatures of Virginia, Delaware, Pennsylvania, New Jersey, and New York." 14 September 1786. This copy of the Annapolis Convention address, which was circulated to the state legislatures, was probably sent to the Massachusetts General Court.

The delegates to the Annapolis Convention then dissolved the meeting and returned home. In Philadelphia Rufus King talked with Hamilton and Benson and reported to Governor Bowdoin his impression of the results of the convention: "Foreign nations had been notified of this convention, the Friends to a good general Government through these states looked to it with anxiety & Hope—; the history of it, will not be more agreeable to the former, than it must be seriously painful to the latter."[45]

The report of the convention was more the result of the delegates' desperation and disappointment than of any preconceived strategy to adopt extreme measures. In any event, the recommendation of the Annapolis Convention galvanized those who supported an effort to strengthen the general government. Within two months of the Convention's address to the states, for example, Virginia's General Assembly adopted a resolution (Figure 4.11) authorizing the appointment of seven deputies or delegates to represent the state at a general convention in Philadelphia to "join with [delegates from the other states] in devising and discussing all such Alterations and farther Provisions as may be necessary to render the Foederal Constitution adequate to the Exigencies of the Union."[46] Virginia, the first state to act, was soon joined by New Jersey, Pennsylvania, and South Carolina; indeed, eight of the twelve states that ultimately sent delegates to Philadelphia in 1787 followed the broad Annapolis formula in defining their authority.

The Confederation Congress delayed acting on the recommendation of the Annapolis Convention, referring its report to a committee on 11 October 1786 but not acting formally until 21 February 1787, when it adopted a more limited resolution authorizing the calling of a convention "for the sole and express purpose of revising the Articles of Confederation and reporting to Congress and the several legislatures such alterations and provisions therein as shall, when agreed to in Congress and confirmed by the states render the federal constitution adequate to the exigencies of government and the preservation of the Union."[47] Four states followed this formula. Thus the convention that was to meet in Philadelphia already had to deal with an uncertain and contradictory mandate, a problem that had plagued nearly every intercolony and interstate convention since the Albany Congress of 1754.

George Washington had no doubts about the task facing the Convention. Writing to Madison in March 1787, he declared his conviction that "a thorough reform of the present system is indispensable." Rejecting the occasional murmuring heard throughout America in favor of adopting a monarchy, he declared that the proposed convention should be at liberty to take whatever steps the delegates might think necessary:

> if the delegates come to [the convention] under fetters, the salutary ends proposed will in my opinion be greatly embarrassed & retarded, if not altogether defeated. I am anxious to know how this matter really is, as my wish is, that the Convention may adopt no temporizing expedient, but probe the defects of the Constitution to the bottom, and provide radical cures, whether they are agreed to or not. A conduct like this, will stamp wisdom and dignity on the proceedings, and be looked on as a luminary, which sooner or later will shed its influence.[48]

For his part, Madison was hard at work preparing for the Convention. Now that Congress and every state but Rhode Island had recognized the need for a revision of the Articles, he was more optimistic about the Convention's chances of success than he had been about those of the Annapolis

Figure 4.11
An Act for Appointing Deputies from This Commonwealth . . . (23 November 1786).

AN ACT

FOR APPOINTING DEPUTIES FROM THIS COMMONWEALTH TO A CONVENTION

PROPOSED TO BE HELD IN THE CITY OF PHILADELPHIA IN MAY NEXT, FOR

THE PURPOSE OF REVISING THE FŒDERAL CONSTITUTION.

WHEREAS the Commissioners who assembled at Annapolis, on the fourteenth of September last, for the purpose of devising and reporting the means of enabling Congress to provide effectually for the Commercial Interest of the United States, have represented the necessity of extending the revision of the foederal system to all its defects; and have recommended, that Deputies for that purpose be appointed by the several Legislatures, to meet in convention in the city of Philadelphia, on the second day of May next; a provision which seems preferable to a discussion of the subject in Congress, where it might be too much interupted by the ordinary business before them; and where it would besides, be deprived of the valuable councils of sundry individuals, who are disqualified by the constitution or laws of particular states, or restrained by peculiar circumstances from a seat in that Assembly:

AND WHEREAS, the General Assembly of this Commonwealth, taking into view the actual situation of the Confederacy, as well as reflecting on the alarming representations made from time to time, by the United States in Congress, particularly in their act of the fifteenth day of February last, can no longer doubt that the crisis is arrived at which the good people of America are to decide the solemn question, whether they will by wise and magnanimous efforts reap the just fruits of that independance which they have so gloriously acquired, and of that Union which they have cemented with so much of their common blood; or whether, by giving way to unmanly jealousies and prejudices, or to partial and transitory interests, they will renounce the auspicious blessings prepared for them by the Revolution, and furnish to its enemies an eventual triumph over those, by whose virtue and valour, it has been accomplished:

AND WHEREAS, the same noble and extended Policy, and the same fraternal and affectionate sentiments, which originally determined the Citizens of this Commonwealth, to unite with their Brethren of the other States, in establishing a foederal Government, cannot but be felt with equal force now as the motives to lay aside every inferior consideration, and to concur in such farther concessions and provisions, as may be necessary to secure the great objects for which that Government was instituted, and to render the United States as happy in Peace, as they have been glorious in war.

Be it therefore enacted, by the General Assembly of the Commonwealth of Virginia, That seven Commissioners be appointed by joint ballot of both Houses of Assembly, who, or any three of them, are hereby authorized as Deputies from this Commonwealth to meet such Deputies as may be appointed and authorized by other states, to assemble in Convention at Philadelphia, as above recommended, and to join with them in devising and discussing all such alterations and farther provisions, as may be necessary to render the foederal Constitution, adequate to the exigencies of the Union, and in reporting such an act for that purpose, to the United States in Congress, as when agreed to by them, and duly confirmed by the several states, will effectually provide for the same.

And be it further enacted, That in case of the death of any of the said Deputies, or of their declining their appointments, the Executive are hereby authorized to supply such vacancies; and the Governor is requested to transmit forthwith a copy of this Act, to the United States in Congress, and to the Executives of each of the states in the Union.

November 9, 1786, read the third time and passed the House of Delegates.

JOHN BECKLEY, c. h. d.

November 23, 1786, passed the Senate.

H. BROOKE, c. s.

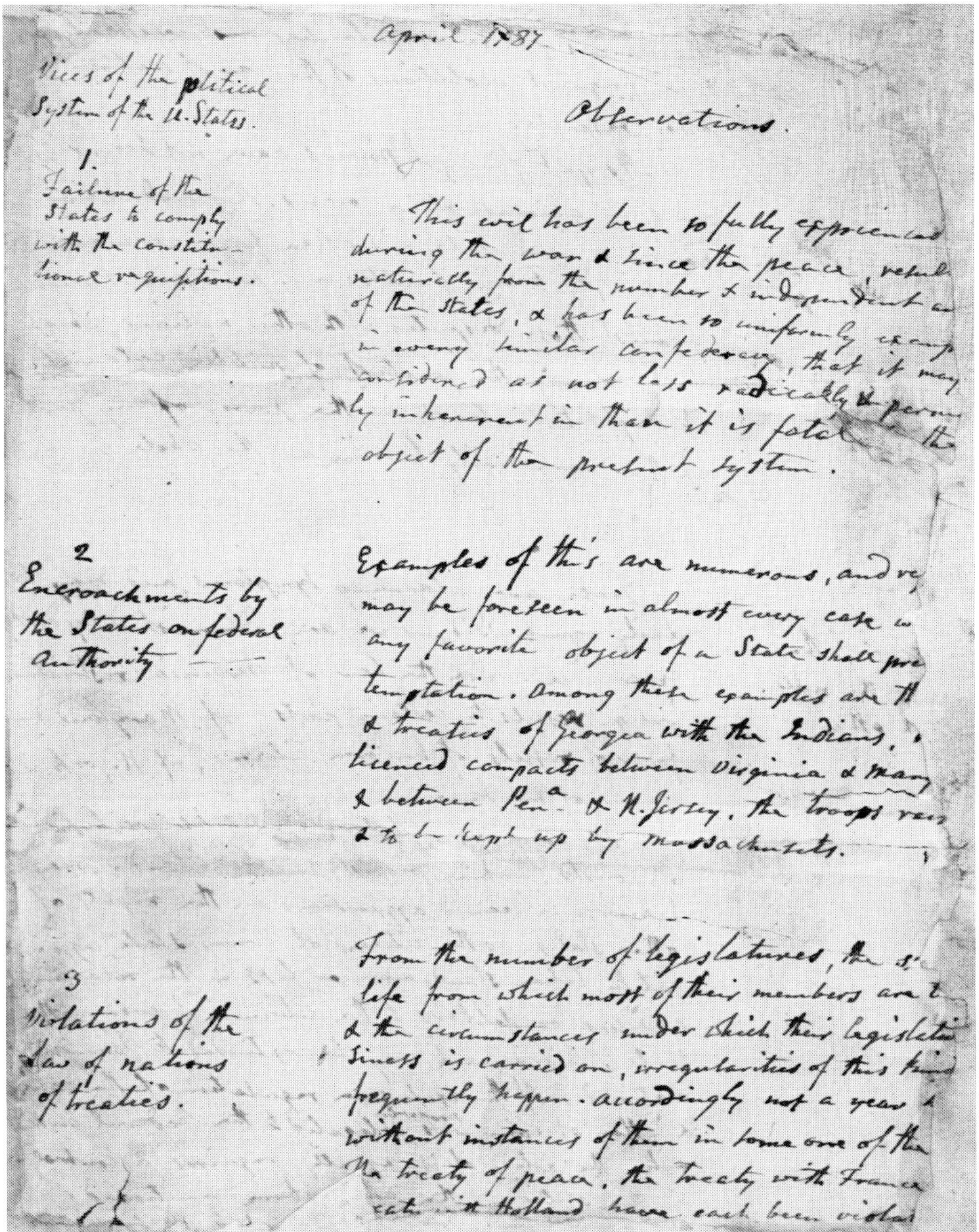

April 1787.

Vices of the political
System of the U. States.

Observations.

1.
Failure of the
States to comply
with the constitu-
tional requisitions.

This evil has been so fully experienced
during the war & since the peace, results
naturally from the number & independence
of the States, & has been so uniformly exemp
in every similar confederacy, that it may
considered as not less radically & perni-
cously inherent in than it is fatal to the
object of the present system.

2
Encroachments by
the States on federal
Authority —

Examples of this are numerous, and o[thers]
may be foreseen in almost every case w[here]
any favorite object of a State shall pre[sent a]
temptation. Among these examples are t[he]
& treaties of Georgia with the Indians, [the]
licensed compacts between Virginia & Mary[land]
& between Pen^a. & N. Jersey, the troops rai[sed]
& to be kept up by Massachusets. —

3
Violations of the
law of nations
of treaties.

From the number of legislatures, the sh[ort]
life from which most of their members are t[aken]
& the circumstances under which their legislati[ve]
business is carried on, irregularities of this kind
frequently happen. accordingly not a year p[asses]
without instances of them in some one of the[m]
Na treaty of peace. the treaty with France [the]
rati with Holland have each been violat[ed]

Convention. His first order of business was to persuade Washington to accept his appointment as a Virginia delegate; the general was uncertain of his health, concerned about the best way to resolve the conflict between his appointment to the Virginia delegation and his duty to preside over the annual convention of the Society of the Cincinnati (which was also meeting in Philadelphia in the spring of 1787), and leery of the risk of committing his prestige to so uncertain a venture. Nonetheless, Madison finally prevailed over Washington's qualms.

Madison also used the months before his journey to Philadelphia to prepare a series of proposals for discussion at the Convention. In several letters, but most fully in his letter of 16 April to Washington, Madison outlined his ideas of "a new system"—indicating that he no longer thought that a mere revision of the Articles would be sufficient. The elements of his proposal were, first, a system of representation recognizing "the inequality of importance" of the states; second, the arming of "the national Government" with "positive and compleat authority in all cases which require uniformity"; third, "a negative *in all cases whatsoever* on the legislative acts of the States"; fourth, a supreme national judiciary and executive; fifth, incorporation of the principles of checks and balances and separation of powers at the national level; and, sixth, ratification by "the people, and not merely from the ordinary authority of the Legislatures."[49]

Madison devoted most of his intellectual energies that spring to the theoretical arguments supporting these proposals. His memorandum, "Vices of the Political System of the U[nited] States" (Figure 4.12), listed the following twelve defects, though he completed analyses of only the first eleven:

1. Failure of the States to comply with the Constitutional requisitions
2. Encroachments by the States on the federal authority
3. Violations of the law of nations and of treaties
4. Trespasses of the States on the rights of each other
5. want of concert in matters where common interest requires it
6. want of Guaranty to the States of their Constitutions & laws against internal violence
7. want of sanction to the laws, and of coercion in the Government of the Confederacy
8. Want of ratification by the people of the articles of Confederation
9. Multiplicity of laws in the several States
10. Mutability of the laws of the States
11. Injustice of the laws of States
12. Impotence of the laws of the States[50]

Figure 4.12
James Madison. "Vices of the Political System of the U. States." Fair copy, April–June 1787. Transcript prepared by Joel Barlow at Monticello, 25 September 1808.

The text of this memorandum indicates that, in Madison's view, the critical task facing the convention was the transformation of a confederation of thirteen sovereign states into one republic. Madison's emphasis on the unfortunate consequences of the states' virtually unchecked sovereignty led him to conclude that it was necessary to erect a sovereign national government to act as a disinterested umpire among the warring interests and factions that were inevitable by-products of human nature; the issues he listed dealing with the "mutability" and "injustice" of state laws provoked his most brilliant theoretical disquisitions. It was in this memorandum that Madison first confronted the teaching of classical political theory that a republic could function only as the government of a small territory, which posed an obvious obstacle to creating an American republic. These ideas, more fully worked out in some of Madison's most important speeches at the Federal Convention and in *Federalist* Nos. 10, 14, and 51, constitute his most important contribution to political theory.[51]

Madison arrived two weeks early in Philadelphia, bringing with him his memorandum on the history of confederacies and the "Vices of the Political System." He was aware—perhaps more so than any of his fellow delegates except Washington—of the critical juncture that American affairs had reached by the spring of 1787. Waiting for the Convention to begin, he was poised on the threshold of performing his greatest service to his country and the cause of liberty and republicanism. Rather than mounting a political counterattack against the American Revolution, he was about to lead his fellow delegates in an arduous, daring, and brilliant campaign to vindicate the Revolution and preserve its achievements.[52]

5

THE GREAT CONFLUENCE

I N THE ERA of the American Revolution, more than at any other time in our history, ideas dominated our politics. The Americans won their independence at the height of the Enlightenment, and the intellectual forces let loose by that age shaped the goals and methods of American political culture.

The Americans were at the same time enlightened and pragmatic statesmen. Fascinated by the patterns of thought of the Enlightenment, the doctrines of the common law and the English constitution, the heritage of Greece and Rome, the principles of classical republicanism, and the lessons of history, they absorbed these constellations of ideas, principles, and information to gain a great end—the preservation of American happiness and freedom, and the fulfillment of America's destiny as the last refuge of liberty.

The discovery of the Americas turned the Europeans' understanding of the world upside down and provoked a long battle of words over whether that discovery was a blessing or a blight on the human prospect. With the emergence of the United States as a source of unsettling political ideas and experiments in self-government, the debate took on a wider focus. At this stage, however, Americans were no longer content to be silent objects of controversy. Benjamin Franklin was the first to enter the fray on a footing of equality and mutual respect, but he was soon joined by others, the most eager and industrious of whom were Thomas Jefferson and John Adams. Jefferson challenged the claims of the great French naturalist the Comte de Buffon, the Abbés Raynal and Corneille de Pauw, and other *philosophes* that nature itself frowned upon the Americas and their flora and fauna, and that its native inhabitants, the Indians, were inferior to white men and women. Jefferson carried on this battle in his classic *Notes on the State of Virginia* as well as on a more prosaic, scientific level, beseeching his friends in America to send him specimens of animals and plants at least as large and healthy as the best European examples cited by Buffon, in order to refute the Frenchman empirically and unanswerably.

John Adams chose a different front in the battle to explain and defend America. Stung by the philosophes' casual dismissal of the American state constitutions as throwbacks unduly influenced by the English constitution,

Adams launched a prodigious one-man research program that consumed years of reading and months of frantic writing. The result—three massive, disorderly, erudite volumes entitled *A Defence of the Constitutions of Government of the United States of America . . .*—maintained that the doctrines of balanced government and separation of powers were necessary to preserve liberty and republican government. To demonstrate the validity of his argument, Adams marshaled the history of all republics.

The Americans' spirited defense of their country, people, and politics turned the European Enlightenment's intellectual and forensic weapons against their source. Following Franklin's example, Jefferson and Adams helped to establish the intellectual independence of the United States, just as they and their colleagues had spearheaded the successful campaign for the political independence of the new republic.

The Americans' Uses of Western Culture

In the decades since the Second World War, specialists in the history of ideas have brought us closer than ever before to a sensitive understanding of the patterns of thought and argument of the Revolutionary generation. Intellectual historians used to emphasize the study of formal, fully articulated systems of political theory—what has been dubbed "the great books approach." In the past four decades, however, historians have shifted their focus to the recovery of the larger context of ideas in which such formal works of political theory are written.[1]

This new study of political culture[2] begins with the recognition that we see the world through a set of conceptual lenses and test our observations and ideas based on those observations against a collection of implicit and explicit generalizations and assumptions. The odds are that, if challenged, we could give only a fragmentary account of our own conceptual lenses, assumptions, and generalizations, because we are too close to them to see them clearly. With the passage of time, however, and the gradual changes in climates of opinion and habits of thought, historians are able to reconstruct earlier generations' patterns of thought and argument, and this project of intellectual reconstruction has produced some of the best scholarship on the creation of the American republic.[3]

Disagreements persist as this project continues—over exactly how the various patterns of thought and argument identified by these historians fitted together in the Revolutionary era, or which of them was central, critical, or dominant.[4] Another, more basic controversy concerns the exact relationship between ideas and political action.[5] Does a politician or polemicist begin with an intellectual framework and allow it to determine his or her goals and actions, or do the goals and preferred courses of action come first, with the intellectual justifications following as effects? Probably the interplay between ideas and goals, between climates of opinion and political actions, is far more complex than either of these polar explanations.

were philosophes and not all philosophes merited the status of philosophers. Rather, the philosophes were theorists of reform, pursuing learning and organizing it to marshal all available knowledge and information in the service of reform.[9]

The Americans found these ways of thinking congenial, and in their own disputes with the British government they invoked and polished them. The controversy with the mother country had begun as a disagreement over the terms of the English constitution—the whole cluster of statues, edicts and proclamations, judicial decisions, common-law rules and principles, customs, usages, and traditions that defined the relationship between government and the people. The Americans saw themselves as Englishmen, with all the rights and privileges of Englishmen. They represented themselves as defenders of the English constitution—the best in the world, the best that ever was or ever could be—against the corruptions that beset the mother country. In their view, the British government's unjustified assertions of authority over the colonies indicated that the treasured constitution had been contaminated at home by designing ministers, complacent legislators, and a people too sunk in corruption and too distracted by trade to recall or defend their heritage of liberty.[10]

As the break with Great Britain approached, the Americans began to make other arguments too. Conscious of the need to consider and win "the opinions of mankind," they included invocations of the laws of Nature and of natural rights while still asserting and defending their understanding of the English constitution. This expanded set of arguments shows up most clearly in the Declaration of Independence. Its famous preamble is an appeal to the spirit of the Enlightenment. Its list of charges against George III alleged specific violations of the English constitution that could be supported by specific English precedents. With their declaration of independence, the Americans embarked on a new course. Compelled to frame their own constitutions of government, they sought to preserve the best of the English constitutional heritage and at the same time to guard against the weaknesses of human nature and government that had corrupted that heritage at home.

The Revolution's exigencies and the Enlightenment's habits of thought combined to encourage Americans in their eclectic, utilitarian approach to Western history and culture. This eclecticism is illustrated by the will of Josiah Quincy, Jr., the brilliant young Boston lawyer who opposed British tyranny as fiercely as did his mentor and friend John Adams, yet who joined with Adams to defend the British soldiers accused of murder in the Boston Massacre trial: "I leave to my son, when he shall have reached the age of fifteen, the works of Algernon Sidney, John Locke, Bacon, Gordon's *Tacitus* and Cato's *Letters*. May the spirit of Liberty rest upon him."[11]

Like Quincy, most Americans assembled intellectual traditions as varied as classical history, the common law, the philosophy of the Enlightenment, and the "Commonwealth" ideology of seventeenth- and eighteenth-century England into a pantheon of Liberty.[12] A thousand or so miles to the south, another young lawyer compiled an equally illuminating list of books. At that

Figure 5.1
Artist unknown. *A Plan of the City of Syracuse Besieged by the Athenians.* Engraving in Charles Rollin, *The Ancient History of the Egyptians, Carthaginians, Assyrians . . .,* vol. III (London: J. and F. Rivington, 1774).

Ogilvie's poems. 5/

Prior's poems. 2.v.12mo Foulis. 6/

Gay's works. 12mo Foulis. 3/

Shenstone's works. 2.v.12mo 6/

Dryden's works. 4.v.12mo Foulis. 12/

Pope's works. by Warburton. 12mo £1.1

Churchill's poems. 4.v.12mo 12/

Hudibras. 3/

Swift's works. 21.v. small 8vo £3.3

Swift's literary correspondence. 3.v. 9/

Spectator. 9.v.12mo £1.7

Tatler. 5.v.12mo 15/

Guardian. 2.v.12mo 6/

Freeholder. 12mo 3/

Ld Lyttleton's Persian letters. 12mo 3/

Criticism on the Fine arts

Ld Kaim's elements of criticism. 2.v.8vo 10/

Burke on the sublime and beautiful 8vo 5/

Hogarth's analysis of beauty. 4to £1.1

Reid on the human mind 8vo 5/

Smith's theory of moral sentiments. 8vo 5/

Johnson's dictionary. 2.v. fol. £3

Capell's prolusions. 12mo 3/

Politicks, Trade

Montesquieu's spirit of laws 2.v.12mo 6/

Locke on government. 8vo 5/

Sidney on government. 4to 15/

Marmontel's Belisarius. 12mo Eng. 3/

Ld Bolingbroke's political works. 5.v.8vo £2.5

Montesquieu's rise & fall of the Roman government 12mo 3/

Steuart's Political oeconomy. 2.v.4to £1.10

Petty's Political arithmetic. 8vo 5/

Religion

Locke's conduct of the mind in search of truth. 12mo 3/

Xenophon's memoirs of Socrates. by Feilding 8vo 5/

Epictetus. by mrs Carter. 2.v.12mo 6/

Antoninus. by Collins. 3/

Seneca. by L'Estrange. 8vo 5/

Cicero's Offices. by Guthrie. 8vo 5/

Cicero's Tusculan questions. Eng. 3/

Ld Bolingbroke's Philosophical works. 5.v.8vo £1.5

Hume's essays. 4.v.12mo 12/

Ld Kaim's Natural religion. 8vo 6/

Philosophical survey of Nature. 3/

Oeconomy of human life. 2/

Sterne's sermons. 7.v.12mo £1.1

Sherlock on death. 8vo 5/

Sherlock on a future state 5/

Law

Ld Kaim's Principles of equity. fol. £1.1

Blackstone's Commentaries. 4.v.4to £4.4

Cuningham's Law dictionary. 2.v.fol. £3.

History. Antients

Bible 6/

Rollin's Antient history. Eng. 13.v.12mo £1.19

Stanyan's Graecian history 2.v.8vo 10/

Livy. (the late translation) 12/

Sallust by Gordon. 12mo 12/

Tacitus by Gordon. 12mo 15/

Caesar by Bladen. 8vo 5/

Josephus. Eng.

Vertot's Revolutions of Rome. Eng. 9/

Plutarch's lives. by Langhorne. 6.v.8vo £1.10

Bayle's Dictionary. 5.v.fol. £7.10.

Jeffery's Historical & Chronological chart. 15/

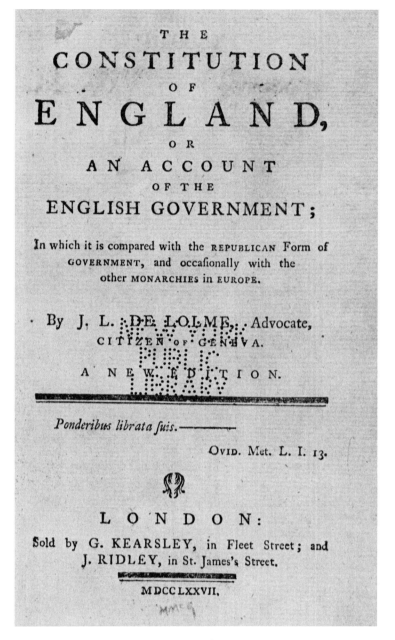

THE
CONSTITUTION
OF
ENGLAND,
OR
AN ACCOUNT
OF THE
ENGLISH GOVERNMENT;

In which it is compared with the REPUBLICAN Form of GOVERNMENT, and occafionally with the other MONARCHIES in EUROPE.

By J. L. DE LOLME, Advocate, CITIZEN OF GENEVA.

A NEW EDITION.

Ponderibus librata fuis.

OVID. Met. L. I. 13.

LONDON:

Sold by G. KEARSLEY, in Fleet Street; and J. RIDLEY, in St. James's Street.

MDCCLXXVII.

time, the summer of 1771, Thomas Jefferson was a twenty-eight-year-old lawyer and planter. Robert Skipwith, Jefferson's friend and neighbor, had asked him for a list of books that would form a basic library for a cultivated Virginia gentleman—and would cost no more than thirty pounds. Jefferson was no stranger to the building of libraries. Since his days at William and Mary, he had loved books, and he had just had to reconstruct his own library, fire having consumed his house the year before. Instead of complying with Skipwith's request, Jefferson drew up a basic book list (Figure 5.2) from which his delighted and astonished friend could make preliminary selections up to his budget and which would serve as a foundation for later

Figure 5.4
William Faithorne. Portrait of
Oliver Cromwell. Engraving,
1656. This portrait of the Lord
Protector appeared in Louis de
Gand de Brachey et de Rome-
cour, *Parallelum Olivae . . .*
(London, 1656).

purchases. This detailed list, filling three double-column pages in Jefferson's minute handwriting, included notes of book prices, the address of his preferred London bookseller, and information on prices and qualities of bookbinding in London.[13]

Jefferson divided his proposed library into nine sections—"Fine Arts" (including poetry, drama, essays, art, gardening, and fiction); "Criticism on the Fine Arts" (including some early works on human psychology as well as Dr. Johnson's *Dictionary*); "Politicks [and] Trade"; "Religion" (which covered mostly what we would call philosophy today); "Law" (Figure 5.3); "History, Antient"; "History, Modern"; "Natural Philosophy, Natural History &c." (what we would call the sciences); and "Miscellaneous." In his accompanying letter Jefferson defended the inclusion of works of fiction and poetry on the ground that "every thing is useful which contributes to fix us in the principles and practice of virtue."[14] This dictum applies equally well to the balance of the books he listed.

Jefferson's list contains most of the books at the heart of the intellectual life of the eighteenth century. Here we find most of the basic works of Greek and Roman history, chief of which were Thomas Gordon's transla-

Sam Garrigues Jr.

COMMENTARIES

ON THE

LAWS

OF

ENGLAND.

IN FOUR BOOKS.

BY

Sir WILLIAM BLACKSTONE, Knt.

ONE OF HIS MAJESTY's JUDGES OF THE COURT OF COMMON PLEAS.

RE-PRINTED FROM THE BRITISH COPY,
PAGE FOR PAGE WITH THE LAST EDITION.

AMERICA:

PRINTED FOR THE SUBSCRIBERS,

By ROBERT BELL, at the late Union Library, in *Third-street,*

PHILADELPHIA. MDCCLXXI.

tions of Tacitus and Sallust, with their detailed pictures of the corruption
of Roman political life, and Charles Rollin's mammoth *Ancient History,* a
popular compilation that served its readers even better than the original
works from which it was drawn. Here, too, appear many works of English
history, focusing on the controversy between the Stuart kings and the House
of Commons that culminated in the English Civil War (Figure 5.4) and the
establishment of the Commonwealth. Under "Religion" Jefferson included
many of the more accessible and widely read works of ancient and contemporary philosophy (though, curiously enough, he listed the Bible as a work
of ancient history): Xenophon on Socrates, Epictetus, Cicero, Bolingbroke,
David Hume, and John Locke. Locke and Hume also appear under "Poli-

ticks [and] Trade," together with Montesquieu, Adam Smith, Bolingbroke, and Algernon Sidney. Jefferson noted only three basic law books, "as a knowledge of the minutiae of that science is not necessary for a private gentleman," but one of these was the formidable *Commentaries on English Law* of Sir William Blackstone (Figure 5.5), the greatest legal treatise produced up to that time (albeit by a lawyer who had not succeeded in practice) and the first to substantiate the view that the law was a science.[15]

The Americans' eclectic approach to the heritage of the West was a natural outgrowth of their practical bent and of their belief, a commonplace of Enlightenment thought, that the study of history of whatever period could disclose principles and lessons of general application. David Hume (Figure 5.6), the great Scottish philosopher, historian, and essayist, declared in his *Enquiry Concerning Human Understanding*:

> Mankind are so much the same, in all times and places, that history informs us of nothing new or strange, in this particular. Its chief use is only to discover the constant and universal principles of human nature, by showing man in all varieties of circumstances and situations, and furnishing us with materials, from which we may form our observations and become acquainted with the regular springs of human action and behavior. These records . . . are so many collections of experiments, by which the politician or moral philosopher fixes the principles of his science, in the same manner as the physician or natural philosopher becomes acquainted with the nature of plants, minerals, and other external objects, by the experiments which he forms concerning them.[16]

John Adams echoed these ideas almost word for word in his *Defence of the Constitutions* decades later.[17]

In the years leading up to the Revolution, the Americans emphasized the lessons to be drawn from English history, as the controversy focused on the terms of and boundaries on power established by the English constitution. In this inquiry they were guided by the interpretations of the English "Whig" historians, who depicted the struggle between Parliament and the Stuart kings as a contest of liberty and constitutionalism against arbitrary power.[18] Most notable of these historians was Catherine Macaulay, whose *History of England* (Figure 5.7) made her famous in America as well as in England. An uncompromising champion of Parliament against the Stuarts in her books, Mrs. Macaulay also supported the American cause against Parliament and the king. Her chief object of devotion was the English constitution, which she defended against assertions of power by whatever institution she viewed as a threat to liberty. Her *History* was read by John Adams and Thomas Jefferson; by George Washington, who hosted Mrs. Macaulay at Mount Vernon during her visit to the United States in 1785; and by countless students at Harvard, Yale, and Brown. Washington praised her in his diary as a lady "whose principles are so much and so justly admired by the friends of liberty and of mankind," and began a correspondence with her that lasted until her death in 1791.[19]

PLATE I
Benjamin West. *The Peace
Commissioners.* Oil on canvas,
1783–84. The artist completed
only the portraits of the American peace delegation (left to
right): Jay, Adams, Franklin,
Laurens (standing), and William
Temple Franklin—the group's
secretary and Franklin's grandson.

PLATE II
Charles Willson Peale. Portrait of
Robert Morris. Oil on canvas,
1782.

PLATE III
Gilbert Stuart. Portrait of John
Jay. Oil on canvas, ca. 1782–83.

PLATE IV
John Toole after Dominic W.
Boudet after John Hesselius.
Portrait of George Mason. Oil on
canvas, 1840–1844.

PLATE V
James Sharples. Portrait of
Thomas Jefferson. Pastel on
paper, ca. 1797. Jefferson is
believed to have posed for this
portrait in Philadelphia shortly
after his inauguration as vice-
president.

PLATE VI
George Washington Parke Custis.
Mount Vernon. Watercolor, ca.
1797. The Washingtons adopted
Custis and his sister after the
death of their father, Martha
Washington's son, in 1781. Custis
created this view of Mount
Vernon, with its famous east
portico, sometime before the
death of his adopted mother in
1802.

PLATE VII
Artist unknown. *View of Annapolis, Maryland.* Watercolor over
pencil, ca. 1800.

PLATE VIII
Pierre Michel Alix after François
Garnerey. Portrait of Charles-
Louis de Secondat, Baron de
Montesquieu. Aquatint, ca. 1801.
This portrait appeared in *Collec-
tion de Portraits, Représentant Les
Personnages Les Plus Célèbres*
(Paris, 1801).

PLATE IX
John Singleton Copley. Portrait
of John Adams. Oil on canvas,
1783. Copley painted this lifesize
portrait in his London studio
shortly after the signing of the
Treaty of Paris. One of the
young diplomat's hands points to
a map of America; the other
holds a document that may
represent the treaty he helped
negotiate. In the background
Britannia symbolically extends an
olive branch.

PLATE X
William Russell Birch and
Thomas Birch. *Back of the State
House, Philadelphia.* Colored
engraving, 1799–1800.

PLATE XI
James Peale after Charles Willson
Peale. Portrait of George Washington. Oil on canvas, ca. 1788.
This portrait recalls Jefferson's
description of Washington as
"easy, erect and noble." The head
and shoulders are based on a
portrait painted by the elder
Peale during the summer of
1787.

PLATE XII
Joseph Sifrède Duplessis. Portrait of Benjamin Franklin. Pastel on paper, 1783. Duplessis painted Franklin from life in Paris in 1778, and that painting (now in the Metropolitan Museum) was the basis for numerous copies by Duplessis and others. It is believed that Franklin commissioned this pastel replica as a gift for his friend, Louis Le Veillard, the mayor of Passy.

PLATE XIII
Charles Willson Peale. Portrait of
Nathaniel Gorham. Oil on
canvas, ca. 1793. After involve-
ment in state and local politics,
Gorham served as a member of
the Continental Congress in
1782, 1783, and between 1785
and 1787. In 1786 he was elected
president of Congress.

PLATE XIV
Robert Edge Pine. Portrait of
Edmund Randolph. Oil on
canvas, 1787. This portrait, until
very recently believed lost, was
presumably painted from life
during the Convention.
Randolph served as Virginia's
attorney general (1776), representative to the Continental
Congress (1779), governor
(1786–87), and delegate to the
Annapolis and the Federal
Conventions; and as U.S. attorney general (1789–1794) and
U.S. secretary of state (1794–95).

PLATE XV
John Wesley Jarvis. Portrait of
William Samuel Johnson. Oil on
canvas, ca. 1814. One of the
Federal Convention's most
respected participants, Johnson
later served as president of
Columbia University (1787–1800)
and as senator from Connecticut
took an active role in the shaping
of the Judiciary Act of 1789.

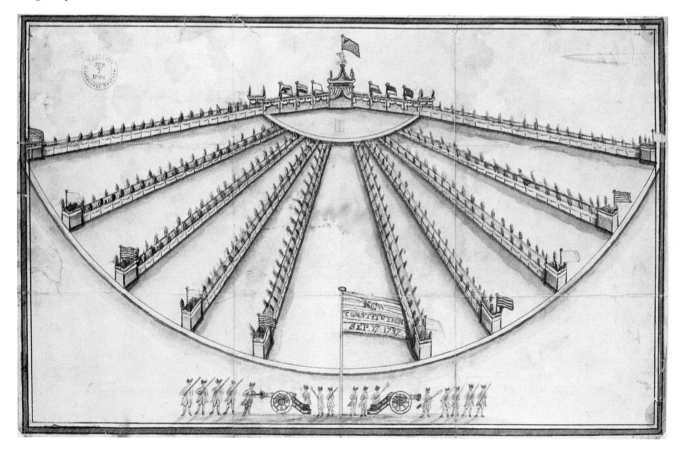

Figure 5.6
Robert Scott. Portrait of David
Hume. Line engraving, ca. 1797.

Once independence was declared, the major problems the Americans
faced were those of framing and administering new constitutions of government, and they turned more and more frequently to the histories of
republics in their study and citation of historical precedents.[20] This was a
matter both of necessity and of preference—of necessity, in that they had
thrown off monarchical institutions and practices along with monarchical
authority and were not anxious to replace them; of preference, in that they
were committed to the values of republicanism.

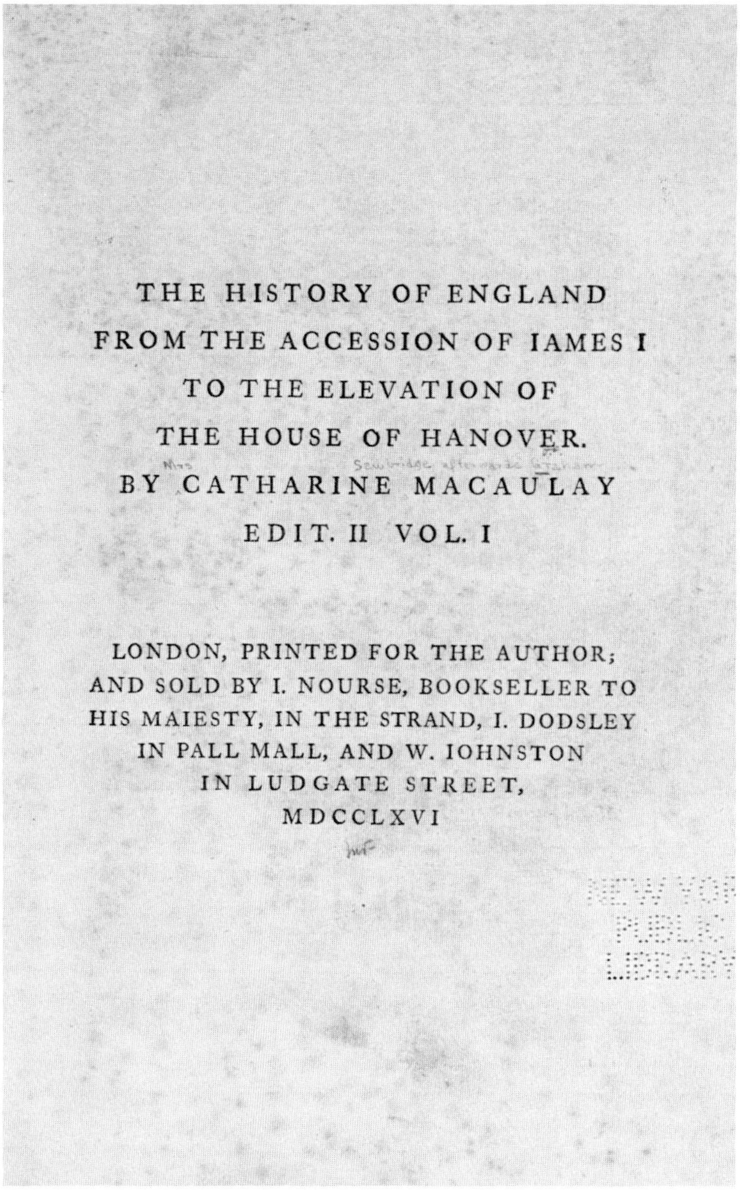

THE HISTORY OF ENGLAND
FROM THE ACCESSION OF IAMES I
TO THE ELEVATION OF
THE HOUSE OF HANOVER.
BY CATHARINE MACAULAY
EDIT. II VOL. I

LONDON, PRINTED FOR THE AUTHOR;
AND SOLD BY I. NOURSE, BOOKSELLER TO
HIS MAIESTY, IN THE STRAND, I. DODSLEY
IN PALL MALL, AND W. IOHNSTON
IN LUDGATE STREET,
MDCCLXVI

Figure 5.7
Catherine Sawbridge Macaulay. *The History of England from the Accession of James I . . .* (London: I. Nourse, 1766).

We have forgotten just how radical the idea of a republican form of government was in the Revolutionary era. Most theorists of government in the eighteenth century were convinced that the republican form—which they defined as a government in which the people had the primary share of governmental power, whether direct or indirect—was a useless relic of classical history. Republics were too unstable to govern anything but small territories, such as the city-states of the classical world and Renaissance Italy or the cantons of Switzerland. And yet the idea of republicanism had a persistent allure that attracted controversialists and students of political theory on both sides of the Atlantic.

Republicanism is an elusive bundle of ideas and doctrines.[21] Some historians have identified as many as two, three, or more kinds of republicanism, but all these variants have some things in common. At the heart of republican thought was a deep concern with public virtue and an obsession with its opposite, corruption. The books the Americans read—Montesquieu's *Considerations on the Grandeur of the Romans and Their Decline,* James Harrington's Utopian treatise *Oceana,*[22] the works of Algernon Sidney, John Trenchard's and Thomas Gordon's *Cato's Letters,*[23] and Gordon's translations of Roman historians—all emphasized the threat of corruption. Just as virtue was the animating principle of republican government, corruption was the characteristic republican disease. It had subverted and toppled every previous republic; it had even taken root in Britain itself, whose constitution enshrined at least some republican principles; and the Americans anxiously scrutinized their own governments for symptoms of the affliction.

The Americans also believed that a republican form of government offered the only real hope for preserving liberty. Going back to Aristotle, classical political theory had identified three "pure" forms of government, each linked to a discrete order or segment of society and aspect of human nature: *monarchy,* or rule by one man; *aristocracy,* or rule by an elite of powerful men; and *democracy,* or rule by the people. Each of these pure forms contained the seeds of degeneration and would undergo a cyclical process of decline and fall—a monarchy would become a tyranny, an aristocracy would slide into oligarchy, and a democracy would collapse into mob rule. Only a "mixed" or "balanced" government, commingling all three pure forms and the segments of society they represented, would have any hope of resisting the otherwise inevitable cycle of decay and decline. And a republic was the form of government most adaptable to this mix and balance of segments of society and pure governmental forms.

Ultimately, Americans turned to the great French judge and philosopher Montesquieu for a definitive and systematic analysis of government.[24] His disorganized, rambling treatise *De l'Esprit des Lois (The Spirit of the Laws)* was the most widely studied and respectfully quoted product of the European Enlightenment. Readers valued *The Spirit of the Laws* for its confident and authoritative treatment of governments in all ages and nations, for its pioneering interdisciplinary approach to the study of politics, and for its glowing tribute to the English constitution as the incarnation of properly balanced government, the apotheosis of the doctrine of separation of powers, and the citadel of liberty. No one worried that Montesquieu's flattering portrait of the English constitution bore little relation to reality; it was the ideal that mattered.

And yet Montesquieu (Plate VIII) posed the greatest challenge to the Americans' attempts to revive republicanism, for he lent the full weight of his immense authority to the traditional understanding that a republic could work only as the government of a small territory.[25] He maintained that, for such a government to function, all the citizens of a republic had to know and have regular contact with one another. Because this was not possible for any polity larger than a city-state, Montesquieu concluded, an extensive territory probably required a military despotism. Each of the American states was larger than the largest republics of antiquity, and the United States was larger than every European nation but Russia. Thus the Americans had to accept Montesquieu's dictum and abandon all hope of creating an energetic national government based on republican principles—keeping the states from succumbing to the diseases of republicanism would be enough of a challenge—or they had to find a sound theoretical and practical basis by which to challenge the authority of the greatest political thinker of the age and the two millennia of accumulated political experience that supported his position.

The Americans proved ingenious enough to refute Montesquieu's arguments on both the theoretical and practical levels. On the practical level they could cite the largely successful record of the state governments in the 1770s and 1780s. On the theoretical level, James Madison provided the most sophisticated refutation of Montesquieu's dictum, finding his inspiration in David Hume's essay "On the Idea of a Perfect Commonwealth."[26] Madison's argument—the theory of the extended republic immortalized in *Federalist* Nos. 10 and 14—is only the best-known instance of the Americans' creative dialogue with the materials of Western history and culture.

One of the most important sources of ideas, influences, and role models for the Americans of the eighteenth century was the literature of Greece and Rome. A classical education was considered the foundation of a first-rate education for intelligent men (Figure 5.8). Benjamin Rush might argue that this continuing dependence on classical learning and languages represented the dead hand of the past stifling Americans' independence and creativity,[27] but he was in a small minority. In addition to sharing the nearly universal belief in the usefulness of a classical education, the Americans valued classical history and literature as peculiarly suited to the inculcation of republican virtue. The histories of the Greek city-states and the Roman Republic were the richest and most instructive sources of information on the pathology of republicanism. In addition, Plutarch's *Lives of the Most Noble Grecians and Romans* (Figure 5.9) was a particularly accessible fount of patterns of political behavior to emulate or guard against; American politicians could try to be like Solon or Lycurgus, Scipio or Brutus. The vocabulary of American political culture resounds with echoes of classical politics; among other terms, *president, Senate,* and *federalism* all have roots in Greek and Roman history. The Americans made use of the language of politics developed in antiquity and of the larger concepts and constellations of values underlying that terminology.[28]

Above all the Americans valued republican virtue (Figure 5.10), and the sternest and most attentive student of virtue and its implications for the emerging American political culture was George Washington.[29] Washington patterned his conduct in politics and in war on that of the great Roman statesman Cincinnatus, who never sought power for himself but instead answered Rome's call when necessary and returned to his plow as soon as the crisis had passed. Washington's example and the general appeal of

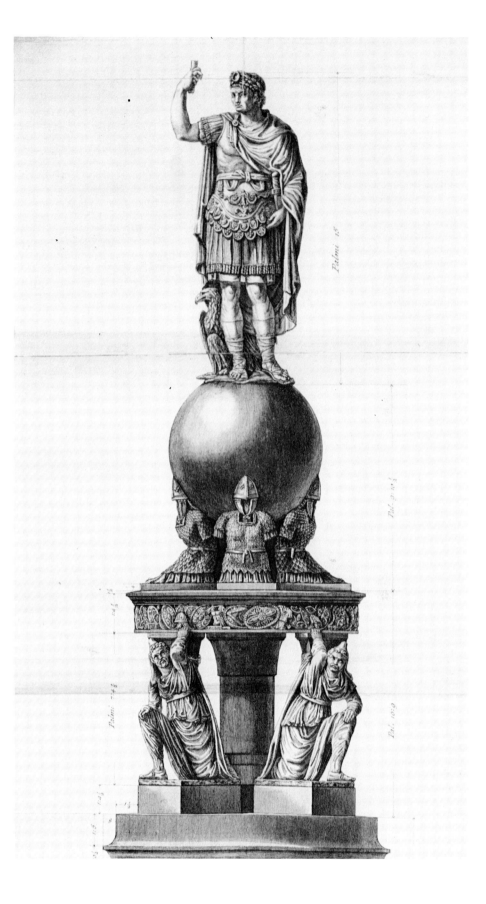

Figure 5.8
Giovanni Battista Piranesi.
Column of Trajan (detail).
Engraving, ca. 1770. The eighteenth century's fascination with
the classical world extended to
the art and architecture of
ancient Rome and Greece.

PLVTARCHS
LIVES

AGRECIAN

ATHENS

AROMAN

ROME

LONDON,
Printed For George Sawbridge
at the Bible upon Ludgate-Hill.
And Thomas Lee
at the Turkes Head in Fleet=
streete over against Fetter-Lane
1676.

Figure 5.10
Peter C. Verger after John Francis Renault. *Triumph of Liberty.* Engraving, 1796. At the center of this complex allegorical print the "Genius of America" stands in front of a tomb dedicated to heroes of the American Revolution. She is attended by Liberty, Justice, Peace, and Plenty. On an obelisk to the right is the goddess of Liberty, with a copy of *The Rights of Man* below. In the foreground a group of kings under the guard of a votary of Liberty turn away from the scene in disgust.

Figure 5.9
Plutarch's Lives, translated by Sir Thomas North (London: George Sawbridge and Thomas Lee, 1676).

Cincinnatus inspired the creation after the Revolution of an organization for officers of the Continental Army. The Society of the Cincinnati quickly drew fire from politicians who feared that it might form the nucleus of a military conspiracy to subvert the liberties of the United States and overthrow the Confederation. Washington's well-known aversion to such ideas eventually eased opposition to the society, which still exists as a memorial to the example of Cincinnatus in the American mind.[30]

The Enlightenment in Europe and America was not a uniform triumph of reason. In several key instances, politicians and political theorists on both sides of the Atlantic not only failed to take advantage of opportunities to extend the battle against prejudice and superstition; they also sometimes used the methodology of the Enlightenment to bolster existing injustices.

For example, the problem of slavery and the plight of most black Americans persisted throughout the Enlightenment, despite the foundation of numerous antislavery and manumission societies by William Wilberforce and others in England, and by Benjamin Franklin, Benjamin Rush, John Jay, and others in America. Jefferson's *Notes on the State of Virginia* presented an eloquent defense of the equality, integrity, and accomplishments of the Indians and a powerful denunciation of slavery as an institution, but it also included his tortured and unconvincing attempts to demonstrate "scientifically" that black men and women were inferior to whites and thus were not suited to freedom on any basis—intellectual, moral, or emotional. Jefferson was not alone in his failure to come to grips with the dilemmas of slavery and race. Most Americans explained different races as the products of different environments and thus believed that racial traits could be altered or even extinguished by a change of environment or by "civilization." Dr. Benjamin Rush even maintained that blackness was a skin disease like leprosy that might eventually be "cured." Jefferson himself expressed the hope that his arguments that black human beings were inferior could be disproved, but he never recanted them despite the efforts of Benjamin Banneker and other black Americans to convince him of his mistake.[31]

Similarly, the position of women in society occasioned some debate during the Enlightenment, but this debate produced only scattered, hesitant reforms.[32] John Adams humorously dismissed his wife's plea for equal political and legal rights for women. And, just after his election as president in 1801, Thomas Jefferson rejected the suggestion of his secretary of the Treasury, the Swiss-born Albert Gallatin, that he consider appointing women to federal office. In *The Spirit of the Laws* Montesquieu touched on the issue of the place of women in politics, as he did on so many other issues, but his comments show the limitations of the philosophers of the Enlightenment, and the tendency of the politicians of that time to act only selectively to reform society. Montesquieu's habit of throwing out suggestions and insights without developing them is exemplified by his comment in Book VII that "it is contrary to reason and nature that women should reign in families . . . but not that they should govern an empire." He based his argument on the comparative physical weakness of women, which in a family would render them unable to maintain authority and discipline but which in government would encourage "leniency and moderation."[33] He also suggested that a republic was the best form of government for women to live under, as they would be free from the tendency of despotic governments to treat them as objects of luxury—a forerunner of our modern term of reproach, "sex objects." Unfortunately, Montesquieu did not offer any suggestion as to how women could bring about a republican form of government or secure political power. And even these casual suggestions were not taken up by the philosophes of Europe or the enlightened statesmen of the United States.

Despite the Enlightenment's failures of imagination and of nerve, despite the Americans' continued refusal to accord blacks or women full political and social equality, John Adams justifiably extolled the age that he and his colleagues had labored so long and hard to bring about:

> According to the few lights that remain to us, we may say that the eighteenth century, notwithstanding all its errors and vices, has been of all that are past, the most honorable to human nature. Knowledge and virtue were increased and diffused; arts, sciences, useful to men, ameliorating their condition, were improved more than in any former equal period.[34]

There was a significant difference between the European and American Enlightenments.[35] Although the philosophes of Europe brimmed over with ideas, suggestions, and proposals for reform or even for revolution, and although some of the rulers of Europe allowed a few the chance to implement their suggestions, the era of the philosophes lasted only a short time. The forces of change that they sought to unleash consumed many of them. Some despots, such as Catherine the Great of Russia, executed these reformers; other philosophes perished as the victims of revolutions that they had helped to bring about, among them the Marquis de Condorcet and Brissot de Warville. Still others, such as Thomas Paine and Joseph Priestley, were forced to flee to America. Those who had had the chance to experiment with society and government saw their hopeful ventures swept away by the forces of reaction, and in fact many of these brave experiments in government were doomed to failure anyway, because of their inventors' almost total lack of experience in government.

By contrast, the achievements of the American philosophes—Franklin, Jefferson, John Adams, Madison, Hamilton, and their colleagues—endured as foundations for the political habits and culture of a new nation. In large part this success resulted from the Americans' solid grounding in political experience. Americans may well have had the single longest unbroken record of experience with popularly elected legislatures and self-government, beginning with the Virginia House of Burgesses in 1619, the Mayflower Compact in 1620, and the Fundamental Orders of Connecticut in 1639. Furthermore, as many philosophes recognized, the people of the United States were singularly blessed by having escaped the baleful influences of feudalism, formal class distinctions, and other corrupting and stultifying Old World influences. Goethe congratulated the Americans on escaping the "ghosts" that had haunted Europe, and Joseph Mandrillon's *The American Spectator* praised the citizens of the United States for their "unsullied virtue," which enabled them to avoid "the tyranny of the passions or the seduction of bad examples" that characterized most of European history.[36] Professor Commager rightly suggests that, whereas the philosophes of Europe had taken the leading role in originating and proposing the doctrines and habits of thought of the Enlightenment, it was the Americans who systematized them, refined them, and put them to work in the new nation.

The Problem of America in European Thought

The discovery of the Americas in the sixteenth century had shaken the Europeans' intellectual world to its foundations. The New World abounded with plants, animals, natural and mineral wealth, and even a race of human beings unknown in the Old. The difficulty of assimilating the existence of this world, and especially of justifying the exploitation of the Americas and their peoples, led many philosophes to conclude that the discovery of the New World might have been a colossal mistake.[37] Thus in his *History of the*

Two Indies the French Jesuit Abbé Guillaume Raynal arraigned European civilization for its crimes in the Americas and in India. Intent on using the flaws of the New World to expose the sins and crimes of the Old, Raynal sponsored an essay contest on the theme "Was America a Mistake?"; and some, like the Comte de Buffon, the most venerated naturalist of his age, saw in the flora and fauna of the Americas confirmation of preconceived theories about the deleterious effects of the American climate.

For the most part the opponents of America focused on the Spanish and Portuguese colonies in Central and South America. They emphasized the death and persecution suffered by the Indians at the hands of the *conquistadores;* the habits of tyranny and brutality produced by the administration of the Latin American colonies; the loss to Europe of those bold, daring men who chose to make their fortunes and careers in America; and the diseases, including syphilis, that the Europeans supposedly caught from the Indians and brought back to ravage the Old World. As for North and South America before their discovery, the critics maintained that the two continents had not developed any worthwhile civilization whatever, that their histories consisted of uncounted centuries of savagery and barbarism, and that both the Americas and Europe would have been better off had the New World never been found.

Americans on both continents could dismiss the Abbé Raynal or the Abbé Corneille de Pauw, whose vicious attacks on America had hardly any basis in fact. But how could one ignore the Comte de Buffon? Of all the critics of America, Buffon was by far the most formidable. His *Histoire Naturelle,* a vast compilation and systematization of all known information on the natural world that took forty years to produce, occupied Buffon and more than thirty collaborators and researchers and filled twenty-nine volumes and seven supplementary volumes, the last of which appeared in 1789, the year after Buffon's death. It was said that when Buffon and Nature disagreed, Nature gave way.

The American Revolution marked a turning point in the European attitude toward America. It appeared to the philosophes that the ideals of the American Revolution offered hope to the Old World and that the Revolution itself might become the catalyst for sweeping away the backward-looking and oppressive governments of Europe and instilling new principles and habits of freedom and equality (Figure 5.11). Second, and perhaps more important, the emissaries from the newly established United States showed personal qualities that could not be squared with the theory of American degeneracy, and they soon mounted a vigorous and effective intellectual counterattack.

The debate over Nature and America had a larger significance than the philosophes' complacent arrogance or the Americans' wounded national pride. Taking inspiration from the theories of Montesquieu, nearly every student of government in the eighteenth century believed that a territory's climate had something to do with its people's culture and form of government.[38] Thus the philosophes' theory of American degeneracy had disturb-

Figure 5.11
Artist unknown. *America trampling on Oppression.* Etching, 1789. Among the most popular European images of the new United States was the female "goddess" of America. Here she holds a liberty pole and stands with one foot crushing the British lion. The plate appeared as the frontispiece of W. D. Cooper's *The History of North America* (London, 1789).

ing implications: if Nature was inimical to America, it would doom the Revolutionary generation's efforts to preserve and vindicate liberty, republicanism, and constitutional government. The presence of Benjamin Franklin and John Adams, and later of Thomas Jefferson, in Europe opened new fronts in the debate over America and eventually routed the arguments of those who maintained that America was a mistake.

All by himself, Franklin represented a complete refutation of the philosophes' strictures against America.[39] He was the best-known American of his time, having won a European reputation as a man of science and of letters and as a distinguished politician and diplomat. In person, whether at the French court at Versailles, in the salons of Paris, or at his small house in Passy, Franklin brilliantly managed Europeans' perceptions of himself and his nation. His complex personality dazzled the philosophes. He was at the same time a sophisticated and experienced man of the world and the epitome of the ingenuous, candid American philosopher fresh from his meditations on the banks of the Delaware. In one celebrated and effective gesture, Franklin and Voltaire met and embraced each other at the French Academy of Sciences. Though this scene may have given indigestion to John Adams, who never understood the protean nature of Franklin's personality, all Europe pronounced it the meeting of Solon and Socrates.[40] In another incident—Franklin's diplomatic stock-in-trade consisted of parables and incidents[41]—he left the case against America in shambles. William Carmichael, who was there, told the story to Thomas Jefferson a few years later:

> I do not know whether Dr. Franklin ever mentioned to you what passed at a Dinner at Paris in which I was present . . . I think the Company consisted of 14 or 15 persons. At Table some one of the Company asked the Doctor what were his sentiments on the remarks made by [the Abbé Corneille de Pauw on American degeneracy]. We were five Americans at table. The Venerable Doctor regarded the Company and then desired the Gentleman who put the question to remark and to judge whether the human race had degenerated by being transported to another section of the Globe. In fact there was not one American present who could not have tost out of the Windows one or perhaps two of the rest of the Company, if this effort depended merely on muscular force. We heard nothing more of Mr. P's work.[42]

Franklin's hallmark as a diplomat and representative of American civilization was tactful wit. Thomas Jefferson, who succeeded Franklin as American minister in Paris, adapted Franklin's style to his own use and added a few elements of his own. The polished and affable Virginian created just as favorable an impression as "the Venerable Doctor" had done. But Jefferson took the controversy over America to the Europeans' own ground. He set out to refute Buffon and his colleagues with empirical evidence and in a scientific manner as authoritative as that of Buffon's *Histoire Naturelle*. Buffon was clearly Jefferson's principal adversary, for even the "Newton of

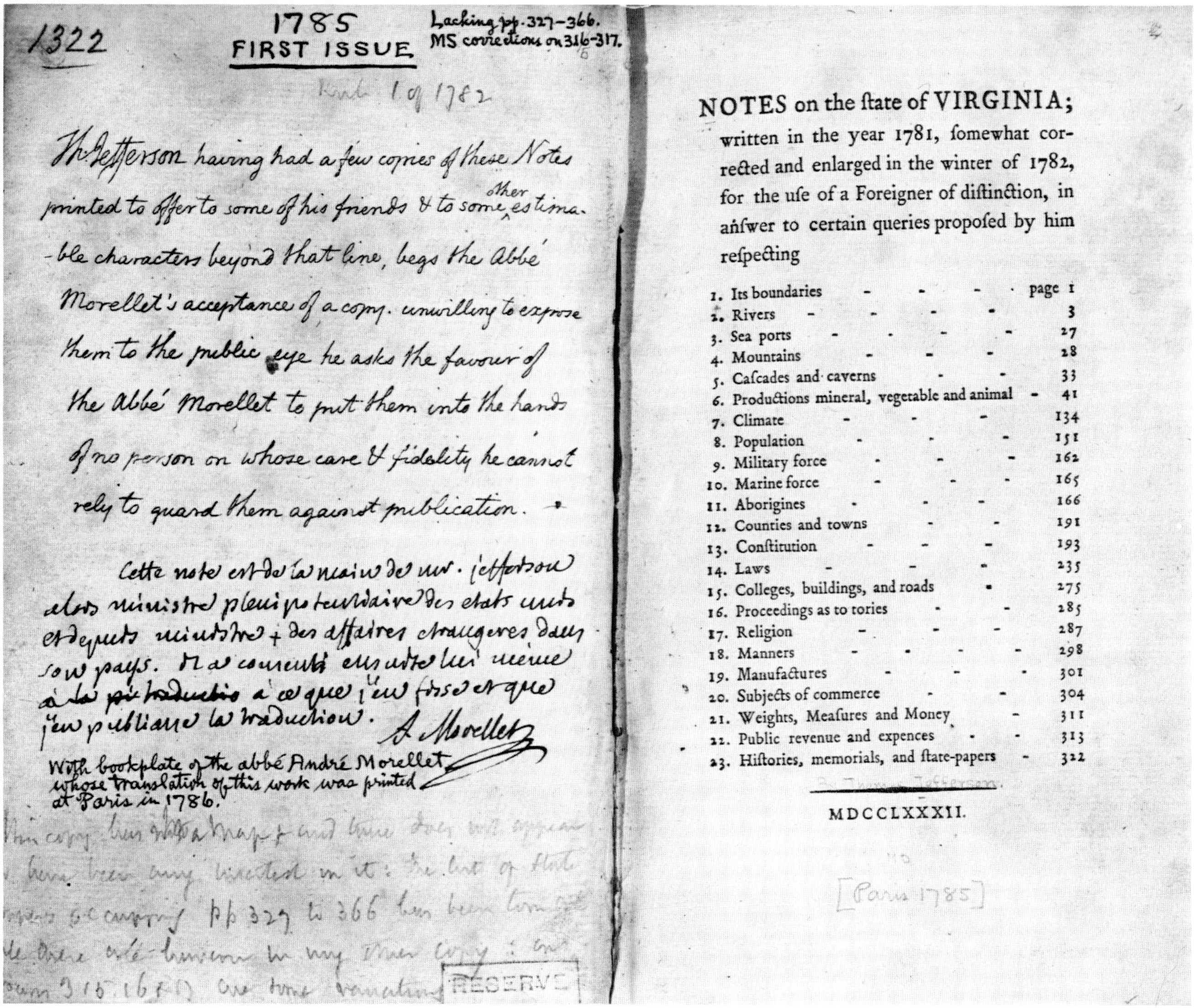

1785
FIRST ISSUE
Lacking pp. 327-366.
MS corrections on 316-317.

[handwritten] 1 of 1782

Th: Jefferson having had a few copies of these Notes printed to offer to some of his friends & to some other estima-ble characters beyond that line, begs the Abbé Morellet's acceptance of a copy. unwilling to expose them to the public eye he asks the favour of the Abbé Morellet to put them into the hands of no person on whose care & fidelity he cannot rely to guard them against publication.

Cette note est de la main de mr. Jefferson alors ministre plenipotentiaire des etats unis et depuis ministre + des affaires etrangeres dans son pays. Il a consenti lui même à la production a ce que j'eu fisse et que j'eu publiasse la traduction. *A Morellet*

With bookplate of the abbé André Morellet, whose translation of this work was printed at Paris in 1786.

[faded handwritten lines, partly illegible] ... pp 329 to 366 ... 315 16 17 ...

NOTES on the ftate of VIRGINIA; written in the year 1781, fomewhat cor-rected and enlarged in the winter of 1782, for the ufe of a Foreigner of diftinction, in anfwer to certain queries propofed by him refpecting

1. Its boundaries - - -	page 1
2. Rivers - - - -	3
3. Sea ports - - -	27
4. Mountains - - -	28
5. Cafcades and caverns -	33
6. Productions mineral, vegetable and animal -	41
7. Climate - - -	134
8. Population - - -	151
9. Military force - - -	162
10. Marine force - - -	165
11. Aborigines - - -	166
12. Counties and towns - -	191
13. Conftitution - - -	193
14. Laws - - - -	235
15. Colleges, buildings, and roads -	275
16. Proceedings as to tories - -	285
17. Religion - - -	287
18. Manners - - -	298
19. Manufactures - - -	301
20. Subjects of commerce - -	304
21. Weights, Meafures and Money -	311
22. Public revenue and expences -	313
23. Hiftories, memorials, and ftate-papers -	322

MDCCLXXXII.

[Paris 1785]

Figure 5.12
Thomas Jefferson. *Notes on the State of Virginia* (Paris, 1782 [1785]). This copy of the original edition of *Notes* was presented by Jefferson to the Abbé André Morellet.

the natural world" had criticized Raynal and Corneille de Pauw for their lack of critical judgment and scientific method. What was needed, Jefferson decided, was an American work fusing the method of the *Histoire Naturelle* and the agenda of the Declaration of Independence, presenting the case for America and the Americans just as the Declaration had presented the case for the break with Great Britain.[43]

Jefferson's opportunity was a series of questions on American condi-tions that the secretary of the French legation in America, François de Barbé-Marbois, had sent to the governors of each of the thirteen American states in 1781, when Jefferson was governor of Virginia. Jefferson was the only recipient of the questionnaire to take it seriously. He worked intermit-tently at the project for three years, taking it with him to Paris when he became American minister. Eventually he produced a book with the modest title *Notes on the State of Virginia* (Figure 5.12). He had it privately printed in an edition of two hundred copies for confidential distribution to a few friends in Europe and America, but the *Notes* soon found a wider audience as a result of its readers' indiscretion and the greed of unscrupulous printers. To Jefferson's dismay, garbled accounts of the book began to circulate, together with the threat of an unauthorized French translation. Jefferson worried that this rumored French edition might, if not preempted by an authentic version, result in an even more corrupted English-language edition based on the garbled French text. He therefore authorized a translation into French by the Abbé André Morellet, one of the book's original recipients. Within two years he revised and expanded the book for its first general English-language edition, published in London in 1787 by John Stockdale. Thus appeared the only full-length work that Jefferson ever wrote.[44]

A model of what his contemporaries called "philosophical history," *Notes on the State of Virginia* took an interdisciplinary approach modeled on that of Montesquieu's *The Spirit of the Laws*. Jefferson first set out to refute the claim that "nature is less active, less energetic on one side of the globe than she is on the other."[45] After describing the fossilized remains of the newly discovered mammoth, which was larger than any known European animal, he counterattacked with ridicule: "As if both sides [of the globe] were not warmed by the same genial sun; as if a soil of the same chemical composition, was less capable of elaboration into animal nutriment; as if the fruits and grains from that soil and sun, yielded a less rich chyle . . ."[46] Next he refuted Buffon's description of American environmental conditions as unduly moist and inhospitable with his own statistics on weather (which, as both a careful scientific observer and a practical farmer, he collected for most of his life). He also presented detailed tables of statures of European and American animals of comparable species. In each instance, he triumphantly concluded, the data refuted Buffon's theory.

Jefferson dealt at greatest length with Buffon's attempt to apply his theory of American degeneracy to human beings, citing as authority his own firsthand observations of the Indians of North America. He conceded some of the Indians' inferiorities as described by Buffon, but he maintained that these were the results of the Indians' circumstances rather than of nature. Physically, intellectually, morally, even sexually—in every way not shaped by their customs, the Indians were the equals if not perhaps the superiors of white men and women. For example, in oratory the Mingo chief Logan had exceeded even the greatest speeches of Demosthenes and Cicero. Have the Indians made no great advances in civilization? Jefferson asked rhetorically and replied that it took the Europeans sixteen centuries to produce Isaac Newton. Nature, he proclaimed, is no partisan of any given section of the earth:

> I am induced to suspect, there has been more eloquence than sound reasoning displayed in support of this theory; that it is one of those cases where the judgment has been seduced by a glowing pen: and whilst I render every tribute of honor and esteem to the celebrated

Zoologist, who has added, and is still adding, so many precious things to the treasures of science, I must doubt whether in this instance he has not cherished error also, by lending her for a moment his vivid imagination and bewitching language.[47]

After this delicate though pointed rebuke of Buffon, Jefferson turned to the question of nature's supposed degenerative effect on Europeans in the New World—a point urged not by Buffon but by Raynal, who in Jefferson's translation declared his astonishment that "America has not yet produced one good poet, one able mathematician, one man of genius in a single art, or a single science."[48] Again, Jefferson pointed out that it had taken the Europeans two millennia and more to produce only two universally revered poets, Homer and Virgil, and he confidently predicted that the appearance of a great American poet was just a matter of time. Jefferson cited the achievements of Washington as a military leader, Franklin as a scientist, and the great Philadelphia astronomer and mathematician David Rittenhouse (whom Jefferson as president would appoint director of the United States Mint). In other fields

> we might show that America, though but a child of yesterday, has already given hopeful proofs of genius, as well as of the nobler kinds, which arouse the best feelings of man, which call him into action, which substantiate his freedom, and conduct him to happiness, as of the subordinate, which serve to amuse him only. We therefore suppose, that this reproach is as unjust as it is unkind; and that, of the geniuses which adorn the present age, America contributes its full share.[49]

Then Jefferson turned the tables on Raynal and his allies. If, as it appeared, American was indeed "contribut[ing] its full share" of genius to the world, what of the two greatest nations of Europe, Great Britain and France? France had six times and Great Britain three times the population of the American states. If America has produced three geniuses, Jefferson calculated, then Great Britain should be able to present nine, and France eighteen. Mindful of his audience, Jefferson acknowledged that France had "produce[d] her full quota of genius," but his anti-British bias led him to conclude that "the sun of [Great Britain's] glory is fast descending to the horizon."[50]

Not content to rest his case on the arguments of the *Notes*, Jefferson also sought actual physical evidence to lay before Buffon.[51] He presented the Frenchman not only with a copy of the first edition of the *Notes*, which the latter received with distant politeness, but also with a fine panther skin, and, later, many other specimens collected by himself and by friends throughout America. Even James Madison, for whom Jefferson had purchased a complete set of Buffon's works, took time from his constitutional and historical researches to reassure his friend, promise him specimens, and develop and extend Jefferson's refutation of Buffon in the *Notes*. Although Buffon died in early 1788 without fully abandoning his position, he and his collaborators took account of many of Jefferson's specific corrections in the supplementary volumes of the *Histoire Naturelle*. Meanwhile, in 1783 Raynal had revised his *History of the Two Indies*, adding apologies to the "Federo-Americans" and qualifications and recantations of his earlier arguments. In the same letter in which he reported Franklin's dinner with the philosophes, William Carmichael complimented Jefferson's campaign for America: "After your [*Notes*] I think that we shall hear nothing more of the opinions of Monsr. Buffon or the Abbé Raynal on this subject."[52]

The publication of *Notes on the State of Virginia* coincided with the publication of books praising the United States by Europeans who had actually traveled in America—such as Johann David Schoepf's *Travels in the Confederation* (Figure 5.13)—or even settled there, such as the French envoy J. Hector St. John de Crèvecoeur's *Letters from an American Farmer*, the greatest foreign book on America before Alexis de Tocqueville's *Democracy in America*.[53] Crèvecoeur's work demolished the theory of American degeneracy put forth by Buffon, Raynal, and Corneille de Pauw. In fact the Americans' lack of a long history seemed a blessing to Crevecoeur, as America was thus spared the millstone of past crimes and follies that weighed down Europe. Soon bookshelves filled with counterblasts against the older philosophes by a new generation of social thinkers and reformers, led by the Marquis de Condorcet and Diderot and encouraged by Jefferson. Inspired by the French-American defeat of Great Britain and by the example of the Marquis de Lafayette's ardent love for America, these young philosophes hailed the new nation as the best hope of mankind and the refuge of liberty. Americans, too, kept up the fire; even in the midst of the debate between supporters and opponents of the Constitution, Alexander Hamilton found space in *Federalist* No. 11 for a few derisive lines aimed straight at Corneille de Pauw.[54]

Although the eminent philosopher and dialectician G. W. F. Hegel gave the theory of American degeneracy a new lease on life at the close of the eighteenth century,[55] the idea no longer occupied a central position in the transatlantic debate over the meaning of America for the world. By the beginning of the twentieth century this theory was little more than an intellectual curiosity, an anomalous relic from the European Enlightenment. The greatest share of credit for stripping this idea of its intellectual respectability rests with the Americans themselves. Led first by Franklin and then by Jefferson, the American intellectual counterattack established the claims of the new republic to intellectual, polemical, and scientific parity with the nations of the Old World.

John Adams Confronts the Philosophes

John Adams (Plate IX) cheered on Jefferson's defense of America from his post as American minister in London, generously suggesting that the writing and publication of the *Notes* had earned the Virginian a place alongside his

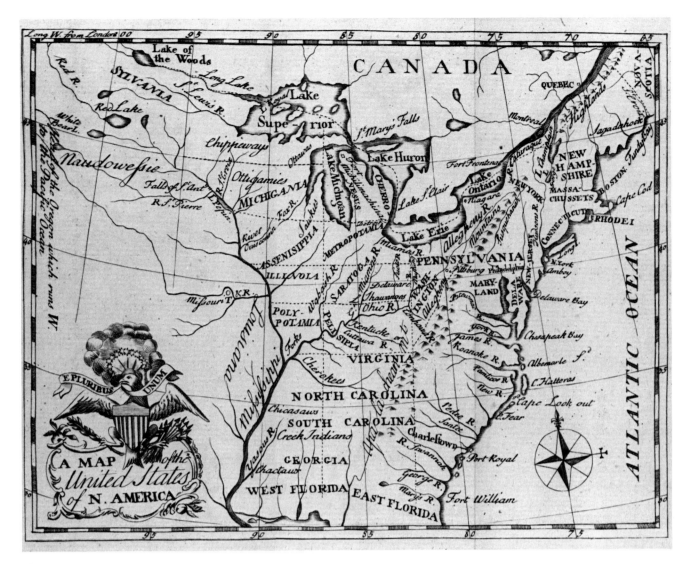

Figure 5.13
Unknown artist after H. D.
Pursell. *A Map of The United States
of N. America.* Engraving in
Johann David Schoepf, *Reise
Durch Einige Der Mittlern Und
Südlichen Vereinigten Nordamerikan-
ischen Staaten,* vol. I (Erlangen: J.
J. Palm, 1788). This small map
originally appeared in *Bailey's
Pocket Almanac* (Philadelphia:
1785).

trio of American geniuses, Franklin, Washington, and Rittenhouse. Adams, too, was embroiled in an intellectual battle in defense of America—a controversy that called on his own peculiar talents and interests. On this front, the natural world was not at issue. The argument focused instead on the Americans' greatest achievements, those of most interest to the European philosophes and politicians—the new states' constitutions.

The American epoch of constitution-making was a matter of keen interest to the Europeans.[56] The French followed this subject in the magazine *Affaires de l'Angleterre et de l'Amérique,* which Benjamin Franklin encouraged and helped to edit. In 1778 this magazine published the Duc de La Rochefoucauld's translations of the constitutions of Pennsylvania, New Jersey, Delaware, Maryland, Virginia, and South Carolina. In 1783, after the publication of a pirated edition of these translations, Franklin supervised an authorized translation of all thirteen states' constitutions and the significant American treaties (Figure 5.14). This compilation appeared in two versions—an inexpensive edition for general circulation and a special, deluxe edition for presentation to heads of state and other eminent political figures. Each presentation copy was richly bound in leather with the recipient's coat of arms stamped in gold on the front and back covers.

The American constitutions attracted the attention of government officials and students of politics all over Europe. Ewald Friedrich Graf von Hertzberg, a minister of the government of Frederick II (the Great) of Prussia, commented on the American constitutions in 1784, in a lecture delivered at the Berlin Academy of Sciences for Frederick's birthday. While acknowledging the intrinsic interest of the American experiments—"Our century by birth of the American Republic has provided us with a new phenomenon"—von Hertzberg sought to reassure his audience that republican government was a thing of the past. The Americans had won their independence and the chance to frame new forms of government thanks only to the mistakes of the British government and the assistance of the French, and the French alliance was motivated more by that nation's commercial rivalry with Great Britain than by agreement with the Americans' political theories. Constrained by his prejudices and those of his audience, confident of the advantages and necessity of the Prussian government and other "enlightened despotisms," von Hertzberg declared: "We will have to wait at least half a century before we know whether and how this new republic, this confederated body, will consolidate the form of its government; at this time its existence does not prove anything in favor of the republican form."[57]

Other Europeans were not so quick to dismiss the ideas of republicanism and the promise of self-government. The citizens of the Netherlands hailed John Adams as a hero when in 1782 he finally succeeded in negotiating a treaty of alliance and securing loans for the American Confederation from the bankers of Amsterdam.[58] The people of France lionized first Franklin and then Jefferson when each arrived to serve as American minister. The philosophes in most European nations welcomed the Americans' attempts to revive republicanism in practice and applauded the efforts of some states to do away with established religions and to foster absolute religious freedom; thus both Jefferson and James Madison (who never visited Europe) became heroes of the cause of liberty on account of their campaign to dissolve the established church in Virginia. Indeed, many philosophes criticized the Americans for not going far enough in certain directions in their new constitutions.

The two men who unknowingly touched off the controversy over the American constitutions were a retired French government official and a British Dissenting minister, philosopher, and controversialist. Born in Paris in 1727, Anne Robert Jacques Turgot was a bold, inventive administrator who as intendant of the province of Limousin from 1761 to 1774 became renowned as an enlightened political thinker for his overhaul of provincial administration and finances. In 1774 Louis XVI named Turgot comptroller general of finance, authorizing him to reorganize and systematize the fi-

Figure 5.14
Constitutions des Treize Etats-Unis de l'Amérique, translated by Louis Alexandre, Duc de La Rochefoucauld d'Enville (Paris: Ph.-D. Pierres and Pissot, 1783).

CONSTITUTIONS

DES

TREIZE ÉTATS-UNIS

DE L'AMÉRIQUE.

A PHILADELPHIE;

Et se trouve A PARIS,

Chez { Ph.-D. Pierres, Imprimeur Ordinaire du Roi, rue Saint-Jacques.
Pissot, pere & fils, Libraires, quai des Augustins.

1783.

nances of France. Turgot proposed six edicts designed to abolish the *corvée* (the hated system of forced labor) and other bastions of feudal privilege and corruption. Although Louis XVI promulgated the edicts and formally endorsed their recommendations, Turgot's enemies conspired to remove him from office. Using forged letters in which Turgot supposedly disparaged the king and queen, they persuaded Louis to force Turgot into early retirement in 1776. In the remaining five years of his life, Turgot saw the dismantling of his edicts and the restoration of the old system. In 1781 his successor, the Swiss-born Jacques Necker, was also forced into retirement for attempting to effectuate the same kinds of reforms that Turgot had championed.[59]

Richard Price was a devout and popular Presbyterian clergyman, an ardent supporter of the American cause, and a notable writer on moral philosophy and economics.[60] His economic writings foreshadowed the concepts of life insurance and old-age pensions, and he was consulted on economic questions by everyone from Turgot through William Pitt to President Joseph Willard of Harvard University. For more than thirty years he corresponded with dozens of Americans, and the leaders of the Revolution venerated him and valued his advocacy of justice for America. He was awarded an honorary doctorate of laws (together with George Washington) by Yale University and was elected a member of the American Philosophical Society and the American Academy of Arts and Letters. The Continental Congress even invited Price to accept American citizenship and emigrate to the United States; though he regretfully declined the offer, he maintained close ties with America and an interest in the new nation's affairs until he died in 1791 at age sixty-eight. When in 1785 the young Noah Webster sent him two of his early books, one on grammar and the other on politics, Price responded with generous praise for both volumes, expressing his hope that "your Sketches of American Policy will contribute to Spread those principles of Governmt and Civil Liberty which I think of the utmost importance, and wish to take root and flourish in the united States in order to render them Examples and blessings to the world."[61]

Price's second pamphlet supporting the Americans contained a few lines criticizing the "want of address" or tactlessness shown by Turgot in proposing his six edicts. On 22 March 1778 Turgot responded in a letter thanking the clergyman for sending him a copy of the pamphlet, and Price deleted the offending passage from later editions. Like most American and European philosophes, Turgot took the opportunity to pen a wide-ranging commentary on politics and particularly on American affairs. Although Price honored Turgot's wishes and kept the letter confidential during the latter's life, he reprinted it, together with his own English translation, in his 1784 pamphlet *Observation on the Importance of the American Revolution, and the Means of Making it a Benefit to the World* (Figure 5.15).[62]

When Price's pamphlet appeared, the appendix containing Turgot's letter attracted the attention of John Adams, who considered himself—with good reason—the prophet of American constitutionalism. Adams's 1776 pamphlet *Thoughts on Government . . .*, with its emphasis on an independent executive and a bicameral legislature as a necessary application of the principles of balanced government and separation of powers, had strongly influenced the framing of many of the state constitutions. The Americans were not unanimous on the necessity or desirability of two legislative houses, however. A few state constitutions, the most famous and influential of which was the Pennsylvania constitution of 1776, vested most governmental power in a unicameral legislature. The influence of the Pennsylvania constitution in Europe flowed from the generally held belief that it was the handiwork of Benjamin Franklin, and indeed it carried Franklin's blessing. Adams repeatedly criticized the Pennsylvania constitution and others following its example as flying in the face of history and all human experience with government. In effect, he saw this controversy in both political and personal terms, as a contest between his version of American constitutionalism as codified in the Massachusetts constitution of 1780, which he had drafted almost single-handed, and Franklin's version as embodied in the Pennsylvania constitution of 1776.[63]

Turgot's letter revived this dispute and expanded it into a transatlantic controversy, in large part because Turgot attributed the defects of most American constitutions to their imitation of "the customs of England." Turgot elaborated on this view, drawing parallels between the Americans' tendency to separate powers among a governor, a council or upper legislative house, and a lower legislative house consisting of a body of representatives, and the British system of King, Lords, and Commons. He maintained that the Americans should "collect all authority into one center," contending that in a republic there was no need for separation of powers. Although his letter continued with a detailed analysis of the defects of the Articles of Confederation, this point was Turgot's central argument:

> [The Americans] endeavour to balance these different powers, as if this equilibrium, which in England may be a necessary check to the enormous influence of royalty, could be of any use in republics founded upon the equality of all the citizens, and as if establishing different orders of men was not a source of divisions and disputes.

Turgot concluded with words of praise for the Americans, describing them as "the hope of the world." He retained his doubts about the Americans' mastery of the arts of government, however, and urged "all enlightened men, all the friends of humanity . . . at this time to unite their lights to those of the American sages and to assist them in the great work of legislation."[64]

When Price's pamphlet appeared in 1784, he sent copies to many friends, including Benjamin Franklin, Thomas Jefferson, and John Adams. Adams focused his critical attention not on Price's text but on the appendix containing Turgot's letter, annotating it at great length and with some irritation. At one point, he exploded in the margin opposite Turgot's comments on the uselessness of separation of powers in a republic:

> Is it possible that the writer of this paragraph should have ever read Plato, Livy, Polybius, Machiavel, Sidney, Harrington; or that he should ever have thought of the nature of man or of society? What does he mean [by] collecting all authority into one center? What does he mean by the center of a nation? Where would he have the [power of] legislation placed? Where the execution? Where the decision of controversies? Emptier piece of declamation I never read: it is impossible to give a greater proof of ignorance.
>
> Is it possible that any good government should exist without an equilibrium?
>
> Would he have no different orders?[65]

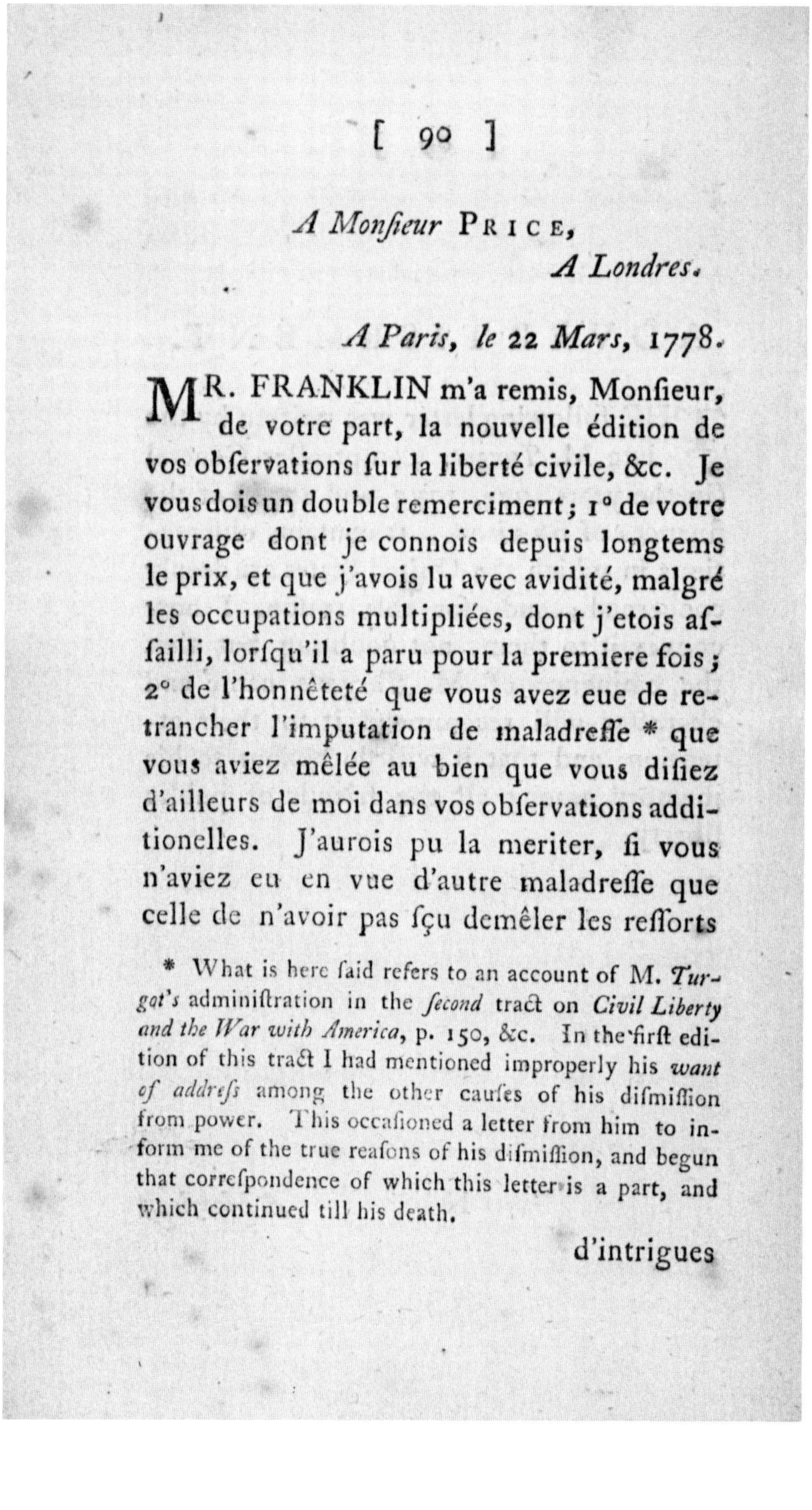

Figure 5.15
Turgot's letter in Richard Price, *Observations on . . . the American Revolution . . .* (London: T. Cadell, 1785). Price presented this copy of his *Observations* to Noah Webster.

[90]

A Monfieur PRICE,

A Londres.

A Paris, le 22 *Mars,* 1778.

MR. FRANKLIN m'a remis, Monfieur, de votre part, la nouvelle édition de vos obfervations fur la liberté civile, &c. Je vous dois un double remerciment; 1° de votre ouvrage dont je connois depuis longtems le prix, et que j'avois lu avec avidité, malgré les occupations multipliées, dont j'etois affailli, lorfqu'il a paru pour la premiere fois; 2° de l'honnêteté que vous avez eue de retrancher l'imputation de maladreffe * que vous aviez mêlée au bien que vous difiez d'ailleurs de moi dans vos obfervations additionelles. J'aurois pu la meriter, fi vous n'aviez eu en vue d'autre maladreffe que celle de n'avoir pas fçu demêler les refforts

---

* What is here faid refers to an account of M. *Turgot's* adminiftration in the *fecond* tract on *Civil Liberty and the War with America,* p. 150, &c. In the firft edition of this tract I had mentioned improperly his *want of addrefs* among the other caufes of his difmiffion from power. This occafioned a letter from him to inform me of the true reafons of his difmiffion, and begun that correfpondence of which this letter is a part, and which continued till his death.

d'intrigues

Figure 5.16
John Adams. *A Defence of the Constitutions of Government of the United States of America,* vol. I (London: C. Dilly, 1787).

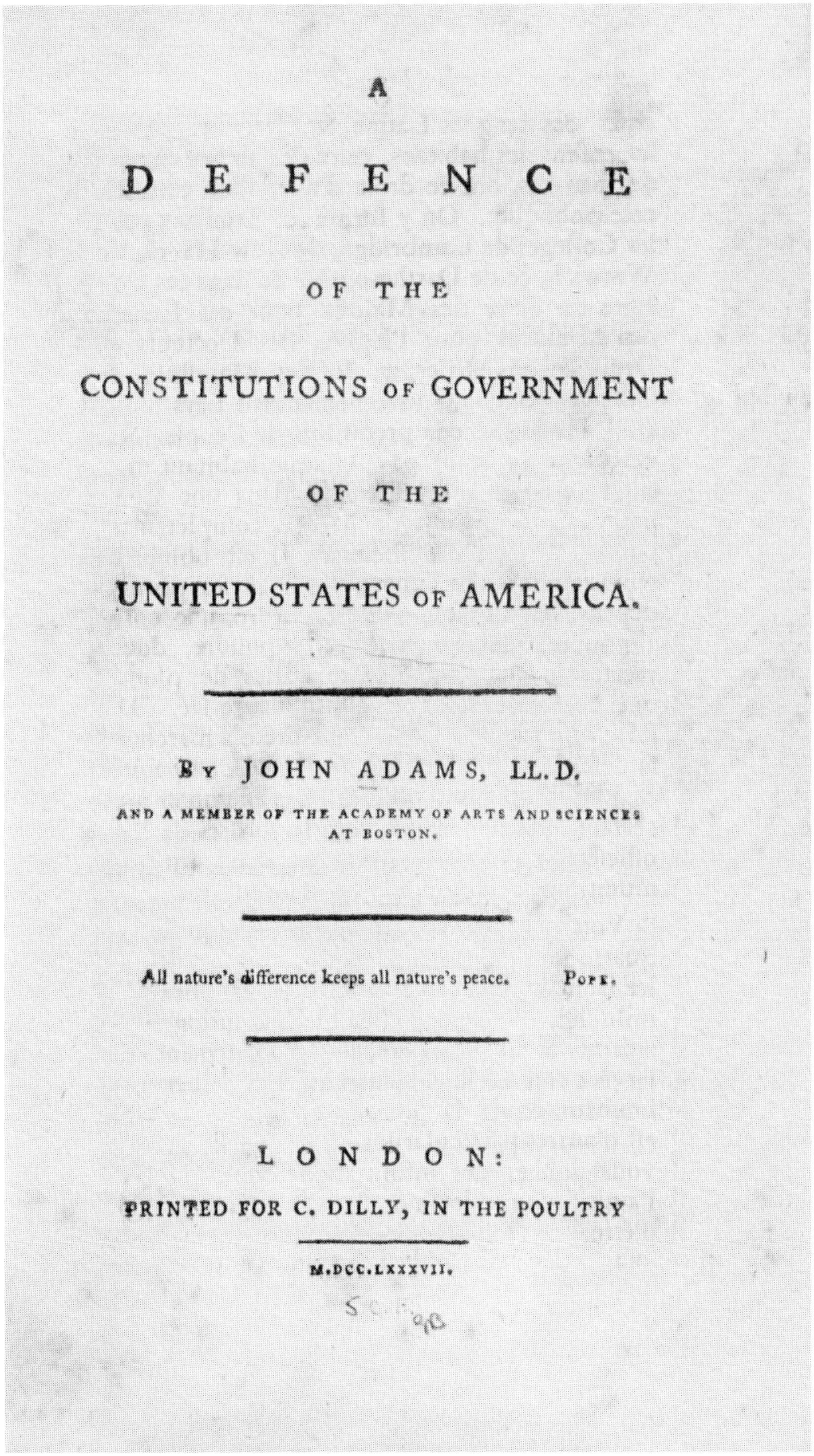

A

D E F E N C E

OF THE

CONSTITUTIONS OF GOVERNMENT

OF THE

UNITED STATES OF AMERICA.

———————

BY JOHN ADAMS, LL.D.

AND A MEMBER OF THE ACADEMY OF ARTS AND SCIENCES
AT BOSTON.

———————

All nature's difference keeps all nature's peace.   POPE.

———————

L O N D O N:

PRINTED FOR C. DILLY, IN THE POULTRY

M.DCC.LXXXVII.

Adams concluded that Turgot, like most of the European philosophes and his American compatriot Benjamin Franklin, "had an honest heart and great theoretical knowledge; but was not a judicious, practical statesman."[66]

In 1786 Adams's mounting frustration with the arrogance of the British and his increasing concern over the unsettled state of American affairs at home prompted him to respond to Turgot's published letter. Assembling a small library of works of ancient and contemporary history, Adams set to work. Drawing on his extensive historical knowledge and reading, and writing at top speed, he began to amass his data, copying out huge chunks from his sources and stitching them together with a few comments of his own. The news of the outbreak of Shays's Rebellion in Massachusetts stimulated Adams to an even more frantic pace. In early 1787 the book finally appeared, with a long and programmatic title typical of the age: *A Defence of the Constitutions of Government of the United States of America, against the Attack of M. Turgot, in his Letter to Dr. Price, dated the twenty-second day of March, 1778* (Figure 5.16). Although the book was complete in itself, Adams continued to expand his research and to amass additional extracts from his sources. He turned out two more huge, disorderly volumes in 1788, ending his third volume with a brief discussion of the United States Constitution, just made public by the Federal Convention.[67]

Adams's great aim in the *Defence* was to identify certain basic, enduring principles of the science of government and to prove them by culling evidence from the whole span of the history of republics. He reasserted and defended the classical political dictum that there were three kinds of "pure" government, each corresponding to a division or order of society—monarchy, aristocracy, and democracy. The mixing or balancing of these three orders and forms of government by constructing a republic with a strong executive and a bicameral legislature was the secret of preserving liberty, one known to the Greeks and the Romans. Adams warned his countrymen and the world that "without these orders, and an effectual balance between them, in every American constitution, [America] must be destined to frequent unavoidable revolutions: if they are delayed a few years, they must come, in time."[68] The book nearly foundered under the weight of all this evidence, as Adams himself came to recognize. But even though he had lost control of his book, he could not stop the process. In his letter to Richard Price of 4 February 1787, Adams acknowledged the book's defects:

> It is but a humble tho' laborious office to collect together so many opinions and examples but it may point out to my young countrymen the genuine sources of information upon a subject more interesting to them if possible than to the rest of the world. A work might be formed upon the plan which would be worthy of the pen and talents of a Hume, a Gibbon, a Price or a Priestley, and I cannot but think that the two former would have employed their whole lives in forming into one system and view all the governments that exist, or are recorded, more

beneficially to mankind than in attacking all the principles of human knowledge, or in painting the ruins of the Roman Empire, instead of leaving such an enterprise to the temerity of an American demagogue worn out with the cares and vexations of a turbulent life.[69]

Ironically, as Gordon S. Wood has shown in his brilliant analysis of John Adams's constitutional thought, the one man who seemed to have the best and most complete understanding of the history and theory of constitutionalism somehow managed to "miss the intellectual significance of the most important event since the Revolution."[70] Adams had briefly believed, as did his contemporaries in America, that the effects of a revolution intended to establish republican governments would also establish republicanism as a source of new social habits and patterns of thinking and behavior, thus fixing the American people in the ways of virtue necessary to preserve republican government. But he came to reject the possibility that America might be different, that his country could escape the forces of history that affected all other governments, nations, and peoples.

The desires, passions, and ambitions that dominated the human race also dominated the Americans, Adams taught. In the scramble for distinction, wealth, and power, those who triumph do so not from any special virtue but only because they have been sufficiently fortunate and ruthless. The doctrines of republicanism offered little hope of moderating these competitive passions and cycles. For this reason Adams espoused the doctrine of the balanced constitution—the only form of government that could control the conflict between the few and the many, the aristocratic and democratic interests of society. By creating two legislative houses, one representing the people (the democratic interest) and the other representing property (the aristocratic interest), with a strong and independent executive holding both houses in balance, such a constitution could prevent society's forces from tearing the polity apart.

In the last pages of his third volume, Adams hailed the new Constitution penned by the Federal Convention as a sign that the American people had absorbed the teachings of history—and his first volume, which had appeared in Philadelphia on the eve of the Convention. The Constitution at first glance seemed to enshrine the principles of balance so dear to Adams. In fact, however, the two-house Congress created by the Constitution differs significantly from the balanced, bicameral legislature advocated by Adams. Convinced that sovereignty was indivisible, Adams did not understand or appreciate the Federal Convention's unique, almost inadvertent development of federalism, with its division and commingling of federal and state sovereignty. Adams also did not share his fellow Americans' understanding of the sources of sovereignty, namely that in the federal Constitution the executive and both houses of the legislature represented the people, whether directly or indirectly. Last, he did not appreciate the potential of the federal judiciary to act as another source of checks and balances in a constitutional

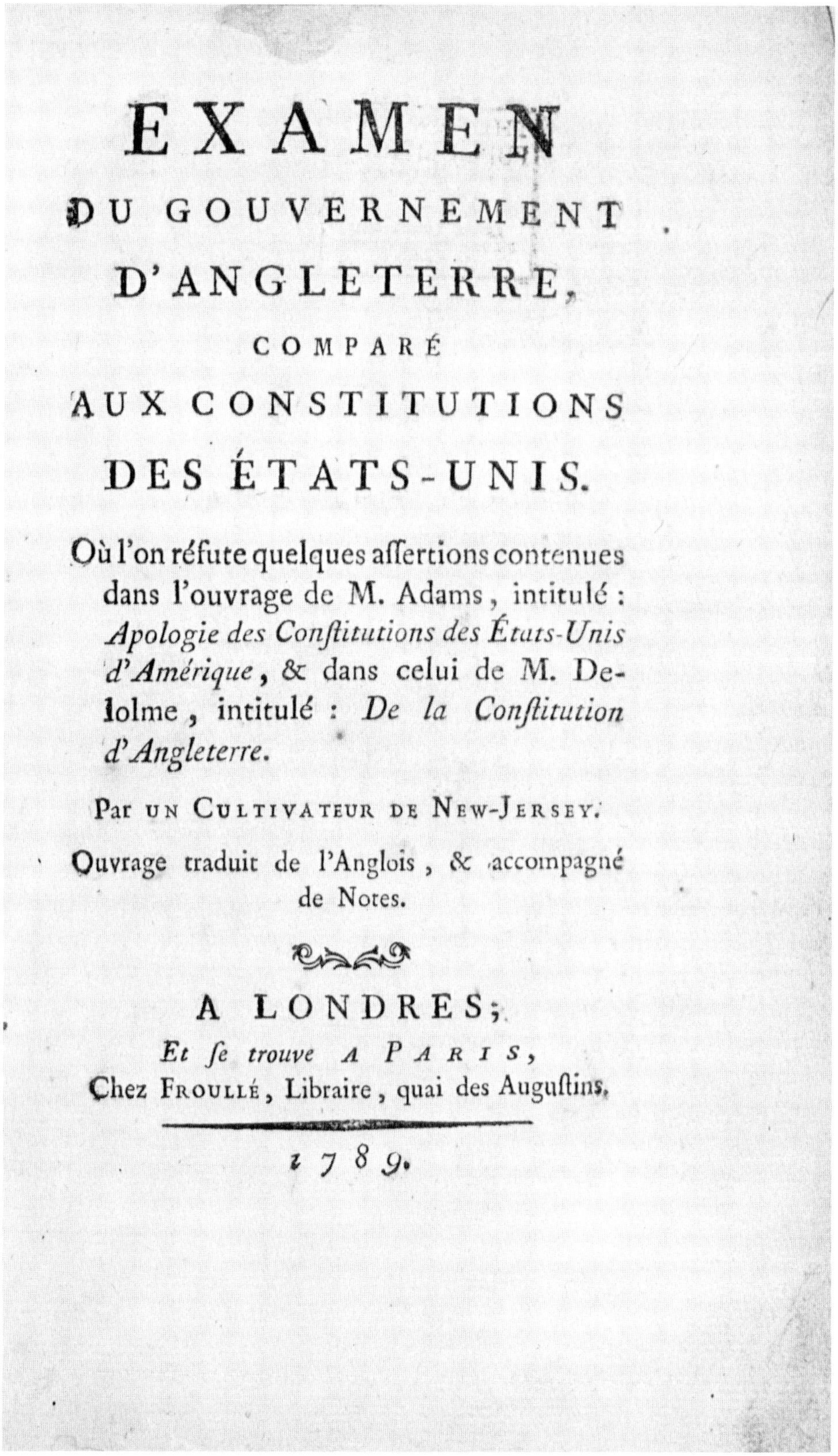

Figure 5.17
[John Stevens, Jr.?] *Examen du Gouvernement d'Angleterre, Comparé aux Constitutions des Etats-Unis* [translated by M. Fabre] (Paris: Froullé, 1789).

EXAMEN

DU GOUVERNEMENT

D'ANGLETERRE,

COMPARÉ

AUX CONSTITUTIONS

DES ÉTATS-UNIS.

Où l'on réfute quelques assertions contenues dans l'ouvrage de M. Adams, intitulé : *Apologie des Constitutions des États-Unis d'Amérique*, & dans celui de M. De-lolme, intitulé : *De la Constitution d'Angleterre*.

PAR UN CULTIVATEUR DE NEW-JERSEY.

Ouvrage traduit de l'Anglois, & accompagné de Notes.

A LONDRES;

Et se trouve A PARIS,

Chez FROULLÉ, Libraire, quai des Augustins.

1789.

Figure 5.18
Raphael Morghen after Georg
Dillis after A. Bronzino. Portrait
of Niccolò Machiavelli. Line
engraving, 1795.

system. Just as the European philosophes had betrayed a faulty understanding of the realities of republican politics and constitution-making by insufficient attention to the lessons of history, Adams had failed to understand the new currents of American constitutional thought embodied in the federal Constitution.

Adams predicted correctly that the *Defence* would make him unpopular, but he was mistaken in his expectation that he would ultimately be vindicated, even though the states with unicameral legislatures did revise their constitutions in the 1790s and afterward adopted the bicameral system. And Adams was not surprised when Condorcet and other philosophes translated the most searching criticism of his work, *Observations on Government,* probably the work of John Stevens of New Jersey (Figure 5.17). Adams also became the target of increasing criticism at home, some of it extending to personal attacks charging him with favoring monarchy. He tried to restate and develop the arguments of the *Defence* in a series of essays called *Discourses on Davila,* modeled loosely on Machiavelli's (Figure 5.18) *Discourses on the First Ten Books of Titus Livius,* one of the classic works of republican political thought. This new book only got him into more trouble, helping to break his friendship with Thomas Jefferson and to stimulate the rise of party politics in the 1790s.

And yet Adams's great book did contain one critical truth unjustly ignored by his contemporaries—his rejection of the emerging doctrine of American exceptionalism, based on his insistence that Americans were subject to the same political afflictions that had beset societies and governments throughout history. The doctrine of American exceptionalism was at the heart of American attempts to revive republicanism in the New World and became an enduring element of American political orthodoxy. Adams resisted this "chimerical" view all his life in hundred of letters to his friends, including Jefferson, with whom he became reconciled in their retirement. Though he may not have dissuaded his contemporaries from their wishful thinking, he became one of the great skeptical figures in the history of American political thought.[71]

6

AN ASSEMBLY OF DEMIGODS?

O N 2 5 MAY 1 7 8 7, picking their way through a driving rain, thirty men representing seven states assembled in the Pennsylvania State House (Plate X), now known as Independence Hall, and the Federal Convention began.[1] The authorizing resolution of the Confederation Congress had fixed the opening date for 14 May, but delegates from only Virginia and Pennsylvania had arrived by that date. Eventually fifty-five men representing twelve states attended at least some sessions of the Convention. Writing from his post in Paris to John Adams, Thomas Jefferson described the delegates as "an assembly of demigods."[2] Other observers, though less adulatory than Jefferson, were also impressed with the range of talent and experience assembled for the Convention. The gathering included states' governors, chief justices, attorneys general, and many delegates to the Confederation Congress, as well as several distinguished Americans who had agreed to come out of retirement to participate one last time in American affairs.[3]

Two of the delegates were regarded by common consent as the greatest living Americans. George Washington (Plate XI) had not had an easy time deciding whether to accept or decline his appointment to the Virginia delegation. For eight grueling, frustrating years he had served his country as commander-in-chief of the Continental Army. He had wrestled with the problems of an ill-trained, poorly equipped, and undisciplined army; a recalcitrant, faction-ridden, and impotent Congress; an erratic, touchy officer corps that had conspired once against his own leadership and another time against Congress itself; and even his elderly, querulous mother, who complained bitterly and unfairly to Congress and anyone else who would listen about her son's neglect of her. At the end of 1783, with American independence won, Washington retired to his estate at Mount Vernon; renouncing power and popularity, he was determined to settle back into the life of a vigorous, hard-riding planter and country squire. And yet he never abandoned his interest in American affairs. For one thing, he was a shrewd land speculator who kept a vigilant eye on all factors that might affect his investments. For another, his experiences during the Revolution had strengthened his belief that the United States needed a stronger, more

Figure 6.1
Gilbert Stuart. Portrait of James Madison. Oil on canvas, 1822. This portrait (based on one done from life in 1804) was originally part of a set of five portraits of presidents painted by Stuart in 1822 for John Doggett, a Boston art dealer.

vigorous government than that provided by the Confederation. His hosting of the Mount Vernon Conference of 1785 and the disheartening news he received from friends such as Alexander Hamilton and James Madison in the Confederation Congress persuaded him that, as he wrote to Madison in March 1787, "the defects of the [Articles]" must be "probe[d] to the bottom."[4]

Washington was the American nation personified and took many pains to shape and restrain his conduct and his relations with others to preserve this eminence.[5] He was—and understood himself to be—his era's embodiment of the classical ideal of disinterested patriotism, like the legendary Roman Cincinnatus, to whom he was often compared. He cultivated a serious dignity and reserve that discouraged levity and familiarity, but he did so out of sensitivity to the importance of his role and the commingling of America's reputation and destiny with his own. For this reason he was cautious almost to a fault in deciding whether or not to represent Virginia at the Federal Convention. That he did so at last was a triumph for James Madison and others favoring efforts to strengthen the government of the

Figure 6.2
James Madison. Notes on the debates in the Federal Convention, 14 July 1787.

Saturday July 14. contin?

from the Eastern States to the Western Country. and he did not wish those remaining behind to be at the mercy of those Emigrants. Besides foreigners are resorting to that Country, and it is uncertain what turn things may take there. — On the question for agreeing to the motion of Mr. Gerry. it passed in the negative.

Mas. ay. Con?. ay. N. J. no. Pa. divd. Del. ay. Md. ay. Va. no. N. C. no. S. C. no. Geo. no.

Mr. Rutlidge proposed to reconsider the ~~clause touching~~ two propositions touching the originating of money bills, & the equality of votes in the first in the second branch.

Mr. Sherman was for the question on the whole at once. It was he said a conciliatory plan, it had been considered in all its parts, a great deal of time had been spent on it, and if any part should now be altered, it would be necessary to go over the whole ground again.

Mr. L. Martin urged the question on the whole. He did not like many parts of it. He did not like having two branches, nor the inequality of votes on the 1st branch. He was willing however to make trial of the plan, rather than do nothing.

Mr. Wilson traced the progress of the report through its several stages, remarking yt on the question concerning an equality of votes, the House was divided, our constituents had they voted as their representatives did, would have stood as ⅔ agst. the equality, and ⅓ only in favor of it. This fact would ere long be known, and th will it appear that this fundamental point has been carried by ⅓ agst. ⅔. What hopes will our constituents entertain when they find that the essential principles of justice have been violated in the outset of the Government. As to the privilege of originating money bills, it was not considered by any as of much merit, and by many as improper in itself. He hoped both clauses wd be reconsidered. The equality of votes was a point of such critical importance, that every opportunity ought to be allowed, for discussing and collecting the mind of the convention on it.

Mr. L. Martin denies that there were ⅔ agst. the equality of votes. The States that please to call themselves large, are the weakest in the Union. Look at Mast. Look at Virga. Are they efficient States? He was for letting a separation take place if they desired it. He had rather there should be two confederacies, than one founded on any other principle than an equality

United States. It was also a signal and reassurance to the American people not only of the need for the Convention but also of the delegates' noble purposes and trustworthiness.

Washington's only possible rival in the estimation of the Western world was Benjamin Franklin (Plate XII). At eighty-one the oldest delegate to the Convention, Franklin could look back on an enormous range of careers and a dazzling constellation of talents and achievements. Printer, inventor, essayist, scientist, public servant, founder of learned societies, propagandist, politician, revolutionary, diplomat, peacemaker—by 1787 the self-educated Franklin was firmly enshrined in the role of sage. At this time, Franklin was visibly old and enfeebled. Almost certainly he realized that his part would be that of conciliator—to ease tensions, turn aside wrath with soft or amusing words, and help to frame compromises. A younger generation would take the lead in the theoretical work.[6]

To forestall any possible contest between Washington and Franklin for preeminence, Franklin and his Pennsylvania colleagues decided to propose Washington for the presidency of the Convention. To Franklin's disappointment, bad weather on the first day prevented him from attending the session to nominate Washington himself; Robert Morris stood in for Franklin, and all who were present understood and welcomed the Pennsylvanians' graceful gesture.

Seated at a desk just in front of the president's chair at this first—and every later—session was the thirty-six-year-old James Madison of Virginia (Figure 6.1).[7] Madison was perhaps the most learned and best prepared delegate; indeed, he had arrived two weeks before the scheduled opening date. Now, as the proceedings got under way, he carried out a resolution that he had made as a result of his careful study of the histories of ancient and modern confederacies. Using a self-taught system of shorthand, he began the single most detailed, authoritative, and reliable record of the Convention's labors (Figures 6.2, 6.3). Each evening he copied out his shorthand notes, occasionally referring to the full texts of speeches lent him by other delegates. Several other delegates kept notes of the debates for their own reference, and the Convention had elected an official secretary, Major William Jackson of Georgia, but he turned out to be lazy and inefficient, and his *Journal*, published in 1819, is unreliable.

The Virginians made good use of the eleven days between the official and actual starting dates. Led by Madison, they prepared a set of resolutions that they hoped would serve as the basis for the deliberations. Thus, when the delegates convened on 25 May, the Virginians awaited the right moment to offer their plan for restructuring the Confederation.

After the election of officers, the Convention appointed a committee consisting of George Wythe of Virginia, Alexander Hamilton of New York, and Charles Pinckney of South Carolina to draft rules of procedure.[8] Most of these were based on the rules of the Confederation Congress[9] and were designed to preserve civility during the debates and to ensure a spirit of

Figure 6.3
John Wayles Eppes and John C. Payne. Notes of debates in the Federal Convention of 1787 by a member. Letterpress copy, 1791–1836. This letterpress copy is one of the only two copies Madison permitted to be made from his notes. The transcript was begun in 1791 by Jefferson's nephew as part of his legal training and was supplemented and corrected in 1836 by Madison's brother-in-law, who prepared the notes for translation and publication abroad. The original Eppes-Payne copy belongs to the Massachusetts Historical Society.

Monday May 14th, was the day fixed for the meeting of the deputies in Convention, for the revising the federal Constitution. On that day a small number only had assembled. Seven States were not convened &c.

Friday 25th of May when the following members appeared viz. from Massachusetts Rufus King, N. York Robert Yates, Alex. Hamilton, N. Jersey David Brearly William Church. ll Houston, William Patterson, Pensa. Robert Morris, Thomas Fitzsimmons, James Wilson Govr. Morris, Delaware George Read, Richard Bassett, Jacob Broom, Virginia, George Washington, Edmd. Randolph John Blair, James Madison, and George Mason, George Wythe James McClurg. North Carolina Alexander Martin, William Richardson Davie, Richard Dobbs Spaight, Hugh Williamson South Carolina, John Rutledge, Charles Cotesworth Pinkney Charles Pinkney, Pierce Butler, Georgia William Few.

Mr. Robert Morris, Informed the members the members assembled that by the instruction & in behalf

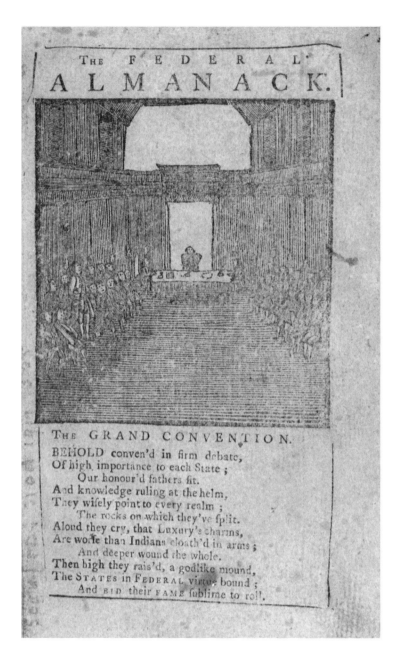

THE FEDERAL
ALMANACK.

THE GRAND CONVENTION.

BEHOLD conven'd in firm debate,
Of high importance to each State;
    Our honour'd fathers fit.
And knowledge ruling at the helm,
They wisely point to every realm;
    The rocks on which they've split.
Aloud they cry, that Luxury's charms,
Are worfe than Indians cloath'd in arms;
    And deeper wound the whole.
Then high they rais'd, a godlike mound,
The STATES in FEDERAL virtue bound;
    And BID their FAME fublime to roll.

Figure 6.4
Attributed to John Norman. *The Grand Convention.* Woodcut, 1787. This imaginary view of the Convention appeared on the cover of *Weatherwise's Federal Almanack* for 1788. The engraver was familiar with the interior of the State House.

harmony, cooperation, and mutual respect. Two, however, require extended discussion.

The rule of secrecy prohibited delegates from making copies of entries in the Convention's journal without leave of the full Convention. Further, only delegates were permitted to examine this journal or to attend meetings of the Convention or of its committees. Finally, delegates were barred from revealing or discussing with outsiders any business of the Convention. This rule of secrecy was consistent with the general practice of legislatures on both sides of the Atlantic until the 1790s.[10] The "public's right to know" did not have the same meaning in 1787 that we give it today. Although there was much good-natured curiosity and well-meant speculation about what

Figure 6.5
Attributed to Elkanah Tisdale. *Convention at Philadelphia.* Engraving, ca. 1823. This imaginary scene of the delegates at work appeared in Rev. Charles A. Goodrich, *A History of the United States of America* (Hartford: Huntington and Hopkins, 1823).

was going on behind the closed doors of the Convention (Figure 6.4), no one inside or out made a serious effort to breach this rule while the Convention was in session (Figure 6.5). The city of Philadelphia did its part by posting armed sentries around the State House to discourage inquisitive passersby and ordering loose dirt to be spread in the streets to muffle the sounds of passing wagons and carriages.

The other important rule adopted by the delegates was what might be called the "rule of mutability." The delegates rejected a proposed rule entitling delegates to require that the yeas and nays be entered in the journal and accepted the proposal of Richard Dobbs Spaight of North Carolina (Figure 6.6) that the Convention grant itself the ability to reconsider votes already taken by a majority. The delegates had reason to congratulate them-

Figure 6.6
Attributed to James Sharples.
Portrait of Richard Dobbs
Spaight. Pastel on paper, ca.
1796–97.

selves on having adopted Spaight's suggestion, for the Convention retraced its steps many times in the course of the summer, backing off from false or hasty starts and reaping the benefit of sober second thoughts.[11]

Most sessions of the Convention were conducted as sessions of the Committee of the Whole, a useful device familiar from English, colonial, and state legislative practice.[12] Meeting as a committee of the whole permitted more informal debate, greater freedom in stating views, and flexibility in adopting and reconsidering decisions and votes. When the delegates met in Committee of the Whole, Washington would convene a session of the full Convention and then relinquish the chair to the able and tactful Nathaniel Gorham of Massachusetts (Plate XIII). The delegates would debate the proposal before them, frequently reviewing it clause by clause. At the end of each major stage, the Committee of the Whole would submit its report to the full Convention, which would then conduct a more formal debate before taking a vote. At times, when the Convention needed to extricate itself from an impasse, or the delegates' ingenuity failed them, or the debate had reached a stage advanced enough to require stock-taking, the Convention would appoint a committee to work out a compromise, to prepare a report embodying the decisions reached up to that point, or to formulate a range of possible solutions to a given problem. Once the committee had completed its task the process would begin again.

This manner of doing business created severe pressures on the delegates. Because of the rule of secrecy, they were unable to thrash out matters, complain to sympathetic friends, or simply release their pent-up emotions. As the Convention dragged on through the summer, delegates began to wilt under the unusually oppressive heat. Laggard delegates kept arriving through the spring and early summer; New Hampshire's delegates did not arrive until 23 July, nearly two months after the Convention had begun, because the state's legislature had failed to appropriate funds to pay their expenses; ultimately John Langdon paid his and Nicholas Gilman's costs out of his own pocket. Many of the late arrivals crossed the paths of those whom Clinton L. Rossiter has called "the dropouts and walk-outs."[13] Some ran out of money and had to write home to their state governments for help.[14] Others were forced to leave because of illness, family crises (Figure 6.7),[15] or the pressures of business. Finally, some delegates could not abide the evolving new system of government. Such men as Luther Martin and John Francis Mercer of Maryland and Robert Yates and John Lansing, Jr., of New York later became active in the Anti-Federalists' campaign against the Constitution.

Despite all the frustrations inherent in attending the Convention and the many temptations to leave Philadelphia for home, more than half the delegates (twenty-nine) attended every or nearly every session, with another ten missing only a few weeks. Forty-two delegates showed up on the last day, including three—Elbridge Gerry of Massachusetts and George Mason and Edmund Randolph of Virginia—who refused to sign the Constitution.

Why were so many so faithful to their duties? First, many delegates sincerely feared for the nation's future under the Articles of Confederation and believed that the Convention provided a last clear chance to restructure the government of the United States to preserve the American experiment. Second, the delegates were aware that the interests of their states and sections as well as those of the United States depended on what the Convention did. They were there as much to safeguard state and local interests under whatever new system was devised by the Convention as "to render the constitution of the federal government adequate to the exigencies of the Union." Third, especially for younger and more intellectual delegates such as James Madison, Alexander Hamilton, and Charles Pinckney, the challenge of framing a new government and participating in deliberations critical to the future of republican government was irresistible.

Fourth, and closely related to the third, participation in the Convention gratified many delegates' desire for fame. Considered the reward of virtuous conduct, fame was the goad to virtuous behavior in public and private life.[16] And, as the delegates knew from their familiarity with Sir Francis Bacon's essay on the subject, the greatest fame and highest honor were reserved for "founders of states and commonwealths."

There was also the hope that distinguishing oneself at so important an assembly and among so remarkable a gathering of notables might well be a spur to one's later political career. Witness Charles Pinckney, whose desperate desire to shine led him to knock five years off his own age (he was twenty-nine) in order to lay claim to the distinction of being the Convention's youngest delegate—an honor properly belonging to twenty-six-year-old Jonathan Dayton of New Jersey. Even more questionable were Pinckney's later claims about his influence at the Convention.[17]

Did the delegates write the Constitution in order to protect their economic interests? In 1913 Charles A. Beard, relying on his research into lists of holders of United States securities in the 1780s, maintained that the delegates to the Convention and the supporters of the Constitution in the state ratification controversy were bent on protecting their holdings in these securities. A strong constitution and powerful federal government, Beard asserted, would guarantee the rights of property against encroachments by radical state governments such as Rhode Island or by armies of desperate debtors such as the Massachusetts farmers led by Daniel Shays.[18] Later research has shattered the foundation of Beard's claims and restored a measure of patriotism to the farmers' motives.[19] But the threats posed to the security of the rights of property by state governments and by the possibility of more debtors' rebellions like Shays's Rebellion galvanized politicians, such as Rufus King and Elbridge Gerry of Massachusetts, who otherwise would not have pursued that object with energy or commitment.

Exercises in Creative Statesmanship

On 29 May 1787, once the Convention had adopted its rules and elected its officers, Governor Edmund Randolph of Virginia (Plate XIV) opened the main business on behalf of his state's delegation. As in the case of the Annapolis Convention, Virginia had taken the leading part in campaigning for this gathering, and the delegates were probably not surprised to see Virginians at the head of this effort as well. Tall, handsome, a polished speaker, Randolph was one of the most popular figures in Virginia politics. In a long and eloquent speech, Randolph decried the unsettled state of the Union, pointed out the many defects of the Articles of Confederation, extolled the advantages of strengthening the general government, and concluded by presenting the fifteen resolutions drawn up by Madison and his colleagues. Later historians have dubbed these resolutions the Virginia Plan.[20]

The first resolution of the Virginia Plan made an obligatory bow to the limiting language of the congressional resolution authorizing the calling of

Figure 6.7
Letter from George Wythe to Edmund Randolph, Williamsburg, 16 June 1787.

G: Wythe to mr Randolph.

Mrs W's state of health is so low, and she
is so emaciated, that my apprehensions are not
a little afflicting, and, if the worst should not
befall, she must linger, i fear, a long time.
in no other circumstances would i withdraw
from the employment, to which i had the honour to be appointed. but, as probably i
shall not
~~come~~ return to Philadelphia; if, sir, to appoint one in my room be judged adviseable,
i hereby authorise you to consider this letter as a resignation, no less valid than a
solemn act for that express purpose.
my best wishes attend you and the other,
most respectable personages with whom
i was thought worthy to be associated.
Williamsburgh, 16 of june, 1787

the Convention, presenting the plan as a set of proposals for amendments to the Articles. The very next day, however, at the urging of Gouverneur Morris of Pennsylvania, Randolph withdrew this first resolution and substituted a set of three new ones. Meeting for the first time in Committee of the Whole, the Convention adopted the third of these: "Resolved, that a national government ought to be established consisting of a supreme Legislative, Executive, and Judiciary."[21]

When the Committee of the Whole adopted this proposal, with surprisingly little debate or disagreement, it chose to scrap the Articles of Confederation and frame a completely new instrument of government for the United States, one having the authority to operate directly on the American people rather than having to rely on the cooperation of the state governments. This resolution was also the foundation of the Convention's effort to create a fully developed system of government. The drafters of the Articles of Confederation had made no effort to embody the principle of separation of powers in that document, because it was intended to be not an instrument of government but a covenant among sovereign states. This resolution brought the cherished constitutional principle of separation of powers to the federal level, after more than a decade of fruitful experimentation in state constitution-making.

The Virginia Plan provided for a national legislature in two branches, each to be apportioned on the basis of population. The members of the first branch would be elected by the people; those of the second would be chosen by the first branch from a list of persons nominated by each state legislature. Members of the national legislature would be ineligible for other state or federal offices. They would receive liberal stipends to be paid by the United States, and thus would not be dependent on the whims of state governments, as were delegates to the Confederation Congress. The national legislature would have the legislative powers vested in Congress by the Articles, as well as the authority to legislate "in all cases to which the separate States are incompetent, or in which the harmony of the United States may be interrupted by the exercise of individual [states'] Legislation" and the power to veto state laws contrary to the new federal charter. The national legislature would also have the power to summon the armed forces of the United States against any state failing to fulfill its duties to the Union.

The Virginia Plan merely sketched the structure of the national executive, not even specifying how many persons would constitute it; but the plan did provide that the executive would be chosen by vote of the national legislature and would join with "a convenient number of the National Judiciary" to exercise a qualified veto power over the national legislature. The national judiciary would include one or more supreme tribunals and several lower courts; the judges of these courts would be named by vote of the national legislature. The national judicial power would extend to piracy, maritime cases, suits involving foreigners or citizens of other states, federal revenue cases, impeachments, "and questions which involve the national peace or harmony." The plan also included a proposal to devise a method to admit new states to the Union, a guarantee of a republican form of government for the states, an amendment procedure more flexible than that of the Articles, a requirement that state officeholders swear to support the new charter of government, and a ratification clause under which the new charter would be submitted to specially chosen assemblies in the states rather than to the state legislatures.

The first incarnation of the Constitution of the United States, the Virginia Plan contained the seeds of most of the issues that agitated the delegates, and some of its omissions proved just as controversial as its terms. For the rest of the Convention, using the Virginia Plan as a basis, the delegates struggled to frame a national charter sufficiently powerful, flexible, and well checked and balanced to hold the nation together without injuring the legitimate rights of the states.

The Dilemma of Representation

The dispute that posed the greatest threat to the unity and harmony of the Federal Convention focused on the system of representation governing the structure of the national legislature. Ever since the First Continental Congress of 1774, every assembly convened to discuss American affairs or to deal with American problems had adhered to the rule that each colony—or, later, state—had one vote, regardless of population or the number of delegates its government appointed. The large states, such as Virginia, Pennsylvania, Massachusetts, and New York, often chafed at this system of representation, which in their view gave an unfair advantage to small states such as Delaware, Rhode Island, and Georgia.

Even before the Convention began, the rule of equal representation posed problems. In the preliminary caucus of Virginia and Pennsylvania delegates, the Virginians had managed to scotch the Pennsylvanians' suggestion that the Convention itself do away with the rule of equal representation. Thus they narrowly averted a catastrophic battle that would have doomed the Convention from the start. Just how explosive the Pennsylvanians' proposal might have been if it had been allowed to reach the floor of the Convention is suggested by an incident in the otherwise pro forma readings of the delegates' credentials on the first day. At the express request of George Read (Figure 6.8), who had presided over the Delaware constitutional convention in 1776 and represented his state at the Annapolis Convention, the Delaware legislature had instructed its delegates to oppose any attempt to change the rule of state equality.[22] On the other hand, the Virginia Plan startled and disturbed the delegations from the smaller states by apportioning *both* houses of the national legislature on the basis of population.

From the vantage point of two centuries' experience, the solution seems obvious. Nonetheless, it took ten weeks of heated debate, false starts, and even threats of disunion and disruption of the Convention before the delegates finally arrived at a compromise.

Figure 6.8
James Barton Longacre after
Robert Edge Pine. Portrait of
George Read. Stipple engraving,
ca. 1834.

For the first few weeks the supporters of the Virginia Plan enjoyed an almost unbroken string of successes, as provision after provision and clause after clause fell into place in Committee of the Whole. On 13 June 1787 the committee reported its revisions of the Virginia Plan to the full Convention (Figure 6.9).[23] This report made several important changes in Randolph's original resolutions. First, the members of the second branch of the national legislature would be elected by the individual legislatures of the several states rather than by the cumbersome multilevel system proposed by the Virginians. Second, the powers of the national legislature were expanded by the addition of a clause permitting it to veto state laws that contravened treaties entered into by the United States—a clear threat to state laws punishing Loyalists and confiscating their land, which were invalid under the Treaty of Paris of 1783. Third, the report included the first suggestion that slaves be counted in some fashion in determining representation in the national legislature; this provision was familiar from earlier practice, and the northern delegates knew from the outset that some such concession was necessary to satisfy the southern delegates. Fourth, the report did away with the shared veto power given to the national executive and a

Figure 6.9
The Virginia Plan as reported
out of the Committee of the
Whole. Working copy, 13 June
1787. This copy belonged to
delegate George Read.

The Resolutions as Reported from the Committee of the whole in Convention on y.e 13.th June 1787.

1.st Resolved that it is the opinion of this Committee that the national Government ought to be established consisting of a supreme Legislative Judiciary and Executive.

2.d Resolved that the national Legislature ought to consist of two Branches.

3.d Resolved that the members of the first Branch of the national Legislature ought to be elected by the People of the several States for the Term of three years, to receive fixed Stipends, by which they may be compensated for the devotion of their time to public Service to be paid out of the national Treasury, to be ineligible to any Office established by a particular State, or under the authority of the United States (except those peculiarly belonging to the functions of the first Branch) during the Term of Service, and under the national Government for the Span of one year after its Expiration.

4.th Resolved that the Members of the Second Branch of the national Legislature ought to be chosen by the individual Legislatures, to be of the age of Thirty years at least, to hold their Offices for a Term sufficient to ensure their Independency namely Seven years, to receive fixed Stipends by which they may be compensated for the devotion of their time to public Service to be "council of revision," instead vesting a qualified veto power solely in the national executive—a change that disappointed James Madison. Fifth, the national executive would consist of a single person.

While these changes were all significant, most delegates focused on the seventh and eighth resolutions:

> Resolved, that the right of suffrage in the first branch of the national Legislature ought not to be according to the rule established in the articles of confederation: but according to some equitable ratio of representation . . .
>
> Resolved, that the right of suffrage in the second branch of the national Legislature ought to be according to the rule established for the first.

This pair of resolutions formed the battleground for the next month of the Convention.

On 14 June, the day after the Committee of the Whole reported its resolutions to the full Convention, William Paterson of New Jersey moved for a recess to allow small-state delegates to submit their own set of proposals for consideration.[24] The result, known as the New Jersey Plan and presented by Paterson the next day, was the work of a group of small-state delegates including Paterson and David Brearly of New Jersey, Roger Sherman of Connecticut (Figure 6.10), and Luther Martin of Maryland. John Lansing, Jr., of New York, whose antinationalist cast of thought allied him with the small-state bloc in opposition to the Virginia Plan, also had a hand in preparing the resolutions.[25]

The New Jersey Plan, like the original version of the Virginia Plan, represented itself as a proposed set of amendments to the Articles of Confederation. A careful consideration of the New Jersey Plan reveals that it would have given the government of the United States almost as energetic a government as that contemplated by the Virginia Plan or the 13 June report of the Committee of the Whole.[26] Like the Virginia Plan, it contemplated the addition of a federal executive and judiciary to complete the traditional grouping of legislative, executive, and judiciary branches. Also like the Virginia Plan, it would have greatly expanded the powers of the United States to levy and collect taxes and customs duties, giving the Confederation an independent source of revenue and the power to operate directly on the American people. In addition, the New Jersey Plan included the following provision:

> Resolved, that all Acts of the United States in Congress made by virtue and in pursuance of the powers hereby & by the articles of Confederation vested in them, and all Treaties made & ratified under the authority of the U. States shall be the supreme law of the respective States so far forth as those Acts or Treaties shall relate to the said States or their Citizens, and that the Judiciary of the several States shall be bound thereby in their decisions, any thing in the respective laws of the Indi-

Figure 6.10
Unknown artist after Ralph Earl. Portrait of Roger Sherman. Watercolor on ivory, ca. 1810–1820.

vidual States to the contrary notwithstanding, and that if any State, or any body of men in any State shall oppose or prevent the carrying into execution such acts or treaties, the federal Executive shall be authorized to call forth the power of the Confederated States, or so much thereof as may be necessary to enforce and compel an obedience to such Acts, or an observance of such Treaties.[27]

Nonetheless, the New Jersey Plan preserved the one-house Confederation Congress, in which each state would have one vote, and this feature became the focus of the delegates' energies. For three days they debated the relative merits of the two plans in Committee of the Whole. Finally, on 19 June, after a brilliant speech by Madison demolishing the New Jersey Plan, the Committee of the Whole voted to retain unaltered its 13 June report to the Convention. The full Convention then began consideration of the 13 June report, and the delegates soon found themselves embroiled in the dispute over representation.[28]

This heated and bitter debate, which dragged on for three weeks, was the critical juncture in the life of the Convention. So frayed did the delegates'

Figure 6.11
William Satchwell Leney after
Joseph Wood. Portrait of Rufus
King. Stipple engraving, 1815. A
veteran of the Continental
Congress, King was one of the
Convention's more polished
speakers.

tempers become that on 28 June the aged Franklin urged his colleagues to
call for the assistance of Heaven:

> In this situation of this Assembly, groping as it were in the dark to find
> political truth, and scarce able to distinguish it when presented to us,
> how has it happened, Sir, that we have not hitherto once thought of
> humbly applying to the Father of lights to illuminate our understand-
> ings? . . . I have lived, Sir, a long time, and the longer I live, the more
> convincing proofs I see of this truth—*that God Governs in the affairs of
> men*. And if a sparrow cannot fall to the ground without his notice, is
> it probable that an empire can rise without his aid? . . .
>
> I therefore beg leave to move—that henceforth prayers imploring
> the assistance of Heaven, and its blessings on our deliberations, be held
> in this Assembly every morning before we proceed to business, and that
> one or more of the Clergy of this City be requested to officiate in that
> Service—[29]

For several reasons—among them the resulting breach of the rule of secrecy,
the possible ill effect of this motion on the public's hopes for the success of

the Convention, and the absence of funds to pay clergymen—the Convention silently let Franklin's motion slide into limbo.

Whether or not Franklin intended his motion merely as a reproof to his colleagues, the tone of debate in the Convention cooled, but only for a few days. In the succeeding weeks some large-state delegates, including Madison, James Wilson of Pennsylvania, and Rufus King of Massachusetts (Figure 6.11), could not resist making sarcastic comments about what they saw as the pretensions of the small states and the desirability of dismantling them. In response, on 1 July, Gunning Bedford, Jr., of Delaware exploded:

> We have been told with a dictatorial air that this is the last moment for a fair trial in favor of a good Government. It will be the last indeed if the propositions reported from the Committee go forth to the people. He was under no apprehensions. The Large States dare not dissolve the Convention. If they do the small ones will find some foreign ally of more honor and good faith, who will take them by the hand and do them justice. He did not mean by this to intimidate or alarm. It was a natural consequence; which ought to be avoided by enlarging the federal powers not annihilating the federal system. This is what the people expect. All agree in the necessity of a more efficient Govt. and why not make such a one; as they desire.[30]

Later Bedford apologized for the warmth of his remarks, asking that "some allowance . . . be made for the habits of his profession"—he was a lawyer and attorney general of Delaware—"in which warmth was natural & sometimes necessary." Bedford also reminded the tactless large-state delegates that they had offered more than ample provocation.[31]

Not until 16 July did the delegates finally arrive at a solution, or, more accurately, a compromise of competing state claims. The Convention's efforts were led by the calm and judicious trio from Connecticut—William Samuel Johnson (Plate XV), Roger Sherman, and Oliver Ellsworth—and guided by a committee of eleven delegates (one from each state, with Rhode Island unrepresented and New York's delegates having left the Convention). Under the resolutions adopted that day, each state would receive an equal vote in the second branch of the legislature of the United States; seats in the first branch would be apportioned on the basis of the number of free inhabitants in each state plus three-fifths of the number of "other persons" (that is, slaves); a census every ten years would allow for adjustment of representation in the lower house according to population growth; the lower house would have the power to originate revenue bills, with the upper house having no power to change them.[32]

Known as the Great Compromise (and sometimes as the Connecticut Compromise, from the crucial role played by the Connecticut delegation), this package of resolutions seemed to resolve the controversy of the preceding weeks. Yet on the very day it was adopted Edmund Randolph nearly exploded the fragile harmony of the Convention by criticizing the delegates' decision to accept state equality in the upper house. He suggested an adjournment, "that the large States might consider the steps proper to be taken in the present solemn crisis of the business, and that the small States might also deliberate on the means of conciliation."[33]

Randolph's speech, breathing the fire of irreconcilable large-state sentiment, galvanized Paterson, who agreed sarcastically with the Virginian: "it was high time for the Convention to adjourn that the rule of secrecy ought to be rescinded, and that our Constituents should be consulted." Randolph's reference to the propriety of a conciliatory gesture by the small states infuriated him, and, he declared, "if Mr. Randolph would reduce to form his motion for an adjournment sine die"—that is, a final adjournment of the Convention—"he would second it will all his heart."[34]

Realizing that he had gone too far, Randolph hastily sought to clarify his meaning, explaining that he only wanted an adjournment till the next day to permit the large-state delegates to consider possible solutions to the dilemma. After another brief skirmish, John Rutledge of South Carolina pointed out the real state of the business: "he could see no need of an adjournment because he could see no chance of a compromise. The little States were fixt. They had repeatedly & solemnly declared themselves to be so. All that the large States then had to do, was to decide whether they would yield or not."[35] Rutledge's assessment was borne out by the large-state delegates' caucus before the Convention the next morning. Nothing came of this strategy session, and the large-state delegates reluctantly abandoned their campaign for proportional representation in both houses of the legislature.[36]

Taken together, the terms of the Great Compromise seem a natural solution to the problems of representation, and indeed they were suggested more than once in the debates of this issue. John Dickinson seems to have been the first delegate to offer such proposals, as early as 2 June, during the first week of debate over the Virginia Plan.[37] A Delaware delegate, Dickinson had spent most of his life in Pennsylvania and won most of his political experience there; thus he could appreciate the claims of large and small states alike.[38] But the most consistent and effective proponents of the Great Compromise were the Connecticut delegates. Amid the hail of citations of classical and European history and tough-minded recitations of the clashing interests of large and small states or of individual states, the calm speech of Oliver Ellsworth of Connecticut on 29 June stands out: "Let a strong Executive, a Judiciary & a Legislative power be created; but Let not too much be attempted; by which all may be lost. He was not in general a half-way man, yet he preferred doing half the good we could, rather than do nothing at all. The other half may be added, when the necessity shall be more fully experienced."[39] As Clinton L. Rossiter has pointed out in his study of the Federal Convention, "The problem . . . was not for constitution-makers to find the solution but for politicians to learn to live with it, and that process of learning . . . was a hard one."[40] Though the summer was far

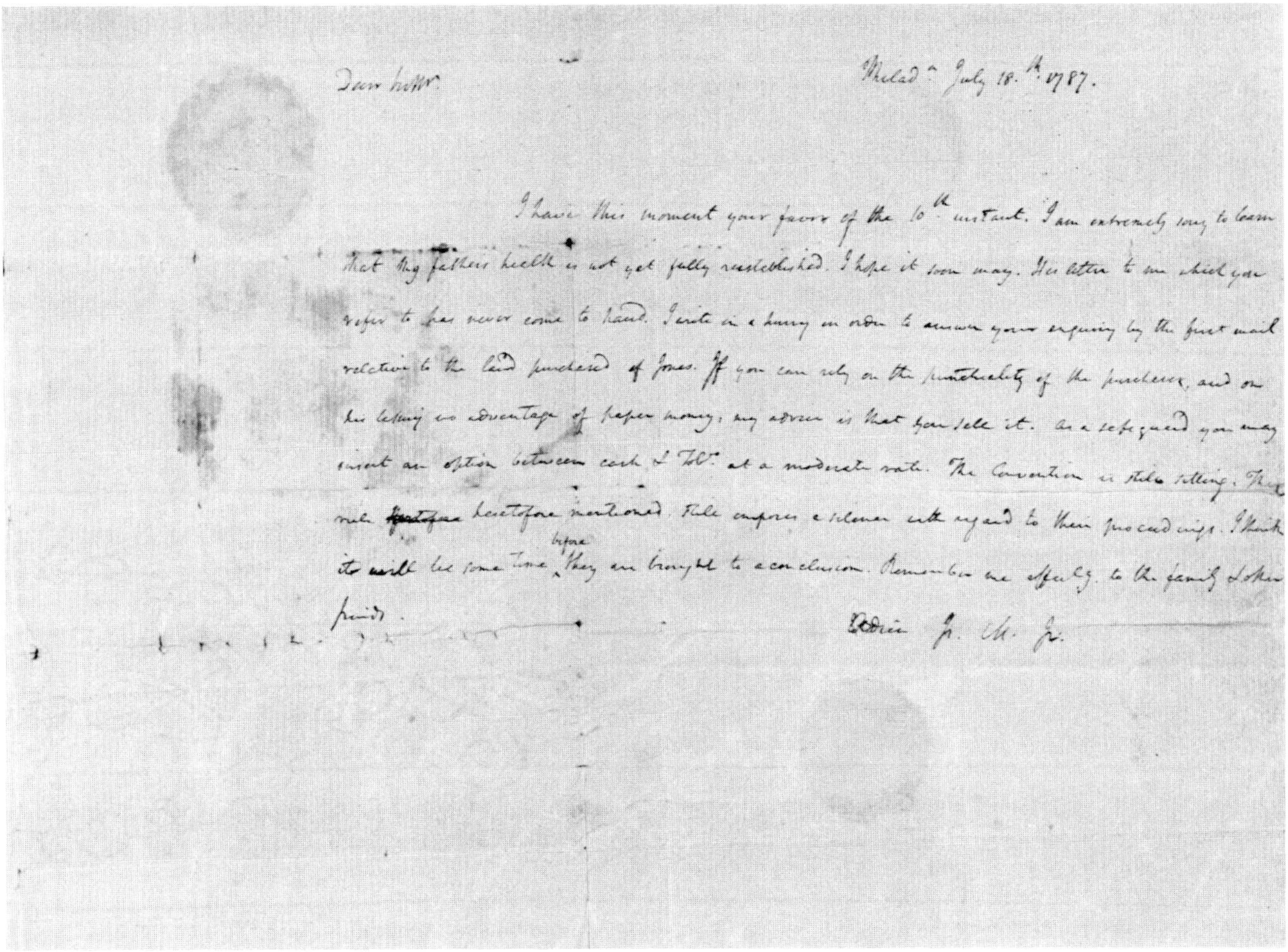

Dear Brother

Philad^a. July 18th. 1787.

I have this moment your favor of the 10th instant. I am extremely sorry to learn that my fathers health is not yet fully reestablished. I hope it soon may. The letter to me which you refer to has never come to hand. I write in a hurry in order to answer your enquiry by the first mail relative to the land purchased of Jones. If you can rely on the punctuality of the purchaser, and on his taking no advantage of paper money, my advice is that you sell it. As a safeguard you may insert an option between cash & Tob^o. at a moderate rate. The Convention is still sitting. The rule ~~heretofore~~ heretofore mentioned still imposes a silence with regard to their proceedings. I think it ~~will~~ will be some time before they are brought to a conclusion. Remember me affec^ly. to the family & other friends.

Adieu Js. M. Jr.

Figure 6.12
Letter from James Madison to Ambrose Madison, Philadelphia, 18 July 1787.

from over (Figure 6.12), the Convention never again approached the abyss as closely as in those critical weeks of late June and early July.

During the struggle with the issues of representation, the delegates interwove high political principle with clear-eyed advocacy of state and sectional interests. Although large-state delegates such as Madison and James Wilson, together with delegates from the deep South, maintained that proportional representation was a matter of simple justice for the American people, they also recognized that this mode of representation would advance the interests of large states such as Virginia, Pennsylvania, and the southern states, where most observers expected the greatest future increases in population.[41]

The fight over representation is also perhaps the best case study of the Convention's working methods. The delegates did not deal with one issue at a time, or even with all aspects of one issue at a time. They would attack an issue piecemeal, debating and deciding on each facet. For example, in constructing their plan for the lower house of the national legislature, the delegates would address first the mode of representation and then turn to the mode of election (whether by the people or the state legislatures), the term of office, and so forth. Often a decision on one issue would require the delegates to reconsider other decisions they had reached on other issues. Thus the delegates traced a tortuous, crisscrossing route, winding through and spiraling around each stage of deliberation, at times pausing in dismay as they realized that their most recent vote had just undone the accomplishments of hours or even days of grueling debate. Nonetheless, as the delegates realized, the Great Compromise of 16 July was the Convention's turning point.

Creating a National Government

From the first days of the Convention, the delegates abandoned the idea of merely framing amendments to the Articles of Confederation. Both in the original Virginia Plan of 29 May and in the Committee of the Whole's report of 13 June, the delegates agreed that they were working to create a *national* government. On 20 June, however, Oliver Ellsworth moved that the Convention replace the word "national" with the phrase "of the United States" wherever appropriate. Randolph agreed to the motion, and the delegates dutifully marked up their copies of the 13 June report to reflect this change.[42]

Despite this rewording the delegates continued to assemble a government that was in fact more "national" than "federal"—a distinction disregarded today but considered significant in the eighteenth century.[43] In the 1780s a federal government was a confederation or league of separate and otherwise independent governments; the federal government would act on the individual governments under it rather than directly on the people of each political unit. By contrast, a national government acted directly on the people and not on intervening governments. Were the United States a completely national government, the states would have the same relation to the national government as counties have to a state: they would function as mere administrative units, with no share in *sovereignty,* or ultimate political rule. It was an axiom of classical political theory that sovereignty could not be divided between two governments or two levels of government claiming authority over the same people and territory.[44]

The Constitution created a completely new kind of government, however—one that, as Madison pointed out in *Federalist* No. 39, was neither completely national nor completely federal but a mixture of both.[45] In some areas, the central government would have final power or sovereignty; in others, the state governments would be supreme; in still others, the federal and state governments would have overlapping, or concurrent, power. This intricate solution to the problem of strengthening the government of the United States while paying due respect to the authority of the state governments evolved more by accident than by design. The consequences of this new form of federal government are shown in one key debate from which emerged the linchpin of the supremacy of the government of the United States in federal-state relations.

One of the principal features of the Virginia Plan was the national legislature's power to veto state laws violating the "articles of Union," a device proposed by James Madison.[46] This assault on state sovereignty alarmed delegates such as Hugh Williamson of North Carolina, John Lansing, Jr., of New York, and Luther Martin of Maryland. In Williamson's words, this provision "might restrain the States from regulating the internal police"[47]—that is, the states would be discouraged from making laws necessary to protect the safety, health, morals, and welfare of their citizens. Lansing and Martin predicted that such a veto power over state laws would provoke resistance by the states, particularly the smaller states, to the entire plan. The proposal also contained disquieting echoes of the old power of the king in council to disapprove laws passed by colonial assemblies, a procedure that had been attacked in the Declaration of Independence.[48]

The delegates substituted for Madison's veto power over state laws an amended version of the provision of the New Jersey Plan making the laws of the United States the supreme law of the land despite the states' laws or constitutions. Originally drafted by Luther Martin as a tactic to head off Madison's proposed negative on state laws, this provision was recast to become what is now the Supremacy Clause of the Constitution (Art. VI, Sec. 1). The Supremacy Clause makes the Constitution, federal laws, and treaties the supreme law of the land, elevating them above state constitutions and laws. The clause thus confers on the federal courts the power to enforce the Constitution against the states, giving implicit sanction to the federal courts' power to declare state laws unconstitutional. Neither Madison nor Martin expected the Supremacy Clause to assume this importance. Madison was the last delegate to give up the fight for a national legislative power to disapprove state laws, and he saw the Supremacy Clause as an inadequate substitute. Martin was taken aback by the Convention's strengthening of his proposal as given in the New Jersey Plan.

Creating a National Executive

After the issue of representation, the most difficult task the Convention faced was the creation of a national executive. At the outset, the Committee of the Whole took a long, hard look at James Wilson's proposal that "a National Executive to consist of a single person be instituted." Madison recorded that the delegates greeted Wilson's motion with "a considerable pause," Finally Benjamin Franklin broke the silence, urging his colleagues to deliver their opinions on the proposal. George Mason and Edmund Randolph argued that a single executive would be the "foetus of monarchy," and Roger Sherman claimed that, because the executive was simply an institution to carry out the will of the legislature, the legislature should have the power to choose the executive *and* to fix its numbers. Ultimately, on 4 June, by a vote of seven states to three, the Committee of the Whole adopted Wilson's motion, and the Convention never reconsidered this decision.[49]

The next major stumbling block was the means of choosing the national executive, an issue closely linked to the duration of his term and his eligibility for reelection. The delegates could not make up their minds, adopting and then dropping several competing proposals. The main choices before them were election by the national legislature as opposed to election by either the state legislatures or some body of "electors" chosen by the states in some way. When the delegates favored electing the executive by the national legislature, they also chose to give the executive a single, relatively long term; seven years was the term most frequently mentioned, though some delegates suggested a term as long as twenty years and Alexander Hamilton favored lifetime tenure "during good behavior." When the delegates supported assigning the choice of the national executive to the states, they also favored a relatively short term—three or four years—with no limit on eligibility for reelection.

Eventually the Convention referred the whole matter to its Committee on Postponed Matters, chaired by David Brearly of New Jersey and including most of the ablest delegates. On 24 August this committee recommended that the president be elected by electors selected by the states—by whatever means they chose—to a four-year term without restrictions on reelection. Each state was assigned electoral votes equal to its combined representation in both houses of Congress. The idea of this "electoral college" had surfaced repeatedly in the Convention's deliberations, but each time the delegates had rejected it. They accepted the committee's recommendation now because they recognized that their ingenuity had reached its limits and that the electoral college was the least objectionable method before them.[50]

Only a handful of delegates favored James Wilson's proposal that the president be chosen by popular vote. Wilson was perhaps the most consistent advocate at the Convention of a strong central government founded directly on the American people.[51] He favored popular election not only of the president but also of both houses of the national legislature, as well as proportional representation in both houses.

A former scholarship student at St. Andrews University, Wilson (Figure 6.13) emigrated from Scotland to Pennsylvania in 1765. He was trained as a lawyer by John Dickinson and became perhaps the foremost legal theorist in America in the 1770s and 1780s. Wilson published notable pamphlets refuting British assertion of authority over the colonies in the years leading up to the Declaration of Independence but was reluctant to take the final step of revolution, though he did sign the Declaration. His opposition to the radical Pennsylvania constitution of 1776 and his generally conservative stands in Pennsylvania state politics earned him the dislike of many of his fellow citizens, some of whom once organized a mob to lay siege to his Philadelphia home, thereafter nicknamed "Fort Wilson." In many respects Wilson fits the pattern of most other self-made Americans of this period.

Figure 6.13
James Barton Longacre after
Jean Pierre Henri Elouis. Portrait
of James Wilson. Watercolor on
artist board, ca. 1825.

Yet in the Federal Convention he outstripped every other delegate in his
commitment to the cause of democratic nationalism. Robert G. McCloskey,
the most astute interpreter of Wilson's life and thought, maintains that of
all the delegates Wilson had the clearest and most accurate vision of America's eventual constitutional development,[52] and most historians of the Convention rank him as second only to Madison in his contributions to the
making of the Constitution.

Wilson may have lost the fight for a popularly elected president, but he
was generally successful in working to create a strong and independent
presidency. He and his fellow delegates were strongly influenced by the New
York and Massachusetts constitutions, which created independent, popularly
elected governors, rejecting the principle of legislative supremacy enshrined
in the constitutions of Virginia and Pennsylvania. They saw the need to
create an executive capable of maintaining the balance of powers in a
government of three coequal branches. Finally, they took courage and inspiration from the silent presence of George Washington. Believing that
Washington would be asked to serve as the nation's first chief executive
under the Constitution, the delegates were willing to entrust greater powers

to the presidency in the expectation that Washington would exercise them responsibly and set unassailable precedents for his successors. Thus, the delegates gave the president the power to appoint judges and other government officials and to negotiate treaties with the advice and consent of the Senate—a survival of the old conception of the upper house of the legislature as a council to advise and act with the executive. They also gave the president the sole power to veto legislation, despite Madison's proposal to league him with a Council of Revision drawn from the national judiciary for that purpose. This veto power was qualified, however; a two-thirds vote by both houses of the national legislature could override a presidential veto. The Constitution thus created a presidency that would be what the holder of the office wanted to make of it.

The Judiciary

Beyond agreeing that there should be a judicial branch of government and one supreme court, the framers gave relatively short shrift to the national judiciary.[53] Some delegates, such as John Rutledge of South Carolina (Figure 6.14), maintained that there should be no lower federal courts at all, on the ground that the state courts would be bound by oath to enforce the Constitution and thus could be relied upon to handle cases involving the United States or its Constitution or laws. Most delegates agreed on the need for a system of lower federal courts but ultimately decided to leave this matter to be worked out by the national legislature.

Much ink has been spilled over whether the delegates to the Federal Convention intended to grant the federal courts the power to declare federal or state laws unconstitutional—what we now call the doctrine of judicial review.[54] Nowhere does the Constitution explicitly confer the power to pass on the constitutionality of federal laws or actions, but references by several delegates to state courts' exercises of the power to review state laws in the 1770s and 1780s suggest that they would not have been surprised by federal courts' assertions of this power in the 1790s and early 1800s. As for the federal courts' power to review the constitutionality of state laws and actions, a stronger case can be made that the delegates expected the federal courts to have and exercise this power under the Constitution. The Supremacy Clause is the locus of this power, clothing the Constitution with supralegal status and commanding its enforcement against contrary state laws or constitutional provisions. In addition, by bringing the Constitution into the sphere of judicially enforceable law, the Supremacy Clause ensures that controversies over the meaning of the Constitution will resolve themselves, sooner or later, into judicial questions coming before the federal judiciary and eventually the Supreme Court.

The Constitution leaves the structure of the federal court system, the number of members of the Supreme Court, and the jurisdiction of all federal courts to the discretion of the national legislature. Article III merely sets forth the maximum grant of jurisdiction beyond which Congress may

not go, but it seems to permit Congress to give the courts less than the full measure of constitutionally authorized jurisdiction. One of the most important acts of the first Congress meeting under the Constitution was the adoption of the Judiciary Act of 1789, which completed the work deliberately left unfinished by the delegates to the Federal Convention.[55]

Sectionalism and Slavery

Although the initial division in the Federal Convention was that between the large and small states, the split that occurred most often and ominously was that between northern and southern states.[56] Two issues became the focal points for these divisions—the apportionment of the lower house of the national legislature (linked with the apportionment of direct taxes) and the regulation of trade.

Some historians have claimed that the South Carolina and Connecticut delegates forged a "deal" early on in the Convention to link these two issues and pursued this strategy throughout the drafting of the Constitution;

Figure 6.15
W. Ralph. *Negroes just landed from a Slave Ship.* Line engraving, 1808. This small engraving was probably originally a book illustration.

Figure 6.16
James Akin after James Earle. *General Pinckney late Envoy Extraordinary to the French Republic.* Stipple engraving, 1799.

through this arrangement they created a consensus on which delegates from both sections could agree.[57] Although such a "deal" would explain neatly the evolution of the compromise between proslavery and antislavery interests, it seems more likely that the delegates worked and argued and dealt their way into the eventual compromise, step by step, without a clear vision of the final result.

The original Virginia Plan contemplated a proportional representation based on the number of free inhabitants of the several states. The 13 June report of the Committee of the Whole modified this ratio to include three-fifths of "other persons," a euphemism for slaves. In this as in all later compromises designed to protect slavery without naming it in the Constitution, the South Carolina delegates took the lead. The "three-fifths" clause survived as part of the Great Compromise. In late August the problem reached a crisis as the delegates from the deep South pressed for limits on the power of the general government to regulate trade, specifically the slave trade. Delegates from northern states, such as Gouverneur Morris and Rufus King, and Virginian delegates such as Madison and George Mason resisted these efforts, fearing that they would interfere with the natural erosion of slavery as a workable institution (Figure 6.15).

To resolve this controversy, the Convention appointed yet another committee, which reported a compromise designed to please no one but to propitiate everyone. The United States could not interfere with the slave trade before 1800—a date later extended by eight years—but could within limits tax the importation of slaves. Further, only a simple majority in both houses of the national legislature would be needed to pass navigation acts—that is, tariffs, quotas, embargoes, and discriminations in favor of local products. This clause was a concession by the South Carolinians, who had previously demanded a two-thirds vote in both houses for the enactment of such laws. To hold this compromise together, the South Carolinians—John Rutledge, Charles Cotesworth Pinckney (Figure 6.16), and Pierce Butler—restrained their colleague Charles Pinckney, who was bent on reintroducing the two-thirds requirement, and delivered fulsome tributes to the virtues of the northern delegates.[58] In this atmosphere of tense and punctilious conciliation, the Federal Convention sidestepped the explosive issue of slavery, wrapping up its work on the issue by adopting a fugitive-slave clause borrowed from the Northwest Ordinance of 1787, enacted the previous month by the Confederation Congress in New York City.[59]

Many later historians and politicians have denounced what they see as the Convention's failure of nerve, moral courage, and ingenuity in dealing with the problem of slavery.[60] Indeed, in the 1830s and 1840s abolitionists such as Wendell Phillips and William Lloyd Garrison staged public burnings of the Constitution, denouncing it as "a covenant with death" for its compromise with the slaveholding states.[61] But the delegates to the Convention were fully aware of the southern states' commitment to their "peculiar institution" and believed Charles Cotesworth Pinckney's threat that South

Carolina and the other deep southern states would leave the Union unless the Constitution contained some protection for slavery.[62] In a choice between striking a blow against slavery and holding the Union together, the delegates decided to preserve the Union. They showed equal sensitivity to the growing antislavery sentiment in the northern states by taking care to avoid mentioning slavery or slaves by name anywhere in the document. Instead they used euphemisms borrowed from the Confederation Congress, most notably its 1783 formula, proposed but not adopted, for requisitions for funds from the states, the source of the "three-fifths" clause.

The delegates knew that a charter that denounced slavery, no matter how mildly, would be rejected by the southern states, at least three of which had economies bound up with the slave system. Similarly, they knew that a charter explicitly recognizing and sanctioning slavery would be defeated in the northern states. On 22 August, the day the Convention appointed its Committee of Eleven to deal with slavery and the question of navigation acts, Elbridge Gerry sketched the delegates' ultimate approach: "he thought we had nothing to do with the conduct of the States as to Slaves, but ought to be careful not to give any sanctions to it."[63] In accommodating the interests of northern and southern states, the delegates kept before them at all times the goal of framing a Constitution that would work on a practical level, and tiptoed around issues of political and moral principle that would blow apart their fragile consensus if faced directly.

The other element of this sectional compromise was the southern delegates' willingness to abandon the requirement of a two-thirds vote by both houses of the national legislature to pass laws regulating foreign trade. This was the South's concession to the New England delegates, whose states conducted most of the United States' "carrying trade" and manufacturing. The southerners would have preferred to make it more difficult for the United States to regulate trade, as this power would increase the price of imported goods on which the South relied.

Virginia, alone of the southern states, stood to gain from the restriction on the slave trade. Although its delegates, such as Madison and Mason, opposed on principle restrictions on the power of the United States to ban or restrict this trade, Virginia enjoyed large profits from the sale of native-born slaves across state lines. Prohibiting or restricting the overseas slave trade would thus benefit Virginians active in the domestic slave trade, for they could be assured of a market in those slaveholding states, such as South Carolina, that otherwise would buy slaves more cheaply from overseas.[64] In this as in other instances, principle was mixed with baser motives for political decision-making in the Convention.

Omission of a Bill of Rights

None of the plans for a new form of government or for amendments to the Articles of Confederation nor any of the drafts produced by the Convention's several committees contained a declaration of rights. Of course, neither did the Articles of Confederation. Although only a few delegates felt that a bill of rights should be incorporated in the Constitution, the Convention's omission of one proved to be the single greatest obstacle to the ratification of the Constitution.

Throughout the late spring and summer of 1787, the delegates focused on devising and adjusting the machinery of government under the Constitution. Few if any—not even such staunch libertarians as James Madison—bothered to think in terms of that government's potential effect on the rights of individual Americans. Some isolated procedural safeguards did find their way into the Constitution, such as the ban on suspending the writ of habeas corpus (a writ commanding an official detaining or incarcerating a person under color of law to bring that person before a judge to explain the legal authority under which the person is being held); the strict definition of a treasonable offense and the standard of evidence needed to support a conviction for treason (the only crime so treated in the Constitution); the guarantee of trial by jury; the bans on bills of attainder (legislative acts imposing punishments on named persons) and *ex post facto* laws (laws making acts criminal though committed before enactment of the law); the omission of property qualifications for holding federal office; and the prohibition on religious test oaths for voting or holding office. Hamilton cited all of these in *Federalist* No. 84 to support his argument that the Constitution itself was a bill of rights.[65]

A few delegates were not convinced, however. George Mason and Elbridge Gerry unsuccessfully raised the issue on 12 September, a few days before the end of the Convention. Their failure to persuade their colleagues to act to recognize individual rights prompted their refusal to sign the Constitution and their later opposition to it in the campaign for ratification.

One of the grand figures of Virginia politics, Mason was born in 1725, the fifth of a long line of rich, powerful planters.[66] Only rarely could Mason be tempted to take part in public life; he preferred to remain at Gunston Hall, his opulent plantation in Tidewater Virginia. His most important contribution to his state and nation was his participation in the convention that drafted the Virginia constitution of 1776; Mason was the principal draftsman of the Virginia Declaration of Rights, a model for all later bills of rights. Mason had served as a delegate to the Mount Vernon Conference of 1785 but had declined appointment to the Virginia delegation to the Annapolis Convention of 1786. To everyone's astonishment, however, he agreed to serve as a senior delegate from Virginia to the Federal Convention. This trip to Philadelphia was the farthest he had ever traveled from Gunston Hall. As a delegate, Mason followed an independent line, voting to strengthen the government of the United States yet opposing efforts to create a single, independent executive. Weeks before the climactic exchange of 12 September, Mason had begun hinting that he might not be able to support the emerging Constitution.

Elbridge Gerry (Figure 6.17), nicknamed the "Grumbletonian" for his supposed refusal to support any measure he did not himself propose, had

Figure 6.17
John Vanderlyn. Portrait of
Elbridge Gerry. Black chalk on
paper, 1798.

also moved away from his early belief in the need for a stronger general
government. A veteran of the Second Continental Congress, a signer of
both the Declaration of Independence and the Articles of Confederation,
in 1785 Gerry had opposed his state legislature's proposal that amendments
to the Articles were necessary. Shays's Rebellion had changed Gerry's mind,
and he accepted appointment as a Massachusetts delegate to the Federal
Convention. Gerry distrusted many of the tendencies he saw in the Constitution, however, and it became clear that he too would not automatically go
along with his fellow delegates.[67]

On 12 September Mason urged the Convention to add a bill of rights
to the Constitution. He pointed out that, by reference to the state bills of
rights (including his own), "a bill might be prepared in a few hours." Gerry
backed Mason's proposal and made a formal motion in its support, which
Mason seconded. Despite Mason's hopeful prediction that a bill of rights
prefixed to the Constitution "would give great quiet to the people," Roger
Sherman argued that such a measure was not needed: he "was for securing

the rights of the people where requisite. The state declarations of rights are not repealed by this Constitution; and being in force are sufficient." No one else spoke to Mason's and Gerry's motion, or to Mason's reply to Sherman that "the laws of the United States are to be paramount to state bills of rights." When the motion was put to a vote, every state present on the floor rejected it, and the move to add a bill of rights to the Constitution perished.[68]

Despite Mason's estimate of how quick and simple it would be to draft a satisfactory bill of rights, his fellow delegates realized that his proposal, if adopted, could add days or even weeks to the life of the Convention. Having spent more than four months in Philadelphia away from their families, business affairs, and political and other commitments, they were eager to finish their work and depart. Having weathered one crisis (over representation) that nearly wrecked the Convention, and another (over slavery and the regulation of trade) that carried with it ominous signs of future sectional divisions, and having exhausted their ingenuity and patience, the delegates were not willing to tackle yet another difficult assignment. Further, the delegates had never included the task of writing a federal bill of rights as part of their mandate, and they did not believe that the Constitution might pose a threat to individual rights.[69] Had they been less exhausted, they might have realized that the creation of a government having the power to operate directly on the people of the United States carried with it at least a potential threat to individual rights. As it was, though they brushed aside the Mason-Gerry proposal, the delegates would have to come to terms with it in the public arena for months thereafter.

The Writing of the Constitution

After the climactic battle over representation that ended with the Great Compromise, the delegates set to work fixing the details of the new system and dealing with the theoretical implications and practical consequences of drafting a Constitution. On 26 July the Convention turned over the resolutions that it had adopted to a Committee of Detail, chaired by John Rutledge and including James Wilson, Edmund Randolph, Oliver Ellsworth, and Nathaniel Gorham. At this point, the Convention adjourned to permit the committee to prepare the draft that would serve as the basis of deliberations.

The committee worked quickly and effectively, with Randolph doing the first draft and James Wilson contributing his legal and jurisprudential talent. The committee supplemented the Convention's resolutions by drawing on state constitutions and plans presented by individual delegates. The committee then entrusted its draft to Dunlap and Claypoole of Philadelphia, the publishers of *The Pennsylvania Packet* and the official printers to the Confederation Congress, to prepare copies for the use of each delegate. This first draft of the Constitution contained twenty-three articles, many of which survive virtually unchanged in the Constitution we know today. In it

Figure 6.18
Attributed to James Sharples.
Portrait of Gouverneur Morris.
Pastel on paper, ca. 1800.

the institutions of government first received the names they bear today—President, House of Representatives, Senate, Supreme Court, and so forth.[70]

The Convention worked with this draft from 6 August until 10 September. Then the delegates appointed a Committee of Style and Arrangement to prepare a new draft, which with a few alterations made in full session was the last before the final text of the Constitution was prepared for signing. The Committee of Style and Arrangement drew on the talents of the Convention's ablest members—Madison, Rufus King, Gouverneur Morris, Hamilton (who had returned for the last few weeks of the Convention), and William Samuel Johnson as chairman. The general consensus, supported by the testimony of Madison, is that Gouverneur Morris (Figure 6.18) was the principal author of this draft, and Madison penned a generous compliment to his ability: "The *finish* given to the style and arrangement of the Constitution fairly belongs to the pen of Mr. Morris; the task having probably been handed over to him by the chairman of the committee, himself a highly respectable member, and with the ready concurrence of the others . . . A better choice could not have been made."[71]

Born in 1752, Morris was in fact a New Yorker, who found a place in the Pennsylvania delegation thanks to the efforts of his friend, mentor, and fellow delegate Robert Morris, the "Financier." Whereas Robert Morris said hardly a word at the Convention, Gouverneur Morris was the most talkative delegate, outstripping even Madison in the number of times he took the floor. Morris missed the opening weeks of the Convention and at times got carried away by his ready eloquence and eagerness to follow his train of thought wherever it went; for example, in the middle of the debate on representation he delivered a long speech urging lifetime tenure during good behavior for members of the upper house. Nonetheless, Morris had many valuable qualities that made him a principal contributor to the Convention: his talent (second only to Franklin's) for wit and conciliation, his willingness to shoulder much hard work and serve on committees, and his readiness to surrender his own opinions on realizing that he had adopted them too quickly.[72]

Morris's greatest contribution to the success of the Federal Convention and the Constitution was his authorship of the final document. He recast the first draft of 6 August into a document of seven articles. Writing with restraint and power, he gave the Constitution a seriousness and eloquence that has rarely been equaled. He especially improved the Preamble, making it a statement of the purposes of the new government as well as including a conveniently ambiguous turn of phrase. Following the model of the Articles of Confederation, the 6 August draft began:

> We the People of the States of New Hampshire, Massachusetts, Rhode Island and Providence Plantations, Connecticut, New-York, New-Jersey, Pennsylvania, Delaware, Maryland, Virginia, North-Carolina, South-Carolina, and Georgia, do ordain, declare, and establish the following Constitution for the Government of Ourselves and our Posterity.

Morris and his colleagues realized that it would be embarrassing if the Preamble listed a state (such as Rhode Island, which had not even sent delegates to Philadelphia) that later refused to ratify the Constitution. Thus, he adopted a phrase that neatly evaded the problem: "We, the people of the United States." Later, Patrick Henry would seize upon the Preamble as evidence of the consolidating tendencies embodied in the Constitution, but this charge is not supported by the Preamble's actual history. More important, Morris drew on various sources to assemble an eloquent list of purposes for the new government: "in order to form a more perfect Union, establish Justice, insure domestic Tranquility, provide for the common Defence, promote the general Welfare, and Secure the Blessings of Liberty to ourselves and our Posterity." Although Morris deserves the most credit for the final draft of the Constitution, the other members of the committee also contributed to the text, and Morris probably asked James Wilson for advice even though Wilson was not a member of the committee.

The Convention debated the Morris draft for four days, adjusting a detail here and there but conscious that their labors were nearly at an end. Finally, on Saturday, 15 September, the longest day of the Convention, the delegates paused to consider their work.[73] Randolph, Mason, and Gerry declared their dissatisfaction, stressing their concerns about the excessive powers granted to the president and the absence of a bill of rights, and Randolph urged that the document be submitted to a second convention. Thinking back over the long, hard road they had traveled to agree on the text before them, the delegates must have shuddered at the mere suggestion of a second convention. Speaking for the majority, Charles Pinckney conceded that everyone had some cause for dissatisfaction with the Constitution, but pointed out that it was the best they could hope for and that a second convention was unlikely to improve it. Then Washington put the question to a vote, and the state delegations present unanimously adopted the document as it stood. The Convention adjourned to permit the preparation of an engrossed copy of the Constitution for signing by the delegates.

Until the late 1930s one of the minor mysteries surrounding the making of the Constitution was the identity of the clerk who prepared the official engrossed copy for the signing ceremony on 17 September. Just in time for the Constitution's sesquicentennial, John C. Fitzpatrick discovered evidence that the Convention's penman was Jacob Shallus, a Pennsylvania German who was assistant clerk to the state's General Assembly. Thomas Fitzsimons, the Speaker of the Pennsylvania General Assembly and a delegate to the Convention, apparently suggested Shallus for the job, for which the clerk was paid thirty dollars.[74]

On 17 September 1787 the delegates assembled for the last time to review and sign the Constitution. Washington called the Convention to order, and the delegates listened to the last full reading of the text. Then Benjamin Franklin rose, secured recognition from the chair, and handed a written speech to James Wilson to read aloud for him. For all practical purposes his last real contribution to American politics, this speech was vintage Franklin—a mixture of gentle wit, political wisdom, pleas for harmony and unanimity, and an endorsement of the Constitution:

> Mr. President—I confess that there are several parts of this constitution which I do not approve, but I am not sure I shall never approve them: For having lived long, I have experienced many instances of being obliged by better information, or fuller consideration, to change opinions even on important subjects, which I once thought right, but found to be otherwise. It is therefore that the older I grow, the more apt I am to doubt my own judgment, and to pay more respect to the judgment of others . . .
>
> In these sentiments, Sir, I agree to this Constitution with all its faults, if they are such; because I think a general Government necessary for us, and there is no form of Government but what may be a blessing to the people if well administered, and believe farther that this is likely to

be well administered for a course of years . . . I doubt too whether any other Convention we can obtain may be able to make a better Constitution. For when you assemble a number of men to have the advantage of their joint wisdom, you inevitably assemble with those men, all their prejudices, their passions, their errors of opinion, their local interests, and their selfish views. From such an assembly can a perfect production be expected? It therefore astonishes me, Sir, to find this system approaching as near to perfection as it does; and I think it will astonish our enemies . . . Thus I consent, Sir, to the Constitution because I expect no better, and because I am not sure, that it is not the best. The opinions I have had of its errors, I sacrifice to the public good. I have never whispered a syllable of them abroad. Within these walls they were born, and here they shall die . . .

On the whole, Sir, I cannot help expressing a wish that every member of the Convention who may still have objections to it, would with me, on this occasion, doubt a little of his own infallibility, and to make manifest our unanimity, put his name to the instrument—[75]

Of all the men gathered in the Convention, Franklin alone had had any part in the first efforts to forge an American union more than thirty years earlier, in the Albany Congress of 1754; it is not hard to imagine the sentiments he felt as he listened to Wilson read this speech to the convention that had finally achieved his dream. Franklin then made a motion, suggested by Gouverneur Morris, that the Convention adopt the Constitution by the unanimous consent of the *states* present—a face-saving formula that apparently persuaded William Blount of North Carolina (and perhaps some others) to sign the document.

Before the delegates could act on this motion, Nathaniel Gorham attempted one last amendment to the plan before them. He suggested that the ratio of representation in the House of Representatives be changed, from not more than one to forty thousand to not more than one to thirty thousand. Daniel Carroll of Maryland and Rufus King seconded this motion. When Washington rose to put the question, he made his first and only substantive contribution to the debates of the Convention, urging the delegates to adopt the motion. Not since his brief and graceful speech accepting the presidency of the gathering had Washington said a word in formal debate, although tradition preserves a few whispered asides attributed to him.[76] As a result, his speech in support of Gorham's motion was doubly effective. The delegates unanimously agreed, and someone scraped away the word "forty" and scratched in "thirty."

The delegates once more took up Franklin's motion. Randolph, Mason, and Gerry resisted all pressures and pleas to sign the Constitution—though, already wavering in his opposition to the new charter, Randolph said that he merely wanted to preserve his freedom to make up his mind later (that is, after he could assess how his Virginian constituents would react to the new document). Gouverneur Morris and Alexander Hamilton recounted their own qualms about the Constitution but pointed out that they were willing to sign it and that a second convention would not do better and might do much worse. The delegates then adopted Franklin's motion (10–0, with the South Carolina delegation evenly divided, and thus losing its vote, because C. C. Pinckney and Pierce Butler opposed "the equivocal form of the signing").[77]

As the delegates signed the Constitution, with Alexander Hamilton writing in the names of the states opposite the delegates' signatures and Mason, Randolph, and Gerry watching grimly, Franklin had the last word. He commented on the difficulty that painters have had distinguishing between a rising and a setting sun. Pointing to the half-sun carved on the back of the president's chair, Franklin observed: "I have . . . often in the course of the Session, and the vicissitudes of my hopes and fears as to its issue, looked at that behind the President without being able to tell whether it was rising or setting: But now at length I have the happiness to know that is is a rising and *not* a setting Sun."[78] The delegates then voted to dissolve the Convention and adjourned en masse to the nearby City Tavern (Plate XVI) for a celebration.

Gorham's motion and Washington's speech caused a minor problem for the Convention's printers. John Dunlap had served, on and off, as the printer to the Continental and Confederation Congresses since 1775, including among his notable assignments the first printings of the Declaration of Independence and the Articles of Confederation. In the latter case, he and his assistant, David C. Claypoole, were obliged to work under an oath of secrecy in printing successive drafts of the Articles, so they did not find it either onerous or unfamiliar to assume a similar obligation with respect to printing the two drafts of the Constitution. After the Convention voted to adopt the Constitution on 15 September, it also moved to have prepared a few hundred printed copies for the use of the delegates and to be sent to state governments and the Confederation Congress. Unfortunately, the Gorham motion changing the ratio of representation made these copies, which apparently were ready by the morning of 17 September, useless, and the printers destroyed the entire printing. As good journalists, though, they salvaged for *The Pennsylvania Packet* an anecdote about the Gorham motion and Washington's speech in its support.

Working in the later afternoon and early evening of 17 September, Claypoole prepared new versions of the final text of the Constitution, together with the Convention's accompanying resolutions and letter to Congress. He then prepared a special issue, dated 19 September 1787, of the *Packet* containing the full text of all three documents. This issue is the first newspaper publication of the Constitution (Figure 6.19).[79] Newspapers throughout the United States soon printed the Constitution and its accompanying documents in special issues, handbills, and pamphlets. Within the month, the Constitution even crossed the ocean, appearing in the London

Figure 6.19
The Pennsylvania Packet and Daily Advertiser. Philadelphia, 19 September 1787.

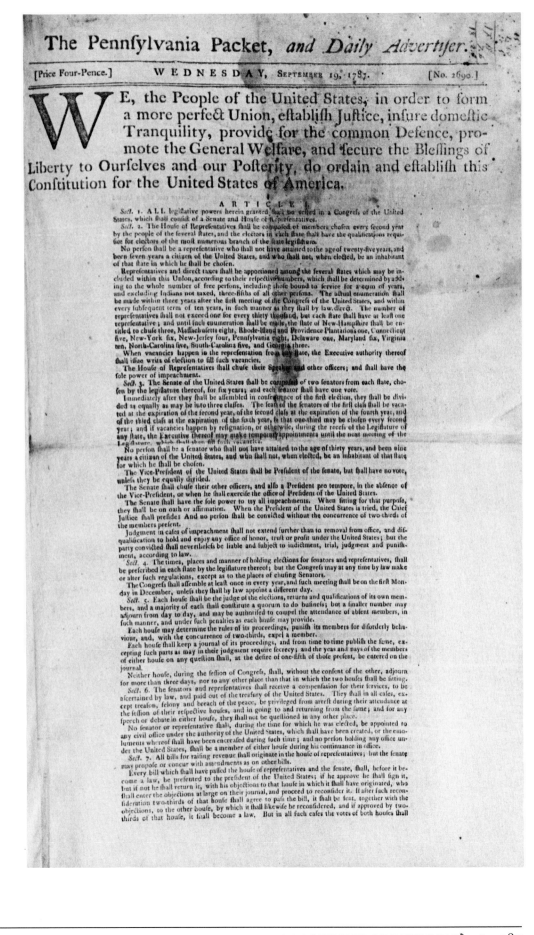

determined by yeas and nays, and the names of the persons voting for and against the bill shall be entered on the journal of each house respectively. If any bill shall not be returned by the President within ten days (Sundays excepted) after it shall have been presented to him, the same shall be a law, in like manner as if he had signed it, unless the Congress by their adjournment prevent its return, in which case it shall not be a law.

Every order, resolution, or vote to which the concurrence of the Senate and House of Representatives may be necessary (except on a question of adjournment) shall be presented to the President of the United States; and before the same shall take effect, shall be approved by him, or, being disapproved by him, shall be repassed by two-thirds of the Senate and House of Representatives, according to the rules and limitations prescribed in the case of a bill.

Sect. 8. The Congress shall have power

To lay and collect taxes, duties, imposts and excises, to pay the debts and provide for the common defence and general welfare of the United States; but all duties, imposts and excises shall be uniform throughout the United States;

To borrow money on the credit of the United States;

To regulate commerce with foreign nations, and among the several states, and with the Indian tribes;

To establish an uniform rule of naturalization, and uniform laws on the subject of bankruptcies throughout the United States;

To coin money, regulate the value thereof, and of foreign coin, and fix the standard of weights and measures;

To provide for the punishment of counterfeiting the securities and current coin of the United States;

To establish post offices and post roads;

To promote the progress of science and useful arts, by securing for limited times to authors and inventors the exclusive right to their respective writings and discoveries;

To constitute tribunals inferior to the supreme court;

To define and punish piracies and felonies committed on the high seas, and offences against the law of nations;

To declare war, grant letters of marque and reprisal, and make rules concerning captures on land and water;

To raise and support armies, but no appropriation of money to that use shall be for a longer term than two years;

To provide and maintain a navy;

To make rules for the government and regulation of the land and naval forces;

To provide for calling forth the militia to execute the laws of the union, suppress insurrections and repel invasions;

To provide for organizing, arming, and disciplining, the militia, and for governing such part of them as may be employed in the service of the United States, reserving to the States respectively, the appointment of the officers, and the authority of training the militia according to the discipline prescribed by Congress;

To exercise exclusive legislation in all cases whatsoever, over such district (not exceeding ten miles square) as may, by cession of particular States, and the acceptance of Congress, become the seat of the government of the United States, and to exercise like authority over all places purchased by the consent of the legislature of the state in which the same shall be, for the erection of forts, magazines, arsenals, dock-yards, and other needful buildings;—And

To make all laws which shall be necessary and proper for carrying into execution the foregoing powers, and all other powers vested by this constitution in the government of the United States, or in any department or officer thereof.

Sect. 9. The migration or importation of such persons as any of the states now existing shall think proper to admit, shall not be prohibited by the Congress prior to the year one thousand eight hundred and eight, but a tax or duty may be imposed on such importation, not exceeding ten dollars for each person.

The privilege of the writ of habeas corpus shall not be suspended, unless when in cases of rebellion or invasion the public safety may require it.

No bill of attainder or ex post facto law shall be passed.

No capitation, or other direct, tax shall be laid, unless in proportion to the census or enumeration herein before directed to be taken.

No tax or duty shall be laid on articles exported from any state. No preference shall be given by any regulation of commerce or revenue to the ports of one state over those of another; nor shall vessels bound to, or from, one state, be obliged to enter, clear, or pay duties in another.

No money shall be drawn from the treasury, but in consequence of appropriations made by law; and a regular statement and account of the receipts and expenditures of all public money shall be published from time to time.

No title of nobility shall be granted by the United States:—And no person holding any office of profit or trust under them, shall, without the consent of the Congress, accept of any present, emolument, office, or title, of any kind whatever, from any king, prince, or foreign state.

Sect. 10. No state shall enter into any treaty, alliance, or confederation; grant letters of marque and reprisal; coin money; emit bills of credit; make any thing but gold and silver coin a tender in payment of debts; pass any bill of attainder, ex post facto law, or law impairing the obligation of contracts, or grant any title of nobility.

No state shall, without the consent of the Congress, lay any imposts or duties on imports or exports, except what may be absolutely necessary for executing its inspection laws; and the net produce of all duties and imposts, laid by any state on imports or exports, shall be for the use of the Treasury of the United States; and all such laws shall be subject to the revision and controul of the Congress. No state shall, without the consent of Congress, lay any duty of tonnage, keep troops, or ships of war in time of peace, enter into any agreement or compact with another state, or with a foreign power, or engage in war, unless actually invaded, or in such imminent danger as will not admit of delay.

II.

Sect. 1. The executive power shall be vested in a president of the United States of America. He shall hold his office during the term of four years, and, together with the vice-president, chosen for the same term, be elected as follows.

Each state shall appoint, in such manner as the legislature thereof may direct, a number of electors, equal to the whole number of senators and representatives to which the state may be entitled in the Congress: but no senator or representative, or person holding an office of trust or profit under the United States, shall be appointed an elector.

The electors shall meet in their respective states, and vote by ballot for two persons, of whom one at least shall not be an inhabitant of the same state with themselves. And they shall make a list of all the persons voted for, and of the number of votes for each; which list they shall sign and certify, and transmit sealed to the seat of the government of the United States, directed to the president of the senate. The president of the senate shall, in the presence of the senate and house of representatives, open all the certificates, and the votes shall then be counted. The person having the greatest number of votes shall be the president, if such number be a majority of the whole number of electors appointed; and if there be more than one who have such majority, and have an equal number of votes, then the house of representatives shall immediately chuse by ballot one of them for president; and if no person have a majority, then from the five highest on the list the said house shall in like manner chuse the president. But in chusing the president, the votes shall be taken by states, the representation from each state having one vote; a quorum for this purpose shall consist of a member or members from two-thirds of the states, and a majority of all the states shall be necessary to a choice. In every case, after the choice of the president, the person having the greatest number of votes of the electors shall be the vice-president. But if there should remain two or more who have equal votes, the senate shall chuse from them by ballot the vice-president.

The Congress may determine the time of chusing the electors, and the day on which they shall give their votes; which day shall be the same throughout the United States.

Figure 6.19 (cont.)

Figure 6.19 (cont.)

No perſon except a natural born citizen, or a citizen of the United States, at the time of the adoption of this conſtitution, ſhall be eligible to the office of preſident ; neither ſhall any perſon be eligible to that office who ſhall not have attained to the age of thirty-five years, and been fourteen years a reſident within the United States.

In caſe of the removal of the preſident from office, or of his death, reſignation, or inability to diſcharge the powers and duties of the ſaid office, the ſame ſhall devolve on the vice-preſident, and the Congreſs may by law provide for the caſe of removal, death, reſignation or inability, both of the preſident and vice-preſident, declaring what officer ſhall then act as preſident, and ſuch officer ſhall act accordingly, until the diſability be removed, or a preſident ſhall be elected.

The preſident ſhall, at ſtated times, receive for his ſervices, a compenſation, which ſhall neither be encreaſed nor diminiſhed during the period for which he ſhall have been elected, and he ſhall not receive within that period any other emolument from the United States, or any of them.

Before he enter on the execution of his office, he ſhall take the following oath or affirmation:

" I do ſolemnly ſwear (or affirm) that I will faithfully execute the office of preſident of the United States, and will to the beſt of my ability, preſerve, protect and defend the conſtitution of the United States."

Sect. 2. The preſident ſhall be commander in chief of the army and navy of the United States, and of the militia of the ſeveral States, when called into the actual ſervice of the United States ; he may require the opinion, in writing, of the principal officer in each of the executive departments, upon any ſubject relating to the duties of their reſpective offices, and he ſhall have power to grant reprieves and pardons for offences againſt the United States, except in caſes of impeachment.

He ſhall have power, by and with the advice and conſent of the ſenate, to make treaties, provided two-thirds of the ſenators preſent concur ; and he ſhall nominate, and by and with the advice and conſent of the ſenate, ſhall appoint ambaſſadors, other public miniſters and conſuls, judges of the ſupreme court, and all other officers of the United States, whoſe appointments are not herein otherwiſe provided for, and which ſhall be eſtabliſhed by law. But the Congreſs may by law veſt the appointment of ſuch inferior officers, as they think proper, in the preſident alone, in the courts of law, or in the heads of departments.

The preſident ſhall have power to fill up all vacancies that may happen during the receſs of the ſenate, by granting commiſſions which ſhall expire at the end of their next ſeſſion.

Sect. 3. He ſhall from time to time give to the Congreſs information of the ſtate of the union, and recommend to their conſideration ſuch meaſures as he ſhall judge neceſſary and expedient : he may, on extraordinary occaſions, convene both houſes, or either of them, and in caſe of diſagreement between them, with reſpect to the time of adjournment, he may adjourn them to ſuch time as he ſhall think proper ; he ſhall receive ambaſſadors and other public miniſters ; he ſhall take care that the laws be faithfully executed, and ſhall commiſſion all the officers of the United States.

Sect. 4. The preſident, vice-preſident and all civil officers of the United States, ſhall be removed from office on impeachment for, and conviction of, treaſon, bribery, or other high crimes and miſdemeanors.

III.

Sect. 1. The judicial power of the United States, ſhall be veſted in one ſupreme court, and in ſuch inferior courts as the Congreſs may from time to time ordain and eſtabliſh. The judges, both of the ſupreme and inferior courts, ſhall hold their offices during good behaviour, and ſhall, at ſtated times, receive for their ſervices, a compenſation, which ſhall not be diminiſhed during their continuance in office.

Sect. 2. The judicial power ſhall extend to all caſes, in law and equity, ariſing under this conſtitution, the laws of the United States, and treaties made, or which ſhall be made, under their authority ; to all caſes affecting ambaſſadors, other public miniſters and conſuls ; to all caſes of admiralty and maritime juriſdiction ; to controverſies to which the United States ſhall be a party ; to controverſies between two or more States, between a ſtate and citizens of another ſtate, between citizens of different States, between citizens of the ſame ſtate claiming lands under grants of different States, and between a ſtate, or the citizens thereof, and foreign States, citizens or ſubjects.

In all caſes affecting ambaſſadors, other public miniſters and conſuls, and thoſe in which a ſtate ſhall be party, the ſupreme court ſhall have original juriſdiction. In all the other caſes before mentioned, the ſupreme court ſhall have appellate juriſdiction, both as to law and fact, with ſuch exceptions, and under ſuch regulations as the Congreſs ſhall make.

The trial of all crimes, except in caſes of impeachment, ſhall be by jury ; and ſuch trial ſhall be held in the ſtate where the ſaid crimes ſhall have been committed ; but when not committed within any ſtate, the trial ſhall be at ſuch place or places as the Congreſs may by law have directed.

Sect. 3. Treaſon againſt the United States, ſhall conſiſt only in levying war againſt them, or in adhering to their enemies, giving them aid and comfort. No perſon ſhall be convicted of treaſon unleſs on the teſtimony of two witneſſes to the ſame overt act, or on confeſſion in open court.

The Congreſs ſhall have power to declare the puniſhment of treaſon, but no attainder of treaſon ſhall work corruption of blood, or forfeiture except during the life of the perſon attainted.

IV.

Sect. 1. Full faith and credit ſhall be given in each ſtate to the public acts, records, and judicial proceedings of every other ſtate. And the Congreſs may by general laws preſcribe the manner in which ſuch acts, records and proceedings ſhall be proved, and the effect thereof.

Sect. 2. The citizens of each ſtate ſhall be entitled to all privileges and immunities of citizens in the ſeveral ſtates.

A perſon charged in any ſtate with treaſon, felony, or other crime, who ſhall flee from juſtice, and be found in another ſtate, ſhall, on demand of the executive authority of the ſtate from which he fled, be delivered up, to be removed to the ſtate having juriſdiction of the crime.

No perſon held to ſervice or labour in one ſtate, under the laws thereof, eſcaping into another, ſhall, in conſequence of any law or regulation therein, be diſcharged from ſuch ſervice or labour, but ſhall be delivered up on claim of the party to whom ſuch ſervice or labour may be due.

Sect. 3. New ſtates may be admitted by the Congreſs into this union ; but no new ſtate ſhall be formed or erected within the juriſdiction of any other ſtate ; nor any ſtate be formed by the junction of two or more ſtates, or parts of ſtates, without the conſent of the legiſlatures of the ſtates concerned as well as of the Congreſs.

The Congreſs ſhall have power to diſpoſe of and make all needful rules and regulations reſpecting the territory or other property belonging to the United States ; and nothing in this Conſtitution ſhall be ſo conſtrued as to prejudice any claims of the United States, or of any particular ſtate.

Sect. 4. The United States ſhall guarantee to every ſtate in this union a Republican form of government, and ſhall protect each of them againſt invaſion ; and on application of the legiſlature, or of the executive (when the legiſlature cannot be convened) againſt domeſtic violence.

V.

The Congreſs, whenever two-thirds of both houſes ſhall deem it neceſſary, ſhall propoſe amendments to this conſtitution, or, on the application of the legiſlatures of two-thirds of the ſeveral ſtates, ſhall call a convention for propoſing amendments, which, in either caſe, ſhall be valid to all intents and purpoſes, as part of this conſtitution, when ratified by the legiſlatures of three-fourths of the ſeveral ſtates, or by conventions in three-fourths thereof, as the one or the other mode of ratification may be propoſed by the Congreſs ; Provided, that no amendment which may be made prior to the year one thouſand eight hundred and eight ſhall in any manner affect the firſt and fourth clauſes in the ninth ſection of the firſt article ; and that no ſtate, without its conſent, ſhall be deprived of its equal ſuffrage in the ſenate.

VI.

All debts contracted and engagements entered into, before the adoption of this Conſtitution, ſhall be as valid againſt the United States under this Conſtitution, as under the confederation.

This conſtitution, and the laws of the United States which ſhall be made in purſuance thereof ; and all treaties made, or which ſhall be made, under the authority of the United States, ſhall be the ſupreme law of the land ; and the judges in every ſtate ſhall be bound thereby, any thing in the conſtitution or laws of any ſtate to the contrary notwithſtanding.

Figure 6.19 (cont.)

The senators and representatives beforementioned, and the members of the several state legislatures, and all executive and judicial officers, both of the United States and of the several States, shall be bound by oath or affirmation, to support this constitution; but no religious test shall ever be required as a qualification to any office or public trust under the United States.

VII.

The ratification of the conventions of nine States, shall be sufficient for the establishment of this constitution between the States so ratifying the same.

Done in Convention, by the unanimous consent of the

States present, the seventeenth day of September, in the year of our Lord one thousand seven hundred and eighty seven, and of the Independence of the United States of America the twelfth. In witness whereof we have hereunto subscribed our Names.

GEORGE WASHINGTON, President,
And Deputy from VIRGINIA.

NEW-HAMPSHIRE. { John Langdon, Nicholas Gilman.

MASSACHUSETTS. { Nathaniel Gorham, Rufus King.

CONNECTICUT. { William Samuel Johnson, Roger Sherman.

NEW-YORK. Alexander Hamilton.

NEW-JERSEY. { William Livingston, David Brearley, William Paterson, Jonathan Dayton.

PENNSYLVANIA. { Benjamin Franklin, Thomas Mifflin, Robert Morris, George Clymer, Thomas Fitzsimons, Jared Ingersoll, James Wilson, Gouverneur Morris.

DELAWARE. { George Read, Gunning Bedford, Junior, John Dickinson, Richard Bassett, Jacob Broom.

MARYLAND, { James M'Henry, Daniel of St. Tho. Jenifer, Daniel Carrol.

VIRGINIA. { John Blair, James Madison, Junior.

NORTH-CAROLINA. { William Blount, Richard Dobbs Spaight, Hugh Williamson.

SOUTH-CAROLINA. { John Rutledge, Charles Cotesworth Pinckney, Charles Pinckney, Pierce Butler.

GEORGIA. { William Few, Abraham Baldwin.

Attest, *William Jackson*, SECRETARY.

IN CONVENTION, Monday September 17th, 1787.
PRESENT

The States of New-Hampshire, Massachusetts, Connecticut, Mr. *Hamilton* from New-York, New-Jersey, Pennsylvania, Delaware, Maryland, Virginia, North-Carolina, South-Carolina and Georgia:

RESOLVED,

THAT the preceding Constitution be laid before the United States in Congress assembled, and that it is the opinion of this Convention, that it should afterwards be submitted to a Convention of Delegates, chosen in each State by the People thereof, under the recommendation of its Legislature, for their assent and ratification; and that each Convention assenting to, and ratifying the same, should give Notice thereof to the United States in Congress assembled.

Resolved, That it is the opinion of this Convention, that as soon as the Conventions of nine States shall have ratified this Constitution, the United States in Congress assembled should fix a day on which Electors should be appointed by the States which shall have ratified the same, and a day on which the Electors should assemble to vote for the President, and the time and place for commencing proceedings under this Constitution. That after such publication the Electors should be appointed, and the Senators and Representatives elected: That the Electors should meet on the day fixed for the Election of the President, and should transmit their votes certified, signed, sealed and directed, as the Constitution requires, to the Secretary of the United States in Congress assembled, that the Senators and Representatives should convene at the time and place assigned; that the Senators should appoint a President of the Senate, for the sole purpose of receiving, opening and counting the votes for President; and, that after he shall be chosen, the Congress, together with the President, should, without delay, proceed to execute this Constitution.

By the unanimous Order of the Convention,

GEORGE WASHINGTON, President.

William Jackson, Secretary.

In Convention, September 17, 1787.

SIR,

WE have now the honor to submit to the consideration of the United States in Congress assembled, that Constitution which has appeared to us the most adviseable.

The friends of our country have long seen and desired, that the power of making war, peace and treaties, that of levying money and regulating commerce, and the correspondent executive and judicial authorities should be fully and effectually vested in the general government of the Union: but the impropriety of delegating such extensive trust to one body of men is evident—Hence results the necessity of a different organization.

It is obviously impracticable in the foederal government of these States, to secure all rights of independent sovereignty to each, and yet provide for the interest and safety of all—Individuals entering into society, must give up a share of liberty to preserve the rest. The magnitude of the sacrifice must depend as well on situation and circumstance, as on the object to be obtained. It is at all times difficult to draw with precision the line between those rights which must be surrendered, and those which may be reserved; and on the present occasion this difficulty was encreased by a difference among the several States as to their situation, extent, habits, and particular interests.

In all our deliberations on this subject we kept steadily in our view, that which appears to us the greatest interest of every true American, the consolidation of our Union, in which is involved our prosperity, felicity, safety, perhaps our national existence. This important consideration, seriously and deeply impressed on our minds, led each State in the Convention to be less rigid on points of inferior magnitude, than might have been otherwise expected; and thus the Constitution, which we now present, is the result of a spirit of amity, and of that mutual deference and concession which the peculiarity of our political situation rendered indispensible.

That it will meet the full and entire approbation of every State is not perhaps to be expected; but each will doubtless consider, that had her interests been alone consulted, the consequences might have been particularly disagreeable or injurious to others; that it is liable to as few exceptions as could reasonably have been expected, we hope and believe; that it may promote the lasting welfare of that country so dear to us all, and secure her freedom and happiness, is our most ardent wish. With great respect,

We have the honor to be, SIR,

Your EXCELLENCY's most

Obedient and humble Servants,

George Washington, President.

By unanimous Order of the CONVENTION.

HIS EXCELLENCY

The President of Congress.

[PRINTED by DUNLAP & CLAYPOOLE.]

Morning Chronicle and in the *Annual Register,* the distinguished British compilation of information, documents, news, and opinions. Although the first foreign-language editions of the Constitution appeared in German-language newspapers serving the Pennsylvania Dutch population, interest in the work of the Convention prompted the translation and republication of the Constitution in other European languages as well.

At first, the close of the Federal Convention and release of the Constitution occasioned celebrations. Soon enough, however, the new charter became the focus of political controversy. The unanimity of September was short-lived.

Frustration and Deadlock in the New York Delegation

Historians of the Federal Convention—particularly those from New York—have viewed the activities of the New York delegation with puzzlement and considerable embarrassment. New York was not the only state to play a less than statesmanlike role in connection with the framing of the Constitution: Maryland's deeply divided delegation included two of the most irreconcilable opponents of the new government, Luther Martin and John Francis Mercer; and Rhode Island did not bother even to send delegates. But when New York's lackluster contribution to the Convention is viewed in relation to the many eminent figures it produced in this period—men such as John Jay, Robert R. Livingston, and Philip Schuyler—or when the disappointing performance of its most distinguished delegate, Alexander Hamilton, is compared with his record of achievement outside the Convention, the state's record is even sorrier.

New York's failure of creativity and nerve at Philadelphia flowed mainly from the ambitions of its political leaders. Governor George Clinton and his allies resisted efforts to strengthen the Confederation because a weak Confederation ensured for New York a more important and powerful role in American politics. New York had long manifested shifting and uncertain attitudes and commitments toward the Confederation. Though valuing the assistance given by other states and the Confederation during the Revolution, when much of the state, including New York City, had been occupied by the British, the New Yorkers also resented the Confederation's unwillingness to serve the state's interests, most notably in the controversy over Vermont. Under the Confederation New York also was able to swell its revenues by taxing interstate commerce. By early 1787, when the states were selecting delegates to the Convention, most Americans perceived New York as at best ambivalent about its ties to the Confederation, and rumors abounded that New York was ready and willing to go its own way should the Union dissolve.[80]

The Clintonian faction could not ignore the call of the Confederation Congress for the Federal Convention, especially as the Annapolis Convention's report urging the need for such a convention was the work of Alexander Hamilton, one of the state's ablest and most fervent nationalists. Therefore, Clinton and his legislative allies determined to skew the state's delegation to Philadelphia—appointing Hamilton, to be sure, but neutralizing him by appointing two delegates who would resist his efforts to strengthen the government of the United States. The Clintonians also defeated attempts by Hamilton's supporters to expand the New York delegation from three members to five. As a result, the delegation appointed to represent New York in the Federal Convention consisted of one man of continental reputation—Alexander Hamilton—and two eminent local politicians whose reputations did not extend beyond the state's borders.[81]

Robert Yates, who had spent most of his political life as a judge, was well regarded by New Yorkers of all political casts; Hamilton described him in 1783 as "upright and respectable in his profession." His experience in the drafting of the New York constitution of 1777 and on the state's supreme court made him a natural choice for the New York delegation to the Federal Convention, and he was the unanimous first choice of both houses of the state's legislature. Yates was also a close friend of Governor Clinton and a cousin and friend of Abraham Yates, Jr., a leading upstate politician and irreconcilable opponent of efforts to strengthen the Confederation. The senior member of the delegation, Yates was forty-nine in 1787.

Thirty-three-year-old John Lansing, Jr., the mayor of Albany, was already an experienced politician, having served four years in the state Assembly and two terms as a New York delegate to the Confederation Congress. He was on close terms with both George Clinton and Philip Schuyler, Hamilton's father-in-law and political ally, but was allied by ties of family and shared views with the Clinton-Yates faction.

Traveling together from New York to Philadelphia, Yates and Hamilton had an opportunity to get to know each other's point of view. They arrived in time to represent their state as part of the first quorum the Convention was able to assemble, on 25 May. Within a week Yates began to express serious doubts about the Convention and its work. Writing to his cousin Abraham, he described his reaction to the quickly developing consensus that the Articles should be scrapped:

> Alas sir! my forebodings . . . are too much realized, & to prevent any member from communicating the future proceedings of Convention additional Rules have since been entered into, one of which strictly prohibits the communication of its business until the final close of it. While I remain a sitting member these rules must be obligatory. How long I shall so remain future events must determine. I keep in the mean while an Exact journal of all its proceedings. This Communication is in the most perfect confidence, in which only one person beside yourself can participate. My Respectfull compliments to the Governor.[82]

Dated 1 June 1787, this letter illustrates Yates's unhappiness with the progression of events in the Convention. The day before, he and Hamilton had split the state's vote on the substituted first resolution of the Virginia Plan, calling for the formation of a national government. This letter is also the first hint Yates gave that he might feel compelled to abandon the Convention.

Yates's letter is also significant for its reference to his "Exact journal." Like Madison, Yates set out to keep a record not only of the Convention's votes but also of principal speeches and debates. His motivations are unknown, though it is likely that he was gathering ammunition to justify his and Lansing's opposition to the Convention. Because Yates and Madison were participating in and observing the Convention from opposed points of view, Yates's notes are a valuable supplement to Madison's fuller but less colorful account of the proceedings. The original manuscript of Yates's journal has long since disappeared, and John Lansing's transcript of the manuscript has also vanished. Our only source for Yates's journal is an edition taken from Lansing's transcript and published in Albany in 1821. Lansing's own notes of the Convention were not published until 1939.[83]

Yates and Lansing disagreed with Hamilton on the basic issue whether the purely federal form of government embodied in the Articles should be replaced with a national government as embodied in the developing plan of the Constitution. Yates and Lansing were also sensitive to the alarming discrepancy between the work of the Convention and their own mandate, based on the congressional resolution of 21 February, which authorized them only to propose revisions to the Articles of Confederation and not to scrap them.

After the Committee of the Whole reported its revisions of the Virginia Plan on 13 June, Lansing joined the small-state delegates in preparing the New Jersey Plan. In the first full day of debate on the competing plans, Lansing pointed out in a major speech that "the power of the Convention was restrained to amendments of a federal nature, and having for their basis the Confederacy in being." Attacking the Convention's decision to violate its mandate, Lansing claimed that "N[ew] York would never have concurred in sending deputies to the convention if she had supposed the deliberations were to turn on a consolidation of the States, and a National Government." He prophesied that the people of New York and the other states would never accept a consolidating, nationalizing plan such as the Virginia Plan, especially as "they had never authorized [us] to propose [such a plan]."[84]

This was the context for Alexander Hamilton's now notorious speech of 18 June.[85] Most historians cannot explain why Hamilton should have chosen this moment, when the Convention's nerves were rubbed raw by the contest between the Virginia and New Jersey Plans, to propound so radically nationalizing, centralizing, and high-toned a system of government as he sketched in this speech. It is usually described as Hamilton's venting of frustration and indignation at the humiliating part he was forced to play in the Convention, watching as Yates and Lansing rendered his presence a nullity by outvoting him on every issue and every occasion. To some extent, this interpretation of Hamilton's speech and plan makes sense. But more in his speech was directly related to the arguments of John Lansing than has been appreciated before.

Hamilton began by conceding not only his comparative youth and inexperience in so distinguished a body but also his delicate position as the perpetual minority member of the New York delegation. He maintained that although the choice between the Virginia and New Jersey Plans was not much of a choice (Yates reported Hamilton as dismissing the Virginia Plan as "pork still, with a little change of the sauce"—a joke that Madison chose not to record)[86]—the Virginia Plan was far better than the New Jersey Plan, because the latter conceded sovereignty to the states. Hamilton then outlined his own idea of an effective government for America. Doubting that a republic could be extended over so great a territory—an argument that Anti-Federalists would maintain in the ratification contest and that Madison would demolish in *Federalist* Nos. 10 and 14—Hamilton declared his extravagant admiration for the British constitution and "doubted much whether anything short of it would do in America." Hamilton knew well that the people would never accept a monarchy, even a limited monarchy on the British model, and thus was willing to recommend that the Convention "go as far in order to attain stability and permanency, as republican principles will admit."

How far Hamilton thought the Convention should go to achieve "stability and permanency" is illustrated by a sketch of his plan. He proposed an executive, to be chosen by electors chosen by the people to serve "during good behaviour," and to be armed with an absolute veto power. His legislature would consist of two houses, the lower house to be chosen by the people and the upper house by indirect election for life or for good behavior. The states would be reduced to mere administrative districts, with governors appointed by the central government and armed with an absolute veto over all laws passed by state legislatures.

In some respects, the extreme degree of centralization embodied in Hamilton's plan supports the traditional view that he was speaking out of frustration and with a desire to shock by disclosing his inmost views of the kind of government that the American crisis required. This is especially true of his view of the states. Having spent none of his early life in America, Hamilton had not formed the local and regional attachments that characterized his colleagues in Philadelphia. Consequently, his national and even continental vision had little in common with most Americans' hopes for the United States. But Hamilton's speech was also a direct response to Lansing, and to Lansing's implication that he and Yates alone spoke for the people of New York and accurately reflected their views. Hamilton expressed the view that "evils operating in the states . . . must soon cure the people of their fondness for democracies . . . [and, once this happens,] they will not be satisfied at stopping where the [Virginia Plan] w[ould] place them, but be ready to as far at least as" Hamilton's proposals.

Figure 6.20
Alexander Hamilton. "Plan of a constitution for America." Draft, September 1787.

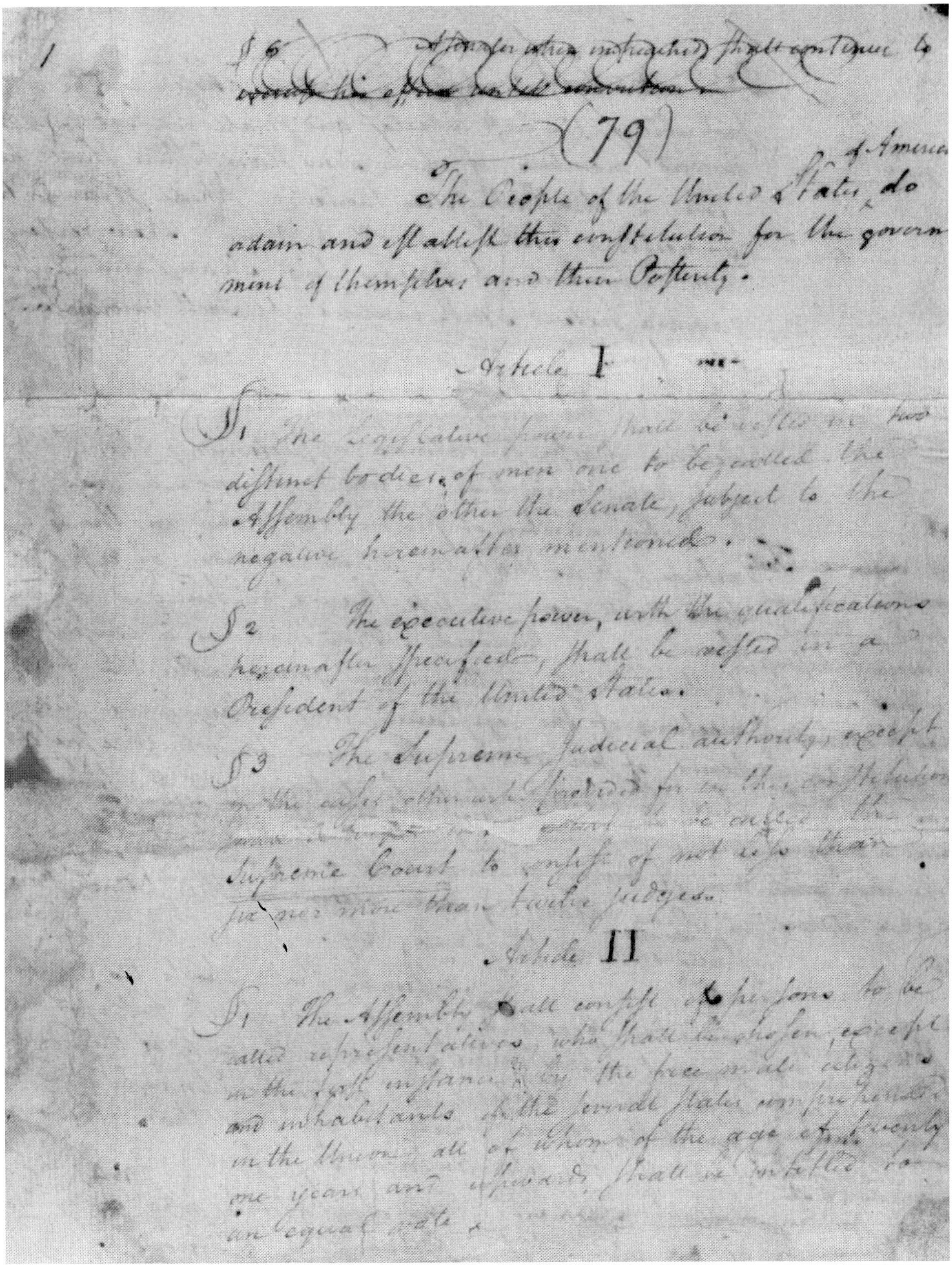

1

§ 6 *[struck through line]* ...shall continue to ... *[struck through]*

(79)

, of America

The People of the United States, do
ordain and establish this constitution for the government of themselves and their Posterity.

Article I

§ 1. The Legislative power shall be vested in two
distinct bodies of men one to be called the
Assembly the other the Senate, subject to the
negative hereinafter mentioned.

§ 2. The executive power, with the qualifications
hereinafter specified, shall be vested in a
President of the United States.

§ 3. The supreme Judicial authority except
in the cases otherwise provided for in this constitution
... ...
Supreme Court to consist of not less than
... nor more than twelve judges.

Article II

§ 1. The Assembly shall consist of persons to be
called representatives who shall be chosen, except
in the first instance by the free male citizens
and inhabitants of the several States comprehended
in the Union all of whom of the age of twenty
one years and upwards, shall be intitled to
an equal vote.

Hamilton's speech also resembles a dissenting opinion of an appellate judge. Such an opinion, reflecting the greater freedom of a dissenter, is often an appeal to posterity, a way to release one's ideas in the hope that future generations will be convinced and accept them in preference to the view held by the majority.[87] Although the debates in the Convention were secret, Hamilton knew that Madison was keeping a detailed record, and he reviewed Madison's account of his speech, making a few verbal changes, doubtless in the expectation that the speech would someday see the light of day. One last possible explanation for Hamilton's outburst is that, like Madison and Charles Pinckney, Hamilton had given a great thought to his own plan of government for America and grasped the first opportunity to place the fruits of his research and thinking before the delegates. In any event Hamilton's speech had no influence at the Convention; it was admired for its eloquence, and Hamilton also demonstrated impressive energy and resilience (estimates of the length of his speech range up to six hours), but no one was convinced.[88]

Toward the end of the Convention, Hamilton prepared a full draft of a constitution for America, based on his earlier plans and on the evolving drafts of the Committee of Detail and the Committee of Style and Arrangement (Figure 6.20). He lent this draft to Madison, who copied and returned it. Madison's leading biographer, Irving Brant, declared of this document: "What Hamilton did, it appears, was to take the printed report of the committee and rewrite it to embody his radically different ideas—not for submission to the convention but as a record of the features in which he regarded the Constitution to be defective."[89]

By the end of June, Hamilton had determined to leave the Convention. He based his decision both on pressing personal and legal business in New York City and on his weariness and frustration with his uncomfortable position in Philadelphia. Yates and Lansing continued to represent New York until 10 July. Their departure ended the state's official participation in the framing of the Constitution.

The departure of Yates and Lansing is generally seen as a final and irreversible declaration that the emerging Constitution was a threat to their political beliefs and a violation of their mandate, but the available evidence indicates that they had not yet come to this conclusion. George Mason recorded that in his view Yates and Lansing had departed to attend the circuit courts in New York; Yates as a judge was obliged to ride the circuit, and Lansing was a rising lawyer with several cases demanding his attention. Hamilton apparently had not given up on his colleagues, either; in late August he wrote to them announcing his intention to return to Philadelphia and invited them to join him. By this time, however, Yates and Lansing had decided to abandon the Convention. As Abraham G. Lansing, the delegate's brother, reported to his close friend and political ally Abraham Yates:

> The Judge [Yates] and my Brother have attended the Circuit in Montgomery County, from which place the former returned but few days

and will in the Morning go to Washington County to hold a Court.—I find but little Inclination in either of them to repair again to Philadelphia and from their General Observations I believe they will not go. early in the Commencement of the business at Philadelphia my Brother informed me that he was in sentiment with a respectable *Minority* of that body, but that they had no prospect of succeeding in the measures proposed and that he was at a Stand whether it would not be proper for him to Leave them. This Circumstance convinces me the more that they will not again attend.—Mr. Hamilton will consequently be disappointed and chagrined.[90]

Abraham Lansing's letter is also a good indicator of the level of rumor spreading through the country as the Convention continued its work behind closed doors:

> we have reports here that Mr. Paine (common sense) is employed to write in favor of the British form of government—and that the system which will be recommended to the states will be similar to that Constitution the Kingly part excepted. Your intercourse with the high prerogative Gentlemen will enable you to learn at least the outlines of the Government which we are in their Ideas to adopt or sink into Oblivion.—the situation of our Country is critical and truly alarming—if we once get fairly in Confusion it is hard to say were [*sic*] we will stop.

Hamilton would have smiled sourly had he been able to read this letter, for one of his greatest differences with the evolving Constitution was precisely that it did not follow closely enough the British constitution, which he extolled throughout his life as the best government on earth.[91]

In any event, Yates and Lansing never returned to the Convention, thus depriving New York of a quorum. Hamilton journeyed to Philadelphia at the beginning of September knowing that he would be officially powerless, restricted to speaking in debate and serving on committees. That his fellow delegates did not hold his 18 June speech against him is evidenced by his appointment to the Committee of Style and Arrangement, the last committee the Convention was to appoint. At the end of the Convention, Hamilton sought to persuade the die-hard Gerry and Mason and wavering Randolph to sign the Constitution. Madison took down his appeal:

> Mr. Hamilton expressed his anxiety that every member should sign. A few characters of consequence, by opposing or even refusing to sign the Constitution, might do infinite mischief by kindling the latent sparks which lurk under an enthusiasm in favor of the Convention which may soon subside. No man's ideas were more remote from the plan than his were known to be; but is it possible to deliberate between anarchy and Convulsion on one side, and the chance of good to be expected from the plan on the other.[92]

Finally, even though he had at best questionable authority to sign the Constitution on behalf of New York, Hamilton added his own name to the instrument and also marked off the state delegations in his own hand during the signing ceremony.

In essence, the story of the New York delegation is one of frustration and deadlock, of delegates who from their differing origins, ideological commitments, and habits of thought were not capable of understanding each other. Yates and Lansing were shaped primarily by their experience of New York politics; Hamilton's political experience was almost entirely at the national level. Hamilton came to the Convention intent on forging a powerful, energetic government for a nation; Yates and Lansing considered themselves bound by the Confederation Congress and the New York legislature to consider only amending the Articles of Confederation. Out of loyalty to their perceived mandate, and refusing to concede Hamilton's argument that the needs of America required the Convention to go beyond the limits of the congressional resolution, Yates and Lansing sought to stem the tide represented by the Virginia Plan. When they failed, their failure combined with other responsibilities to compel them to leave the Convention. Reflection convinced them that they could not in good conscience return to Philadelphia. Hamilton, on the other hand, felt that the Convention would not take strong enough measures to cope with the problems of America. Nonetheless, he was willing to accept the Constitution as better than a continuation of the Articles of Confederation, and returned to take part in the last stages of the writing of the Constitution and declare himself one of its supporters. The conflict between Hamilton, on the one side, and Yates and Lansing, on the other, represented in miniature and in caricature the conflict that would dominate American politics for the next year, as the Constitution came before the American people.

7

THE STRUGGLE FOR
RATIFICATION

THE CLOSE of the Federal Convention marked the first step in the
making of the Constitution. The Convention had no authority to impose the result of its work on the American people; it could only recommend
the charter it had drafted to the Confederation Congress. Although the
people eventually did adopt the Constitution, this process was neither au-
tomatic nor unopposed. The campaign for and against the Constitution
raged in state legislatures and ratifying conventions, in newspaper essays
and pamphlets (Figure 7.1), in streets and taverns and coffeehouses. As
hard-fought as any battle of the Revolution, it was a contest of words and
arguments and votes, of parades and bonfires, with an occasional riot thrown
in for good measure.

The ratification controversy was both a direct, unabashed contest for
votes and a complex, impressive argument about politics and constitutional
theory. It acted as a catalyst for the creation of a national political community, transforming the ways Americans thought of themselves and encouraging the growth and popularity of national loyalties.

The First National Political Campaign

The delegates to the Federal Convention set forth the means by which the
new Constitution would be adopted in Article VII and in a set of resolutions
adopted together with the new charter. They designed a four-stage procedure: transmission of the Constitution and resolutions to the Confederation
Congress; transmission of the Constitution and resolutions by Congress to
the state legislatures; election of delegates to special ratifying conventions
in each state to consider the Constitution; and ratification of the Constitution
by the conventions of at least nine states.

This ratification process differed significantly from the amending process specified in the Articles of Confederation. Under the Articles, any
amendment had to be proposed by Congress to the state legislatures, and
all thirteen state legislatures had to approve the amendment for it to go
into effect. The ratification process made adoption of the Constitution more
likely, especially as every attempt to amend the Articles under their own
terms had failed.

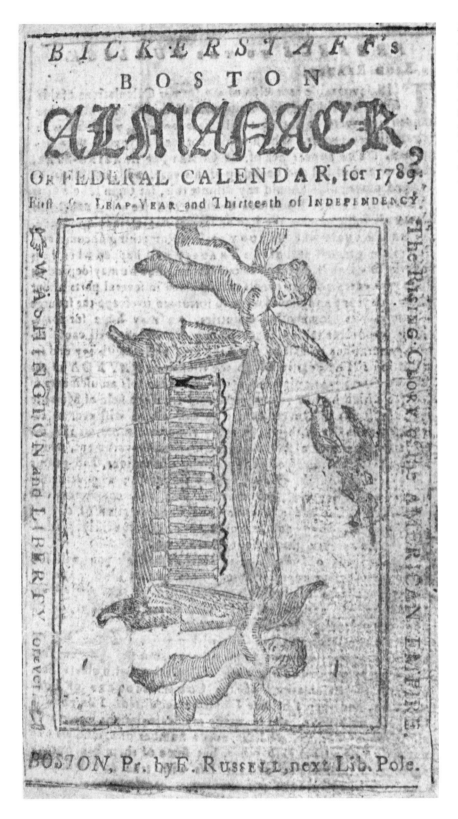

Figure 7.1

Artist unknown. *The Rising Glory of the AMERICAN EMPIRE*. Woodcut, 1788. In this crude woodcut, on the cover of *Bickerstaff's Boston Almanack* for 1789, two cherubs and an angel hail the ratification of the Constitution, represented by thirteen upright pillars, a recurrent popular image. Washington's endorsement of the document was one of the Federalists' strongest weapons—and the woodcut proclaims "Washington and Liberty forever."

The delegates' decision to adopt the ratification process was based on their judgment of the Constitution's prospects and on substantive political principles. Committing the Constitution to specially chosen state ratifying conventions would circumvent the expected hostility of state governors and legislators jealous of their states' sovereignty. The delegates also viewed the Constitution as a fundamental law that had to be adopted in a manner more solemn and significant and less vulnerable to the shifts of public opinion than would be involved in adoption by the state legislatures. This method of making and adopting constitutions was derived from the Massachusetts constitution of 1780. Finally, the ratification process encouraged the people of each state to look beyond their borders in choosing to support or reject the new Constitution. Also, a pattern of quick votes for ratification in the first state conventions might stimulate momentum that would be difficult to resist.

The ratification process was studded with potential stumbling blocks, however. First, the Confederation Congress might refuse to send the Constitution to the states, on the ground that the Convention had violated its limited mandate to propose amendments to the Articles. Second, Congress might try to rewrite the Constitution or to submit it to a second general convention. Third, the states might accept the argument that the Convention had violated its mandate and refuse to hold elections for the ratifying conventions. Fourth, enough state conventions might reject the Constitution to prevent it from going into effect. Fifth, a negative vote by the legislatures or ratifying conventions of any or all of four key states—Massachusetts, New York, Pennsylvania, and Virginia—might cripple efforts to put the Constitution into effect even if the required nine states did ratify it. These possibilities shaped the struggle for ratification that dominated American politics in late 1787 and 1788.

The term *Federalists* is used to designate the Constitution's supporters and *Anti-Federalists* to designate the Constitution's opponents.[1] This nomenclature arose in the early 1780s, when disputes over proposals to give the Confederation Congress more power divided the nation into Federalists— those favoring additional power for the federal government—and Anti-Federalists. Thus, when the Constitution's supporters adopted the name Federalists, they could claim consistency with the word's earlier usage. But the Constitution's opponents argued that they had at least as valid a claim to be called Federalists. Invoking the traditional distinction between federal and national government, they denounced the Constitution as a nationalizing, consolidating charter that would destroy the sovereignty of the states, individual liberties, and republican government. However, the Constitution's supporters won the tug-of-war over nomenclature by linking the Constitution with the idea of Union; they maintained that the American people could preserve the Union only by adopting the Constitution. The next step in this war of words, which they portrayed as simply a logical consequence of celebrating the Constitution as the bulwark of Union and Federalism, was that the new charter's opponents, the Anti-Federalists, were willing or even eager to dissolve the Union. These terms soon passed into general usage.

However, neither the Federalists nor the Anti-Federalists were modern political parties as we understand them.[2] Loose and shifting coalitions of interests, voters, and officeholders had existed in America since the foundation of the earliest colonial legislatures in the seventeenth century, but they lacked the organization, discipline, and articulated political programs that we now associate with parties. The Federalists and Anti-Federalists were an intermediate step in the evolution of organized political parties. They were more structured than their colonial counterparts, and they even attempted to function on the national level, but, unlike modern parties, they had coalesced only on the basis of a single national issue. In some states the split between Federalists and Anti-Federalists superimposed itself on preexisting factions. The best example is Pennsylvania, where supporters of the state's radical, democratic constitution of 1776 generally became Anti-Federalists and its opponents became Federalists.[3] Even there, however, the most prominent backer of the Pennsylvania constitution, Benjamin Franklin, was well known as a supporter of the federal Constitution. And most linkages between national and state factional positions were rarely as solid and coherent as those in Pennsylvania. Though some historians maintain that the Federalists and Anti-Federalists of 1787–88 evolved into the Federalists and Republicans of the 1790s,[4] the course of party development was more complicated and the continuities between the two sets of parties were much more attenuated than the traditional wisdom would suggest. Consistent realignment of political forces at national and state levels awaited the next decade.

The first two steps in the ratification process were completed by the end of September 1787. On 20 September the Constitution, the Convention's resolutions, and its formal letter to Congress, signed by George Washington, arrived in New York City. The Confederation Congress heard these documents read aloud on the same day and set 26 September for formal debate on the proper disposition of the Convention's report. Almost immediately opponents of the Constitution charged that the Convention had exceeded its mandate. Led by Richard Henry Lee of Virginia and Nathan Dane of Massachusetts, these delegates urged that Congress either refuse to send the Constitution to the states or send along with it a resolution pointing out the several ways in which the Convention had violated its mandate and the Articles' amending process. Lee and his allies also suggested that Congress could rewrite the Constitution or attach a set of amendments, including a declaration of rights, before sending it to the states. James Madison led those delegates who supported the Constitution. He and his colleagues sought a favorable congressional resolution to accompany it; they also resisted Lee's various proposals to hamstring the new charter. Finally, after three days of debate, Congress worked out a compromise. It sent the Constitution to the states without comment but recommended that the states hold elections for ratifying conventions as provided for by the Convention's resolutions.[5]

The Federalists tried to build momentum for the Constitution by inducing the state legislatures to hold elections for the ratifying conventions as soon as possible. In some states their roughshod tactics provided Anti-Federalists with powerful ammunition in their campaign against the new charter. In Pennsylvania the Federalists rushed the election bill for the ratifying convention through the General Assembly, so that representatives from the western part of the state, expected to oppose the Constitution, could not arrive in Philadelphia in time to take part in the debate. The few Anti-Federal legislators who were present realized that they could prevent the majority from having its way by absenting themselves from the legislature, thus depriving it of a quorum (Figure 7.2). When the Federalists figured out what the Anti-Federalists' empty seats signified, Speaker Thomas Fitzsimons, a signer of the Constitution, ordered the sergeant-at-arms to find two absent members and bring them to the State House to make up the quorum. Followed by a cheering mob, the sergeant-at-arms cornered two Anti-Federal legislators in their rooming house, and the crowd carried them back to the Assembly, where they were forced to remain in their seats long enough to register the presence of a quorum and watch the majority enact the election bill.[6]

Federalist methods in other states were more subtle, although Anti-Federalists repeatedly charged that their opponents were rushing things through the legislatures to prevent reasoned consideration. They also claimed that the Federalists were using bribery, chicanery, and outright fraud to dominate the state legislatures' consideration of election bills and to rig the elections to the state ratifying conventions.[7]

The Federal and Anti-Federal strategies took shape in the fall and winter of 1787.[8] In states in which they could be reasonably certain that the Constitution would be adopted, the Federalists campaigned and lobbied for a quick election for the ratifying conventions and a speedy vote on the Constitution. In states where the outlook was less certain or where opposition to the Constitution would defeat a push for early ratification, the Federalists chose to go slowly, hoping that speedy ratifications in other states would sap the strength of the Anti-Federalists. This strategy worked well. Generally, the states that adopted the Constitution quickly were relatively weak ones that had reason to welcome the creation of a stronger central government. In Georgia, for example, the fourth state to ratify, the convention met in the capital, Augusta, which was an armed camp ringed with a wooden palisade to guard against the ever-present danger of Indian attacks. The siege mentality that pervaded Augusta was a constant reminder of the weakness of the Confederation Congress and the promise of security offered by the Constitution.[9] By contrast, those states that delayed ratifying conventions were strong, rich, and powerful, whose politicians wondered if they

To the CITIZENS of PHILADELPHIA.

Friends, Countrymen, Brethren and Fellow Citizens,

THE important day is drawing near when you are to elect delegates to represent you in a Convention, on the result of whose deliberations will depend, in a great measure your future happiness.

This convention is to determine whether or not the commonwealth of Pennsylvania shall adopt the plan of government proposed by the late convention of delegates from the different states, which sat in this city.

With a heart full of anxiety for the preservation of your dearest rights, I presume to address you on this important occasion—In the name of sacred liberty, dearer to us than our property and our lives, I request your most earnest attention.

The proposed plan of continental government is now fully known to you. You have read it I trust with the attention it deserves—You have heard the objections that have been made to it—You have heard the answers to these objections.

If you have attended to the whole with candor and unbiassed minds, as becomes men that are possessed and deserving of freedom, you must have been alarmed at the result of your observations. Notwithstanding the splendor of names which has attended the publication of the new constitution, notwithstanding the sophistry and vain reasonings that have been urged to support its principles; alas! you must at least have concluded that great men are not always infallible, and that patriotism itself may be led into essential errors.

The objections that have been made to the new constitution, are these:

1. It is not merely (as it ought to be) a CONFEDERATION of STATES, but a GOVERNMENT of INDIVIDUALS.

2. The powers of Congress extend to the *lives*, the *liberties* and the *property* of every citizen.

3. The *sovereignty* of the different states is *ipso facto* destroyed in its most essential parts.

4. What remains of it will only tend to create violent dissentions between the state governments and the Congress, and terminate in the ruin of the one or the other.

5. The consequence must therefore be, either that the *union* of the states will be destroyed by a violent struggle, or that their sovereignty will be swallowed up by silent encroachments into a universal aristocracy; because it is clear, that if two different *sovereign powers* have a co-equal command over the *purses* of the citizens, they will struggle for the spoils, and the weakest will be in the end obliged to yield to the efforts of the strongest.

6. Congress being possessed of these immense powers, the liberties of the states and of the people are not secured by a bill or DECLARATION OF RIGHTS.

7. The *sovereignty* of the states is not expresly reserved, the *form* only, and not the SUBSTANCE of their government, is guaranteed to them by express words.

8. TRIAL BY JURY, that sacred bulwark of liberty, is ABOLISHED IN CIVIL CASES, and Mr. WILSON, one of the convention, has told you, that not being able to agree as to the FORM of establishing this point, they have left you deprived of the SUBSTANCE. Here are his own words—*The subject was involved in difficulties. The convention found the task* TOO DIFFICULT *for them, and left the business as it stands.*

9. THE LIBERTY OF THE PRESS is not secured, and the powers of congress are fully adequate to its destruction, as they are to have the trial of *libels*, or *pretended libels* against the United States, and may by a cursed abominable STAMP ACT (as the *Bowdoin administration* has done in Massachusetts) preclude you effectually from all means of information. *Mr. Wilson has given you no answer to these arguments.*

10. Congress have the power of keeping up a STANDING ARMY in time of peace, and Mr. Wilson has told you THAT IT WAS NECESSARY.

11. The LEGISLATIVE and EXECUTIVE powers are not kept separate as every one of the American constitutions declares they ought to be; but they are mixed in a manner entirely novel and unknown, even to the constitution of Great Britain; because,

12. In England the king only, has a *nominal negative* over the proceedings of the legislature, which he has NEVER DARED TO EXERCISE since the days of *King William*, whereas by the new constitution, both the *president general* and the *senate* TWO EXECUTIVE BRANCHES OF GOVERNMENT, have that negative, and are intended to *support each other in the exercise of it.*

13. The representation of the lower house is too small, consisting only of 65 members.

14. That of the *senate* is so small that it renders its extensive powers extremely dangerous: it is to consist only of 26 members, two-thirds of whom must concur to conclude any *treaty or alliance* with foreign powers: Now we will suppose that five of them are absent, sick, dead, or unable to attend, *twenty-one* will remain, and eight of these (*one-third*, and *one* over) may prevent the conclusion of any treaty, even the most favorable to America. Here will be a fine field for the intrigues and even the *bribery* and *corruption* of European powers.

15. The most important branches of the EXECUTIVE DEPARTMENT [illegible] the hands of a *single magis*[illegible] The

16. Should the *senate*, by the intrigues of foreign powers, become devoted to foreign influence, as was the case of late in *Sweden*, the people will be obliged, as the *Swedes* have been, to seek their refuge in the arms of the *monarch* or PRESIDENT GENERAL.

17. ROTATION, that noble prerogative of liberty, is entirely excluded from the new system of government, and great men may and probably will be continued in office during their lives.

18. ANNUAL ELECTIONS are abolished, and the people are not to re-assume their rights until the expiration of *two*, *four* and *six* years.

19. Congress are to have the power of fixing the *time*, *place* and *manner* of holding elections, so as to keep them forever subjected to their influence.

20. The importation of slaves is not to be prohibited until the year 1808, and SLAVERY will probably resume its empire in Pennsylvania.

21. The MILITIA is to be under the immediate command of congress, and men *conscienciously scrupulous of bearing arms*, may be compelled to perform military duty.

22. The new government will be EXPENSIVE beyond any we have ever experienced, the *judicial* department alone, with its concomitant train of *judges, justices, chancellors, clerks, sheriffs, coroners, escheators, state attornies and solicitors, constables, &c.* in every state and in every country in each state, will be a burden beyond the utmost abilities of the people to bear, and upon the whole.

23. A government partaking of MONARCHY and aristocracy will be fully and firmly established, and liberty will be but a name to adorn the *short* historic page of the halcyon days of America.

These, my countrymen, are the objections that have been made to the new proposed system of government; and if you read the system itself with attention, you will find them all to be founded in truth. But what have you been told in answer?

I pass over the sophistry of Mr. Wilson, in his equivocal speech at the state house. His pretended arguments have been echoed and re-echoed by every retailer of politics, and *victoriously* refuted by several patriotic pens. Indeed if you read this famous speech in a cool dispassionate moment, you will find it to contain no more than a train of pitiful sophistry and evasions, unworthy of the man who spoke them. I have taken notice of some of them in stating the objections, and they must, I am sure, have excited your *pity* and *indignation*. Mr. Wilson is a man of sense, learning and extensive information, unfortunately for him he has never sought the more solid fame of *patriotism*. During the late war he narrowly escaped the effects of popular rage, and the people seldom arm themselves against a citizen in vain. The whole tenor of his political conduct has always been strongly tainted with the spirit of *high aristocracy*, he has never been known to join in a truly popular measure, and his talents have ever been devoted to the patrician interest. His lofty carriage indicates the lofty mind that animates him, a mind able to conceive and perform great things, but which unfortunately can see nothing great out of the pale of power and worldly grandeur; despising what he calls the inferior order of the people, popular liberty and popular assemblies offer to his exalted imagination an idea of meanness and contemptibility which he hardly seeks to conceal—He sees at a distance the pomp and pageantry of courts, he sighs after those stately palaces and that apparatus of human greatness which his vivid fancy has taught him to consider as the supreme good. Men of sublime minds, he conceives, were born a different race from the rest of the sons of men, to them, and them only, he imagines, high heaven intended to commit the reins of earthly government, the remaining part of mankind he sees below at an immense distance, they, he thinks were born to serve, to administer food to the ambition of their superiors, and become the footstool of their power—Such is Mr. Wilson, and fraught with these high ideas, it is no wonder that he should exert all his talents to support a form of government so admirably contrived to carry them into execution—But when the people, who possess collectively a mass of knowledge superior to his own, inquire into the principles of that government on the establishment or rejection of which depend their dearest concerns, when he is called upon by the voice of thousands to come and explain that favorite system which he holds forth as an object of their admiration, he comes—he attempts to support by reasoning what reason never dictated, and finding the attempt vain, his great mind, made for nobler purposes, is obliged to stoop to mean evasions and pitiful sophistry; himself not deceived, he strives to deceive the people, and the treasonable attempt delineates his true character, beyond the reach of the pencil of a *West* or *Peale*, or the pen of a *Valerius*.

And yet that speech, weak and insidious as it is, is the only attempt that has been made to support by argument that political monster THE PROPOSED CONSTITUTION. I have sought in vain amidst the immense heap of trash that has been published on the subject, an argument worthy of refutation, and I have not been able to find it. If you can bear the disgust which the reading of those pieces must naturally occasion, and which I have felt in the highest degree, [illegible] hands upon your hearts) whether there is any thing in them that can impress unfeigned conviction upon your unprejudiced minds.

One of them only I shall take notice of, in which I find that argument is weakly attempted. This piece is signed "AN AMERICAN CITIZEN" and has appeared with great pomp in four succeeding numbers in several of our newspapers. But if you read it attentively, you will find that it does not tell us what the new constitution IS, but what it IS NOT, and extolls it on the sole ground that it does not contain ALL the principles of tyranny with which the European governments are disgraced.

But where argument entirely failed, nothing remained for the supporters of the new constitution but to endeavor to inflame your passions—The attempt has been made and I am sorry to find not entirely without effect. The great names of WASHINGTON and FRANKLIN, have been taken in vain and shockingly prostituted to effect the most infamous purposes. What! because our august chieftain has subscribed his name in his capacity of president of the convention to the plan offered by them to the states, and because the venerable sage of Pennsylvania, has *testified* by his signature that *the majority of the delegates of this state* assented to the same plan, will any one infer from this that it has met with their entire approbation, and that they consider it as the master piece of human wisdom? I am apt to think the contrary, and I have good reasons to ground my opinion on.

In the first place we have found by the publication of *Charles Cotesworth Pinckney*, Esquire, one of the *signing* members of the convention, who has expressed the most pointed disapprobation of many important parts of the new plan of government, that all the members whose names appear at the bottom of this instrument of tyranny have not concurred in its adoption. Many of them might conceive themselves bound by the opinion of the majority of their state, and leaving the people to their own judgment upon the form of government offered to them, might have conceived it impolitic by refusing to sign their names, to offer to the world the lamentable spectacle of the disunion of a body on the decisions of whom the people had rested all their hopes. We KNOW, and the long sitting of the convention tells us, that, (as it is endeavoured to persuade us) concord and unanimity did not reign exclusively among them. The thick veil of secrecy with which their proceedings have been covered, has left us entirely in the dark, as to the *debates* that took place, and the unaccountable SUPPRESSION OF THEIR JOURNALS, the highest insult that could be offered to the majesty of the people, shews clearly that the whole of the new plan was entirely the work of an *aristocratic majority*.

But let us suppose for a moment that the proposed government was the unanimous result of the deliberations of the convention—must it on that account preclude an investigation of its merits? Are the people to be dictated to without appeal by any set of men, however great, however dignified? Freedom spurns at the idea and rejects it with disdain—We appeal to the collective wisdom of a great nation, we appeal to their general sense which is easily to be obtained through the channel of a multitude of free presses, from the opinions of *thirty-nine* men, who secluded from the rest of the world, without the possibility of conferring with the rest of their fellow-citizens, have had no opportunity of rectifying the errors into which they may have been led by the *most designing* among them. We have seen names not less illustrious than those of the members of the late convention, subscribed to the present *reprobated* articles of confederation, and if those patriots have erred, there is no reason to suppose that a succeeding set should be more free from error. Nay the very men, who advocate so strongly the new plan of government, and support it with the infallibility of Doctor Franklin, affect to despise the present constitution of Pennsylvania, which was dictated and avowed by that venerable patriot—They are conscious that he does not entirely approve of the new plan, whose principles are so different from those he has established in our ever-glorious constitution, and there is no doubt that it is the reason that has induced them to leave his respected name out of the *ticket* for the approaching election.

Now then my fellow-citizens, my brethren, my friends, if the sacred flame of liberty be not extinguished in your breasts, if you have any regard for the happiness of yourselves, and your posterity, let me entreat you, earnestly entreat you by all that is dear and sacred to freemen, to consider well before you take an awful step which may involve in its consequences the ruin of millions yet unborn—You are on the brink of a dreadful precipice;—in the name therefore of holy liberty, for which I have fought and for which we have all suffered, I call upon you to make a solemn pause before you proceed. One step more, and perhaps the scene of freedom is closed forever in America. Let not a set of aspiring despots, *who make us* SLAVES *and tell us 'tis our* CHARTER, wrest from you those invaluable blessings, for which the most illustrious sons of America have bled and died—but exert yourselves, like men, like freemen and like Americans, to transmit unimpaired to your latest posterity those rights, those liberties, which have ever been so dear to you, and which it is yet in your [illegible]

[illegible] Philadelphia, November [illegible] 1787.

could perhaps go their own way. The exception to this pattern was Pennsylvania, where the Federalists experimented only once with flagrant strong-arm tactics.

The Anti-Federalists' strategy reflected the divisions in their ranks, which included both die-hard opponents of the Constitution and moderates who favored parts of the new plan of government but sought amendments to remove troubling or objectionable features or to fill holes. Their initial plan of attack was to call for delay to prevent the Constitution from being "hurr[ied] down our Throats, before we have opened our mouths," as one Anti-Federal newspaper essayist put it.[10] The Anti-Federalists never quite gave up hope that the voters would accept their argument that the Convention had violated its mandate and the Articles and thus that the Constitution was not properly before the people; but this contention failed time and time again.

The Anti-Federalists' first fallback position was to urge that the Constitution be submitted to a second convention.[11] Conceding that there were many good things in the Constitution, many Anti-Federalists maintained nonetheless that various flaws and omissions required amendment. They urged that state conventions adopt amendments as conditions of ratification; the Constitution, together with these conditional amendments, should be submitted to a second general convention with a clearly defined mandate—to bring the Constitution into conformity with the wishes of the people as codified in the conditional amendments.

The potential weaknesses of the Anti-Federalists' position were apparent even at the time to all but the most optimistic opponents of the Constitution. The Federalists had identified a problem—the weakness of the Confederation—and had propounded a full-scale systemic reform to solve that problem. The Anti-Federalists had to concede the flaws of the Confederation, but in so doing they had to accept the basis of the argument over the Constitution on the Federalists' terms. By setting the agenda, the Federalists had half the battle won.

The Anti-Federalists were also plagued by problems of leadership, organization, and communication. The esteem in which most of the delegates to the Federal Convention were held, especially Washington and Franklin, made it difficult for Anti-Federalists to attack the Convention's motives and actions. The Federalists realized the tactical advantage inherent in Washington's and Franklin's endorsements of the Constitution and constantly reminded the voters that the two greatest Americans favored the new plan of government, even though neither man took an active role in the ratification campaign. More important, from service together in the Continental Army, the Confederation Congress, and the Federal Convention the Federalist leaders knew one another and kept in close touch, funneling news of the ratification campaign back and forth and coordinating their activities. Alexander Hamilton even paid out of his own pocket for express riders to bring the news of ratifications from New Hampshire and Virginia to New York during the summer of 1788.

Figure 7.2
[William Findley?] *To the Citizens of Philadelphia.* Broadside, 1787. Findley, a state representative from western Pennsylvania, refused his seat on the Pennsylvania delegation to the Federal Convention and became one of the state's leading Anti-Federalists. This broadside was an attempt to influence the election of delegates to the Pennsylvania ratification convention in December 1787.

The Anti-Federalists had no such network of leadership and information. With only a handful of exceptions, they had received their political training, earned their political experience, and acquired their patterns of thought in state politics. They had had little opportunity to deal with their counterparts in other states or to acquire a national reputation. As a result their attempts to establish links with potential allies in other states were fumbling and uncertain. Moreover, in an age without nationwide mass media or rapid and dependable communication and transportation, news traveled slowly and often arrived garbled when it arrived at all. Plagued by undependable mail service, which some embittered Anti-Federalists charged had been deliberately subverted by the Federalists,[12] the opponents of the Constitution could not form an accurate picture of the campaign even within their home states. For example, Melancton Smith, a New York delegate to the Confederation Congress and Anti-Federal leader, complained on 28 January 1788 to Abraham Yates, Jr.:

> All sides are waiting here with anxious expectations for the determination of the Convention of Massachusetts. Both the favourers and opposers say that they have a majority. Each party speak as they would have it, and I believe the information received from Massachusetts differs according to the sentiments of the Men who give it . . . It is impossible in this variety of reports to form an opinion that may be relied upon. I am not sanguine. I think it best always to reckon the strength of your adversaries as much as it is.[13]

By contrast, James Wilson's letter of that same week to Samuel Wallis gleefully reported:

> Appearances with Regard to the new federal Constitution are very favourable on every Side. Its Friends increase in Virginia. In Maryland, Opposition has ceased almost everywhere. The Convention of Connecticut have adopted it by a Majority of more than three to one. It is more than probable that, by this Time, it is adopted by the Convention of Massachusetts . . . Some agreeable Pieces of Intelligence have been lately received from New York; but we know not what the Assembly will do; tho' there seems greater Reason for Hope than for Apprehension.[14]

As Smith's and Wilson's letters show, both Federalists and Anti-Federalists watched the campaign in Massachusetts keenly. The Federalists had taken a calculated risk by rushing the Constitution through in Pennsylvania, provoking charges of foul play. But that ratification, along with the equally quick ratifications by Delaware (the first state to ratify), New Jersey, Georgia, and Connecticut, had given the Constitution the momentum the Federalists had hoped for.

The Massachusetts convention posed the greatest threat to the adoption of the Constitution up to that time.[15] The Anti-Federalists there, especially

Figure 7.3
Artist unknown. *The Federal Pillars.* Woodcut, 1 March 1788. From January to August 1788, to mark each state's ratification of the Constitution, *The Massachusetts Centinel* published a small allegorical illustration: an upright column emblazoned with the state's name and the prediction "It will yet rise." This woodcut accompanied a printing of the Federalist anthem "The Raising" (also called "The New Roof"), by Francis Hopkinson.

in western Massachusetts, the seedbed of Shays's Rebellion, were determined and organized. A vote to reject the Constitution early in the ratification contest, especially by a large and important state, could have ended the Federalists' hopes then and there. But the elections for the ratifying convention gave both groups cause for celebration and concern. The Anti-Federalists apparently had a majority, but their potential leaders, Elbridge Gerry and James Warren, were humiliated at the polls. This lack of leadership hobbled the Anti-Federal delegates. Two other potential leaders, John Hancock and Samuel Adams, did not fill the vacuum left by the defeat of Gerry and Warren. Governor Hancock chose to wait and see what the prevailing currents were before committing himself; Adams was largely silent during the convention.

The Federalists had learned from Pennsylvania's controversial ratification. They no longer demanded that the conventions accept or reject the Constitution as it was. Instead, in Massachusetts they took an inspired gamble. They agreed that the convention should propose amendments to the Constitution but suggested that these be offered as recommendations attached to a vote for ratification, rather than as conditions of ratification. This formula was the salvation of the Constitution, swaying undecided votes in many states and reconciling moderate Anti-Federalists to ratification, especially when Federalist leaders pledged to support amendments when the new national legislature should convene. Just as important was the Anti-Federal delegates' reaction to the close vote in the Massachusetts convention—187 to 168 for ratification. The defeated delegates' gracious pledges to accept the decision of the convention and to work for peaceful implementation of the Constitution and its subsequent amendment eliminated concerns that the divisions spawned by the ratification controversy were irreparable.

Figure 7.4
Paul Sandby after Governor
Thomas Pownall. *A View in
Hudson's River of Pakepsey & the
Catts-Kill Mountains.* Line engraving, 1761. The New York
ratifying convention met at Van
Kleck's tavern.

Massachusetts became the sixth state to ratify the new Constitution on 6 February 1788 (Figure 7.3). Aware that they were outnumbered at the New Hampshire convention, the Federalists secured an adjournment to allow pressure for ratification to build.[16] By the end of May, Maryland ratified unconditionally, and South Carolina followed Massachusetts' example of ratifying with recommendatory amendments. June marked the climax of the ratification process; with eight states having adopted the Constitution, three states' conventions were in session at once: New Hampshire's reconvened in Concord on 18 June; Virginia's met at Richmond on 2 June; and New York's began in Poughkeepsie (Figure 7.4) on 17 June.

Throughout the spring, Anti-Federalists had attempted to organize across state lines, but their efforts were too little, too late. In their letters to each other in June, George Mason and Robert Yates gingerly explored the possibility that New York and Virginia might both reject the Constitution and demand its amendment before they consented to ratify; the terms of the required amendments, Yates and Mason hoped, could be drawn up in a manner agreeable to both states' Anti-Federalists. Had this happened, the course of American history might have been different. But in his letter to Mason of 21 June Yates conceded that the chance was past:

> We are happy to find that your Sentiments with respect to the Amendments correspond so nearly with ours, and that they stand on the Broad

Figure 7.5
Charles Balthazar Julien Fevret de Saint-Mémin. *View of Richmond.* Etching with wash, 1804–1807.

Basis of securing the Rights and equally promoting the Happiness of every Citizen in the Union . . .

Such has been the Spirit and Independency of the Yeomanry of this State and the Danger they apprehend from an Adoption of this Constitution, that by a Majority of at least two to one, their Sentiments at the Election are truly brought into the Representation. We have therefore the fullest Reliance that neither Sophistry Fear nor Influence will effect any Change in their Sentiments.

We would willingly open a Correspondence with your Convention but the doubtful Chance of your obtaining a Majority—and the possibility that we will compleat our Determinations before we could avail ourselves of your Advice, are the Reasons that we pursue the present Mode of Correspondence.[17]

Yates could only offer cheering news from New York and sympathy. And, though he did not know it, his consoling letter was already too late. On the day he wrote to Mason, New Hampshire ratified the Constitution and proposed recommendatory amendments.[18] As the ninth state to ratify, New Hampshire put the Constitution into effect as the new form of government of the United States. By the time Mason received the letter, Virginia had ratified as well, also with recommendatory amendments, though the delegates were unaware of New Hampshire's action at the time.

Figure 7.6
Lawrence Sully. Portrait of
Patrick Henry. Watercolor on
ivory, 1795. This is the only
known life portrait of the famed
orator and foe of the Constitution.

The Virginia convention was one of the classic political battles of American history.[19] Meeting in Richmond (Figure 7.5), the delegates were aware that the Anti-Federalists, led by Patrick Henry (Figure 7.6) and George Mason with able support from younger delegates such as James Monroe, were in the majority. But this majority was soft, and the Federalists knew that they might be able to sway enough wavering delegates to win ratification. Led by James Madison, Edmund Pendleton, and George Wythe, and drawing on emerging political talents such as the young John Marshall, the Virginia Federalists scored early triumphs with the election of Pendleton as the convention's president and Wythe as the president of the Committee of the Whole. Pendleton, a venerable figure in Virginia politics and the perennial president or chairman of every state convention since the beginning of the Revolution, handed the Federalists another victory as well. When Patrick Henry tried to attack the illegality of the Convention's actions and the illegitimacy of the Constitution, Pendleton ruled from the chair that the Confederation Congress, the state legislatures, and the voters had all accepted the Constitution as at least worthy of discussion, and the convention was obliged to limit debate to consideration of the merits and defects of the new charter. Two more victories for the Federal delegates were the last-minute announcement by Governor Edmund Randolph that he now backed the Constitution and the adoption of a rule requiring clause-by-clause debate. Randolph was particularly effective at exposing the exaggerations and inconsistencies of Anti-Federal objections. The clause-by-clause form of debate was designed to restrain the oratorical flights of Patrick Henry, who was all too apt to engage in passionate wholesale denunciations of the Constitution that might stampede his fellow delegates.

Essentially, the Virginia convention was a forensic duel between Patrick Henry, esteemed as the greatest orator of the day, and James Madison, who impressed fellow delegates on both sides with his logic and information. As a speaker, Madison was no match for the flamboyant Henry, but the clause-by-clause discussion enabled him to draw on his matchless familiarity with the Constitution and the debates of the Federal Convention. Further, it enabled him to speak in the manner that displayed his principal talents—the patient, reasoned elucidation of complex matters and the presentation of explosive issues in orderly, logical fashion. Driving himself mercilessly to answer Henry, Madison pushed his frail health and weak voice up to and beyond their limits, allowing his friends to spell him when necessary.

At last the Federalists scented victory. Henry and Mason showed signs of "despair," as Madison reported,[20] and the Federal delegates then brought forward the idea of recommendatory amendments to accompany a vote for ratification. Henry, Mason, and their colleagues sat, despondent and shaken, as the convention voted, eighty-nine to seventy-nine, for George Wythe's motion to ratify the Constitution in this form. Not even the Federalists' concession of appointing all the leading Anti-Federal delegates to frame the set of recommended amendments could relieve their gloom. Despite earlier veiled threats of military resistance to the implementation of the Constitution, Henry and Mason and their allies agreed, as had Anti-Federalists in every other state convention, to abide by the result.

New York at first seemed to be another matter.[21] From the beginning, the New York Anti-Federalists were sure of their margin of victory. Led by Alexander Hamilton, John Jay, Robert R. Livingston, Philip Schuyler, and James Duane, the Federalists agreed to delay the call for an election until after the beginning of 1788. Once more, both Federalists and Anti-Federalists saw advantages in delaying New York's convention. Federalists hoped that the accumulating ratifications of other states would impress New York's delegates with the inevitability of the Constitution; Anti-Federalists hoped that another large state, most likely Virginia, would reject the Constitution and share the responsibility for blocking its adoption.[22]

Although New York politicians on both sides of the issue were surprisingly quiet in the weeks before the convention, the Anti-Federalists were confident,[23] for they had swept the elections for delegates to the ratifying convention in nearly every county. Governor George Clinton (Figure 7.7) led the Anti-Federalists and presided over the convention as well. In re-

Figure 7.7
Charles Balthazar Julien Fevret
de Saint-Mémin. Portrait of
Governor George Clinton. Black
and white crayon on paper with
wash, ca. 1797–98.

sponse the Federalists adopted a grim and brilliant strategy of delay, confident that New Hampshire and Virginia would both ratify the Constitution. They persuaded the majority to agree to clause-by-clause debate, which allowed the Anti-Federalists to air all arguments against the new charter and the Federalists to answer with arguments of their own while they awaited the expected good news from New Hampshire and Virginia. New Hampshire's ratification had little effect on the New York Anti-Federalists, but Virginia's vote for the Constitution left them badly shaken. The Federalists then changed their tactics and remained silent, allowing the Anti-Federalists to continue to speak against the Constitution and to get used to their defeats in the other two states. Then they put the issue bluntly: The Constitution was already in effect, with ten states having ratified it; it remained for the New York convention to decide whether New York would join the other states under the new government or not.

The Anti-Federalists insisted that the Constitution had to be amended before they would accept it, but the Federalists insisted that neither the other states nor Congress would accept a conditional ratification or previous amendments. Motions for conditional ratification and for previous amendments got nowhere; the Federalists remained obdurate, allowing the pressure of the other ten ratifications to build. Finally, Melancton Smith, the Anti-Federal floor leader and one of the convention's ablest speakers against the new charter, conceded defeat. He accepted a compromise proposed by John Jay, whose tact and behind-the-scenes maneuvering were at least as responsible as the combative eloquence of Alexander Hamilton for the Federalist victory in New York.[24] On 26 July the Convention voted narrowly to accept the Constitution and a list of recommendatory amendments drawn up by the Anti-Federal delegates (Figure 7.8). John Jay prepared the other element of the compromise—a circular letter to the other states suggesting a second general convention to consider amendments—which the convention adopted unanimously.

Although the New York call for a second convention alarmed Madison and other Federalists outside the state, the New York Federalists realized that it was not as bad as a formal resolution demanding a second convention as a condition of ratification would have been. In addition, thanks to the pledges of moderate Federalists in Virginia, Massachusetts, New York, and other states to work for amendments in the first Congress to meet under the Constitution, a second convention probably would not take place.[25]

Thus by August 1788 the Constitution had won the support of eleven states, including all four critical states. Rhode Island had refused even to call a convention, instead submitting the new Constitution to its town meetings; because Federalists boycotted these meetings in protest, the ten-to-one margin by which the towns rejected the Constitution was even more lopsided than the actual divisions in the state.[26] In North Carolina the Anti-Federalists commanded an unbreakable majority in the ratifying convention.[27] Led by Willie Jones, the Patrick Henry of his state, the North Carolina convention voted 185–84 not to accept the Constitution. Instead, they passed a set of amendments that had to be adopted before they would consent to ratify the new charter (Figure 7.9). Despite these defeats, supporters of the Constitution could look with satisfaction upon the results of their efforts. The Articles of Confederation had been replaced with a new, stronger, and more energetic government that would preserve the Union, safeguard the rights of private property, and make the United States worthy of respect at home and abroad. The "wayward sisters," as North Carolina and Rhode Island were called, could not long remain outside the Union.

The Federalists' preferred form of celebration was the ceremonial parade,[28] in which usually a ship (Figure 7.10), representing the Union, was towed in the place of honor. The New York parade included "the Federal Ship *Union*," followed by a frigate dubbed the *Hamilton,* honoring the most visible and eloquent advocate of the Constitution (Figure 7.11). In addition,

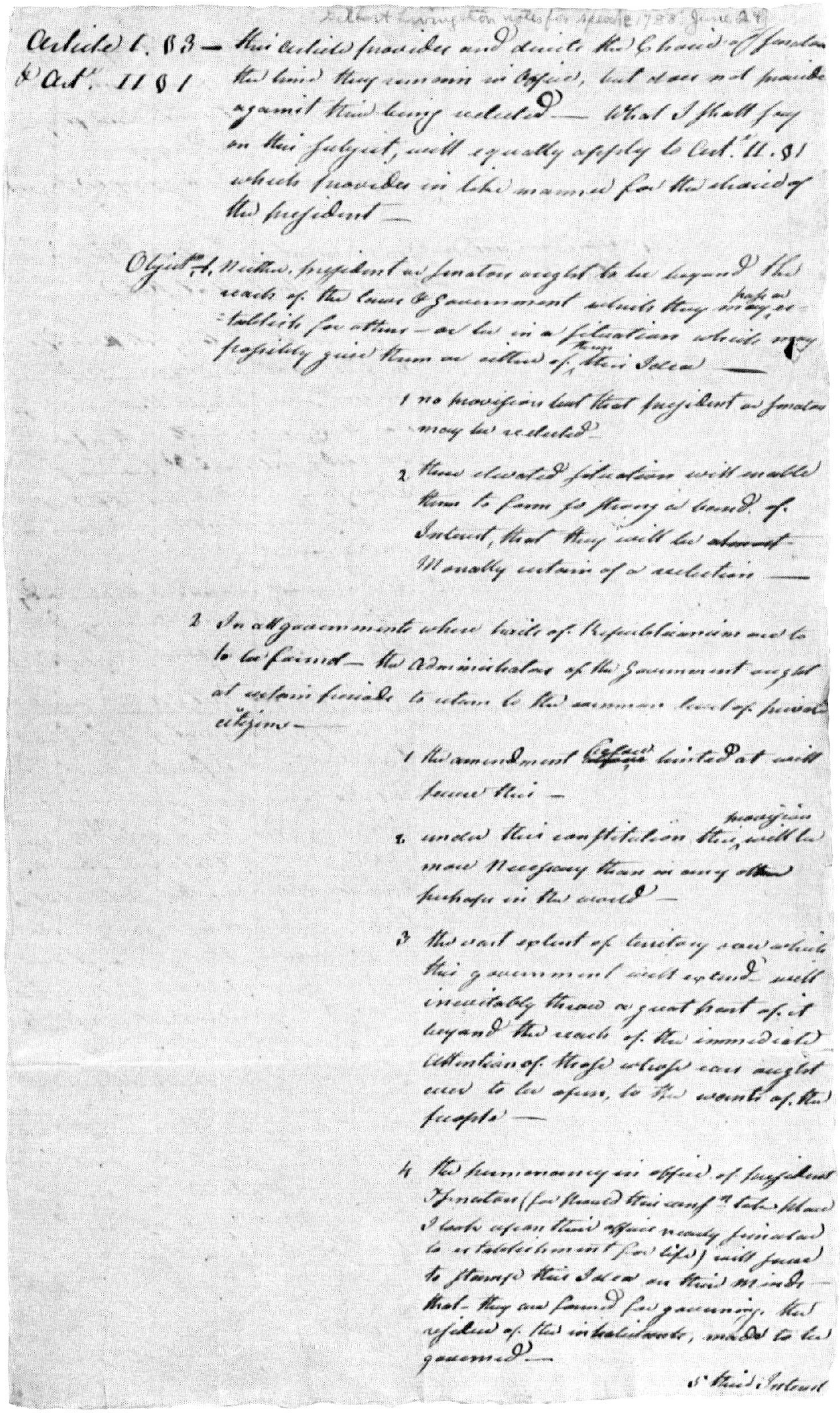

Figure 7.8
Gilbert Livingston. "Notes for a speech," 24 June 1788. The notes of Livingston, a delegate from Dutchess County, are the most complete surviving record of the New York ratifying convention.

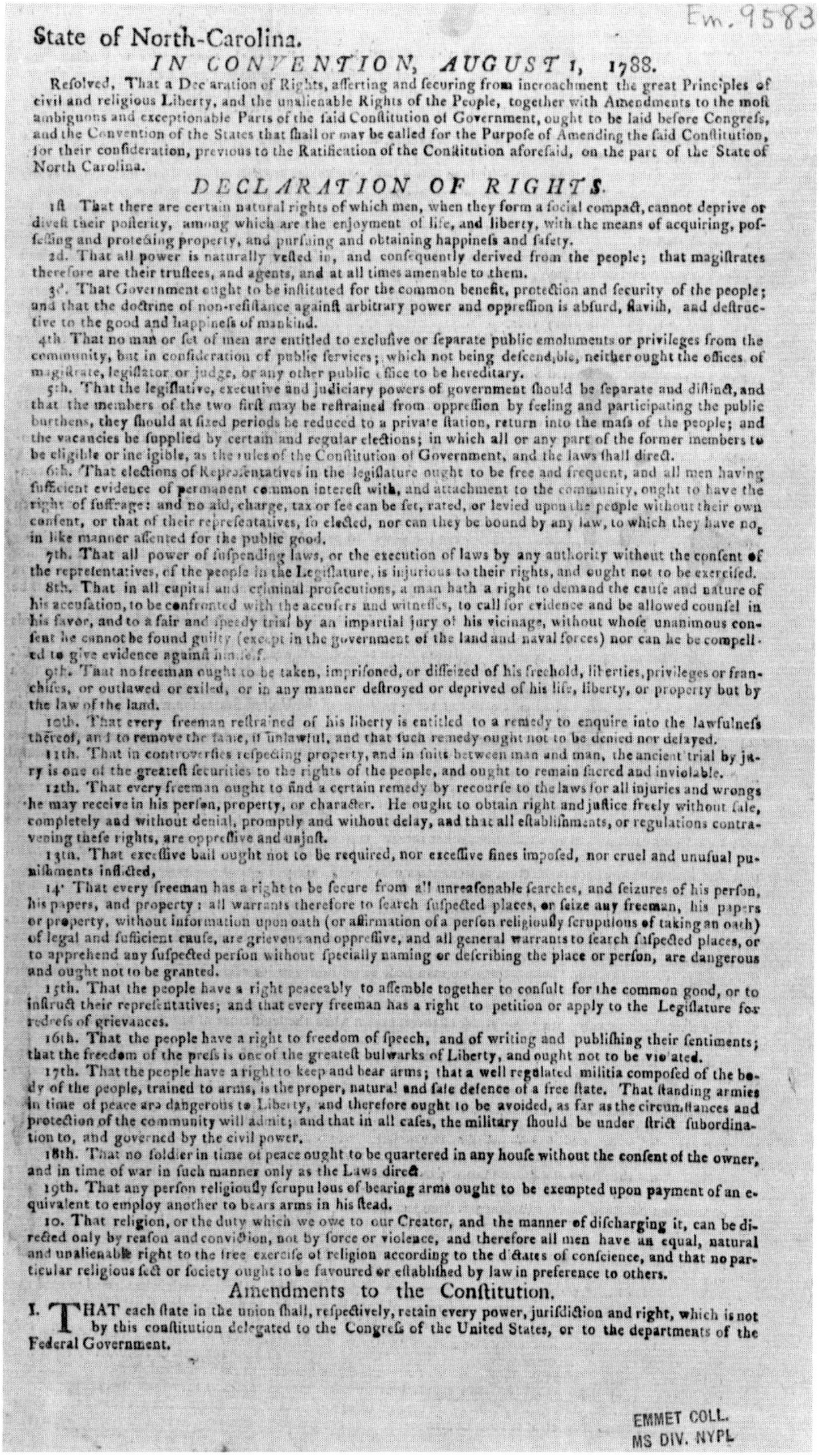

Figure 7.9
North Carolina's call for a Declaration of Rights. Broadside,
1788.

State of North-Carolina.

IN CONVENTION, AUGUST 1, 1788.

Resolved, That a Declaration of Rights, asserting and securing from incroachment the great Principles of civil and religious Liberty, and the unalienable Rights of the People, together with Amendments to the most ambiguous and exceptionable Parts of the said Constitution of Government, ought to be laid before Congress, and the Convention of the States that shall or may be called for the Purpose of Amending the said Constitution, for their consideration, previous to the Ratification of the Constitution aforesaid, on the part of the State of North Carolina.

DECLARATION OF RIGHTS.

1st That there are certain natural rights of which men, when they form a social compact, cannot deprive or divest their posterity, among which are the enjoyment of life, and liberty, with the means of acquiring, possessing and protecting property, and pursuing and obtaining happiness and safety.

2d. That all power is naturally vested in, and consequently derived from the people; that magistrates therefore are their trustees, and agents, and at all times amenable to them.

3d. That Government ought to be instituted for the common benefit, protection and security of the people; and that the doctrine of non-resistance against arbitrary power and oppression is absurd, slavish, and destructive to the good and happiness of mankind.

4th. That no man or set of men are entitled to exclusive or separate public emoluments or privileges from the community, but in consideration of public services; which not being descendible, neither ought the offices of magistrate, legislator or judge, or any other public office to be hereditary.

5th. That the legislative, executive and judiciary powers of government should be separate and distinct, and that the members of the two first may be restrained from oppression by feeling and participating the public burthens, they should at fixed periods be reduced to a private station, return into the mass of the people; and the vacancies be supplied by certain and regular elections; in which all or any part of the former members to be eligible or ineligible, as the rules of the Constitution of Government, and the laws shall direct.

6th. That elections of Representatives in the legislature ought to be free and frequent, and all men having sufficient evidence of permanent common interest with, and attachment to the community, ought to have the right of suffrage: and no aid, charge, tax or fee can be set, rated, or levied upon the people without their own consent, or that of their representatives, so elected, nor can they be bound by any law, to which they have not, in like manner assented for the public good.

7th. That all power of suspending laws, or the execution of laws by any authority without the consent of the representatives, of the people in the Legislature, is injurious to their rights, and ought not to be exercised.

8th. That in all capital and criminal prosecutions, a man hath a right to demand the cause and nature of his accusation, to be confronted with the accusers and witnesses, to call for evidence and be allowed counsel in his favor, and to a fair and speedy trial by an impartial jury of his vicinage, without whose unanimous consent he cannot be found guilty (except in the government of the land and naval forces) nor can he be compelled to give evidence against himself.

9th. That no freeman ought to be taken, imprisoned, or disseized of his freehold, liberties, privileges or franchises, or outlawed or exiled, or in any manner destroyed or deprived of his life, liberty, or property but by the law of the land.

10th. That every freeman restrained of his liberty is entitled to a remedy to enquire into the lawfulness thereof, and to remove the same, if unlawful, and that such remedy ought not to be denied nor delayed.

11th. That in controversies respecting property, and in suits between man and man, the ancient trial by jury is one of the greatest securities to the rights of the people, and ought to remain sacred and inviolable.

12th. That every freeman ought to find a certain remedy by recourse to the laws for all injuries and wrongs he may receive in his person, property, or character. He ought to obtain right and justice freely without sale, completely and without denial, promptly and without delay, and that all establishments, or regulations contravening these rights, are oppressive and unjust.

13th. That excessive bail ought not to be required, nor excessive fines imposed, nor cruel and unusual punishments inflicted.

14. That every freeman has a right to be secure from all unreasonable searches, and seizures of his person, his papers, and property: all warrants therefore to search suspected places, or seize any freeman, his papers or property, without information upon oath (or affirmation of a person religiously scrupulous of taking an oath) of legal and sufficient cause, are grievous and oppressive, and all general warrants to search suspected places, or to apprehend any suspected person without specially naming or describing the place or person, are dangerous and ought not to be granted.

15th. That the people have a right peaceably to assemble together to consult for the common good, or to instruct their representatives; and that every freeman has a right to petition or apply to the Legislature for redress of grievances.

16th. That the people have a right to freedom of speech, and of writing and publishing their sentiments; that the freedom of the press is one of the greatest bulwarks of Liberty, and ought not to be violated.

17th. That the people have a right to keep and bear arms; that a well regulated militia composed of the body of the people, trained to arms, is the proper, natural and safe defence of a free state. That standing armies in time of peace are dangerous to Liberty, and therefore ought to be avoided, as far as the circumstances and protection of the community will admit; and that in all cases, the military should be under strict subordination to, and governed by the civil power.

18th. That no soldier in time of peace ought to be quartered in any house without the consent of the owner, and in time of war in such manner only as the Laws direct.

19th. That any person religiously scrupulous of bearing arms ought to be exempted upon payment of an equivalent to employ another to bear arms in his stead.

10. That religion, or the duty which we owe to our Creator, and the manner of discharging it, can be directed only by reason and conviction, not by force or violence, and therefore all men have an equal, natural and unalienable right to the free exercise of religion according to the dictates of conscience, and that no particular religious sect or society ought to be favoured or established by law in preference to others.

Amendments to the Constitution.

I. THAT each state in the union shall, respectively, retain every power, jurisdiction and right, which is not by this constitution delegated to the Congress of the United States, or to the departments of the Federal Government.

Figure 7.10
Artist unknown. *The federal Ship Union.* Woodcut in *American Museum,* vol. IV (Philadelphia: Mathew Carey, 1788).

Figure 7.11
Artist unknown. *The Federal Procession in New York, 1788.* Engraving in Martha J. Lamb, *History of the City of New York* (New York: A. S. Barnes & Co., 1877).

ceremonial arches were built in New York (Plate XVII) and Philadelphia (Figure 7.12), and bonfires in every city and most towns welcomed the new Constitution.

The Argument over the Constitution

Losers generally get a bad press, for the first histories of a conflict are usually written by the winners, who seek to legitimate their triumph and make it appear inevitable. The Anti-Federalists may well be the unluckiest losers in our history. Not until this century was their opposition to the Constitution taken seriously and their right to be counted among the framers of the Constitution firmly established.[29] Further, the Anti-Federal-

Figure 7.12
In Honour of American Beer and Cyder. In *American Museum,* vol. IV (Philadelphia: Mathew Carey, 1788). Philadelphia saluted the Constitution on 4 July 1788 with a large parade and lavish ceremony. More than 17,000 citizens assembled peacefully on the green behind the State House to enjoy "those invaluable FEDERAL liquors," beer and cider.

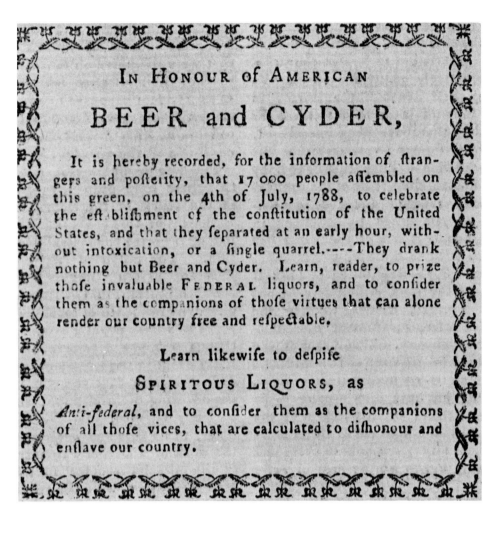

In Honour of American
BEER and CYDER,

It is hereby recorded, for the information of ſtrangers and poſterity, that 17 000 people aſſembled on this green, on the 4th of July, 1788, to celebrate the eſtabliſhment of the conſtitution of the United States, and that they ſeparated at an early hour, without intoxication, or a ſingle quarrel.----They drank nothing but Beer and Cyder. Learn, reader, to prize thoſe invaluable FEDERAL liquors, and to conſider them as the companions of thoſe virtues that can alone render our country free and reſpectable.

Learn likewiſe to deſpiſe

SPIRITOUS LIQUORS, as

Anti-federal, and to conſider them as the companions of all thoſe vices, that are calculated to diſhonour and enſlave our country.

ists' distrust of large and energetic government and their concern for individual rights are echoed in modern political controversy, as Herbert Storing's analysis demonstrates:

> The Anti-Federalists were committed to both union and the states; to both the great American republic and the small, self-governing community; to both commerce and civic virtue; to both private gain and the public good. At its best, Anti-Federal thought explores these tensions and points to the need for any significant American political thought to confront them; for they were not resolved by the Constitution but are inherent in the principles and traditions of American political life.[30]

The ratification controversy was a war of words as well as of votes. As the Constitution came before the public and the state legislatures voted to call ratifying conventions, writers for and against the work of the Federal Convention poured forth newspaper essays, broadsides, and pamphlets extolling or denouncing the new charter. Even before the close of the Convention, Thomas Fitzsimons, a Pennsylvania delegate and powerful figure in the Federal camp, commissioned young Noah Webster to write in support of the Constitution, appealing to Webster's patriotism and vanity. Already known as a versatile writer and polemicist, Webster duly produced his essay within the month (Figure 7.13).[31]

The short periodical essay or series of essays was the preferred form of eighteenth-century literary expression on both sides of the Atlantic.[32] By late 1787, when the Constitution was the focus of American political debate, the essay was the principal means of airing ideas and arguments about political issues. Most of those who signed their pamphlets and essays were delegates to the Federal Convention who had refused to sign the Constitution. Edmund Randolph (Figure 7.14), Robert Yates, John Lansing, Jr., Luther Martin, Elbridge Gerry, George Mason, and John Francis Mercer all published letters, essays, or reports giving their reasons for opposing the Constitution. Most essays, however, were published under pen names.[33]

Writers generally chose pen names to communicate, either directly or subliminally, another layer of meaning in addition to their formal arguments. Several pamphleteers used simple pseudonyms requiring little background or learning for their point to get across. For example, the most important Anti-Federal pamphleteer styled himself "the Federal Farmer." Others called themselves "An Old Soldier," "A Federalist," "A Federal Republican," "An American," "A Watchman," "A Son of Liberty," "A Countryman," and any number of "Farmers." Still others took the names of the great leaders of the English House of Commons in the seventeenth century—such as "Hampden" and "Sydney" (also spelled "Sidney")—to remind their readers of these heroes' battles against the tyranny of the Stuart kings. Most writers, however, preferred to use pseudonyms from classical Greece and the Roman Republic, a frequent and convenient source being Plutarch's *Lives*. Even when they made up their own classical-sounding pen names, such as "Republicus," "Brutus, Jr.," "Philadelphiensis," and even "Aristocritis," they sought to preserve the flavor and connotations of Republican Rome.[34]

Herbert Storing, the leading student of Anti-Federal thought, reminds us that the purposes of pseudonyms in this period were different from what we would expect today:

> A pseudonym was used not merely or even mainly to enable the author to conceal his opinion or to protect himself; it was a convention aimed at directing attention at the arguments rather than at personalities. A public figure might well declare his own position in a speech or letter and go on to publish a longer, more analytical piece over a pseudonym.[35]

Identifying the authors of these pseudonymous publications is difficult or impossible today.[36] Thus although we now know that Mercy Otis Warren rather than Elbridge Gerry wrote the *Observations on the New Constitution . . . by a Columbian Patriot,* we know only that Richard Henry Lee probably did

Figure 7.13
[Noah Webster.] *A Examination into the Leading Principles of the Federal Constitution* . . . (Philadelphia: Prichard & Hall, 1787). This copy of the pamphlet was Webster's own.

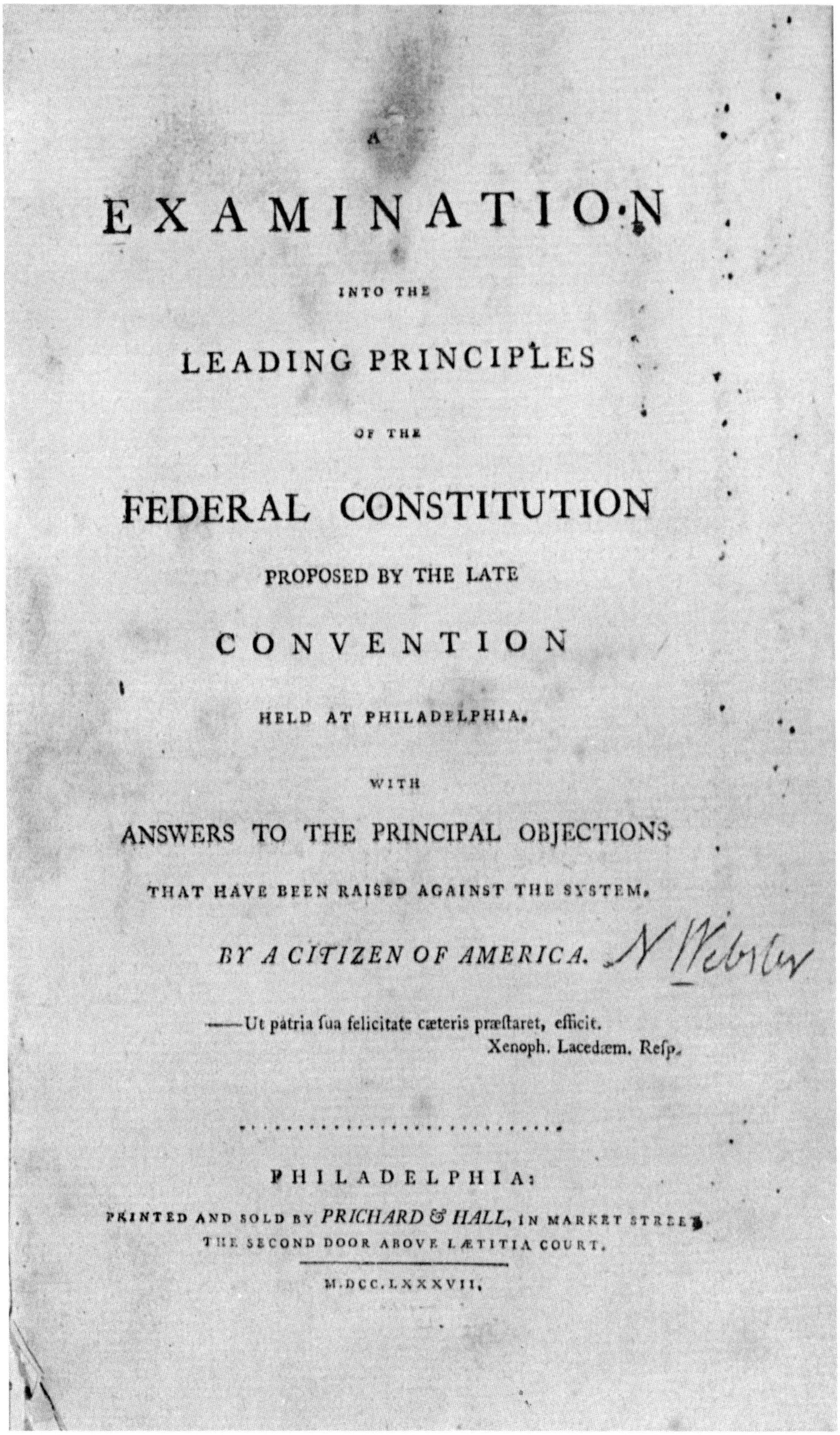

A

EXAMINATION

INTO THE

LEADING PRINCIPLES

OF THE

FEDERAL CONSTITUTION

PROPOSED BY THE LATE

CONVENTION

HELD AT PHILADELPHIA.

WITH

ANSWERS TO THE PRINCIPAL OBJECTIONS

THAT HAVE BEEN RAISED AGAINST THE SYSTEM.

BY A CITIZEN OF AMERICA. N Webster

——Ut pátria ſua felicitate cæteris præſtaret, efficit.
Xenoph. Lacedæm. Reſp.

PHILADELPHIA:

PRINTED AND SOLD BY *PRICHARD & HALL*, IN MARKET STREET,
THE SECOND DOOR ABOVE LÆTITIA COURT.

M.DCC.LXXXVII.

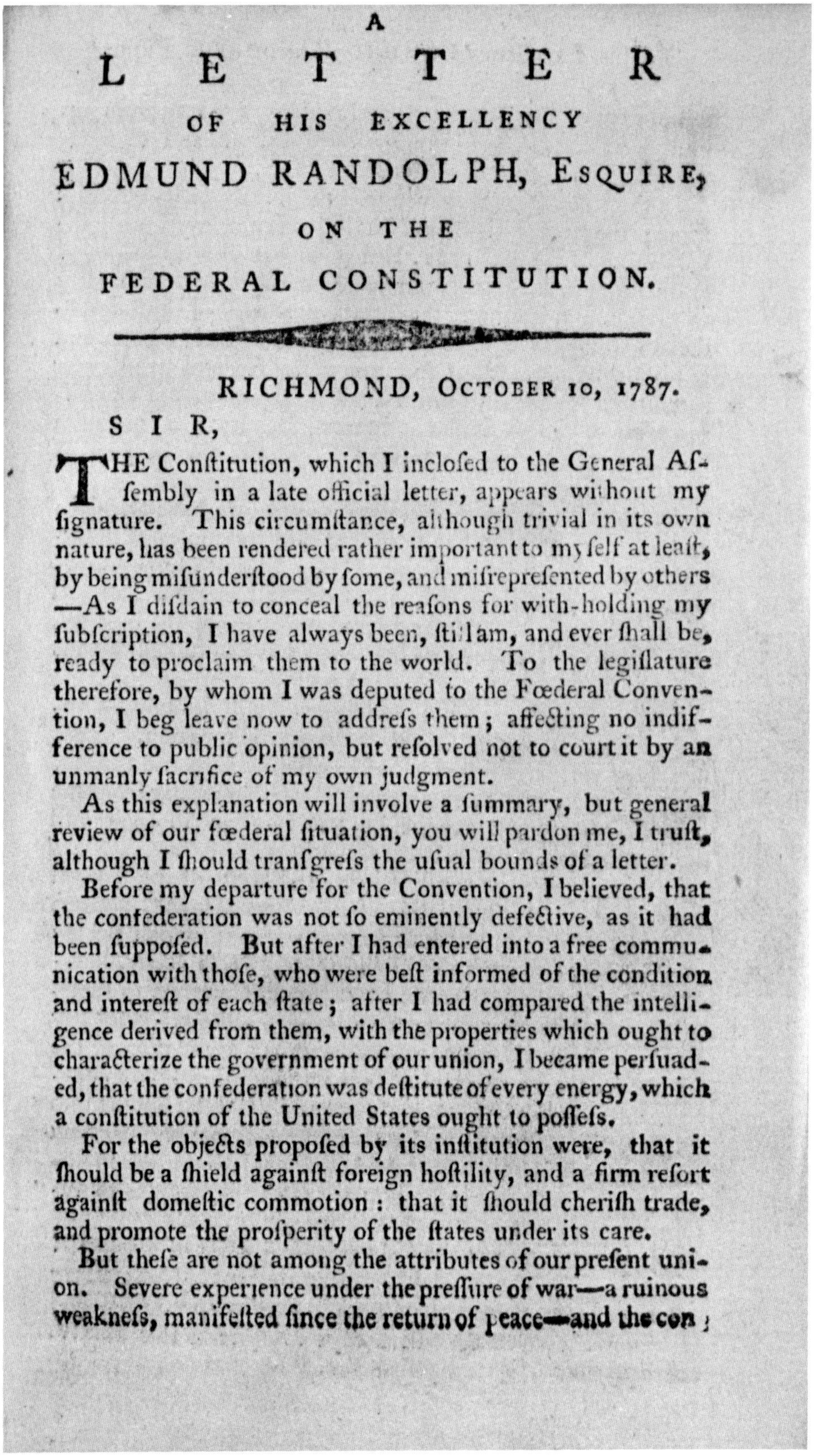

Figure 7.14
A Letter of His Excellency Edmund Randolph, Esquire, on the Federal Constitution (Richmond: A. Davis, 1787).

A LETTER

OF HIS EXCELLENCY

EDMUND RANDOLPH, Esquire,

ON THE

FEDERAL CONSTITUTION.

RICHMOND, October 10, 1787.

S I R,

THE Conftitution, which I inclofed to the General Affembly in a late official letter, appears without my fignature. This circumftance, although trivial in its own nature, has been rendered rather important to myfelf at leaft, by being mifunderftood by fome, and mifreprefented by others —As I difdain to conceal the reafons for with-holding my fubfcription, I have always been, ftill am, and ever fhall be, ready to proclaim them to the world. To the legiflature therefore, by whom I was deputed to the Fœderal Convention, I beg leave now to addrefs them; affecting no indifference to public opinion, but refolved not to court it by an unmanly facrifice of my own judgment.

As this explanation will involve a fummary, but general review of our fœderal fituation, you will pardon me, I truft, although I fhould tranfgrefs the ufual bounds of a letter.

Before my departure for the Convention, I believed, that the confederation was not fo eminently defective, as it had been fuppofed. But after I had entered into a free communication with thofe, who were beft informed of the condition and intereft of each ftate; after I had compared the intelligence derived from them, with the properties which ought to characterize the government of our union, I became perfuaded, that the confederation was deftitute of every energy, which a conftitution of the United States ought to poffefs.

For the objects propofed by its inftitution were, that it fhould be a fhield againft foreign hoftility, and a firm refort againft domeftic commotion: that it fhould cherifh trade, and promote the profperity of the ftates under its care.

But thefe are not among the attributes of our prefent union. Severe experience under the preffure of war—a ruinous weaknefs, manifefted fince the return of peace—and the con not write as the Federal Farmer, George Clinton did not write the *Cato* letters, and Alexander Hamilton did not write the *Caesar* essays.[37] Although we may find this lack of information frustrating, Storing reminds us that "these eighteenth-century Americans, while sharing with the rest of humankind a curiosity and disposition to gossip about personalities, really did think that what counts most (or at least what ought to count most) in political debate is what is said rather than who said it."[38]

The arguments in the pamphlets on both sides of the ratification controversy range from well-reasoned and judicious presentation of political issues to unbridled mudslinging. A noteworthy example of the latter is Oliver Ellsworth's pseudonymous *Landholder* series.[39] Ellsworth directed much of his rhetoric against Luther Martin and Elbridge Gerry, two non-signing delegates to the Federal Convention who published major pamphlets explaining their opposition to the Constitution.

The Federalist (discussed extensively later in this chapter) tends to overshadow other major pamphlets for and against the Constitution because of its detailed exposition and commentary. Its authors deliberately chose this method in order to make their contribution distinct from most other Federal and Anti-Federal essays and to produce a "debater's handbook" for Federalists in the Virginia and New York ratifying conventions. Because *The Federalist* is far longer and more detailed than any other contribution to the debate over ratification, it was not generally popular with contemporary readers, who preferred shorter works. Several of these warrant mention.[40]

On the Federalist side, the most popular and widely read pamphlet was John Jay's *Address to the People of the State of New-York . . .* (Figure 7.15),[41] a modest essay in which Jay presented the arguments that his illnesses prevented him from making in *The Federalist*. Jay emphasized the defects of the Articles of Confederation and the resulting weaknesses of the United States, the value of the Union and the desirability of preserving it, the absence in the Constitution of any threat to personal liberty, and the many flaws in Anti-Federal demands for a second general convention. Jay stressed the critical nature of the choice before the American people not merely for their own future, but for the future of liberty and republican government everywhere. His peroration typifies the spirit of the Federalists in its most generous and reasonable form:

> Consider then, how weighty and how many considerations advise and persuade the people of America to remain in the safe and easy path of Union; to continue to move and act as they hitherto have done, as a *band of brothers;* to have confidence in themselves and in one another; and since all cannot see with the same eyes, at least to give the Constitution a fair trial, and to mend it as time, occasion and experience may dictate. It would little become us to verify the predictions of those who ventured to prophesy, that *peace,* instead of blessing us with happiness and tranquility, would serve only as the signal for factions, discords and civil contentions to rage in our land, and overwhelm it with misery and distress.

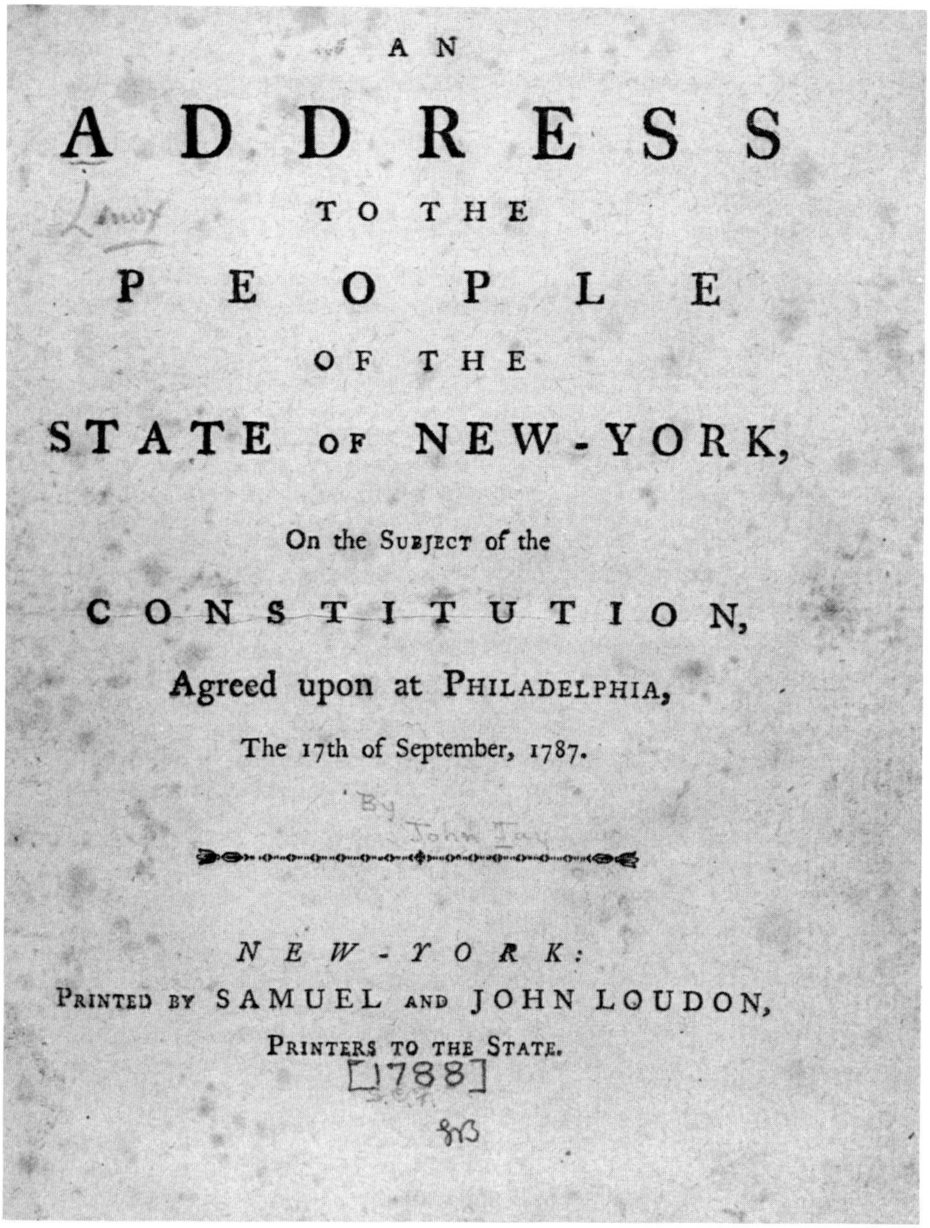
AN
ADDRESS
TO THE
PEOPLE
OF THE
STATE OF NEW-YORK,
On the SUBJECT of the
CONSTITUTION,
Agreed upon at PHILADELPHIA,
The 17th of September, 1787.

NEW-YORK:
PRINTED BY SAMUEL AND JOHN LOUDON,
PRINTERS TO THE STATE.
[1788]

Figure 7.15
[John Jay.] *An Address to the People of the State of New-York, On the Subject of the Constitution . . .* (New York: Samuel and John Loudon, 1788).

Let us also be mindful that the cause of freedom greatly depends on the use we make of the singular opportunities we enjoy of governing ourselves wisely; for if the event should prove, that the people of this country either cannot or will not govern themselves, who will hereafter be advocates for systems, which however charming in theory and prospect, are not reducible to practice? If the people of our nation, instead of consenting to be governed by laws of their own making, and rulers of their own choosing, should let licentiousness, disorder, and confusion reign over them, the minds of men every where, will insensibly become alienated from republican forms, and prepared to prefer and acquiesce in Governments, which, though less friendly to liberty, afford more peace and security.[42]

Several Anti-Federal pamphlets performed the same function that Jay's anonymous *Address* served for the Federal side. Of these, the most reasonable and sophisticated were the two pamphlets produced by the Federal Farmer (Figure 7.16).[43] Printed by Thomas Greenleaf, New York City's leading Anti-Federal printer, they were distributed throughout the United States and extracts were reprinted in a few newspapers. The Federal Farmer is the only Anti-Federal writer referred to by *The Federalist*.[44]

The Federal Farmer was typical in his presentation of the Anti-Federal case. First, he stressed the need for calm and unhurried deliberation over the proposed Constitution, attacking the Federalists' demands for quick adoption. He rejected the Federalists' assertions that the ills besetting the United States were the direct result of the flaws of the Articles of Confederation and concluded that, because the Articles were not the source of American problems, there was no need to replace them with the Constitution.

The Federal Farmer's major substantive argument against the Constitution was that the states could not be consolidated into one entire government on free principles. Spurning the Federalists' claim that the Constitution would in fact establish an energetic federal government rather than a national government, the Federal Farmer maintained, citing Montesquieu and other eminent political thinkers of the period, that the size of the United States, the resulting diversity of interests, customs, and habits among its citizens, and the inability of the general government to enforce its laws in outlying areas would require a resort to military force, which would lead to the establishment of a despotism.

The Federal Farmer also criticized the mode of representation of the people and states in Congress. Adopting the traditional division of society into three orders or classes—monarchy, aristocracy, and democracy—the Federal Farmer claimed that the House of Representatives was too small to represent the aristocratic and democratic interests and would thus be dominated by the aristocracy. He questioned the new charter's blending of governmental powers, the eligibility of the president for reelection, and the excessive powers of the federal judiciary.

Most important, not just for the Federal Farmer but for all Anti-Federal thought, was the Constitution's omission of a bill of rights. Even moderate Federalists such as Virginia's revered Edmund Pendleton were troubled by the omission of a bill or declaration of rights from a constitution that established a government with the power to exert force directly on the citizens of the United States.[45]

Just as Federalists made constant use of Washington's and Franklin's support of the Constitution, Anti-Federal writers repeatedly invoked the

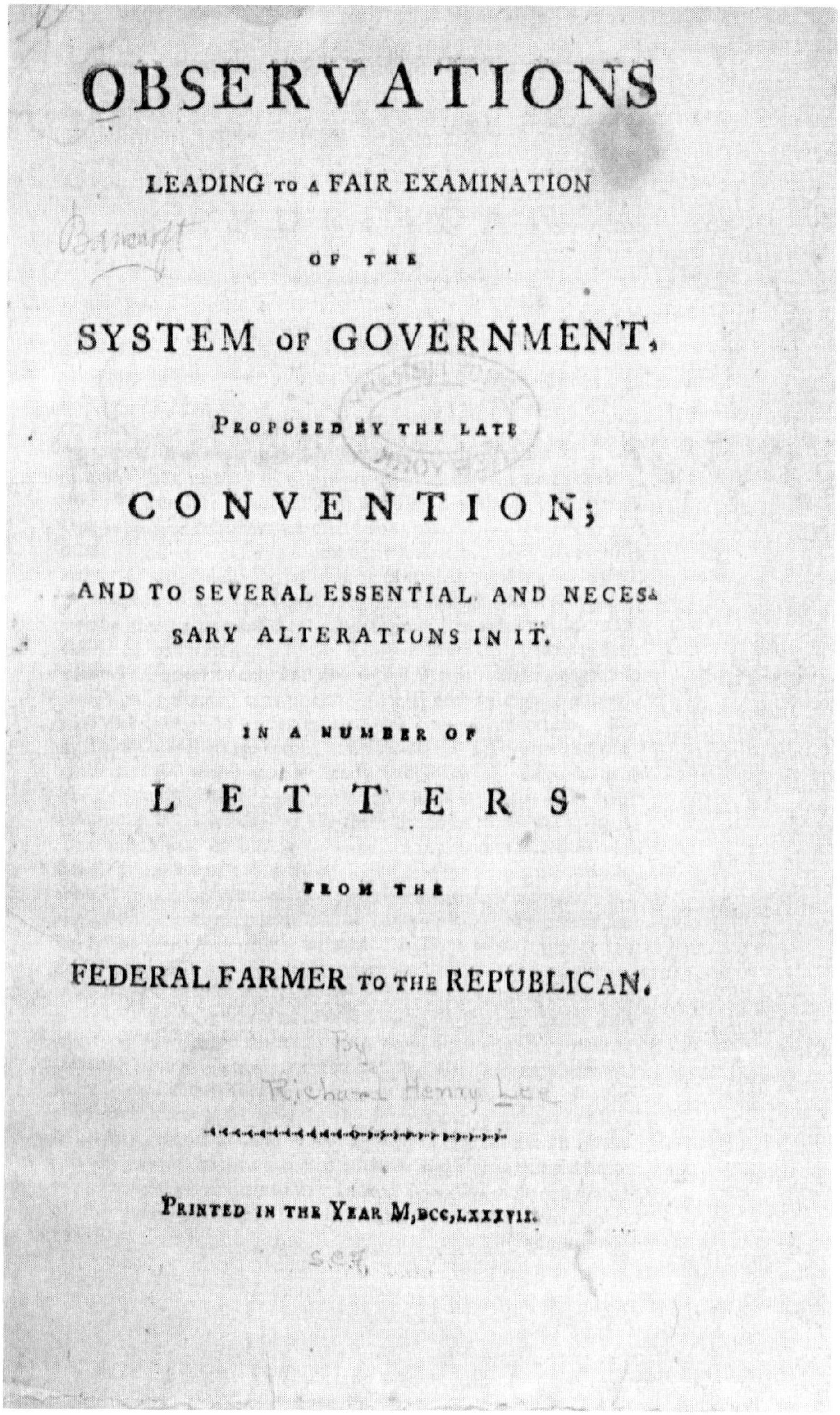

OBSERVATIONS

LEADING TO A FAIR EXAMINATION

OF THE

SYSTEM OF GOVERNMENT,

PROPOSED BY THE LATE

CONVENTION;

AND TO SEVERAL ESSENTIAL AND NECES-
SARY ALTERATIONS IN IT.

IN A NUMBER OF

LETTERS

FROM THE

FEDERAL FARMER TO THE REPUBLICAN.

By

Richard Henry Lee

PRINTED IN THE YEAR M,DCC,LXXXVII.

Figure 7.16
Observations Leading to a Fair Examination of the System of Government . . . in a Number of Letters from the Federal Farmer to the Republican ([New York: Thomas Greenleaf,] 1787).

lack of a bill of rights as their most telling argument against the Constitution. George Mason led off with this point in his *Objections . . .* :

> There is no Declaration of Rights; and the Laws of the general Government being paramount to the Laws and Constitutions of the several States, the Declaration[s] of Rights in the separate States are no security. Nor are the people secured even in the Enjoyment of the Benefits of the common-Law: which stands here upon no other Foundation than it's having been adopted by the respective Acts forming the Constitutions of the several States.[46]

The lack of a bill of rights, as well as other aspects of the Constitution, raised the perennial issue of federal versus national government as the best protector of the people's liberties. The Anti-Federal writers denounced the Constitution as a strange mingling of types of government; because it was neither fish nor fowl, it was destined to fail. Luther Martin (Figure 7.17) refuted the common Federalist objection that the Articles of Confederation did not have a bill of rights by pointing out that the Articles created a purely federal government with no power to violate individual rights. Because the system contemplated by the Constitution would be a new and unstable blending of federal and national principles, he warned, it would endanger liberty, which could be protected only by a truly federal government.[47]

Similarly, in her *Observations on the New Constitution, and on the Foederal and State Conventions, by a Columbian Patriot* (Figure 7.18), Mercy Otis Warren directed withering scorn at the Federalists' arguments justifying the Constitution's blend of federal and national elements:

> The most sagacious advocates for the party have not by fair discussion, and rational argumentation, evinced the necessity of adopting this many-headed monster; of such motley mixture, that its enemies cannot trace a feature of Democratick or Republican extract; nor have its friends the courage to denominate it a Monarchy, an Aristocracy, or an Oligarchy, and the favoured bantling must have passed through the short period of its existence without a name, had not Mr. *Wilson*, in the fertility of his genius, suggested the happy epithet of a *Federal Republic*.[48]

Long thought to be the work of Elbridge Gerry, Mrs. Warren's pamphlet is the only contribution on either side of the debate over the Constitution known to have been written by a woman. Mrs. Warren, the wife of James Warren, a noted Massachusetts politician and Anti-Federalist, was a prolific author in her own right, producing plays and poems emphasizing the roles, rights, and quandaries of women in times of political change and upheaval. Two decades later she published an impressive account, from the Anti-Federal point of view, of the nation's political development under the Constitution.[49]

Many Anti-Federalists were troubled by the proposed federal judicial branch. They had two basic reasons for their distrust of a federal judiciary:

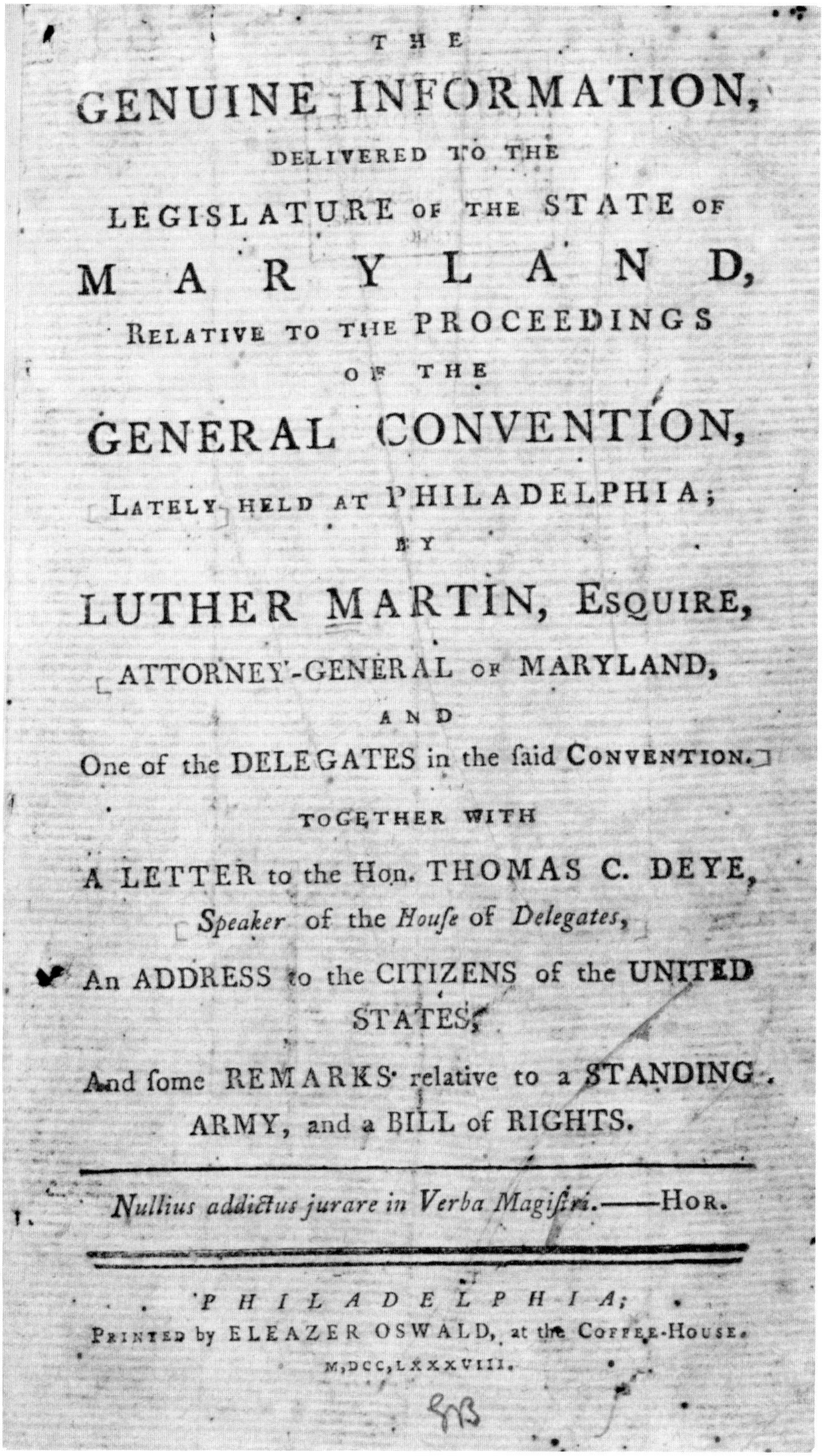

THE
GENUINE INFORMATION,
DELIVERED TO THE
LEGISLATURE OF THE STATE OF
MARYLAND,
RELATIVE TO THE PROCEEDINGS
OF THE
GENERAL CONVENTION,
LATELY HELD AT PHILADELPHIA;
BY
LUTHER MARTIN, ESQUIRE,
ATTORNEY-GENERAL OF MARYLAND,
AND
One of the DELEGATES in the said CONVENTION.
TOGETHER WITH
A LETTER to the Hon. THOMAS C. DEYE,
Speaker of the House of Delegates,
An ADDRESS to the CITIZENS of the UNITED
STATES,
And some REMARKS relative to a STANDING
ARMY, and a BILL of RIGHTS.

Nullius addictus jurare in Verba Magistri.——HOR.

PHILADELPHIA;
PRINTED by ELEAZER OSWALD, at the COFFEE-HOUSE.
M,DCC,LXXXVIII.

Figure 7.17
Luther Martin. *The Genuine Information . . . Relative to the Proceedings of the General Convention, Lately Held at Philadelphia* (Philadelphia: Eleazer Oswald, 1788).

Figure 7.18
[Mercy Otis Warren.] *Observations on the New Constitution, and on the Federal and State Conventions* (New York, reprint, 1788).

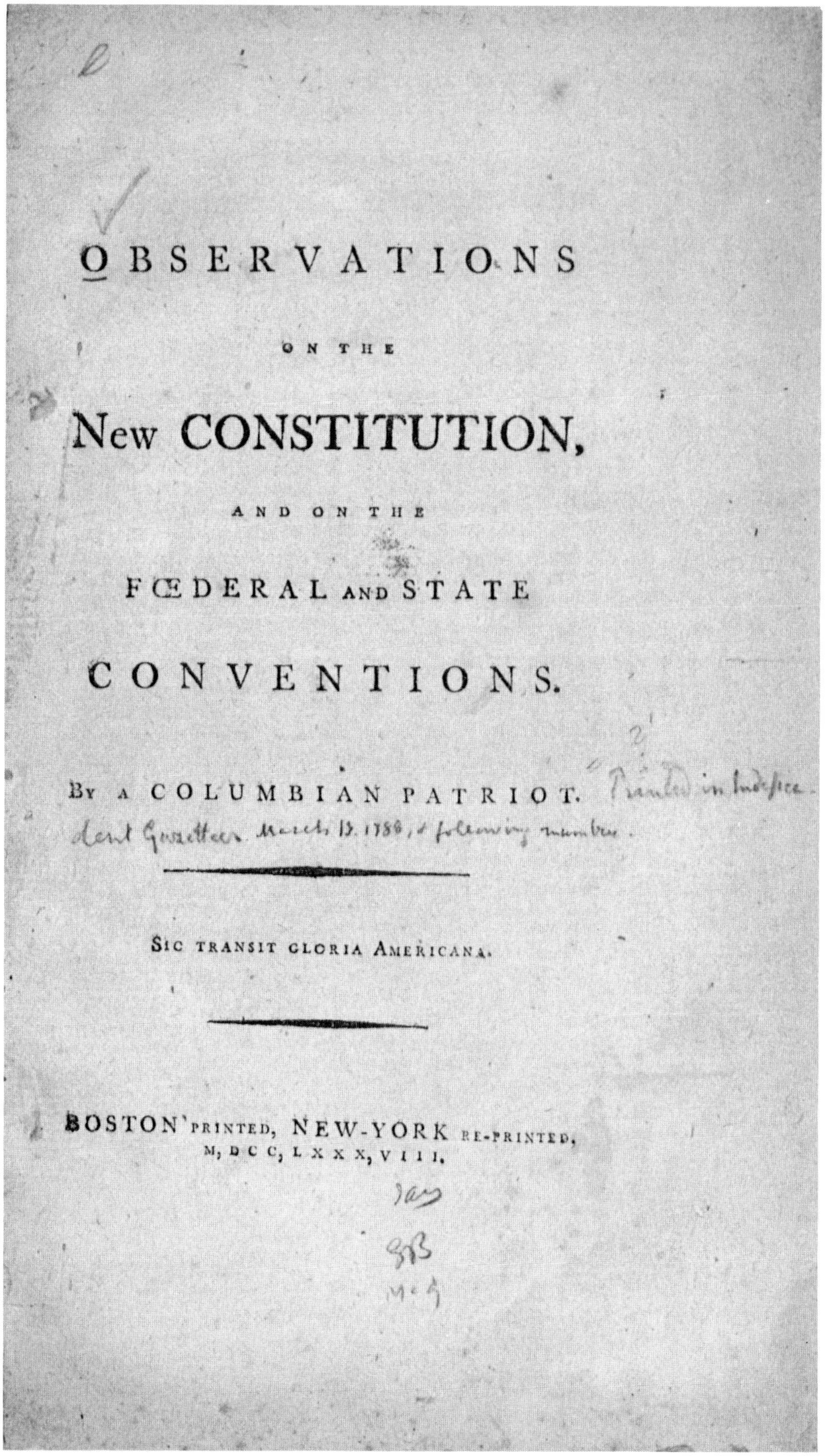

OBSERVATIONS

ON THE

New CONSTITUTION,

AND ON THE

FŒDERAL AND STATE

CONVENTIONS.

BY A COLUMBIAN PATRIOT.

SIC TRANSIT GLORIA AMERICANA.

BOSTON PRINTED, NEW-YORK RE-PRINTED,
M, DCC, LXXX, VIII.

first, a federal court system would compete with and swallow up the state courts, whose existence made a second court structure unnecessary; second, a court system whose judges were not responsible to the people and did not share their interests would give rise to an oppressive aristocracy. In his *Objections,* Mason charged that they were likely to "render . . . Law as tedious intricate and expensive, and Justice as unattainable, by a great part of the Community, as in England, and enabling the Rich to oppress and ruin the Poor."[50] Similarly, in January 1788 Melancton Smith of New York asked his friend and ally Abraham Yates, Jr., for advice on the proposed judiciary article in preparation for the ratification struggle:

> I wish you . . . would favour me, as your leisure and opportunities will permit, with your observations on this system, especially on the Judicial powers of it, about which very little has yet been written. It appears to me this part of the system is so framed as to *clinch* all the other powers, and to extend them in a silent and imperceptible manner to any thing and every thing, while the Court who are vested with these powers are totally independent, uncontroulable and not amenable to any other power in any decisions they may make.
>
> What are the cases in *equity* arising under the Constitution? Will not the supreme court under this clause have a right to enlarge the extent of the powers of the general government—and to curtail that of the States at pleasure?
>
> What are the cases of equity under Treaties? Will they not under this power be authorized to reverse all acts of attainder heretofore passed by the States, and to set aside all Judgements of Confiscation?[51]

Not surprisingly, Benjamin Austin, the author of a famous 1786 series of newspaper essays denouncing the legal profession,[52] became a vigorous and ardent opponent of the new Constitution, and one of the most common Anti-Federal arguments against the new charter was to point out that most lawyers favored its adoption.

As several delegates to the Federal Convention had predicted, the presidency drew extensive fire from Anti-Federal writers. The Federal Farmer stressed the dangers of allowing a president to be reelected without limit, bewailed the extensive power vested in him to make treaties and appoint the officers of government, and suggested that he either would become a tyrant or would fall under the domination of the Senate. Similarly, George Mason denounced the creation of the vice-presidency, calling it a dangerous and useless office that would be the source of contests for power and usurpations of authority.

Melancton Smith, writing as "A Plebeian," tackled the Federalists' alleged willingness to accept recommendatory amendments as the price of ratification.[53] Smith derided the Federalists' promises to work for amendments after the Constitution's adoption: "it is much to be feared, that we shall hear nothing of amendments from most of the warm advocates for adopting the new government, after it gets into operation." He also rejected the Federalists' plea to try the new government in actual operation before looking to frame amendments to the Constitution, declaring, "When we consider the nature and operation of government, the idea of receiving a form radically defective, under the notion of making the necessary amendments, is evidently absurd." Eventually, however, despite the telling arguments in the Plebeian's pamphlet, Smith abandoned his demands for "Making Amendments to the Constitution . . . Previous to its Adoption" at the Poughkeepsie convention.

Like the Federalists, the Anti-Federalists stressed that the decision to adopt or reject the Constitution was a watershed not only for Americans, but for men and women everywhere who valued freedom. George Mason's gloomy prediction of the fate of the United States should the American people adopt the Constitution is typical: "This Government will commence in a moderate Aristocracy; it is at present impossible to foresee whether it will, in it's Operation, produce a Monarchy, or a corrupt oppressive Aristocracy; it will most probably vibrate some Years between the two, and then terminate in the one or the other."[54] And Mercy Otis Warren painted a horrifying picture of the fate of the nation and of freedom-loving Americans in a United States governed by the Constitution:

> But if after all, on a dispassionate and fair discussion, the people generally give their voice for a voluntary dereliction of their privileges, let every individual who chooses the active scenes of life, strive to support the peace and unanimity of his country, though every other blessing may expire—And while the statesman is plodding for power, and the courtier practicing the arts of dissimulation without check—while the rapacious are growing rich by oppression, and fortune throwing her gifts into the lap of fools, let the sublimer characters, the philosophic lovers of freedom who have wept over her exit, retire to the calm shades of contemplation, there they may look down with pity on the inconsistency of human nature, the revolutions of states, the rise of kingdoms, and the fall of empires.[55]

Although the Anti-Federalists failed, they are entitled to their just share of credit in the making of the Constitution. The adoption of the Constitution provoked, indeed required, a searching dialogue about the basic principles of the American polity—about the task of framing an instrument of government for a nation any one of whose states was larger and more diverse than any European nation, about traditional and new conceptions of government and governmental institutions, about the new and untried system of dual federalism, and about the place of individual rights in constitutional government. The Anti-Federalists forced the Constitution's supporters to engage in this dialogue and to explain and justify the new charter clause by clause. In resisting the Constitution, they compelled the American people to think more deeply than any other people, before or since, about what the basic principles of their government should be and how they should be put into effect. Most important, the Anti-Federalists compelled James Madison and other Federalists to pledge themselves to work for the framing and adoption of a bill of rights.

The Federalist

Occasionally a literary, philosophical, or political classic emerges as if by accident. So it was with *The Federalist*.[56] Although Alexander Hamilton, James Madison, and John Jay intended *The Federalist* to be a major component of their strategy to win ratification of the Constitution, they did not expect it to become the single most authoritative exposition of the new charter of government.

The Federalist grew out of the "pamphlet wars" raging in New York City and throughout the nation in the fall of 1787, after the Confederation Congress voted on 28 September to submit the Constitution to the people of the several states. This debate assumed particular importance in New York City, the capital of the United States.

In June 1787, during the Convention, there had already been a brief, acrimonious newspaper skirmish in New York City between Alexander Hamilton and the partisans of Governor George Clinton, who was thought to oppose efforts to strengthen the Articles of Confederation.[57] Five days after the first publication of the Constitution in New York City, a battle between "Cato" and "Caesar" began.[58] Cato appeared in the *New-York Journal*, edited by Thomas Greenleaf; without taking a clear position for or against the work of the Federal Convention, he implied in his dull, pedantic essay that he was opposed to the Constitution, and he promised a full examination of the proposed new charter. Caesar rushed into print a few days later. Displaying thinly veiled contempt for the people, he tactlessly urged adoption of the Constitution as a stopgap measure to strengthen the government of the United States. Caesar clearly wanted a consolidated national government that would replace the Articles of Confederation and subordinate the state governments, reducing them to mere administrative departments. Cato's second essay ponderously set out to demolish Caesar and again promised a point-by-point, unanswerable critique of the Constitution.

Cato's promise to review and criticize the Constitution clause by clause was echoed in a series of newspaper essays by "Brutus," probably Robert Yates. Brutus's reasonable tone and devastating logic persuaded Hamilton of the need for a major series of essays supporting the Constitution and written in a tone and at a level distinct from most other contributions to the ratification controversy.

Hamilton made six strategically crucial decisions. First, the new series of essays should present a comprehensive defense of the Constitution, meeting the challenges of its opponents as they arose and expounding on the structure and functions of the proposed government. Second, the essays should avoid the demagoguery and personal attacks that had disfigured other essays for and against the Constitution. Third, the new series should appear both in the newspapers and as a separate compilation to ensure the widest possible circulation. Fourth, the use of the politically popular word *Federalist* as the general title for the series would help supporters of the Constitution to appropriate the term on their own behalf and use it to their advantage.

Fifth, Hamilton took great pains to select an appropriate pen name for the essay series. Drawing on his familiarity with Plutarch, Hamilton hit upon Publius Valerius, the great Roman leader who, after Lucius Brutus overthrew Tarquin, the last king of Rome, fulfilled the promise of the revolution by establishing a just and stable republican government. Just as Yates had chosen the pen name Brutus (taken from Lucius Brutus and his descendant Marcus Junius Brutus, the leader of the plot to assassinate Julius Caesar) to symbolize opposition to emerging or actual tyranny, Hamilton chose Publius, whom the people of Rome honored with the surname Publicola, meaning "people-lover," to symbolize commitment to the values of republicanism and constitutional government.

This fascination with classical Greek and Roman civilization, and especially Roman political values, is exemplified by the marble bust of Alexander Hamilton by Giuseppe Ceracchi (Plate XVIII), one of his series of portraits of "American Heroes."[59] This bust may justly be regarded as a portrait of Publius, the pseudonymous author of *The Federalist*.

Hamilton's last and most important decision was the choice of collaborators in what promised to be a major literary effort. As a successful lawyer with a thriving practice, a New York delegate to the Confederation Congress, and the leader of New York's Federalists, Hamilton knew that he could not produce *The Federalist* all by himself. But it was not enough just to enlist others to write as Publius; Hamilton had to find coauthors who could maintain both the pace and the quality that *The Federalist* needed to be an effective propaganda device. Eventually he invited four men to join him, but only two actually contributed to *The Federalist*. Gouverneur Morris declined Hamilton's invitation. William Duer wrote several brief essays, which the disappointed Hamilton tactfully judged to be unsuited in tone for *The Federalist*. John Jay (Figure 7.19) accepted Hamilton's invitation and indeed wrote four of the first five essays, but repeated and crippling attacks of rheumatism cut short his participation in the series; after essays 2 through 5, Jay wrote only one more, No. 64 (Figure 7.20). In No. 64 Jay explained and defended the Constitution's assignment to the Senate of the responsibility for ratifying treaties—a subject with which he was familiar because of his service as one of the new nation's first diplomats and as the Confederation's secretary for foreign affairs from 1784 to 1789. At some point during the initial planning of the series, Hamilton and Jay approached James Madison, who was in

Figure 7.19
Cornelius Tiebout after Gilbert Stuart. Portrait of John Jay. Stipple engraving, 1795.

JOHN JAY.

New York City as a Virginia delegate to the Confederation Congress. For most of the series, Hamilton and Madison shared the burden of writing *The Federalist*; unfortunately, in March 1788 Madison finally had to heed Edmund Randolph's warning that he must return home to ensure his election to the Virginia ratifying convention. With Madison's departure (which he delayed until the last moment), Hamilton was forced to write the rest of *The Federalist* by himself.[60]

The Federalist appeared first in the newspapers of New York City.[61] No. 1 was published on 27 October 1787 in the *Independent Journal* and a few days later in the *New-York Packet*. The *Daily Advertiser* and even the Anti-Federal *New-York Journal* soon followed suit. Thus, by the time the essayists hit their stride, Publius addressed "the People of the State of New York" twice a week in four of the city's five newspapers. On 1 January 1788, however, the *Journal* published a letter from "Twenty-Seven Subscribers" protesting that Thomas Greenleaf, the *Journal*'s publisher, was "cramming

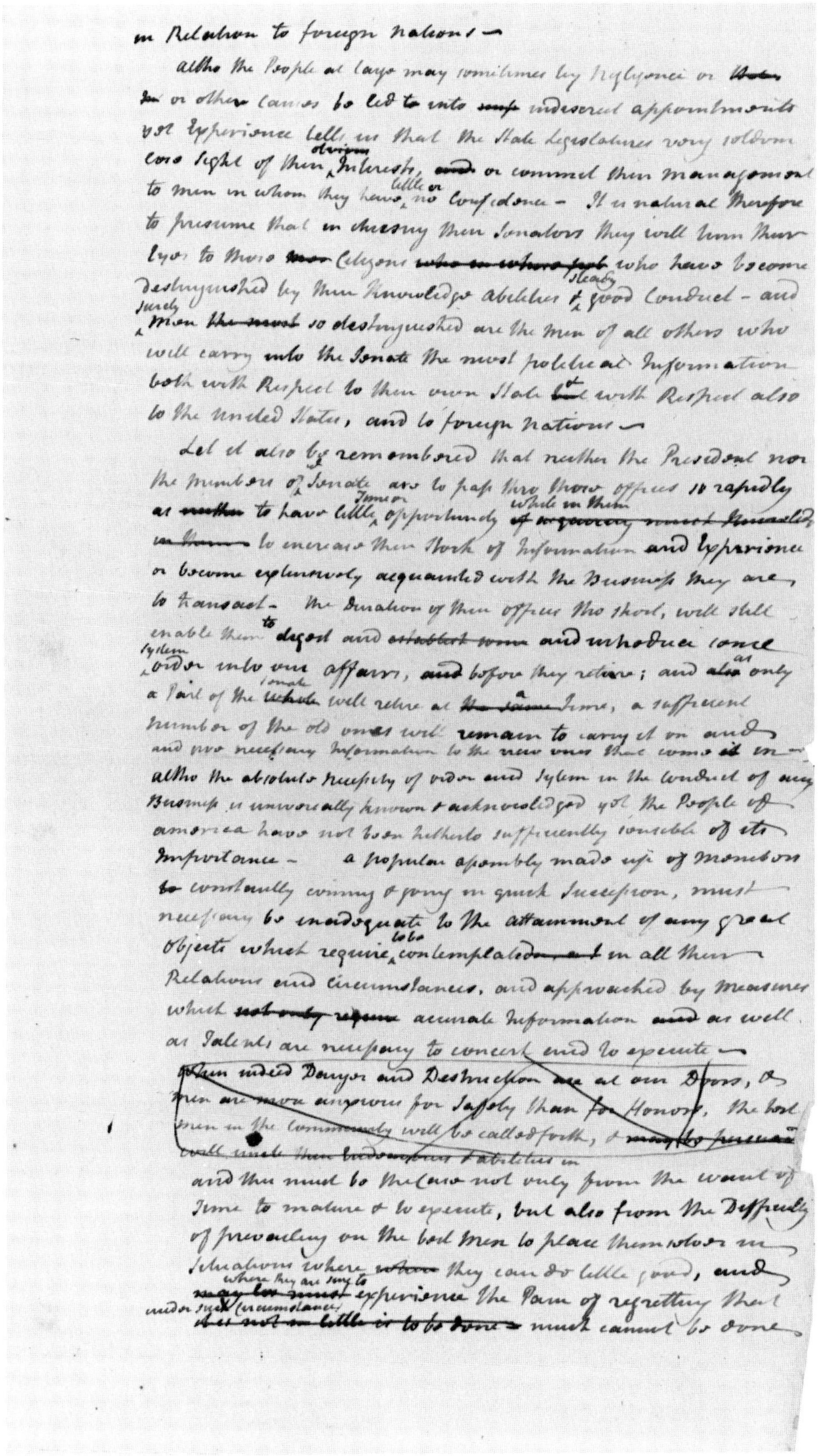

Figure 7.20
[John Jay.] *The Federalist* No. 64.
Draft, 1787–88.

in Relation to foreign nations —

altho the People at large may sometimes by Negligence or ... or other causes be led to into ... undeserved appointments yet Experience tells us that the State Legislatures very seldom lose sight of their Interests, or commit their management to men in whom they have little or no confidence — It is natural therefore to presume that in chusing their Senators they will turn their Eyes to those Citizens who have become distinguished by their Knowledge Abilities & steady good Conduct — and men the so distinguished are the men of all others who will carry into the Senate the most political Information both with Respect to their own State & with Respect also to the United States, and to foreign nations —

Let it also be remembered that neither the President nor the members of Senate are to pass thro' those offices so rapidly as to have little opportunity while in them to increase their Stock of Information and Experience or become extensively acquainted with the Business they are to transact — The duration of their offices tho' short, will still enable them to digest and establish and introduce some system & order into our affairs, before they retire; and as only a Part of the Senate will retire at the same time, a sufficient number of the old ones will remain to carry it on and and no necessary Information to the new ones that come in —

altho the absolute necessity of order and system in the conduct of any Business is universally known & acknowledged yet the People of america have not been hitherto sufficiently sensible of its Importance — a popular assembly made up of members constantly coming & going in quick Succession, must necessary be inadequate to the attainment of any great objects which require to be contemplated in all their Relations and circumstances, and approached by measures which require accurate Information as well as Talents are necessary to concert and to execute —

and this must be the case not only from the want of time to mature & to execute, but also from the difficulty of prevailing on the best Men to place themselves in situations where they can do little good, and when they are sorry to experience the Pain of regretting that much cannot be done us with the voluminous PUBLIUS." *The Federalist*, the letter continued, "has become nauseous, by having been served up to us no less than in two other papers on the same day."[62] Greenleaf dropped *The Federalist* from his paper within the month, but Publius continued to appear in the *Independent Journal*, the *Packet*, and the *Daily Advertiser*. Some of the essays appeared in other newspapers in New York State and in a few newspapers and periodicals in Pennsylvania, Virginia (where they were reprinted through the efforts of George Washington), and some of the New England states, but none appeared in any newspaper or magazine in Connecticut, New Jersey, Delaware, Maryland, North Carolina, South Carolina, or Georgia.[63]

The Federalist quickly burst the bounds envisioned for it by its authors and its printers, John and Andrew McLean; it swelled from a modest pamphlet to two stout volumes (Figure 7.21). In fact the last eight essays, including Hamilton's pathbreaking defense of the doctrine of judicial review in No. 78, appeared first in the second volume of the McLean edition and then in the newspapers. James Madison brought copies of the first volume back to Virginia with him in March 1788, and Hamilton arranged to supply him with enough copies of both volumes (the second appeared in May 1788) to arm every prominent Federalist in the Virginia ratifying convention with a set. John Dixon, an enterprising printer in Richmond, Virginia, had planned to publish his own book-length compilation of Publius but abandoned the project, probably because the McLean edition had become available; only two fragments of this otherwise unknown edition (Figure 7.22) survive.[64]

In his old age James Madison reminisced about the breakneck pace at which *The Federalist* had to be written and the difficulties it caused:

> The haste with which many of the papers were penned, in order to get thro the subject whilst the Constitution was before the public, and to comply with the arrangement, by which the printer was to keep his paper open for four numbers every week [that is, two numbers appearing in two different newspapers], was such that the performance must have borne a very different aspect without the aid of historical and other notes which had been used in the Convention and without the familiarity with the whole subject produced by the discussions there. It frequently happened that whilst the printer was putting into type parts of a number, the following parts were under the pen, & to be furnished in time for the press.[65]

The printer probably set type from the final drafts and threw them away when he was finished.

None of the eighty-five essays that make up *The Federalist* has survived in final manuscript form, and only four manuscript drafts—all of them by John Jay—are known to exist.[66] The requirements of the printers explain the disappearance of any final manuscript versions of Publius' essays. As for Hamilton's and Madison's rough drafts, it is likely that the two men

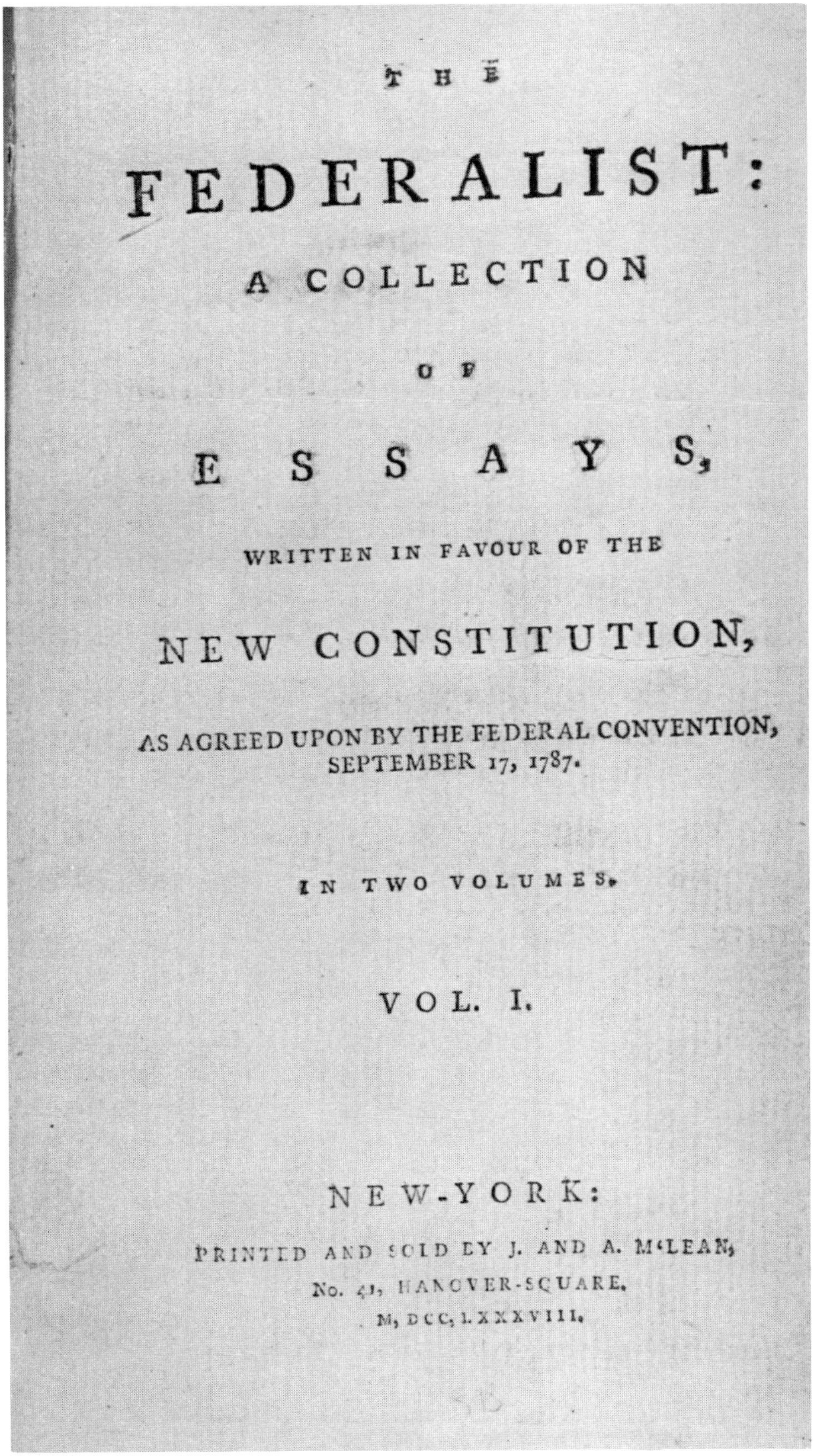

THE

FEDERALIST:

A COLLECTION

OF

ESSAYS,

WRITTEN IN FAVOUR OF THE

NEW CONSTITUTION,

AS AGREED UPON BY THE FEDERAL CONVENTION, SEPTEMBER 17, 1787.

IN TWO VOLUMES.

VOL. I.

NEW-YORK:

PRINTED AND SOLD BY J. AND A. M'LEAN,
No. 41, HANOVER-SQUARE.
M,DCC,LXXXVIII.

Figure 7.21
[Alexander Hamilton, James Madison, and John Jay.] *The Federalist: A Collection of Essays Written in Favour of the New Constitution* . . . , vol. I (New York: J. & A. M'Lean, 1788).

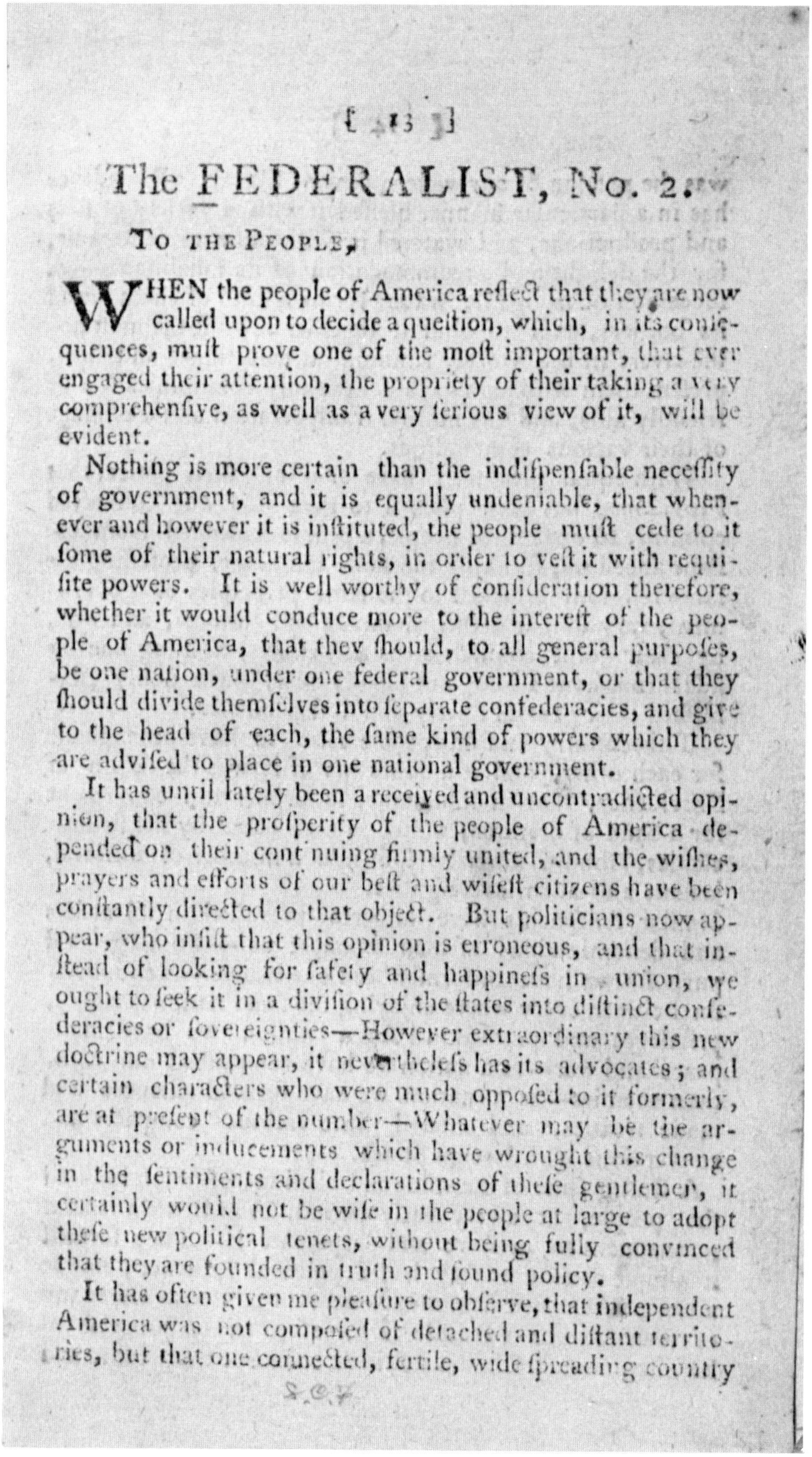

Figure 7.22
[John Jay.] *The Federalist* No. 2 (fragment) [Richmond: John Dixon, 1787?].

{ 13 }

The FEDERALIST, No. 2.

TO THE PEOPLE,

WHEN the people of America reflect that they are now called upon to decide a question, which, in its consequences, must prove one of the most important, that ever engaged their attention, the propriety of their taking a very comprehensive, as well as a very serious view of it, will be evident.

Nothing is more certain than the indispensable necessity of government, and it is equally undeniable, that whenever and however it is instituted, the people must cede to it some of their natural rights, in order to vest it with requisite powers. It is well worthy of consideration therefore, whether it would conduce more to the interest of the people of America, that they should, to all general purposes, be one nation, under one federal government, or that they should divide themselves into separate confederacies, and give to the head of each, the same kind of powers which they are advised to place in one national government.

It has until lately been a received and uncontradicted opinion, that the prosperity of the people of America depended on their continuing firmly united, and the wishes, prayers and efforts of our best and wisest citizens have been constantly directed to that object. But politicians now appear, who insist that this opinion is erroneous, and that instead of looking for safety and happiness in union, we ought to seek it in a division of the states into distinct confederacies or sovereignties—However extraordinary this new doctrine may appear, it nevertheless has its advocates; and certain characters who were much opposed to it formerly, are at present of the number—Whatever may be the arguments or inducements which have wrought this change in the sentiments and declarations of these gentlemen, it certainly would not be wise in the people at large to adopt these new political tenets, without being fully convinced that they are founded in truth and sound policy.

It has often given me pleasure to observe, that independent America was not composed of detached and distant territories, but that one connected, fertile, wide spreading country prudently destroyed them. For one thing, all three authors agreed that the persuasive force of Publius' arguments would be heightened if the identity of the authors was kept secret, for citizens of Virginia would not follow meekly the political advice of New Yorkers such as Hamilton and Jay, and New Yorkers would be suspicious of a Virginian "foreigner" such as Madison. Further, *The Federalist* contained arguments that Hamilton or Madison might not wish to be associated with, both because it was not always possible for the two men to consult with each other before their essays were published and because, with the rise of political parties in the 1790s and the widening ideological rift between them, such revelations could have embarrassing consequences. Hamilton and Madison probably agreed that any potentially revealing clue to the authorship of *The Federalist* would be better off destroyed.[67]

The lack of incontrovertible evidence of the authorship of individual essays has fueled debate since the early 1800s.[68] In a memorandum (now lost) prepared and left with his friend Egbert Benson just before his fatal duel with Aaron Burr in 1804, Hamilton claimed to have written more than two-thirds of the eighty-five essays. Fourteen years later, in answering the questions of Jacob Gideon, a Washington, D.C., printer planning his own edition of Publius, Madison claimed as his own work fifteen of the essays also claimed by Hamilton (Nos. 18–20, 49–58, 62, and 63). In fact the dispute was not one of veracity but of memory, probably compounded by a simple mistake made by Hamilton in reading the Roman numerals used in most early editions to number the essays.[69] In the 1940s Douglass G. Adair put an end to the controversy. After close examination of the internal and other available evidence, he showed that Madison had written all the disputed essays; in the early 1960s computer-assisted textual analysis substantiated Adair's reasoning.[70] It is now agreed that Hamilton wrote Nos. 1, 6–9, 11–13, 15–17, 21–36, 59–61, and 65–85; that Madison wrote Nos. 10, 14, 18–20 (with reference to some material provided by Hamilton), 37–58, 62, and 63; and that Jay wrote Nos. 2–5 and 64.

Hamilton outlined the argument of *The Federalist* in his first essay:

> I propose, in a series of papers, to discuss the following interesting particulars:—*The utility of the* UNION *to your political prosperity—The insufficiency of the present Confederation to preserve that Union—The necessity of a government at least equally energetic with the one proposed, to the attainment of this object—The conformity of the proposed Constitution to the true principles of republican government—Its analogy to your own State constitution—and lastly, The additional security which its adoption will afford to the preservation of that species of government, to liberty, and to property.*[71]

By beginning with the virtues of the Union Publius shrewdly implied that the Anti-Federalists wished to break it up, either into three or four regional confederacies or into its individual components, the states. Although disunionist sentiment was present in the United States in 1787 and 1788, it

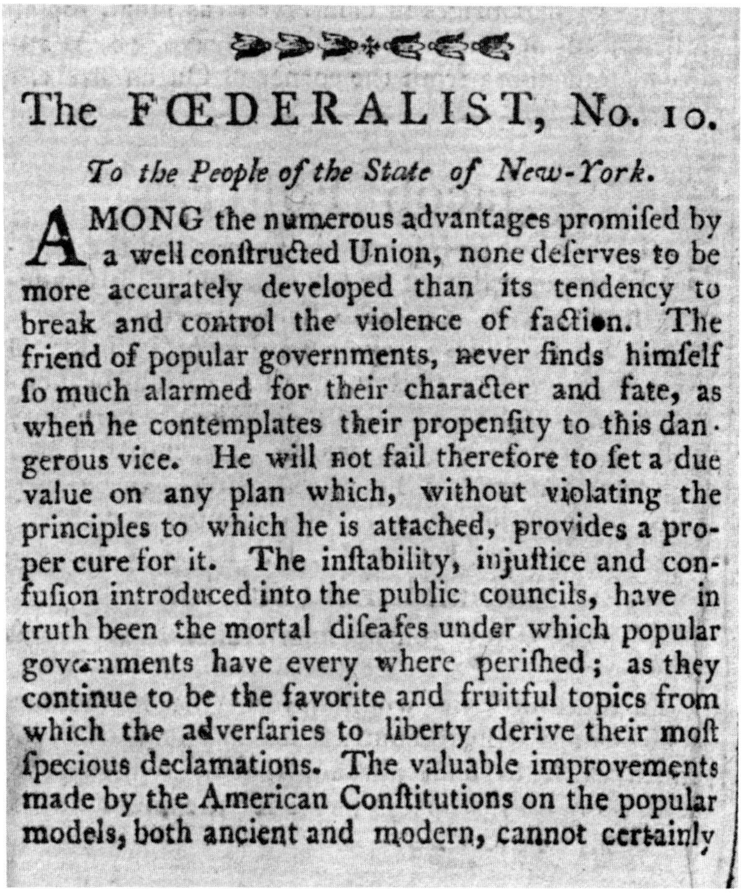

The FŒDERALIST, No. 10.

To the People of the State of New-York.

AMONG the numerous advantages promised by a well constructed Union, none deserves to be more accurately developed than its tendency to break and control the violence of faction. The friend of popular governments, never finds himself so much alarmed for their character and fate, as when he contemplates their propensity to this dan-gerous vice. He will not fail therefore to set a due value on any plan which, without violating the principles to which he is attached, provides a proper cure for it. The instability, injustice and confusion introduced into the public councils, have in truth been the mortal diseases under which popular governments have every where perished; as they continue to be the favorite and fruitful topics from which the adversaries to liberty derive their most specious declamations. The valuable improvements made by the American Constitutions on the popular models, both ancient and modern, cannot certainly

Figure 7.23
[James Madison.] *The Federalist* No. 10 (detail), in *The New-York Packet,* 23 November 1787.

was by no means so widespread as Publius implied, nor was it the ultimate objective of most opponents of the Constitution. This tactic allowed Publius to link the idea of Union with the proposed Constitution, and the authors of *The Federalist* built upon that foundation in their extensive case against the Articles of Confederation.

When John Jay was forced to drop out of the project and James Madison assumed a correspondingly greater responsibility as coauthor, the series of essays changed its emphases. Madison brought to the writing of *The Federalist* the fruit of his intensive historical and philosophical research in 1786 and 1787 on the history of ancient and modern confederacies (embodied in *Federalist* Nos. 18–20) and the adaptation of republicanism to American affairs. Accordingly, he focused on the work of the Federal Convention and the evolving principles of republican government.

Madison's studies had persuaded him that classical political teaching on the fragility and limitations of republican government was wrong on several grounds, but in none so much as in the ancient dictum that a republican form of government was suitable only to a small territory. In *Federalist* Nos. 10 (Figure 7.23) and 14 Madison turned classical political wisdom on its head, and in No. 10 he made what is now regarded as perhaps the greatest single American contribution to political theory.[72] In considering the reasons for the failure of liberty and of republican governments, Madison emphasized factionalism—the tendency of human beings to divide into groups animated by selfish, short-term interests. Ever since Aristotle, most writers on politics had condemned faction as fatal to republican government and thus to liberty. Challenging this conventional wisdom, Madison argued that extending a republican form of government over a large territory would ensure a diversity of interests and factions and thus prevent any one faction from dominating a majority of the people, taking over the government, and injuring the interests of the nation as a whole.

In *Federalist* No. 51 Madison recognized that merely guarding against factionalism in society was not enough. Even within a constitutional republic, ambition could easily lead government officials to enlarge their powers and even to usurp power, subvert individual liberty, and overthrow the republic. In a memorable passage, Madison summarized the arguments for a system of checks and balances designed to pit government officials against each other and neutralize ambition's threat to the republic:

> But the great security against a gradual concentration of the several powers in the same department consists in giving to those who administer each department the necessary constitutional means and personal motives to resist encroachments of the others. The provision for defense must in this, as in all other cases, be made commensurate to the danger of attack. Ambition must be made to counteract ambition. The interest of the man must be connected with the constitutional rights of the place. It may be a reflection on human nature that such devices should be necessary to control the abuses of government. But what is government itself but the greatest of all reflections on human nature? If men were angels, no government would be necessary. If angels were to govern men, neither external nor internal controls on government would be necessary. In framing a government which is to be administered by men over men, the great difficulty lies in this: you must first enable the government to control the governed, and in the next place oblige it to control itself. A dependence on the people is, no doubt, the primary control on the government; but experience has taught mankind the necessity of auxiliary precautions.[73]

David Hume's essays inspired Madison's arguments on factionalism in *Federalist* No. 10,[74] but *The Federalist* as a whole epitomizes the political thought and political optimism, tempered by a mature understanding of the strengths and weaknesses of human nature, of the Americans of the 1780s: the belief that human nature is animated by general principles and motives that are identifiable in every epoch and every nation; the view of government as a great Newtonian machine in which each part should operate to check and balance the others to maintain that equilibrium needed to preserve liberty; the awareness that practical political decisions also have a larger significance for political theory; and so forth.

The great innovation in political thought embodied in the Constitution and *The Federalist* is the idea that government can be constructed to *guard against* the dangers to liberty and to republican government that are inherent in human nature. In contrast to almost all earlier political theorists, who had concluded that human nature eventually corrupts and topples every form of government, no matter how well constructed at the outset, Hamilton, Madison, Jay, and their colleagues maintained that it was possible to preserve a republic by constructing its government to take account of human nature and, indeed, by using the flaws of human nature to preserve the structure of government and the liberties of the people.[75] One of the remarkable features of *The Federalist* is the authors' habit, even when making the most mundane and hard-headed practical point, of developing and exploring its larger significance and elevating the discussion to the level of high principle.[76] This unique linking of political theory and practical application gives *The Federalist* a continuing freshness and immediacy lacking in more formal works of political theory.

Hamilton concluded *The Federalist* as he had begun it, by emphasizing the importance of the choice before the American people—not only for themselves but for humanity—and warning them against the motives of the opponents of the Constitution. In particular, Hamilton decried the Anti-Federalists' call for a second constitutional convention, to which the Constitution would be submitted for further revision:

> A NATION, without a NATIONAL GOVERNMENT, is, in my view, an awful spectacle. The establishment of a Constitution, in time of profound peace, by the voluntary consent of a whole people, is a PRODIGY, to the completion of which I look forward with trembling anxiety. I can reconcile it to no rules of prudence to let go the hold we now have, in so arduous an enterprise, upon seven out of the thirteen States, and after having passed over so considerable a part of the ground, to recommence the course. I dread the more the consequences of new attempts because I know that POWERFUL INDIVIDUALS, in this and in other States, are enemies to a general national government in every possible shape.[77]

It is difficult to assess the influence of *The Federalist* on the ratification campaign. Writing in the glow of the centennial celebrations of 1887–1889, John Fiske argued that Publius played a critical role in securing ratification in New York and in arguing the Federalist cause in other key states.[78] Others, today, suggest that *The Federalist* was useful mainly as a comprehensive and authoritative "debater's handbook" of Federalist arguments.[79] In the crucial states of New York and Virginia, proponents of the Constitution were well primed with arguments drawn from *The Federalist*, and Anti-Federalists such as George Clinton complained that the Federalists were merely repeating parts of Publius learned by heart.

Once the Constitution was ratified and put into effect, *The Federalist* began its metamorphosis from partisan propaganda into universally re-

LE FÉDÉRALISTE,

OU

*Collection de quelques Écrits en faveur de
la Constitution proposée aux États - Unis
de l'Amérique , par la Convention convoquée
en 1787 ;*

Publiés dans les États-Unis de l'Amérique par
MM. HAMILTON, MADISSON et GAY,
Citoyens de l'État de New-York.

TOME PREMIER.

———

A PARIS,

Chez BUISSON, Libraire, rue Hautefeuille,
n°. 20.

———

1792.

spected constitutional commentary. The first foreign-language edition, a French translation in 1792 (Figure 7.24), first revealed the identities of Publius as "MM. HAMILTON, MADISSON, ET GAY, Citoyens de l'Etat de New York." Since then and especially in the aftermath of World War II, the essays have been published in French, Italian, German, Spanish, Portuguese, Arabic, Bengali, Assamese, Korean, Vietnamese, and Japanese.[80]

Originally read as a commentary on the Constitution or as a specialized study of the problems of federal government, *The Federalist* is now justly recognized as a classic exposition of the principles of republican government and the possibility of constructing such a government to preserve individual rights. When Alexander Hamilton sent a copy of *The Federalist* to George Washington in 1788, Washington in acknowledging the gift predicted the enduring significance of Publius:

> When the transient circumstances and fugitive performances which attended this Crisis shall have disappeared, That Work will merit the notice of posterity; because in it are candidly and ably discussed the principles of freedom and the topics of government, which will be always interesting to mankind so long as they shall be connected in Civil Society.[81]

8

UNDER THE CONSTITUTION

T HE CONSTITUTION is not a self-executing document. Even before they won the struggle for ratification, the Federalists confronted the staggering task of putting the new system of government into effect and making it work.

With the adoption of the Constitution by the necessary nine states, the Confederation Congress managed a final burst of energy and purpose in preparing the way for a smooth transition to the new government. On 13 September 1788 it chose New York City as the temporary national capital (Plate XIX). It also drew up a schedule for the transition, directed the states to hold elections for the new House of Representatives and to choose Senators and the electors who would select the first president and vice-president, all before 10 October 1788. It never managed afterward to muster a quorum; all that remained of the Confederation were John Jay, the long-suffering secretary for foreign affairs, a few clerks, and a mountain of debt.

The new national government itself had a shaky start, missing its official inception date by more than a month. It faced a daunting array of old problems and new challenges. It would have to find some way to deal with the crushing national and state debts dating back to the earliest days of the Revolution, and to create a national revenue system and a national system of trade regulation and customs duties. It would have to flesh out those parts of the structure of government deliberately left vague or incomplete in the Constitution—the executive departments, which would become the roots of a federal administrative structure, and, for the first time in American history, a federal court system. And it would have to take action on the Federalists' campaign pledge that in several states had been the price for ratifying the Constitution: the proposing of constitutional amendments, including a declaration of rights.

Two more general and in some ways more daunting problems also confronted the members of the new government. The first was simple uncertainty as to what controversies might arise from the functioning or malfunctioning of the new system, as well as from partisan or sectional issues. The second was their awareness that the new government would be operating under hostile scrutiny. First, the Anti-Federalists, only partly reconciled to their defeat in the ratification campaign, would be vigilant against any apparent violation of the Constitution's limits on federal power and would also be looking for a chance to revive their calls for a second convention. Second, the people of North Carolina and Rhode Island would base their postponed decisions to ratify or reject the Constitution on their evaluation of the new government's performance. Third, the skeptical rulers of Europe would be watching for signs of American weakness and of the role that the United States would choose to play in international affairs. Fourth, the philosophes would be looking for evidence to bolster their arguments for or against the success of republican government. Fifth, the American people themselves would be wary of the untried new system. Sixth and finally, every measure or action or failure to act would have incalculable precedential value for posterity.

By December 1791 the new government had somehow met these challenges and gained the firm respect and admiration of the American people. To the disappointment of President George Washington, the new fiscal policies had created factional divisions that would lead to the formation of political parties. The revival of factionalism seemed to Washington, Hamilton, Madison, and other leaders to threaten the continued existence of the new government. But despite their fears, American political culture assimilated the emerging party system into the larger reshaping of habits of political thought and action begun by the Federal Convention.

The Beginnings of Government

On 30 April 1789 George Washington took office as the first president of the United States (Figure 8.1) in a solemn yet joyous ceremony in New York City. The city had renovated its old City Hall, at the corner of Wall and Broad streets, and presented it to the nation as Federal Hall (Figure 8.2) to serve as the capitol. Standing on the balcony of the small structure, clad in a suit of brown American broadcloth to symbolize his support of American manufactures, Washington swore the oath prescribed in the Constitution on a Bible borrowed at the last moment from a nearby Masonic lodge. At the end of the ceremony, Chancellor Robert R. Livingston, who had administered the oath, shouted to the assembled crowd, "Long live George Washington, President of the United States!" The jubilant crowd ignored Livingston's echo of the traditional cry welcoming a newly crowned king; for the rest of the day, cheers and the sound of church bells filled the air, and that evening New Yorkers and President Washington witnessed the most spectacular display of fireworks yet seen in the United States.[1]

Despite his reluctance to leave retirement, Washington accepted his unanimous election as president, determined to help make the new government work. He spent most of his first year in office occupied with largely ceremonial duties and with a continuous stream of office seekers hoping to find favor with the new administration. Washington took pains to handle

Figure 8.1
James Trenchard after Charles Willson Peale. *An East View of Gray's Ferry, near Philadelphia, with the Triumphal Arches, &c. erected for the Reception of General Washington, April 20th 1789.* Line engraving, 1789.

such applicants and their supporters with tact and reserve. In a letter to Joseph Jones two weeks after his inauguration he observed:

> That part of the President's duty which obliges him to nominate persons for offices is the most delicate and in many instances will be, to me, the most unpleasing, for it may frequently happen that there will be several applicants for the same office, whose merits and pretensions are so nearly equal that it will almost require the aid of supernatural intuition to fix upon the right. I shall, however, in all events, have the consolation of knowing that I entered upon my office unconfined by any engagements, and uninfluenced by any ties, and that no means in my power will be left untried to find out and nominate those characters who will discharge the duties of their respective offices to the best interest and highest credit of the American Union.[2]

Washington governed his appointments policy by reference to three criteria. First, he sought the ablest men available. Second, he preferred to appoint those whom he knew to be warm friends of the Constitution and sincerely committed to its success. Third, aware of the touchy sensibilities of the several states and sections of the United States, he strove for geographic balance in his appointments to national office. In his conduct as president, Washington sought to maintain his personal dignity and reserve in the hope that it would come to be associated with the office he held, so

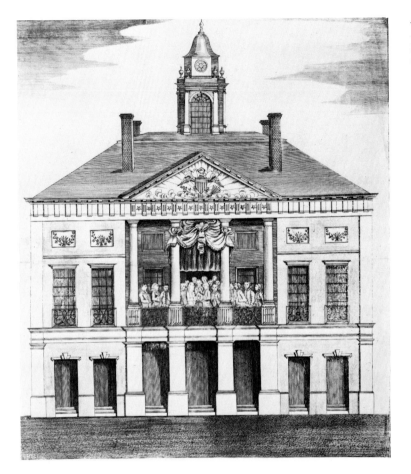

Figure 8.2
Amos Doolittle after Peter LaCour. *Federal Hall The Seat of Congress.* Line engraving, 1790. Pierre L'Enfant refurbished Federal Hall for Washington's inauguration, adding a large frieze displaying the arms of the United States and, as described by the *Columbian Magazine,* "tablets over the windows, filled with thirteen arrows and the olive branch united, [to] mark it as a building set aside for national purposes."

that the personal respect he enjoyed would also attach itself to the presidency (Figure 8.3). In all these ways, Washington sought to embody the ideal of nonpartisan executive leadership, a central element of republican political thought.[3]

In his letter to Joseph Jones, Washington also assured his friend, a noted Virginia politician whose moderate Anti-Federalism had not injured his friendships with Washington and Madison, of the harmony and consensus prevailing in Congress: "Your observation upon the necessity there is for good dispositions to prevail among the Gentlemen of Congress, are extremely just; and, hitherto, everything seems to promise that the good effects which are expected from an accommodating and conciliating spirit in that body, will not be frustrated."[4]

Congress, and particularly the House of Representatives, was the focus of public attention and the fount of governmental activity in the first several months.[5] In 1789 the House took the lead in formulating and fulfilling the national legislative agenda. The Senate lost the initiative and its chance for a share of the political limelight for three reasons. First, unlike the House, it chose to conduct its debates behind closed doors, thereby forfeiting any chance for attracting the direct interest of the public. Second, it quickly lost

Figure 8.3
Artist unknown. *Washington
Giving the Laws to America.* Etch-
ing and engraving, ca. 1800.

itself in the morass of protocol. Because Vice-President John Adams and many Senators believed that an elaborate system of titles and etiquette was needed to stimulate popular respect for the new government, the Senate spent weeks debating the merits of such grandiloquent proposed titles as "His Highness the President of the United States and Protector of the Rights of the Same." Rumors of this debate, coupled with the House's refusal to accept any title for the president other than that given in the Constitution itself, not only disposed of the titles bill but also made the vice president (dubbed "His Rotundity") and the Senate into figures of fun. Third, and most significant, the Senate was generally seen as a council for representation of the states, whereas the House was elected by the people to represent them and act in their name. Thus America's first popularly elected national legislative body had first claim on the people's attention and loyalty.

The Representatives in this period operated largely in a vacuum. No formal party organization, no permanent committee system, and no seniority system existed for nearly a decade; thus the first House of Representatives had none of the signposts or determinants of legislative leadership or structures of doing business that we know today. The Speaker was simply the House's presiding officer and parliamentarian, called upon only to rule on procedural questions. Frederick Augustus Muhlenberg's colleagues elected him Speaker largely because of their respect for him and his previous service as Speaker of the Pennsylvania General Assembly.

Informal processes of leadership operated in the absence of formal institutions, offices, and structures. This tendency was encouraged by the general method used to transact House business. Like most state legislatures of the time, the House did most of its work in Committee of the Whole and appointed short-lived select committees to prepare key bills, work out compromises, or write reports. Two distinct methods of leadership can be identified. Representatives such as Fisher Ames and Theodore Sedgwick of Massachusetts, Elias Boudinot of New Jersey, and William Loughton Smith of South Carolina came forward as articulate, vigorous advocates of the interests of their states or sections or of powerful economic groups among their constituents. James Madison of Virginia emerged as the only practitioner of legislative leadership striving for disinterested achievement of the public good, as envisioned by republican thought. Madison dominated the House in its first session through his extensive legislative experience at the state and national levels, his sheer capacity for hard work, his reputation and authority as a principal architect and champion of the Constitution, and his commitment to the success of the new system of government.

Madison's legislative methods flowed naturally from the pathbreaking theories of factional politics set forth in *Federalist* No. 10. He reasoned that the interplay of factions and interests in the national political system would enable politicians with a genuine interest in the general or national good to achieve that good. Having surveyed the list of his colleagues in the House, he concluded that few would be willing to assume a major share of the burdens of legislative business. Just as he had done in preparing for the Federal Convention, Madison drew up a comprehensive agenda directed to completing, energizing, and financing the new government. Time and again he proposed key measures, cut through legislative tangles by offering coherent compromises, persuaded his colleagues to accept sacrifices on behalf of their states and other interests in the service of the national interest, and shepherded bill after bill through the House and House-Senate conferences. Under his leadership, the House dominated the creation of the first national revenue and trade regulation systems and the Departments of State, Treasury, and War.

A key House debate in this first session resulted in a major victory for the independence of the executive branch in the constitutional system.[6] At issue was a provision of the bill creating the Department of Foreign Affairs declaring that the president had sole power to remove the secretary. Four views of the power to remove executive officers emerged in the long debate that followed: (1) the Senate had a share in the removal power equal to its constitutional share in the appointment power; (2) in its legislation creating executive positions, Congress could specify the modes of appointment *and* removal of executive officers; (3) the president had sole power under the Constitution to remove executive officers; and (4) executive officers, once appointed, could not be removed except by impeachment. Eventually Egbert Benson of New York offered a compromise provision, supported by Madison, that in essence embodied a legislative recognition of the third, or "constitutional grant," approach.[7]

Congress remained wary of the executive departments it had created, and of the Treasury in particular. The bitter controversies of the early 1780s over the conduct of Robert Morris as the Confederation's superintendent of finance[8] were still fresh in the memories of most Representatives and Senators, and some of them vainly championed the creation of a three-member Treasury Board rather than a single secretary of the Treasury. Finally the House and Senate decided to create a single head of the Treasury but hedged the office about with restrictions. The secretary would have no direct contact with the money actually in the Treasury. In addition, to bring the secretary within the control of Congress, the legislation establishing the department contained a provision requiring the secretary to satisfy any House requests for reports on the public credit or the business of the Treasury.[9]

The Treasury Department was the largest and most active of the three executive departments created by Congress. Not only did it have the largest staff—nearly thirty people; its mandate gave it the direct responsibility for dealing with the most urgent problems facing the nation. Except for dealing with Indian tribes on the frontier, the War Department had little to do. Because Thomas Jefferson, Washington's choice for secretary of state, had to be persuaded by Madison to accept the post and then delayed assuming office, John Jay ran the fledgling department as a caretaker operation until March 1790.

In appointing the heads of the new departments, Washington followed his principles of seeking able and honest men friendly to the Constitution and from different sections of the nation. Henry Knox of Massachusetts, the first secretary of war, was an old friend from the earliest days of the Continental Army. John Jay, offered a choice between the offices of chief justice and secretary of state, chose the judiciary. Edmund Randolph, the attorney general, had no administrative responsibility, since there was no Department of Justice. His sole tasks were to prepare legal opinions at the request of the president and to represent the United States before the Supreme Court.

Washington's most important adviser, as both the head of the largest and most powerful department and a trusted friend and protégé, was

Alexander Hamilton of New York, the first secretary of the Treasury.[10] Hamilton had long made economics and finance his special interests, just as Madison had specialized in the theory and organization of republican governments and federations. Drawing on his wide reading in economic literature and his familiarity with the British and French experiences in dealing with their national debts, Hamilton prepared to reshape the nation's economic life. Hamilton regarded the restrictions and responsibilities built into his office as superb opportunities. Freed from day-to-day administration of the nation's money, he could concentrate on larger issues of fiscal policy. Furthermore, he could use his responsibility to prepare reports for Congress to advance his plans for restructuring and systematizing the finances of the United States (Figure 8.4). He also benefited from Washington's trust and confidence, a legacy from the days when he was a young officer on Washington's staff during the Revolution. Finally, Hamilton turned to his advantage the malfunctioning of the revenue system created by the House in its first session. That system, a crazy-quilt of sectional and regional compromises, did not yield the amount of revenue its draftsmen had hoped for, and this did little to reduce the debt of the United States.

The debt problem perplexed most politicians. The debt amounted to more than $50 million, nearly $13 million of which represented back interest payments. Most members of Congress believed that the debt should be paid off eventually, though they did not agree how this should be done. Some favored using revenues from sales of western lands, though these would be insufficient; others favored tax increases, though new taxes would exacerbate sectional rivalries by falling unevenly on different interests and commodities; a few daring politicians thought that the new government should repudiate part or all of the debt.

Hamilton's chance came toward the end of the first session, in September 1789. The House received a memorial from creditors of the United States residing in Pennsylvania urging that the outstanding debt of the United States be paid in full. No one in the House or the Senate was willing to tackle so potentially divisive an issue so close to the end of the session. To shift the burden, a select committee chaired by Madison proposed that the whole matter be referred to the secretary of the Treasury, and the House gratefully complied, directing the secretary to prepare a report on the public credit for the opening of the next session.

Hamilton devoted the next few months to composing his now-classic *Report Relative to a Provision for the Support of Public Credit,* which he delivered to the House on 14 January 1790 (after a brief parliamentary skirmish over whether he should appear on the floor himself to explain it and answer questions). In his *Report* Hamilton argued that the entire debt should eventually be paid off. He took special pains to refute the idea that the government should somehow discriminate against investors who had purchased public securities for a fraction of their face value from Revolutionary War veterans and their families desperate for cash. Such a plan would not only

Figure 8.4
Reports of Alexander Hamilton, Esq.
. . . (London: J. Debrett, 1795).

REPORTS

OF

ALEXANDER HAMILTON, Esq.

SECRETARY OF THE TREASURY,

READ IN THE

HOUSE OF REPRESENTATIVES

OF THE

UNITED STATES,

JANUARY 19th, 1795;

CONTAINING,

I. A PLAN for the further Support of PUBLIC CREDIT.

II. For the Improvement and better Management of the REVENUES of the UNITED STATES:

TO WHICH IS ANNEXED,

The Copy of an ACT for making Provifion for the Support of PUBLIC CREDIT and the Redemption of the DEBT.

———

Printed by Order of the HOUSE of REPRESENTATIVES.

———

LONDON:

REPRINTED FOR J. DEBRETT, OPPOSITE BURLINGTON-HOUSE, PICCADILLY,

———

1795.

impugn the honor of the United States but also render public securities nonnegotiable, thereby jeopardizing the credit of the new government.

Hamilton also rejected the idea that the public debt should be liquidated as soon as possible. Instead he proposed that the debt be consolidated, amalgamating both the principal and the arrears in interest, and that the entire recalculated debt be turned into a fund—that is, a continuing obligation to which a set portion of the national revenue would be devoted each year to retire interest and part of the principal. By stabilizing public securities in this manner, the nation could increase the amount of capital in circulation and thus provide a needed boost in resources available for investment in the new nation's economy, specifically in commercial and manufacturing enterprises. Properly funded, Hamilton argued, a national debt would prove to be a national blessing rather than a burden or curse.

Hamilton's *Report* also maintained that the federal government should assume the outstanding debts of the states and oversee the settlement of state accounts with the United States—that is, state advances to the United States and United States loans to the states during the Revolution. In this way the government could put an end to competition between the federal and state governments for tax revenues, remove the injustices attendant upon differences in states' tax bases, and shift to the government of the American people the burden of paying debts contracted for their common benefit.

Hamilton recommended that new securities be issued in the name of the United States for the entire amount of the domestic debt. He also set forth complex and ingenious proposals for a gradual assumption of the state debts and a step-by-step method of dealing with the debts owed to foreign creditors. He also proposed an overhaul of the revenue system adopted in mid-1789, incorporating gradual increases in taxes on alcoholic beverages, designed both to reduce consumption and to bring in needed revenues. Finally, Hamilton proposed the creation of a "sinking fund" for purchasing public securities as long as they circulated below their par value; its dual objective was to dispose of part of the public debt in an inexpensive fashion and, more important, to drive up the price of securities to their par value.

Hamilton's system was similar to the British system for funding the national debt incurred to finance their wars against the French earlier in the eighteenth century. Hamilton greatly admired the British system but diverged from it in several important respects; his sinking fund, for example, was not designed primarily to retire the debt, unlike the British version.[12]

Hamilton's *Report* provoked confusion and outrage in Congress.[13] Although many speculators who had bought public securities at depreciated prices were delighted, others, who had hoped to make fortunes by purchasing western lands with depreciated securities, resisted the proposals. Representatives from the tobacco states were seeking to ease burdens on their constituents, whose chief cash crop had been half wiped out by an unexpected frost and who would not welcome increased taxes of any sort. Finally, many Representatives believed that the only way to sustain republicanism was to preserve the American economy's primary dependence on agriculture, the only calling that preserved the virtue of the people.[14] Hamilton's encouragement of commercial activity as a major part of American economic life thus struck at a major premise of his opponents' political philosophy.

James Madison emerged as the leader of the opposition to Hamilton's program. He based his resistance on Hamilton's seeming indifference to the plight of those original holders of public securities who had been forced to sell them for a fraction of their face value, and on the consequences he foresaw for the nation and its republican form of government should Hamilton's system be adopted. Madison also believed that Hamilton's system would give the speculating, commercial, and manufacturing interests of the new nation's cities an undue voice in determining American fiscal and economic policy, whereas other interests would be shunted aside or excluded from policy decisions. Madison felt obliged to represent those excluded special interests in order to preserve the full calculus of interests that he had envisioned in *Federalist* No. 10.

Madison's principal move in opposition to the Hamiltonian system was his proposal for discrimination.[15] In a major speech to the House, Madison identified four categories of holders of public securities and would pay them varying amounts. Purchasers of securities at discounted prices should not receive a windfall. Instead, present holders should be issued new certificates equal to the highest price their old ones had reached in the market, and original holders who could prove their status should receive certificates for the difference between that highest market price and the face value of the securities. This proposal had the semblance of justice to recommend it but posed insuperable difficulties of administration and struck at the heart of a basic principle of commercial law—that a negotiable instrument, the equivalent of currency, must be for a "sum certain" stated on its face.

Madison's proposal was defeated, thirty-six to thirteen—his first major defeat on the floor of the House. But Hamilton's proposal soon bogged down in debate and in contention among regions and interests. Southern politicians felt that northern commercial interests would benefit at the South's expense if Hamilton's policies were adopted as they stood. Accordingly, they sought concessions on the sticky issues of the calculation of state accounts and the site of the nation's permanent capital (Figure 8.5).[16]

Recalling the Confederation Congress's frequent and often embarrassing journeys from city to city during the Revolution, the delegates to the Federal Convention had agreed that a permanent site ten miles square, to be called the "Federal District," would be chosen as the seat of government for the United States. The location of the Federal District soon became a matter of fierce sectional interest and republican principle. Southerners

Figure 8.5
Artist unknown. *Cong[re]ss Embark'd on board the Ship Constitution of America . . .* Engraving, 1790. In this cartoon a devil lures an unsuspecting Robert Morris ("This way Bobby") and his crew of supporters toward a deadly waterfall en route to Philadelphia. In the background an unhampered path leads to a southern location for the nation's capital on the Potomac River.

wanted the capital located as far south as possible—in order to reduce the distance and inconvenience of travel between their districts and the seat of government and to guard against the likelihood that northern speculators, merchants, and manufacturers would exert undue influence, by fair means and foul, on the determination of national policy. Northerners espoused the mirror image of the southern position; their substantive concern was that the capital should not be at the mercy of undue pressures exerted by agrarian interests.

Hamilton had nothing to offer in exchange for votes to secure passage of the assumption bill. Assumption of the states' debts by the federal government was difficult for southern Representatives to swallow, although Richard Bland Lee of Virginia had hinted broadly about a trade of southern votes for assumption in exchange for northern support for a southern location for the Federal District, the permanent seat of government. But the New Englanders refused to consider such a trade.

Senator Robert Morris of Pennsylvania and Secretary of State Thomas Jefferson entered the picture to untangle the mess. Morris generally supported Hamilton's proposals but was also interested in securing at least a temporary location for the new capital in Philadelphia, and perhaps a permanent site on the banks of the Delaware River—where he had made extensive real estate investments. Similarly, President Washington's investments in land on the banks of the Potomac inclined him to favor a site for the capital on that river, close to Mount Vernon.

Jefferson had no personal interests to advance; he had made no speculative investments in land and had no special hope for profit based on the location of the Federal District. But he appreciated the critical state to which the impasse over assumption might bring the new government and wanted it resolved as soon as possible. He also was concerned about the political situation in Europe; in the event of an outbreak of war there, the United States could preserve its neutrality only if its internal stability were not damaged by the failure of Hamilton's proposals.

In a complex and still-controversial series of deals and maneuvers, including dinner hosted by Jefferson at which both Hamilton and Madison were guests, these leaders and their colleagues (with Washington's silent blessing) hammered out what has come to be called the Compromise of 1790.[17] Under this plan, the temporary capital would move from New York to Philadelphia in late 1790; it would stay there for ten years before final relocation to a site on the banks of the Potomac. Robert Morris would arrange for the votes needed in the Senate to support the assumption and Federal District bills. Madison would mount only token opposition in the House, and a few key Representatives would switch their votes to support assumption. In return, Hamilton would modify the system for calculating the state and national debts to provide more sympathetic accounting of the Virginian debts and otherwise ensure that the state would not have to worry about paying more than it would receive under the assumption system. The various measures embodying the Compromise of 1790 were all enacted before Congress adjourned its second session.

The next major factional split was provoked by another House request for a report on the public credit for the opening of its third session in Philadelphia in December 1790. This resolution was an invitation to Hamilton to follow through on his proposals for additional taxes and for a national bank. But by the time Hamilton submitted this report, his thinking on the proper role of such a bank had changed. He now thought of this institution as a counterpart of the Bank of England—as the chief adjunct of the Treasury, as the depository of the funds of the federal government and the source of a stable and negotiable national currency. The government would support the Bank, in that stock in the institution could be purchased with government securities. The Bank would support the government in that it would have an interest in supporting the credit of the government so that the securities it received in payment for its stock would rise in value.[18]

The proposal to create a bank raised the first important constitutional issue in American history: whether the Constitution authorized Congress to charter a bank.[19] Madison had argued in *Federalist* No. 44 that the "necessary and proper" clause of Article I, Section 8 conferred power on Congress to adopt measures not specifically authorized by the Constitution if they would achieve ends recognized by the Constitution and were not plainly forbidden by that document.[20] Under this broad reading of that clause, Hamilton's proposal was constitutional. Nonetheless, in early February 1791 Madison denounced the Bank bill on the floor of the House as a violation of the Constitution. He declared that it stretched the grant of implied powers so far that it would nullify the general principle enshrined in Article I that Congress had only limited powers to legislate: "If implications thus remote and thus multiplied, can be linked together, a chain may be formed that will reach every object of legislation, every object within the whole compass of political economy."[21] Madison's opposition was unavailing; the House and Senate enacted a Bank bill that corresponded closely to the proposals in Hamilton's report.

The constitutional debate surrounding the Bank bill had not escaped Washington's attention. When the bill reached him, he submitted it to Attorney General Randolph for a formal opinion on its constitutionality. Randolph argued much as Madison had, recommending that the president veto the bill. Not satisfied, Washington then sought Jefferson's view, and the secretary of state obliged with a now-classic statement of the doctrine of strict construction of the Constitution,[22] following the lines of Madison's speeches in the House and adding a sheaf of arguments that the Bank violated a dizzying array of common-law doctrines. Bending to the disapproving voices of three of his closest advisers, Washington sent Randolph's and Jefferson's opinions to Hamilton with a note inviting him to submit a defense of the proposed legislation. Meanwhile, Washington asked Madison to prepare a veto message.

Hamilton's opinion on the constitutionality of the Bank[23] is justly regarded as a masterpiece of legal and constitutional argument. Hamilton began his analysis by pointing out the difference between ends and means. Implied powers were legitimate means to obtain ends expressly authorized by the Constitution. Congress clearly could exert implied powers to achieve the authorized ends of collecting taxes, regulating foreign and interstate commerce, and supervising the national currency, and had done so in the Bank bill. Second, Hamilton rejected Jefferson's emphasis on the word *necessary* in the "necessary and proper" clause: "If the end be clearly comprehended within any of the specified powers, and if the measure have an obvious relation to that end, and is not forbidden by any particular provision of the Constitution—it may safely be deemed to come within the compass of the national authority."[24] Having refuted Randolph's and Jefferson's constitutional arguments, Hamilton demolished their purely legal arguments. He concluded by establishing the political necessity of the Bank legislation.

The bill fixing the site of the Federal District was approaching a crisis at about the same time as the administration's internal debate over the Bank bill. Washington accepted Hamilton's arguments and signed the Bank bill, and Congress preserved the Compromise of 1790 by passing the bill creating the Federal District on the banks of the Potomac.[25]

Notwithstanding the traditional understanding that Hamilton and Jefferson emerged early as the leaders of the Federalist and Republican parties, respectively, the contest over the Bank bill was a purely internal matter within the executive branch. None of the crucial legal opinions was made public at the time. But party feeling was emerging in the spring of 1791, and Hamilton was coming more and more to be identified as the "Colossus of Federalism." His third great state paper, the *Report on Manufactures,* challenged the core doctrines of Jefferson's and Madison's political and economic thinking, and thus helped to precipitate the formal emergence of political parties.[26]

Hamilton urged that the United States expand its economic base to include manufacturing as well as agriculture. Manufacturing, he argued, was just as productive as agriculture, and indeed would benefit the farmers of America. He rejected the arguments of the revered Adam Smith that, if left to itself, the economy would naturally produce the most beneficial results for itself and for society. Rather, Hamilton contended, government should seek to influence economic activity for society's benefit rather than permitting economic activity to continue untouched in the hope that society would benefit from it.

Hamilton proposed that the United States launch an ambitious and multifaceted program of encouraging local manufactures—by enacting tariffs to protect fledgling industries until they were securely established; by awarding prizes for new developments in technology; by strictly controlling or even prohibiting the export of raw materials; by subsidizing key industries or projects; by building a system of roads and canals to open new and more expeditious channels for internal economic activity; by adopting a system for regulating the quality of manufactured products; and by encouraging inventions. Based on exhaustive research by Hamilton and his friend Tench Coxe, the assistant secretary of the Treasury, this report has become "the Bible of those who have advocated government aid to encourage industry."[27] It was the capstone of the intellectual structure set forth by Hamilton's reports on the public credit and the Bank.

Neither Hamilton's political opponents nor his allies shared his vision of the possibilities for encouraging manufacturing. The Society for Encouraging Useful Manufactures, founded less than two weeks before Hamilton released his report, had set out to create a model community in New Jersey, named Paterson after the eminent New Jersey Federalist William Paterson, but within five years the experiment proved a costly failure. Similarly, most of Hamilton's friends and allies preferred to invest in speculative ventures promising an easy and lucrative return rather than in manufacturing and industrial ventures that could promise returns only in the long term. And Hamilton's political opponents, including Jefferson and his former ally Madison, could not accept his arguments for the virtues of manufacturing as an appropriate, moral, and beneficial form of economic activity. The vision

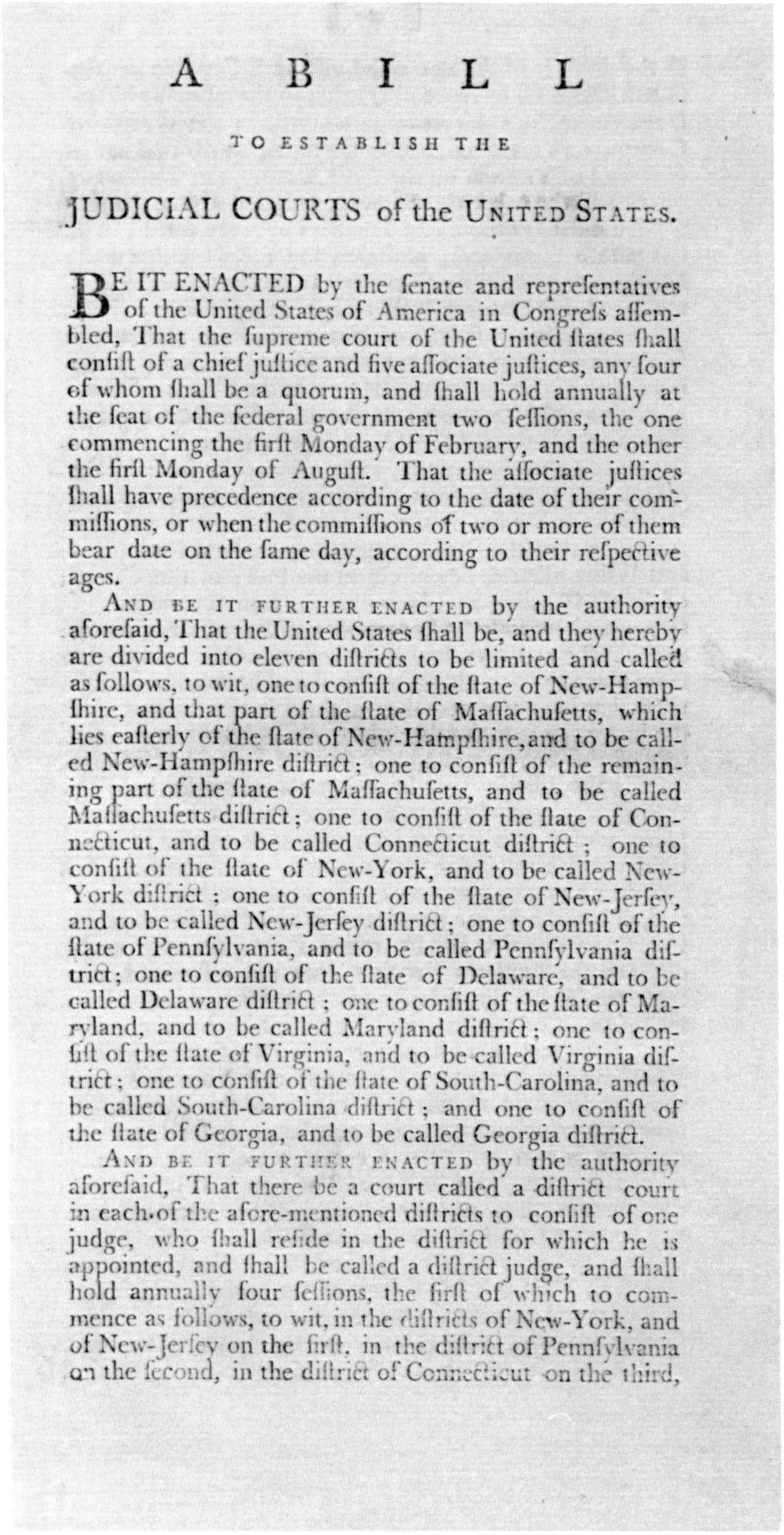

Figure 8.6
A Bill to Establish the Judicial
Courts of the United States (New
York: Thomas Greenleaf, 1789).

A   B I L L

TO ESTABLISH THE

JUDICIAL COURTS of the UNITED STATES.

BE IT ENACTED by the senate and representatives of the United States of America in Congress assembled, That the supreme court of the United states shall consist of a chief justice and five associate justices, any four of whom shall be a quorum, and shall hold annually at the seat of the federal government two sessions, the one commencing the first Monday of February, and the other the first Monday of August. That the associate justices shall have precedence according to the date of their commissions, or when the commissions of two or more of them bear date on the same day, according to their respective ages.

AND BE IT FURTHER ENACTED by the authority aforesaid, That the United States shall be, and they hereby are divided into eleven districts to be limited and called as follows, to wit, one to consist of the state of New-Hampshire, and that part of the state of Massachusetts, which lies easterly of the state of New-Hampshire, and to be called New-Hampshire district; one to consist of the remaining part of the state of Massachusetts, and to be called Massachusetts district; one to consist of the state of Connecticut, and to be called Connecticut district; one to consist of the state of New-York, and to be called New-York district; one to consist of the state of New-Jersey, and to be called New-Jersey district; one to consist of the state of Pennsylvania, and to be called Pennsylvania district; one to consist of the state of Delaware, and to be called Delaware district; one to consist of the state of Maryland, and to be called Maryland district; one to consist of the state of Virginia, and to be called Virginia district; one to consist of the state of South-Carolina, and to be called South-Carolina district; and one to consist of the state of Georgia, and to be called Georgia district.

AND BE IT FURTHER ENACTED by the authority aforesaid, That there be a court called a district court in each of the afore-mentioned districts to consist of one judge, who shall reside in the district for which he is appointed, and shall be called a district judge, and shall hold annually four sessions, the first of which to commence as follows, to wit, in the districts of New-York, and of New-Jersey on the first, in the district of Pennsylvania on the second, in the district of Connecticut on the third, presented in Hamilton's *Report on Manufactures* remained unfulfilled for at least a generation.[28]

Although Congress and the executive branch were the most active and prominent agencies of the new government, the federal judiciary had the greatest day-to-day contact with the American people.[29] The creation of the nation's court system was the Senate's only major contribution to completing the new structure of government. Led by Oliver Ellsworth, William Paterson, and Caleb Strong, all of whom had been delegates to the Federal Convention and supporters of the Constitution (Ellsworth and Paterson later became members of the Supreme Court), the Senate framed the Judiciary Act of 1789 (Figure 8.6). Amended only in a few technical matters by the House, this statute may well be the most significant and enduring law ever adopted by Congress.[30]

The Judiciary Act created a three-tier system of federal courts and established their jurisdictions within the limits spelled out by Article III of the Constitution. It created thirteen district courts, one for each of the eleven states plus one for Maine (then part of Massachusetts) and one for the territory of Kentucky. Later amendments to the Judiciary Act created district courts for North Carolina and Rhode Island when they ratified the Constitution. The district courts were specialized trial courts with narrow grants of jurisdiction. Each district also had a U.S. attorney, a member of the bar whose salary was covered by court fees and who was allowed to maintain his private practice. There was no department of justice, and the attorney general had no responsibility to supervise the U.S. attorneys; in fact, until the 1790s they were under the jurisdiction of the Department of State.

The statute also divided the nation into three circuits: the Eastern (including New England and New York), the Middle (including the states from New Jersey through Virginia), and the Southern (South Carolina and Georgia). When North Carolina and Rhode Island ratified the Constitution, Congress amended the Judiciary Act to assign them to the Southern and Eastern circuits, respectively. Two justices of the Supreme Court would be assigned to each circuit and would sit with the U.S. district judge as a circuit court in each district twice a year. These circuit courts were the principal trial courts of the federal judiciary.

At the top of the system the Judiciary Act established the United States Supreme Court, consisting of a Chief Justice and five Associate Justices. The Justices were required to serve on the circuit courts, and the rigors of travel in this period took their toll; Justice James Iredell, for example, estimated that he had to travel twelve hundred miles twice a year to perform his duties on the Southern Circuit. Regrettably, the Justices' repeated complaints to Congress and the attorney general were ignored, and this arrangement continued for decades. In addition to the Justices' circuit-riding responsibilities, the Supreme Court had its own institutional jurisdiction, both for appeals from the lower federal courts and highest state courts and for cases that could begin in the Court itself.

Within two days of the enactment of the Judiciary Act of 1789, President Washington appointed and the Senate confirmed the first justices of the Court.[31] The president named James Wilson and two other delegates to the Federal Convention, John Rutledge and John Blair, to serve with Chief Justice John Jay. Completing the roster were William Cushing, a noted Massachusetts jurist who had presided over the Massachusetts ratifying convention, and Robert Hanson Harrison, a prominent Maryland judge and comrade-in-arms of Washington from the early days of the Revolution. Harrison declined his appointment, citing his fragile health and his recent appointment as chancellor of Maryland; he died in early 1790, just as the Court was about to hold its first session. By this time North Carolina had ratified the Constitution, and Washington nominated James Iredell, the leader of the state's Federalists, to fill the sixth seat. As with his nominations to the executive department, Washington based his choices for the Court on the nominees' abilities, their support of the Constitution, and geographic balance.

The federal courts' first years were uneventful.[32] John Rutledge resigned after little more than a year without ever having joined his colleagues in a session of the Court, although he did fulfill his responsibilities on the Southern Circuit. The Supreme Court had almost no business before it; most of the federal caseload was handled by the circuit courts. The opening of each circuit term was an occasion for showing the dignity and authority of the government. The presiding Justice delivered a charge to the grand jury at the opening of each session, explaining not merely the duties and powers of the grand jurors but also the basic principles underlying the Constitution, the government it created, the laws enacted under its authority, and the rights and responsibilities of its citizens.[33]

The federal courts were impartial forums for the claims of out-of-state plaintiffs against in-state defendants, especially suits to enforce the rights of British subjects and Loyalists to recover debts owed by Americans. As several Anti-Federalists had feared, the circuit courts upheld the rights of these plaintiffs under the Treaty of Paris of 1783, setting aside state laws enacted to bar such suits or to limit recoveries. In May 1791 Chief Justice Jay, Associate Justice Cushing, and District Judge Richard Law, sitting as the U.S. Circuit Court for the District of Connecticut, overturned a Connecticut law barring British or Loyalist creditors from recovering interest accrued during the Revolution on otherwise recoverable debts. This case was followed by others striking down similar laws in South Carolina and Georgia, and by cases invalidating Rhode Island and Vermont laws deemed to violate the clause of the Constitution that barred states from impairing the obligations of contracts.[34]

These cases provoked little controversy and no challenges to the courts' constitutional authority to render such decisions. They laid the groundwork for the great decisions of the Supreme Court under Chief Justice John Marshall in the early nineteenth century, that the Court has not only the right but also the responsibility to give authoritative interpretations of the Constitution and to strike down federal and state laws inconsistent with or contradicting the Constitution. Judicial review had been practiced, with varying degrees of success, by the state courts in the 1770s and 1780s; during the ratification controversy, Alexander Hamilton had argued in *Federalist* No. 78 that the federal courts, especially the Supreme Court, would have this power. Led by Chief Justice Jay, the federal courts vindicated Hamilton's position.[35]

The Adoption of the Bill of Rights

Most Anti-Federalists gave up the struggle after Virginia and New York ratified the Constitution. Abandoning the campaign for a second convention, they turned their attention instead to the impending elections for the new government, thus conceding the legitimacy of the Constitution and working within its limits. Patrick Henry and George Clinton and their followers were not so easily reconciled to the Federalists' triumph. In July 1788 New York's ratifying convention had adopted a circular letter to the other states calling for a second general convention, and in November the Virginia legislature, under Henry's leadership, endorsed it.[36]

The proponents of a second convention had two major goals: a declaration of rights, and amendments to limit the powers of the federal government and to safeguard state sovereignty. During the ratification campaign the Federalists had altered their strategy to take account of the Anti-Federal and popular demand for a declaration of rights but had resisted efforts to strip the general government of the grants of authority and jurisdiction conferred by the Constitution. Now that the new form of government had been adopted and was being put into effect, the lines of contention gradually shifted. In February 1789 the New York legislature resolved "in behalf of our Constituents in the most earnest and Solemn manner" to apply to Congress for a second general convention (Figure 8.7). Their application was couched in dignified language masking a subtle threat:

> the People of the State of New York having ratified the Constitution . . . [were] in the fullest Confidence of obtaining a Revision of the said Constitution, by a general Convention; and in Confidence that certain Powers in and by the said Constitution granted would not be exercised until a Convention should have been called and Convened for proposing Amendments to the said Constitution . . . a Majority of the Members of [the New York ratifying convention] conceived several Articles of the Constitution so exceptionable that nothing but such Confidence, and an invincible Reluctance to Separate from our Sister States could have prevailed upon a sufficient number to assent to it without stipulating for previous Amendments . . . the Apprehensions and Discontents which those Articles occasion cannot be removed or allayed unless an

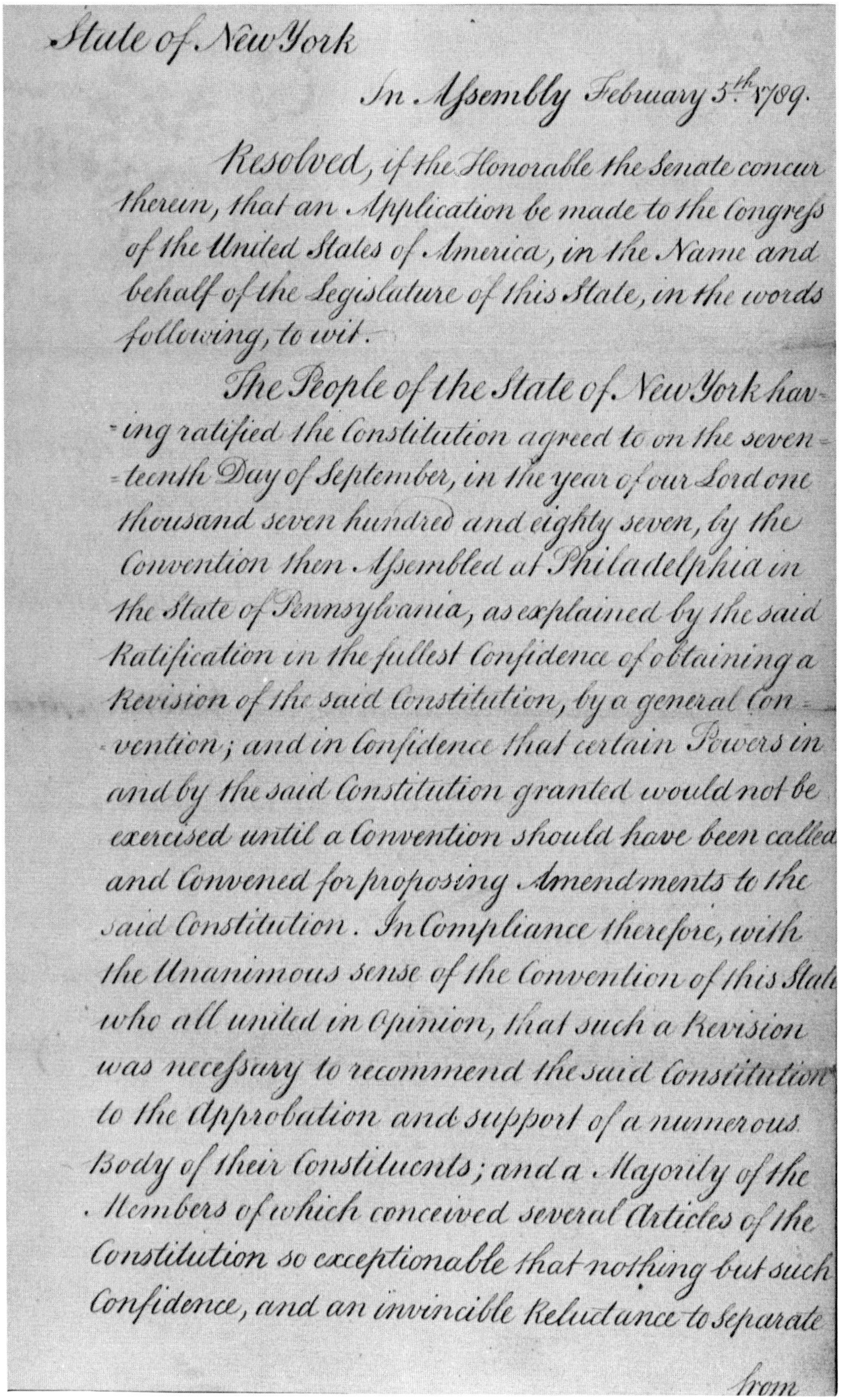

Figure 8.7
Resolution by the New York Assembly to apply to Congress for a convention to amend the Constitution. Albany, 5 February 1789.

State of New York

In Assembly February 5th 1789.

Resolved, if the Honorable the Senate concur therein, that an Application be made to the Congress of the United States of America, in the Name and behalf of the Legislature of this State, in the words following, to wit.

The People of the State of New York having ratified the Constitution agreed to on the seventeenth Day of September, in the year of our Lord one thousand seven hundred and eighty seven, by the Convention then Assembled at Philadelphia in the State of Pennsylvania, as explained by the said Ratification in the fullest Confidence of obtaining a Revision of the said Constitution, by a general Convention; and in Confidence that certain Powers in and by the said Constitution granted would not be exercised until a Convention should have been called and Convened for proposing Amendments to the said Constitution. In Compliance therefore, with the Unanimous sense of the Convention of this State who all united in Opinion, that such a Revision was necessary to recommend the said Constitution to the Approbation and support of a numerous Body of their Constituents; and a Majority of the Members of which conceived several Articles of the Constitution so exceptionable that nothing but such Confidence, and an invincible Reluctance to separate

from

Act to revise the said Constitution, be among the first that shall be passed by the new Congress.[37]

In the months before the inception of the new government, the Federalists began to differ among themselves. Some, such as the acidulous Representative Fisher Ames of Massachusetts, favored ignoring the clamor for amendments of any kind; having won adoption of a vigorous, energetic new form of government, they were satisfied, and regarded any favorable response to the popular demand for amendments as a sign of weakness and a bid for popularity.[38] Other, more moderate Federalists, led by James Madison, began to consider the demand for amendments seriously.[39] Madison had been swayed by Thomas Jefferson's appeals for the adoption of a bill of rights, which Jefferson described as something that "the people are entitled to against every government on earth, general or particular, and [that] no government should refuse, or rest on inference."[40] In the Virginia ratifying convention, and again in his hotly contested campaign for election to the House of Representatives against James Monroe, Madison repeatedly promised to work for the adoption of a bill of rights—giving the promise at first as part of the price of ratification and a way to head off the campaign for a second convention, but later out of his own emerging conviction that Jefferson was right.

In the first years of his administration Washington turned repeatedly to Madison for advice and for help in drafting speeches and official messages. His first inaugural address was largely Madison's work, and it contained only one substantive recommendation to the new Congress: to consider the question of amendments to the Constitution. The speech is both a clear statement of the moderate Federalist position on amendments and a useful example of Washington's manner of seeking to influence Congress while carefully deferring to its primary role in the legislative process:

> Besides the ordinary objects submitted to your care, it will remain with your judgment to decide, how far an exercise of the occasional power delegated by the Fifth article of the Constitution is rendered expedient at the present juncture by the nature of objections which have been urged against the System, or by the degree of inquietude which has given birth to them. Instead of undertaking particular recommendations on this subject, in which I would be guided by no lights derived from official opportunities, I shall again give way to my entire confidence in your discernment and pursuit of the public good: For I assure myself that whilst you carefully avoid every alteration which might endanger the benefits of an United and effective Government, or which ought to await the future lessons of experience; a reverence for the characteristic rights of freemen, and a regard for the public harmony, will sufficiently influence your deliberations on the question how far the former can be more impregnably fortified, or the latter be safely and advantageously promoted.[41]

Within a week of Washington's inauguration, Madison made his first move in the House to fulfill both his campaign pledge and the president's recommendations. On 4 May 1789 he announced his plan to propose constitutional amendments in three weeks. His statement was adroitly timed. The very next day, his Anti-Federal colleague Theodorick Bland presented Virginia's formal application for a second general convention. Led by Madison, the House voted that this petition be "laid on the table"—that is, shelved without discussion—until enough states had filed applications to require the calling of a second convention under Article V of the Constitution. New York's application arrived the next day and was treated in the same way.[42]

Madison's announcement is generally regarded as having given the death blow to the movement for a second convention. The next step in his campaign for amendments came on 8 June 1789, when he finally acted on his promise of 4 May. He had been forced to postpone this move for two weeks because of protracted wrangling over the import bill, but he felt that the matter of amendments could not be safely postponed any longer, even though the import debate was still in full swing. Thus he urged that the House resolve itself into a committee of the whole to consider proposals for amendments. To his consternation, many of his fellow Representatives, both extreme Federalists and Anti-Federalists, resisted his motion on the grounds that all of the new government's institutional framework should be established before amendments were considered. Madison fought attempts to bury his proposals. After hours of debate the House let him explain his proposed amendments and then agreed to place them on the agenda of the Committee of the Whole for later discussion.

Madison had culled his proposals from a compilation of the various state conventions' lists of recommendatory amendments and systematized and rewritten them. In drafting his list of proposed amendments he followed the principles elaborated in Washington's inaugural address, promoting the defense of individual liberties while rejecting ideas that would have weakened the government.[43] Several of Madison's proposals were substantially the same as the amendments now known as the Bill of Rights. In addition he made four proposals that Congress eventually rejected: a general statement of the origins of republican government and the proper relations between government and the people; a provision barring states from violating the rights of conscience, or freedom of the press, or trial by jury in criminal cases—a provision that Madison considered the most important and valuable of the lot; a provision limiting appeals of lower-court decisions; and a statement of the doctrine of separation of powers.

In July Madison again reminded the House of his pending proposals but achieved only the appointment of a select committee consisting of one Representative from each state, with himself representing Virginia. This committee's report, delivered a week later, preserved Madison's proposals with only a few changes in wording. The House delayed consideration until mid-August, and even then seemed more interested in debating the necessity

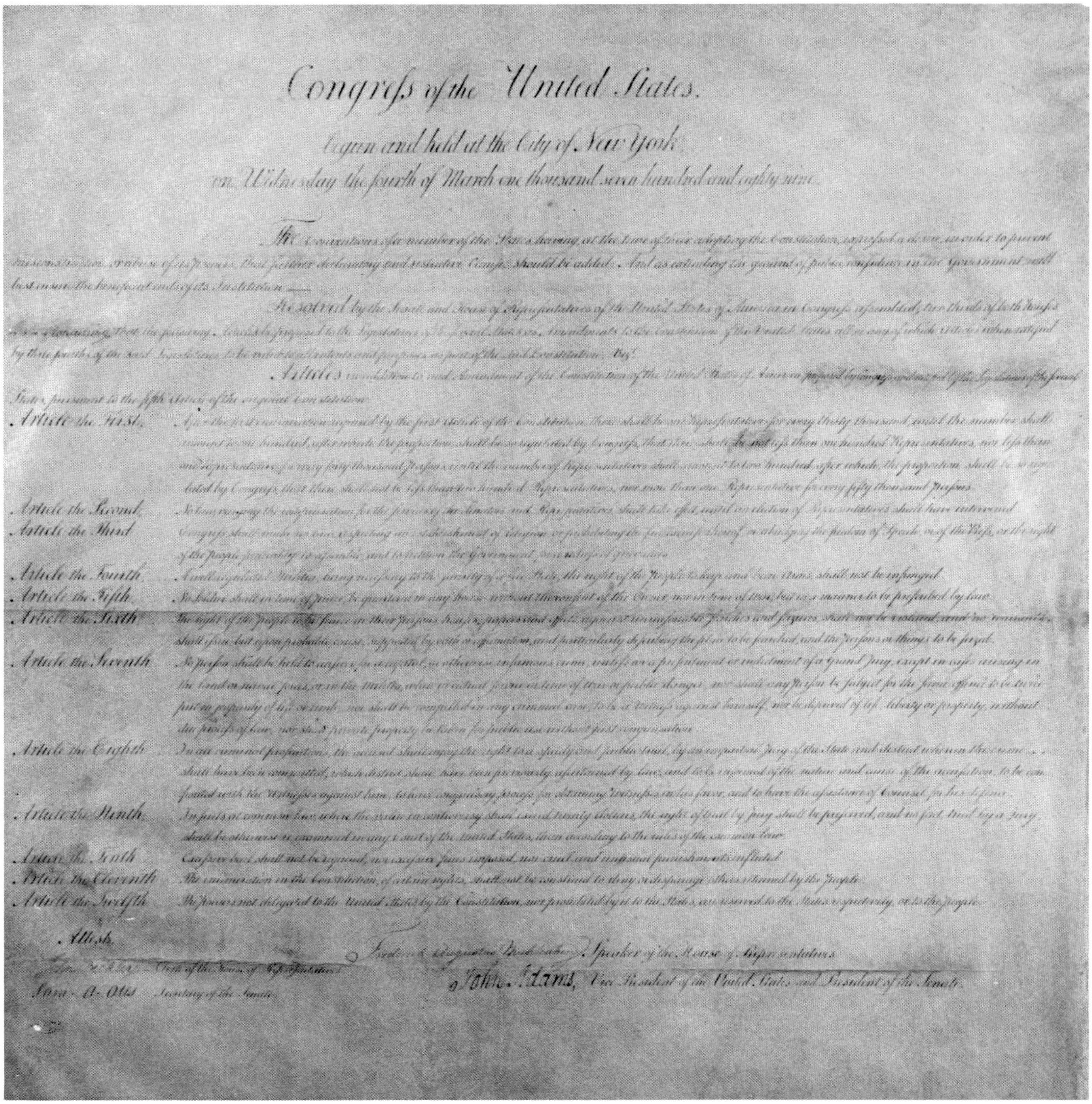
Congress of the United States,
begun and held at the City of New-York,
on Wednesday the fourth of March one thousand seven hundred and eighty nine.

Article the First
Article the Second
Article the Third
Article the Fourth
Article the Fifth
Article the Sixth
Article the Seventh
Article the Eighth
Article the Ninth
Article the Tenth
Article the Eleventh
Article the Twelfth

Attest,
Speaker of the House of Representatives.
John Adams, Vice President of the United States, and President of the Senate.

Figure 8.8
The Bill of Rights. Engrossed copy, September 1789.

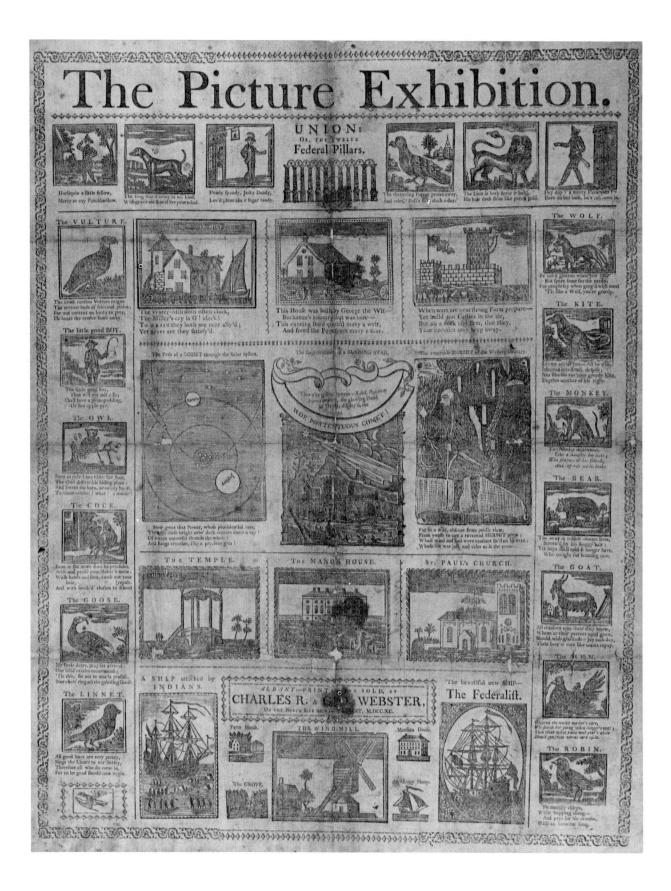

of amendments than their substance. The records of the debates offer little indication of what the Representatives thought about the proposed amendments' meaning or consequences. On 24 August 1789, after further revision, the House finally passed seventeen proposed amendments, most of which incorporated the substance of Madison's original proposals.

Because the Senate met in closed session there are few records of what its members thought of the House proposals.[44] Some Senators resisted the whole project, and most seemed to treat the matter lightly. The Senate proposed several alterations, dropping the purely theoretical provisions, the limit on appeals, and the amendment limiting state powers to infringe individual rights. It also dropped a clause from the amendment protecting the right to bear arms that would have recognized the rights of conscientious objectors; weakened the clause dealing with separation of church and state; and reshaped the seventeen House proposals into twelve amendments. On 9 September the Senate sent the proposals back to the House, which accepted some changes, rejected others, and called for the appointment of a House-Senate conference committee to resolve the differences between the two versions. Madison served on this committee, and under his leadership the House members managed to restore stronger and more definite language, especially regarding separation of church and state. Congress adopted the version produced by the conference committee and sent it to the states on 25 September 1789.[45] Two of the proposed amendments, dealing with modes of apportioning the House and with congressional salaries, were not adopted. The remaining ten were ratified and are now known as the Bill of Rights (Figure 8.8).

Although most Americans welcomed the proposed amendments, opposition developed in some key states.[46] Disgruntled Anti-Federalists complained that the amendments were a sham that did not address or remedy the dangers posed by the powerful new government created by the Constitution. Extreme Federalists, who dominated the legislatures of Massachusetts and Connecticut, managed to prevent them from taking final action on the proposed amendments.[47]

Most states moved quickly, however, and by the end of June 1790 nine states had ratified the Bill of Rights. Of these, the most important were North Carolina and Rhode Island. The failure of these states to ratify the Constitution had placed them in a strange position with respect to the United States. The new government chose not to impose tonnage duties and other tariffs on the "wayward sisters" for the moment, in the hope that this gesture of goodwill would persuade them to ratify the Constitution.[48]

North Carolina maintained observers in New York City to keep the state government informed of the Constitution's progress. The state seemed more and more eager for a chance to reconsider the Constitution, and Congress's proposal of amendments to the states provided that opportunity. In late November 1789 North Carolina's second ratifying convention ap-

Figure 8.9
The Picture Exhibition. Broadside (Albany: Charles R. and George Webster, 1790). This instructional broadside, intended for children, celebrates North Carolina's ratification of the Constitution in late 1789.

proved the Constitution by a margin of nearly three to one (Figure 8.9), and a few weeks later its legislature ratified the Bill of Rights.[49]

Rhode Island was a more difficult matter.[50] The state legislature repeatedly refused to call an election for a ratifying convention and kept itself at arm's length from the United States—an attitude reciprocated by the new national government. When President Washington made an official tour of New England (Figure 8.10), Rhode Islanders learned to their deep chagrin that he had bypassed their state. Jabez Bowen, the state's leading Federalist, wrote his old friend several times, urging him to treat Rhode Island with more friendliness. In his reply (Figure 8.11), Washington laid the blame entirely on the Anti-Federal majority in the state legislature and implied that the leniency with which the United States was treating Rhode Island could not last forever:

> As it is possible that the conduct of Rhode Island (if persevered in) may involve questions in Congress which will call for my official decisions, it is not fit that I should express more than a wish, in reply to your letter, that the Legislature at the coming session would consider *well* before it again rejects the proposition for calling a Convention to decide on their accession to or rejection of the present Government.—The adoption of it by No. Carolina has left them *entirely* alone.[54]

Figure 8.10
Samuel Hill after Jonathan Edes. *View of the triumphal Arch and Colonnade, erected in Boston.* Line engraving with wash, 1790. To celebrate President Washington's visit to Boston during his triumphal tour of the Northeast, the city erected a large arch across from the State House. The arch bore the inscription "To the Man Who Unites All Hearts" and a twenty-foot-high canopy surmounted by a huge eagle.

Figure 8.11
Letter from George Washington to Jabez Bowen, New York, 27 December 1789.

New York Dec.r 27.th 1789.

Sir

The letters with which you have
been pleased to favor me, dated in Oct.r
and the 15.th of the present month came
duly to hand, and are entitled to my
thanks for the communications contain=
ed in them. —

As it is possible that the conduct
of Rhode Island (if persevered in) may
involve questions, which in express which
will call express for my official decisions,
it is not fit that I should express more
than a wish — in reply to your letter — that
the Legislature at the coming session would
consider well before it ———— again re=
jects the proposition for calling a convention
to decide on their accession to or rejection
of the present Government. — The adopt=
on of it by N.o Carolina has left them entirely
alone. —

I am much obliged to you for your
good wishes, and with esteem & regard
I am — Sir
Y.r most Obed.t & hble Serv.
G.o W.

The Hon.ble
Jabez Bowen.

Ratification of the Conftitution of the United States by the Convention of the State of Rhode-Ifland and Providence-Plantations.

WE the DELEGATES of the PEOPLE of the STATE of RHODE-ISLAND AND PROVIDENCE-PLANTA-TIONS, duly elected and met in CONVENTION, having maturely confidered the CONSTITUTION for the UNITED STATES of AMERICA, agreed to on the Seventeenth Day of September, A. D. 1787, by the Convention then affembled at Philadelphia, in the Commonwealth of Pennfylvania (a Copy whereof precedes thefe Prefents) and having alfo ferioufly and deliberately confidered the prefent Situation of this State, DO DECLARE and MAKE KNOWN,

1ft. THAT there are certain natural rights, of which men, when they form a focial compact, cannot deprive or diveft their pofterity, among which are the enjoyment of life and liberty, with the means of acquiring, poffeffing, and protecting property, and purfuing and obtaining happinefs and fafety.

2. That all power is naturally vefted in and confequently derived from the people ; that magiftrates therefore, are their truftees and agents, and at all times amenable to them.

3. That the powers of government may be reaffumed by the people whenfoever it fhall become neceffary to their happinefs. That the rights of the State refpectively to nominate and appoint all State officers, and every other power, jurifdiction and right, which is not by the faid Convention clearly delegated to the Congrefs of the United States, or to the department of government thereof, remains to the people of the feveral States or their refpective State governments to whom they may have granted the fame ; and that thofe claufes in the Conftitution which declare that Congrefs fhall not have or exercife certain powers, do not imply that Congrefs is entitled to any powers not given by the faid Conftitution ; but fuch claufes are to be conftrued either as exceptions to certain fpecified powers, or as inferted merely for greater caution.

4. That religion, or the duty which we owe to our Creator, and the manner of difcharging it, can be directed only by reafon and conviction, not by force or violence, and therefore all men have an equal natural and unalienable right to the free exercife of religion according to the dictates of confcience ; and that no particular religion, fect or fociety ought to be favoured or eftablifhed by law in preference to others.

5. That the legiflative, executive and judiciary powers of government fhould be feparate and diftinct ; and the members of the two firft may be reftrained from oppreffion by feeling and participating the public burthen, they fhould at fixed periods be reduced to a private ftation, return into the mafs of the people, and the vacancy be fupplied by certain and regular elections, in which all or any part of the former members to be eligible or ineligible, as the rules of the Conftitution of Government and the Laws fhall direct.

6. That elections of reprefentatives in the legiflature ought to be free and frequent ; and all men having fufficient evidence of permanent common intereft with, and attachment to the community, ought to have the right of fuffrage ; and no aid, charge, tax or fee can be fet, rated, or levied upon the people, without their own confent or that of their Reprefentatives fo elected ; nor can they be bound by any law to which they have not, in like manner, affented for the public good.

7. That all power of fufpending laws, or the execution of laws by any authority, without the confent of the Reprefentatives of the people in the Legiflature, is injurious to their rights, and ought not to be exercifed.

8. That in all capital and criminal profecutions a man hath a right to demand the caufe and nature of his accufation, to be confronted with the accufers and witneffes, to call for evidence, and to be allowed council in his favor, and to a fair and fpeedy trial by an impartial jury of his vicinage, without whofe unanimous confent he cannot be found guilty (except in the government of the land and naval forces) nor can he be compelled to give evidence againft himfelf.

9. That no freeman ought to be taken, imprifoned or diffeized of his freehold, liberties, privileges or franchifes, or outlawed or exiled, or in any manner deftroyed, or deprived of his life, liberty or property, but by the trial by jury or by the law of the land.

10. That every freeman reftrained of his liberty is entitled to a remedy, to enquire into the lawfulnefs thereof, and to remove the fame if unlawful, and that fuch remedy ought not to be denied or delayed.

11. That in controverfies refpecting property, and in fuits between man and man, the antient trial by jury as hath been exercifed by us and our anceftors from the time whereof the memory of man is not to the contrary, is one of the greateft fecurities to the rights of the people, and ought to remain facred and inviolate.

12. That every freeman ought to obtain right and juftice freely and without fale, completely and without denial, promptly and without delay ; and that all eftablifhments or regulations contravening thefe rights are oppreffive and unjuft.

13. That exceffive bail ought not to be required, nor exceffive fines impofed, nor cruel or unufual punifhments inflicted.

14. That every perfon has a right to be fecure from all unreafonable fearches and feizures of his perfon, his papers, or his property, and therefore that all warrants to fearch fufpected places, or to feize any perfon, his papers, or his property, without information upon oath or affirmation, of fufficient caufe, are grievous and oppreffive, and that all general warrants (or fuch in which the place or perfon fufpected are not particularly defignated) are dangerous and ought not to be granted.

15. That the people have a right to freedom of fpeech, and of writing and publifhing their fentiments ; that the freedom of the prefs is one of the greateft bulwarks of liberty, and ought not to be violated.

16. That the people have a right peaceably to affemble together to confult for their common good, or to inftruct their reprefentatives ; and that every perfon has a right to petition or apply to the Legiflature for redrefs of grievances.

17. That the people have a right to keep and bear arms ; that a well regulated militia, including the body of the people capable of bearing arms, is the proper, natural and fafe defence of a free State ; that the militia fhall not be fubject to martial law, except in time of war, rebellion, or infurrection ; that ftanding armies in time of peace are dangerous to liberty, and ought not to be kept up, except in cafes of neceffity ; and that at all times the military fhould be under ftrict fubordination to the civil power ; that in time of peace no foldier ought to be quartered in any houfe without the confent of the owner ; and in time of war only by the civil magiftrate, in fuch manner as the law directs.

18. That any perfon religioufly fcrupulous of bearing arms ought to be exempted, upon payment of an equivalent to employ another to bear arms in his ftead.

UNDER thefe impreffions, and declaring that the rights aforefaid cannot be abridged or violated, and that the explanations aforefaid, are confiftent with the faid Conftitution, and in confidence that the amendments hereafter mentioned, will receive an early and mature confideration, and conformably to the fifth article of faid Conftitution, fpeedily become a part thereof ; WE, the faid DELEGATES, in the Name and in the Behalf of the PEOPLE of the STATE OF RHODE-ISLAND AND PROVIDENCE-PLANTATIONS, do by thefe Prefents, affent to and ratify the faid Conftitution. IN FULL CONFIDENCE, neverthelefs, that until the amendments hereafter propofed fhall be agreed to and ratified, in purfuant to the aforefaid fifth article, the militia of this State will not be continued in fervice out of this State for a longer term than fix weeks, without the confent of the Legiflature thereof ; that the Congrefs will not make or alter any regulation in this State refpecting the times, places and manner of holding elections for Senators or Reprefentatives, unlefs the Legiflature of this State fhall neglect or refufe to make laws or regulations for the purpofe, or from any circumftance be incapable of making the fame ; and that in thofe cafes fuch power will only be exercifed until the Legiflature of this State fhall make provifion in the premifes ; that the Congrefs will not lay direct taxes within this State

but when the monies arifing from the impoft, tonnage, and excife fhall be infufficient for the public exigencies ; nor until the Congrefs fhall have firft made a requifition upon this State to affefs, levy, and pay the amount of fuch requifition made agreeable to the cenfus fixed in the faid Conftitution in fuch way and manner as the Legiflature of this State fhall judge beft, and that the Congrefs will not lay or make any capitation or poll tax.

DONE IN CONVENTION, at Newport, in the County of Newport, in the State of Rhode-Ifland and Providence-Plantations, the 29th Day of May, in the Year of our Lord One Thoufand Seven Hundred and Ninety, and the Fourteenth Year of the Independence of the United States of America.

BY ORDER,

DANIEL OWEN, PRESIDENT.

ATTEST,

DANIEL UPDIKE, SECRETARY.

AND the CONVENTION DO, in the Name and Behalf of the PEOPLE of the STATE OF RHODE-ISLAND AND PROVIDENCE-PLANTATIONS, enjoin it upon the Senators and Reprefentative or Reprefentatives which may be elected to reprefent this State in Congrefs to exert all their influence and ufe all reafonable means to obtain a ratification of the following amendments to the faid Conftitution in the manner prefcribed therein ; and in all laws to be paffed by the Congrefs in the mean time to conform to the fpirit of the faid amendments, as far as the Conftitution will admit.

AMENDMENTS.

1. THE United States fhall guarantee to each State its fovereignty, freedom, and independence, and every power, jurifdiction and right, which is not by the Conftitution exprefsly delegated to the United States.

2. That Congrefs fhall not alter, modify or interfere in the times, places and manner of holding elections for Senators and Reprefentatives, or either of them, except when the Legiflature of any State fhall neglect, refufe, or be difabled by invafion or rebellion, to prefcribe the fame ; or in cafe when the provifion made by the State is fo imperfect as that no confequent election is had ; and then only until the Legiflature of fuch State fhall make provifion in the premifes.

3. It is declared by the Convention that the judicial power of the United States, in cafes in which a State may be a party, does not extend to criminal profecutions, or to authorize any fuit by any perfon againft a State ; but to remove all doubts or controverfies refpecting the fame, that it be efpecially expreffed as a part of the Conftitution of the United States, that Congrefs fhall not directly or indirectly, either by themfelves or through their judiciary, interfere with any one of the States in the redemption of paper money already emitted and now in circulation, or in liquidating or difcharging the public fecurities of any one State ; that each and every State fhall have the exclufive right of fuch laws and regulations for the before-mentioned purpofes, as they fhall think proper.

4. That no amendments to the Conftitution of the United States hereafter to be made, purfuant to the fifth article, fhall take effect, or become a part of the Conftitution of the United States after the year 1793, without the confent of eleven of the States heretofore united under one Confederation.

5. That the judicial power of the United States fhall extend to no poffible cafe where the caufe of action fhall have originated before the ratification of this Conftitution, except in difputes between States about their territory, difputes between perfons claiming lands under grants of different States, and debts due to the United States.

6. That no perfon fhall be compelled to do military duty, otherwife than by voluntary enliftment, except in cafes of general invafion ; any thing in the fecond paragraph of the fixth article of the Conftitution, or any law made under the Conftitution to the contrary notwithftanding.

7. That no capitation or poll tax fhall ever be laid by Congrefs.

8. In cafes of direct taxes Congrefs fhall firft make requifitions on the feveral States to affefs, levy, and pay their refpective proportions of fuch requifitions in fuch way and manner as the Legiflatures of the feveral States fhall judge beft ; and in cafe any State fhall neglect or refufe to pay its proportion purfuant to fuch requifition, then Congrefs may affefs and levy fuch State's proportion, together with intereft at the rate of fix per cent. per annum, from the time prefcribed in fuch requifition.

9. That Congrefs fhall lay no direct taxes without the confent of the Legiflatures of three fourths of the States in the union.

10. That the journals of the proceedings of the Senate and Houfe of Reprefentatives fhall be publifhed as foon as conveniently may be, at leaft once in every year, except fuch parts thereof relating to treaties, alliances, or military operations, as in their judgment require fecrecy.

11. That regular ftatements of the receipts and expenditures of all public monies fhall be publifhed at leaft once a year.

12. As ftanding armies in times of peace are dangerous to liberty and ought not to be kept up except in cafes of neceffity, and as at all times the military fhould be under ftrict fubordination to the civil power—that therefore no ftanding army or regular troops fhall be raifed or kept up in time of peace.

13. That no monies be borrowed on the credit of the United States without the affent of two thirds of the Senators and Reprefentatives prefent in each Houfe.

14. That the Congrefs fhall not declare war without the concurrence of two thirds of the Senators and Reprefentatives prefent in each houfe.

15. That the words " without the confent of Congrefs," in the feventh claufe in the ninth fection of the firft article of the Conftitution, be expunged.

16. That no Judge of the Supreme Court of the United States fhall hold any office under the United States, or any of them ; nor fhall any officer appointed by Congrefs, or by the Prefident and Senate of the United States, be permitted to hold any office under the appointment of any of the States.

17. As a traffic tending to eftablifh or continue the flavery of any part of the human fpecies is difgraceful to the caufe of liberty and humanity, that Congrefs fhall, as foon as may be, promote and eftablifh fuch laws and regulations as may effectually prevent the importation of flaves of every defcription into the United States.

18. That the State Legiflatures have power to recall, when they think it expedient, their Federal Senators, and to fend others in their ftead.

19. That Congrefs have power to eftablifh an uniform rule of inhabitancy or fettlement of the poor of the different States throughout the United States.

20. That Congrefs erect no company with exclufive advantages of commerce.

21. That whenever two members fhall move that the yeas and nays on any queftion fhall be taken, the fame fhall be entered on the journals of the refpective Houfes.

IN CONVENTION, MAY 29, 1790.

RESOLVED, That three hundred copies of the Ratification of the Conftitution of the United States by the Convention of this State, including the Bill of Rights and the propofed Amendments, be printed : That one copy be fent to each Member of this Convention, one to each Member of the Upper and Lower Houfes of Affembly, and one to each Town-Clerk in this State, for the general information of the people ; and that they be fent to the Sheriffs of the feveral Counties to be diftributed.

The foregoing is a true Copy.

By Order of the Convention,

DANIEL UPDIKE, SECRETARY.

Eventually Rhode Island's Federalists persuaded the legislature to call elections for a ratifying convention. The convention met in March 1790, but, after weeks of debate dominated by an Anti-Federal majority, adjourned until 24 May. Meanwhile, signs in Congress of growing impatience with Rhode Island's intransigence multiplied. Also, the town meeting of Providence adopted a resolution that, if the convention should reject the Constitution, it would apply to Congress to be placed under the authority and protection of the United States. This implied threat of secession had its effect. When it reassembled in late May, the convention immediately adjourned for a few days so that the delegates could consult their town meetings once again. On 29 May, the convention at last ratified the Constitution by the narrow vote of thirty-four to thirty-two (Figure 8.12). Two weeks later the state legislature ratified the Bill of Rights.

In March 1791 Vermont became the first new state to be admitted to the Union, resolving its fourteen-year-old controversy with New York. Several months later Vermont ratified the Bill of Rights. But with Vermont's admission eleven state ratifications were needed to put the Bill of Rights into effect. With the Federalists of Massachusetts and Connecticut resisting, and Georgia's state legislature inexplicably failing to act, the matter depended on Virginia.

The Virginian Anti-Federalists were stunned by Madison's great exertions to secure the passage of amendments; they could only charge that he had co-opted the drive for amendments and had framed a useless set of crowd-pleasing proposals in order to distract the people from the necessity to limit the powers of the government. The lower house of the Virginia legislature adopted the amendments, but the state senate under Henry's leadership remained obdurate. After pointing out that the Anti-Federalists had demanded amendments but now were the sole obstacle to their adoption, the Federalists shelved their campaign and waited to allow popular pressure to build for ratification. The impasse dragged on until the end of 1791, when the legislature exhumed the amendments and adopted them on 15 December, providing the necessary eleventh ratification.[53]

On 1 March 1792, Secretary of State Jefferson formally announced that the Bill of Rights was now part of the Constitution. This announcement marked the end of the making of the Constitution of the United States and the culmination of the process of enshrining individual rights as legally enforceable constitutional guarantees, a process that had begun in 1776 with the adoption of the Virginia Declaration of Rights. The Bill of Rights restrained only the federal government, however; individuals seeking to vindicate their rights against the actions of state or local governments had only the protection of state declarations of rights. Nonetheless, the Bill of Rights complemented the creation of a national government by recognizing its citizens' individual liberties. Once the balance between the federal government and the states was radically reshaped by the Civil War and the

Figure 8.12
Ratification of the Constitution of the United States by the Convention of the State of Rhode-Island and Providence-Plantations (Newport, 1790).

adoption of the Fourteenth Amendment, most of the rights guaranteed in the first ten amendments were extended to protect Americans against government infringements at all levels, and the vigor of the national government could be harnessed to protect and vindicate those rights.

THE ADOPTION of the Bill of Rights ended only the first stage of the history of the Constitution. Since 1791 the nation's charter has been amended sixteen times and shaped by judicial interpretation and by the evolution of informal practices and traditions and nonconstitutional institutions such as the Cabinet and political parties.

The nation the Constitution was intended to govern has also changed dramatically. The thirteen states and four million inhabitants of the 1780s have grown to fifty states and more than two hundred twenty million Americans whose diversity of races, creeds, and national origins would have been inconceivable two centuries ago. The vast but fragile new republic has become the most powerful nation on the globe. American culture, once mocked by European writers as sterile and derivative, now exerts a universal fascination. We have experienced several wars, major and minor, declared and undeclared, including a Civil War that threatened to destroy the work of the Revolutionary generation.

Despite these changes, the evolution of American politics and society continues to be shaped by the Constitution and by the principles and doctrines built into it by the men who drafted it.[54] Even the tensions and disagreements that later generations of Americans had to resolve were forecast in that early era. The framers of the Constitution and the Bill of Rights always acted with an eye toward the interests of posterity and with the hope that their descendants would approve their labors. That the Constitution has worked as well as it has is a tribute to its flexibility and to the foresight of those who created it. That it may still be defective or capable of improvement is a challenge to us to equal the courage, imagination, and versatility of the Revolutionary generation of Americans.

ABBREVIATIONS

AP   Art, Prints and Photographs Division,
New York Public Library

APEC   Emmet Collection, Art, Prints and Photographs Division,
New York Public Library

APMC   McAlpin Collection, Art, Prints and Photographs Division,
New York Public Library

APSC   Stokes Collection, Art, Prints and Photographs Division,
New York Public Library

BC   Berg Collection, New York Public Library

GRD   General Research Division, New York Public Library

GWP   George Washington Papers, New York Public Library

MD   Map Division, New York Public Library

RB   Rare Books and Manuscripts Division, New York Public Library

RBAYP Abraham Yates, Jr., Papers, Rare Books and Manuscripts Division,
New York Public Library

RBBC   Bancroft Collection, Rare Books and Manuscripts Division,
New York Public Library

RBEC   Emmet Collection, Rare Books and Manuscripts Division,
New York Public Library

RBMC   Myers Collection, Rare Books and Manuscript Collection,
New York Public Library

CHRONOLOGY

1634

19 May | Organization of New England Confederation (lasted until 1684)

1686

20 December | Sir Edmund Andros arrives in Boston to organize Dominion of New England

1689

10 January to 25 July | Glorious Revolution in New England topples Andros and leads to dissolution of Dominion of New England

1751

March | Benjamin Franklin offers first proposal for union of British colonies in North America

1754

19 June to 10 July | Albany Congress

1765

22 March | Parliament and King George III enact Stamp Act

7 October to 25 October | Stamp Act Congress meets in New York City

1766

18 March | Parliament repeals Stamp Act
Parliament declares its authority to make laws binding American colonies "in all cases whatsoever"

1767

29 June | Parliament and George III enact Townshend Acts

5 November | John Dickinson publishes first "Letter from a Pennsylvania Farmer" denouncing British policy

1772

2 November   Founding in Boston of first Committee of Correspondence

1774

5 September   First Continental Congress convenes in Philadelphia

28 September   Joseph Galloway proposes plan of union at First Continental Congress

14 October   First Continental Congress adopts Declaration and Resolves

18 October   Non-Importation Association of 1774 adopted by First Continental Congress

1775

19 April   Battles of Lexington and Concord

10 May   Second Continental Congress convenes in Philadelphia

15 June   George Washington named commander-in-chief of Continental Army on motion of John Adams

5 July   Congress adopts Olive Branch Petition

23 August   George III proclaims colonies to be in state of open rebellion, rejecting Olive Branch Petition

1776

5 January   New Hampshire adopts provisional constitution

9 January   Publication of Thomas Paine's *Common Sense*

26 March   South Carolina adopts provisional constitution

April   Publication of John Adams's *Thoughts on Government*

May   Rhode Island revises colonial charter to remove all references to Great Britain and the king

10 May   Congress adopts resolution (with preamble by John Adams added on 15 May) calling on colonies to draft new constitutions

7 June   Richard Henry Lee of Virginia offers resolutions in Congress for declaring American independence, framing a confederation of the American states, and seeking foreign alliances

29 June   Virginia convention adopts constitution and Declaration of Rights

2 July   Congress adopts Lee's resolutions
New Jersey adopts constitution

4 July   Congress adopts Declaration of Independence

12 July   Congress begins review of draft of Articles of Confederation, prepared by John Dickinson

21 September	Delaware adopts constitution
26 September	Congress appoints commissioners to negotiate treaties of alliance and commerce with European nations
28 September	Pennsylvania adopts constitution
October	Connecticut revises charter to delete references to Great Britain and the king
8 November	Maryland adopts constitution
18 December	North Carolina adopts constitution

1777

5 February	Georgia adopts constitution
20 April	New York adopts constitution
2 July	Vermont adopts constitution as independent republic
17 October	"Convention of Saratoga" confirms American military victory at Battle of Saratoga (New York)
15 November	Congress adopts Articles of Confederation and submits them to the states for ratification

1778

6 February	French-American treaties of alliance and of amity and commerce signed in Paris

1779

18 June	Thomas Jefferson, Edmund Pendleton, and George Wythe submit Report of Committee of Revisors of the Laws to the Virginia legislature

1780

16 June	Massachusetts constitutional convention announces ratification of Massachusetts constitution of 1780

1781

2 January	Virginia cedes claims to western lands to secure Maryland's ratification of Articles of Confederation
3 February	Congress adopts proposed amendment to Articles of Confederation granting power to levy an impost
20 February	Congress appoints Robert Morris superintendent of finance
1 March	Maryland ratifies Articles of Confederation, putting them into effect as first instrument of government of United States of America
26 May	Congress approves charter of Bank of North America

14 June	Congress restructures delegation to peace talks, appointing Benjamin Franklin, John Jay, Thomas Jefferson, and Henry Laurens to join John Adams
20 December	Thomas Jefferson prepares first draft of *Notes on the State of Virginia*
31 December	Congress charters Bank of North America

1782

27 September	Negotiations begin on Preliminary Articles of Peace
1 November	Rhode Island rejects proposed impost of 1781

1783

20 January	Effective date of Preliminary Articles of Peace
10 March to 15 March	Newburgh Conspiracy arises and is defused by General Washington
15 April	Congress ratifies Preliminary Articles of Peace
14 June	Congress adopts second proposed amendment to Articles of Confederation granting power to levy an impost
25 November	British evacuate New York City
23 December	George Washington resigns as commander-in-chief of Continental Army

1784

23 April	Congress adopts Jefferson's Land Ordinance of 1784
7 May	John Jay becomes secretary for foreign affairs
28 May	Congress establishes Treasury Board to replace office of superintendent of finance resigned by Robert Morris
1 July	Rhode Island rejects proposed impost of 1783

1785

24 February	Congress appoints John Adams first American minister to Great Britain
10 March	Congress appoints Thomas Jefferson American minister to France to succeed Benjamin Franklin
28 March	Mount Vernon Conference
10 May	Thomas Jefferson publishes first edition of *Notes on the State of Virginia* for private distribution
20 May	Congress adopts Land Ordinance of 1785
June	James Madison prepares and distributes "Memorial and Remonstrance against Religious Assessments" to be submitted to Virginia legislature
June to September	Low point of depression of 1785

1786

16 January	Virginia legislature enacts Virginia Statute for Religious Freedom
20 July	Jay-Gardoqui talks begin
15 August	Protest meeting at Worcester, Massachusetts, signals outbreak of Shays's Rebellion
29 August	Congress authorizes Jay to "forbear" American navigation rights on Mississippi River in talks with Gardoqui, but southern states' opposition renders negotiations futile
11 September to 14 September	Annapolis Convention
October	John Adams begins writing *Defence of the Constitutions*

1787

February	Publication of first general-circulation edition of Jefferson's *Notes on the State of Virginia* Publication of first volume of John Adams's *Defence of the Constitutions*
4 February	Shaysites routed by Massachusetts militia at Petersham in last formal military engagement of Shays's Rebellion
21 February	Congress adopts resolution calling for national convention to meet in Philadelphia to revise Articles of Confederation
March	Massachusetts legislature pardons all participants in Shays's Rebellion except Daniel Shays
14 May	Scheduled opening date of Federal Convention in Philadelphia
25 May	Quorum of seven state delegations assembles to begin Federal Convention Election of George Washington as Convention president Appointment of committee to prepare rules
28 May	First report of committee on rules
29 May	Second report of committee on rules Edmund Randolph presents Virginia Plan Charles Pinckney of South Carolina proposes Pinckney Plan
30 May to 13 June	Committee of the Whole debates Virginia Plan
13 June	Report of Committee of the Whole
15 June	William Paterson of New Jersey presents New Jersey Plan
16 June to 19 June	Committee of the Whole debates New Jersey Plan
18 June	Alexander Hamilton presents his plan of a constitution for America
19 June	Committee of the Whole rejects New Jersey Plan Full Convention begins review of committee report
28 June	Benjamin Franklin asks that Convention open its sessions with prayer

2 July	Appointment of Grand Committee on Representation
5 July	Report of Grand Committee on Representation
6 July	Appointment of committee on apportionment of lower house
10 July	Report of committee on apportionment of lower house New York delegates Robert Yates and John Lansing, Jr., leave Convention, depriving New York of official representation
13 July	Confederation Congress adopts Northwest Ordinance
16 July	Adoption of Great Compromise on representation and taxation
17 July	Large-state delegates abandon resistance to Great Compromise
26 July	Appointment of Committee of Detail to prepare first draft of Constitution
26 July to 5 August	Convention in recess
6 August	Convention reconvenes Committee of Detail reports first draft of Constitution
22 August	Appointment of Committee of Eleven on navigation acts and slave trade
23 August	Report of Committee of Eleven submitted to and adopted by Convention
31 August	Appointment of Committee on Postponed Matters
1 September	First report of Committee on Postponed Matters
4 September	Second report of Committee on Postponed Matters
6 September	Appointment of Committee on Style and Arrangement to prepare revised draft of Constitution
12 September	Report of Committee on Style and Arrangement Convention rejects proposal by George Mason and Elbridge Gerry to prepare a declaration of rights
15 September	Edmund Randolph proposes submission of the Constitution to a second convention Convention rejects Randolph's proposal Convention adopts Constitution
17 September	Benjamin Franklin urges all delegates to sign Constitution Randolph, Mason, and Gerry refuse to sign Constitution Delegates sign engrossed copy of Constitution Convention dissolves
19 September	First newspaper publication of Constitution in *Pennsylvania Packet*
20 September	Confederation Congress receives Constitution and Convention's resolutions governing mode of ratification
28 September	Congress submits Constitution and resolutions to the states
27 October	*Federalist* No. 1 appears in *New-York Independent Journal*
7 December	Delaware ratifies Constitution unanimously

| 12 December | Pennsylvania ratifies Constitution, 46–23 |
| 18 December | New Jersey ratifies Constitution unanimously |

1788
——

2 January	Georgia ratifies Constitution unanimously, 128–40
9 January	Connecticut ratifies Constitution unanimously, 128–40
6 February	Massachusetts ratifies Constitution, 187–168, and adopts list of recommendatory amendments
24 March	Rhode Island town meetings reject Constitution, 2,708–237
28 April	Maryland ratifies Constitution, 63–11
23 May	South Carolina ratifies Constitution, 149–73, and adopts list of recommendatory amendments
13 June	Massachusetts legislature pardons Daniel Shays
21 June	New Hampshire ratifies Constitution, 57–47, and adopts list of recommendatory amendments
25 June	Virginia ratifies Constitution, 89–79, and adopts list of recommendatory amendments
2 July	President Cyrus Griffin announces New Hampshire's ratification to Confederation Congress and declares Constitution to be in effect Congress appoints committee to plan transition to new system of government
8 July	Committee reports draft of transition legislation to Confederation Congress
26 July	New York ratifies Constitution, 30–27, and adopts list of recommendatory amendments and circular letter to other states calling for second convention to consider amendments
28 July	Confederation Congress sets effective date of Constitution and dates for elections of Representatives, choosing of Senators, selection of presidential electors, and elections of president and vice-president
2 August	North Carolina postpones vote on ratification, 185–84, and proposes list of amendments to be adopted before convention will ratify Constitution
13 September	Confederation Congress selects New York City as first temporary capital of United States under Constitution
30 September (to 16 July 1789)	States choose Senators
10 October	Last day on which Confederation Congress is able to muster a quorum
10 November (to 11 May 1789)	States hold elections for House of Representatives
20 November	Virginia legislature adopts resolution calling for second convention

7 January	All states except New York have chosen presidential electors by this date
4 February	Electors vote for president
5 February	New York legislature adopts resolution calling for second convention
4 March	Effective date of Constitution
1 April	House of Representatives achieves quorum, begins first session
6 April	Senate achieves quorum, begins first session House and Senate meet in joint session to hear presidential election results George Washington declared unanimously elected first president of the United States John Adams declared first vice-president, with 34 of 69 electoral votes cast
30 April	Inauguration of George Washington and John Adams
4 May	James Madison announces to the House his plan to introduce proposals for constitutional amendments
1 June	First law enacted under Constitution, prescribing oath to support Constitution to be taken by federal, state, and local officeholders
8 June	Madison proposes amendments in House, including first version of Bill of Rights
4 July	Tariff Act enacted
27 July	Law creating office of secretary of state enacted
7 August	Law creating War Department and office of secretary of war enacted
2 September	Law creating Treasury Department and office of secretary of the Treasury enacted
11 September	Alexander Hamilton becomes first secretary of the Treasury
12 September	Henry Knox becomes first secretary of war
18 September	Law creating Department of State enacted
24 September	Judiciary Act of 1789 enacted
25 September	Congress proposes twelve amendments to Constitution to the states
26 September	Senate confirms appointments of first justices of U.S. Supreme Court
29 September	Enactment of first appropriations measures
1 November	First district court session under Judiciary Act of 1789
20 November	New Jersey ratifies Bill of Rights
21 November	North Carolina's second ratifying convention ratifies Constitution, 194–77, and adopts list of recommendatory amendments
30 November	Maryland ratifies Bill of Rights
8 December	North Carolina ratifies Bill of Rights

1790

1 January	New Hampshire ratifies Bill of Rights by this date
14 January	Hamilton submits *Report on the Public Credit* to Congress
19 January	North Carolina ratifies Bill of Rights
28 January	Delaware ratifies Bill of Rights
2 February	First session of U.S. Supreme Court under Judiciary Act of 1789 Edmund Randolph becomes first attorney general
22 March	Thomas Jefferson becomes first secretary of state
4 April	First circuit court session under Judiciary Act of 1789
29 May	Rhode Island ratifies Constitution, 34–32, and adopts list of recommendatory amendments
15 June	Rhode Island ratifies Bill of Rights
20 June	Compromise of 1790 negotiated by this date
16 July	Enactment of Residence Act
4 August	Enactment of Funding Act
14 December	Hamilton submits *Report on a National Bank*

1791

12 February to 23 February	Washington receives opinions from Randolph, Jefferson, and Hamilton on constitutionality of Bank of the United States and draft of veto message from Madison
25 February	Washington signs Bank legislation into law
3 March	Enactment of Excise Act
14 March	Vermont admitted to the Union
30 March	Washington proclaims location of permanent national capital on banks of Potomac River
4 July	Sale of stock of Bank of the United States begins
3 November	Vermont ratifies Bill of Rights
22 November	Incorporation of Society for Establishing Useful Manufactures
5 December	Hamilton submits *Report on Manufactures*
12 December	Bank of the United States opens for business
15 December	Virginia ratifies Bill of Rights

1792

1 March	Secretary of State Jefferson announces ratification of Bill of Rights

DELEGATES TO
THE FEDERAL CONVENTION
OF 1787

States are listed geographically from north to south; delegates are listed in order of seniority; * = signer of the Constitution.

NEW HAMPSHIRE

John Langdon (1741–1819)*
Nicholas Gilman (1755–1814)*

MASSACHUSETTS

Nathaniel Gorham (1738–1796)*
Caleb Strong (1745–1819)
Elbridge Gerry (1744–1814)
Rufus King (1755–1827)*

CONNECTICUT

William Samuel Johnson
    (1727–1819)*
Roger Sherman (1721–1793)*
Oliver Ellsworth (1745–1807)

NEW YORK

Robert Yates (1738–1801)
John Lansing, Jr. (1754–1829)
Alexander Hamilton (1755–1804)*

NEW JERSEY

William Livingston (1723–1790)*
David Brearly (1745–1790)*
William Paterson (1745–1806)*
William Churchill Houston
    (ca. 1746–1788)
Jonathan Dayton (1760–1824)*

PENNSYLVANIA

Benjamin Franklin (1706–1790)*
Robert Morris (1734–1806)*
George Clymer (1739–1813)*
Thomas Fitzsimons (1741–1811)*
James Wilson (1742–1798)*
Thomas Mifflin (1744–1800)*
Jared Ingersoll (1749–1822)*
Gouverneur Morris (1752–1816)*

DELAWARE

John Dickinson (1732–1807)*
George Read (1734–1798)*
Richard Bassett (1745–1815)*
Gunning Bedford, Jr. (1747–1812)*
Jacob Broom (1752–1809)*

MARYLAND

Daniel of St. Thomas Jenifer
    (1723–1790)*
Daniel Carroll (1730–1796)*
James McHenry (1753–1816)*
John Francis Mercer (1759–1821)
Luther Martin (ca. 1748–1826)

VIRGINIA

George Washington (1732–1799)*
George Mason (1725–1792)
George Wythe (1726–1806)
John Blair (1732–1800)*
Edmund Randolph (1753–1813)
James McClurg (ca. 1746–1823)
James Madison, Jr. (1751–1836)*

NORTH CAROLINA

Hugh Williamson (1738–1819)*
Alexander Martin (1740–1807)
William Richardson Davie
    (1756–1820)
William Blount (1749–1800)*
Richard Dobbs Spaight (1758–1802)*

SOUTH CAROLINA

John Rutledge (1739–1800)*
Charles Cotesworth Pinckney
    (1746–1825)*
Charles Pinckney (1757–1824)*
Pierce Butler (1744–1822)*

GEORGIA

Abraham Baldwin (1754–1807)*
William Few (1748–1828)*
William Houstoun
    (ca. 1755–1813 or 1833)
William Pierce (ca. 1740–1789)

NOTES

1. Prologue

1. Christopher Collier and James Lincoln Collier, *Decision in Philadelphia: The Constitutional Convention of 1787* (New York: Random House/Reader's Digest Press, 1986), chap. 2; Edwin J. Perkins, *The Economy of Colonial America* (New York: Columbia University Press, 1980), chap. 1; see also the first volume of a major multivolume work, Bernard Bailyn, *The Peopling of British North America: An Introduction* (New York: Alfred A. Knopf, 1986). See also Henry Adams, *History of the United States of America during the Administrations of Thomas Jefferson* (1889–90; reprint, New York: Library of America, 1986), 5–125, reprinted separately as *The United States in 1800* (Ithaca: Cornell University Press, 1962). On cities in this period, see Gary B. Nash, *The Urban Crucible: Social Change, Political Consciousness, and the Origins of the American Revolution* (Cambridge, Mass.: Harvard University Press, 1979). A fine work of synthesis is Richard Hofstadter, *America at 1750: A Social Portrait* (New York: Alfred A. Knopf, 1971).
2. Jacob E. Cooke, *Tench Coxe and the Early Republic* (Chapel Hill: University of North Carolina Press, 1978).
3. See generally John J. McCusker and Russell R. Menard, *The Economy of British America, 1607–1789* (Chapel Hill: University of North Carolina Press, 1985); Drew R. McCoy, *The Elusive Republic: Political Economy in Jeffersonian America* (Chapel Hill: University of North Carolina Press, 1980); Douglass G. Adair, "The Intellectual Origins of Jeffersonian Democracy: Republicanism, Class Struggle, and the Virtuous Farmer" (Ph. D. diss., Yale University, 1943).
4. Perkins, *Economy*, chap. 8. On the impact of economic abundance on American history, see the classic study by David M. Potter, *People of Plenty: Economic Abundance and the American Character* (Chicago: University of Chicago Press, 1954).
5. See J. R. Pole, *Political Representation in England and the Origins of the American Republic* (New York: Macmillan, 1966); Chilton Williamson, *American Suffrage from Property to Democracy* (Princeton: Princeton University Press, 1960).
6. Robert H. Wiebe, *The Opening of American Society: From the Adoption of the Constitution to the Eve of Disunion* (New York: Alfred A. Knopf, 1984), chap. 1; John B. Kirby, "Early American Politics—The Search for Ideology: An Historical Analysis and Critique of the Concept of 'Deference,'" *Journal of Politics*, 32 (1970), 808–838; Joy B. Gilsdorf and Robert R. Gilsdorf, "Elites and Electorates: Some Plain Truths for Historians of Colonial America," in David H. Hall, John M. Murrin, and Thad W. Tate, eds., *Saints and Revolutionaries: Essays on Early American History* (New York: W. W. Norton, 1984), 207–244.
7. Henry Steele Commager, *Freedom and Order* (New York: George Braziller, 1966), 215–223.

8. On Franklin, see P. M. Zall, *Benjamin Franklin Laughing* (Berkeley: University of California Press, 1980), 1–7.

9. See Bernard Sheehan, *Seeds of Extinction: Jeffersonian Philanthropy and the American Indian* (Chapel Hill: University of North Carolina Press, 1973); Francis Paul Prucha, *The Great Father: The U. S. Government and the American Indian*, 2 vols. (Lincoln: University of Nebraska Press, 1984), I, 5–60.

10. See Edmund S. Morgan, *American Slavery, American Freedom: The Ordeal of Colonial Virginia* (New York: W. W. Norton, 1974).

11. David Brion Davis, *The Problem of Slavery in Western Culture* (Ithaca: Cornell University Press, 1966); idem, *The Problem of Slavery in the Age of Revolution, 1770–1823* (Ithaca: Cornell University Press, 1975); Winthrop D. Jordan, *White over Black* (Chapel Hill: University of North Carolina Press, 1968).

12. A. Leon Higginbotham, Jr., *In the Matter of Color—Race and the American Legal Process: The Colonial Period* (New York: Oxford University Press, 1978); William M. Wiecek, "The Statutory Law of Slavery and Race in the Thirteen Mainland Colonies of British North America," *William and Mary Quarterly*, 3d ser., 34 (1977), 258–280.

13. On the antislavery movement see Davis, *Age of Revolution*; on the racial attitudes of opponents and supporters of slavery, see generally Jordan, *White over Black*.

14. Linda K. Kerber, *Women of the Republic: Intellect and Ideology in Revolutionary America* (Chapel Hill: University of North Carolina Press, 1980). The following paragraphs draw heavily on Kerber's analysis of these issues.

15. For one example see L. H. Butterfield, ed., *The Book of Abigail and John* (Cambridge, Mass.: Harvard University Press, 1976), a one-volume edition of the correspondence of Abigail and John Adams during the American Revolution.

16. The term is Alexander Hamilton's, from *Federalist* No. 6.

17. Abbot E. Smith, *Colonists in Bondage* (Chapel Hill: University of North Carolina Press, 1947); Richard B. Morris, *Government and Labor in Early America* (1946; reprint, Boston: Northeastern University Press, 1981), 310–512; David W. Galenson, *White Servitude in Colonial America, an Economic Analysis* (Cambridge: Cambridge University Press, 1981).

18. Peter J. Coleman, *Debtors and Creditors in America* (Madison: State Historical Society of Wisconsin, 1974). This discussion is also based on a survey of the records of the U. S. circuit courts from 1790 to 1793; these documents will be presented in Richard B. Morris and Ene Sirvet, eds., *John Jay: Chief Justice and Federalist Statesman, 1789–1829* (New York: Harper & Row, forthcoming).

19. See Henry Steele Commager, *Jefferson, Nationalism, and the Enlightenment* (New York: George Braziller, 1975).

20. Sydney E. Ahlstrom, *A Religious History of the American People* (1972; 2-vol. reprint, New York: Image Books/Doubleday, 1975), I, 329–470, 615–697.

21. Lawrence M. Cremin, *American Education: The Colonial Experience, 1607–1783* (New York: Harper & Row, 1970), 251–570; idem, *American Education: The National Experience, 1783–1865* (New York: Harper & Row, 1980), 103–245.

22. Russel B. Nye, *The Cultural Life of the New Nation* (New York: Harper & Row, 1963), 70–96.

23. The classic treatment is J. Franklin Jameson, *The American Revolution Considered as a Social Movement* (1926; reprint, Princeton: Princeton University Press, 1967). See also Stephen G. Kurtz and James H. Hutson, eds., *Essays on the American*

Revolution (Chapel Hill: University of North Carolina Press, 1973); Jackson Turner Main, *The Social Structure of Revolutionary America* (Princeton: Princeton University Press, 1965); Rhys Isaac, *The Transformation of Virginia, 1740–1790* (Chapel Hill: University of North Carolina Press, 1982); Ralph Ketcham, *From Colony to Country: The Revolution in American Thought* (New York: Macmillan, 1974); Charles Royster, *A Revolutionary People at War* (Chapel Hill: University of North Carolina Press, 1980).

2. A New Government for a New Nation

1. The best account of American colonial history in one volume is R. C. Simmons, *The American Colonies* (1978; reprint, New York: W. W. Norton, 1981).

2. See generally Robert C. Newbold, *The Albany Congress and Plan of Union of 1754* (New York: Vantage, 1955); Harry M. Ward, *"Unite or Die": Intercolony Relations, 1690–1763* (Port Washington, N. Y.: Kennikat, 1971); idem, *The United Colonies of New England, 1643–90* (New York: Vantage Press, 1961).

3. Quoted in Newbold, *Albany Congress*, 47.

4. Ward, *"Unite or Die,"* 12–15, Leonard W. Labaree, ed., *The Papers of Benjamin Franklin*, 24 vols. to date (New Haven: Yale University Press, 1959–: cited hereafter as *Franklin Papers*), V, 272–275.

5. *Franklin Papers*, V, 335–341.

6. "Short Hints. . . ," Committee report, RB; reprinted in *Franklin Papers*, V 357–364.

7. Ibid, 361.

8. Newbold, *Albany Congress*, 72–119; Bernard Bailyn, *The Ordeal of Thomas Hutchinson* (Cambridge, Mass.: Harvard University Press, 1974), 14–15; *Franklin Papers*, V, 366–392.

9. Newbold, *Albany Congress*, 134–178; *Franklin Papers*, V, 397–417, 441–447, 449–451.

10. Edmund S. Morgan and Helen M. Morgan, *The Stamp Act Crisis* (Chapel Hill: University of North Carolina Press, 1953); Bernhard Knollenberg, *Origins of the American Revolution 1759–1766*, rev. ed. (New York: Free Press, 1961); Merrill Jensen, *The Founding of a Nation: A History of the American Revolution, 1763–1776* (New York: Oxford University Press, 1968); Simmons, *American Colonies*, chap. 13.

11. Morgan and Morgan, *Stamp Act Crisis*, 144–206; Peter Shaw, *American Patriots and the Rituals of Revolution* (Cambridge, Mass.: Harvard University Press, 1981).

12. Lawrence Henry Gipson, *The Coming of the Revolution, 1763–1775* (New York: Harper & Row, 1954), 228–230; Julian P. Boyd, "Joseph Galloway's Plans of Union for the British Empire, 1774–1788," *Pennsylvania Magazine of History and Biography*, 64 (1940), 492–515.

13. Olive Branch Petition, RB; reproduced in Cornelius W. Wickersham and Gilbert H. Montague, eds., *The Olive Branch* (New York: New York Public Library, 1954), 15–21.

14. Wickersham and Montague, *Olive Branch*, 19–20.

15. Richard B. Morris, ed., *John Jay: The Making of a Revolutionary. Unpublished Papers 1745–1780* (New York: Harper & Row, 1975), 147–154 (draft at 152–154).

16. Arthur Lee and Richard Penn to unknown person, 2 September 1775, RB; reproduced in Wickersham and Montague, *Olive Branch*, 30.

17. Peter Shaw, *The Character of John Adams* (Chapel Hill: University of North Carolina Press, 1976), 89–92, gives a perceptive account of the controversy occasioned by the publication of Adams's letter. See also the account in L. H. Butterfield, ed., *The Diary and Autobiography of John Adams*, 4 vols. (Cambridge, Mass.: Harvard University Press, 1961), II, 174 and n. The letter quoted in the text—John Adams to James Warren, 24 July 1775 ("In Confidence")—appears in Massachusetts Historical Society *Collections*, vol. 73: *The Warren-Adams Letters*, 2 vols. (Boston: Massachusetts Historical Society, 1917-25), I, 88–89.

18. See generally James Thomas Flexner, *George Washington and the American Revolution, 1775-1783* (Boston: Houghton Mifflin, 1968).

19. See the discussion in Chapter 3.

20. The literature on this document is enormous. See, for example, Henry Steele Commager, "The Declaration of Independence: An Expression of the American Mind," in *Jefferson, Nationalism, and the Enlightenment* (New York: George Braziller, 1975), 77–89; Carl L. Becker, *The Declaration of Independence* (1926; reprint, New York: Vintage, 1955); Dumas Malone, *Jefferson the Virginian* (Boston: Little, Brown, 1948), 214–231; Garry Wills, *Inventing America: Jefferson's Declaration of Independence* (New York: Doubleday, 1978).

21. On this point see the challenging essay by John Phillip Reid, "The Irrelevance of the Declaration," in Hendrik Hartog, ed., *Law in the American Revolution and the Revolution in the Law* (New York: New York University Press, 1981), 46–89.

22. Merrill Jensen, *The Articles of Confederation: An Interpretation of the Social-Constitutional History of the American Revolution, 1774-1781* (Madison: University of Wisconsin Press, 1940), and Jack N. Rakove, *The Beginnings of National Politics: An Interpretive History of the Continental Congress* (New York: Alfred A. Knopf, 1979), provide the most extensive discussions from contrasting views. See also the discussions by Richard B. Morris, *The American Revolution Reconsidered* (New York: Harper & Row, 1967), chap. 4, and Alfred H. Kelly, Winfred Harbison, and Herman Belz, *The American Constitution: Its Origins and Development*, 6th ed. (New York: W. W. Norton, 1982), 79–85.

23. Jennings B. Sanders, *The Presidency of the Continental Congress, 1775-1789: A Study in American Institutional History* (Chicago: University of Chicago Press, 1930); Charles C. Thach, *The Creation of the Presidency, 1775-1789* (Baltimore: Johns Hopkins University Press, 1922).

24. See generally J. C. Bancroft Davis, "Federal Courts Prior to the Adoption of the Constitution," 131 U.S., Appendix, xix-xlix (1889); Peter S. Onuf, *The Origins of the Federal Republic: Jurisdictional Controversies in the United States, 1776-1787* (Philadelphia: University of Pennsylvania Press, 1983); Julius Goebel, Jr., *The Oliver Wendell Holmes Devise History of the Supreme Court of the United States, I: Antecedents and Beginnings to 1801* (New York: Macmillan, 1971), 182–195.

25. See Henry J. Bourguignon, *The First Federal Court: The Federal Appellate Prize Court of the American Revolution 1775-1787*, Memoirs of the American Philosophical Society, vol. 122 (Philadelphia: American Philosophical Society, 1977); Davis, "Federal Courts," l-lxiii; J. Franklin Jameson, "The Predecessor of the Supreme Court," in J. Franklin Jameson, ed., *Essays in the Constitutional History of the United States* (Boston: Houghton Mifflin, 1889), 1–45; Goebel, *Antecedents*, 149–181.

26. Jennings B. Sanders, *Evolution of the Executive Departments of the Continental Congress, 1774-1789* (Chapel Hill: University of North Carolina Press, 1935); Rakove, *Beginnings*, 297–359.

27. On the issue of western lands see also Thomas P. Abernethy, *Western Lands and the American Revolution* (1938; reprint, New York: Russell & Russell, 1958), and Onuf, *Origins*.

28. Kelly, Harbison, and Belz, *The American Constitution*, 80.

29. Onuf, *Origins*, 88–94; Abernethy, *Western Lands*, 242–246; Jensen, *Articles*, 226–228; Rakove, *Beginnings*, 352–354.

30. See generally Merrill Jensen, *The New Nation: A History of the United States during the Confederation, 1781-1789* (New York: Alfred A. Knopf, 1950). Jensen's generally optimistic view of the Confederation period has been challenged ably by Richard B. Morris, *The American Revolution Reconsidered*, chap. 4, but Morris agrees that the Confederation's accomplishments should not be discounted; see also idem, "The Forging of the Union Reconsidered: A Historical Refutation of State Sovereignty over Seabeds," *Columbia Law Review*, 74 (1974), 1054-93. See also the account in Rakove, *Beginnings*. [Eric M. Freedman,] "Note: The United States and the Articles of Confederation: Drifting toward Anarchy or Inching toward Commonwealth?" *Yale Law Journal*, 88 (1978), 142–166, gives a provocative analysis of the accomplishments of the Confederation government significantly at odds with Jensen's interpretation of the Articles as enshrining the principle that sovereignty be lodged as close to the people as possible rather than at the national level.

31. See generally Don Higginbotham, *The American War for Independence* (Bloomington: Indiana University Press, 1971); Charles Royster, *A Revolutionary People at War* (Chapel Hill: University of North Carolina Press, 1980); Lawrence D. Cress, *Citizens in Arms* (Chapel Hill: University of North Carolina Press, 1982); Christopher Ward, *The War of the Revolution*, 2 vols. (New York: Macmillan, 1952).

32. George Washington to the Officers of the Army, 15 March 1783, in John C. Fitzpatrick ed., *The Writings of George Washington*, 39 vols. (Washington, D.C.: U.S. Government Printing Office, 1931-44), XXVI, 222–227; reprinted in Richard B. Morris, ed., *Basic Documents on the Confederation and Constitution* (1970; reprint, Malabar, Fla.: Robert E. Krieger, 1985), 46–50 (quotation at 50). The best account of the Conspiracy is Richard H. Kohn, *Eagle and Sword: The Federalists and the Creation of the Military Establishment in America, 1783-1802* (New York: Macmillan, 1971), 17–39; see also Royster, *A Revolutionary People at War*, 333–341.

33. The authoritative study is Richard B. Morris, *The Peacemakers: The Great Powers and American Independence* (New York: Harper & Row, 1965), supplemented by Richard B. Morris and Ene Sirvet, eds., *John Jay—The Winning of the Peace: Unpublished Papers 1780-1784* (New York: Harper & Row, 1980); see also Morris, *The American Revolution Reconsidered*, chap. 3; Jonathan Dull, *The Diplomacy of the American Revolution* (New Haven: Yale University Press, 1985); Samuel Flagg Bemis, *The Diplomacy of the American Revolution* (New York: Henry Holt, 1935).

34. Morris, *Peacemakers*, passim.

35. On this subject see Chapter 3.

36. See generally Sanders, *Evolution of Executive Departments*.

37. See Jensen, *The New Nation*, 366–374, and E. James Ferguson, *The Power of the*

Purse: A History of American Public Finance, 1776-1790 (Chapel Hill: University of North Carolina Press, 1961).

38. Quoted in Jensen, *The New Nation,* 369. In addition to the works cited in note 37 above, see generally E. James Ferguson and John Catanzariti, eds., *The Papers of Robert Morris, 1781-1784,* 5 vols. to date (Pittsburgh: University of Pittsburgh Press, 1973–).

39. On the Mississippi controversy see Richard B. Morris, *Witnesses at the Creation: Hamilton, Madison, Jay, and the Constitution* (New York: Holt, Rinehart & Winston, 1985), 152–159; Frederick W. Marks III, *Independence on Trial: Foreign Affairs and the Making of the Constitution* (Baton Rouge: Louisiana State University Press, 1973), 21–32, 105–106; Joseph L. Davis, *Sectionalism in American Politics, 1774-1787* (Madison: University of Wisconsin Press, 1977), 109–126; Rakove, *Beginnings,* 349–350; and Jensen, *The New Nation,* 170–173. See generally Samuel Flagg Bemis, *Pinckney's Treaty: America's Advantage from Europe's Distress, 1783-1800,* rev. ed. (New Haven: Yale University Press, 1960); and Arthur P. Whitaker, *The Spanish-American Frontier, 1783-1795* (Boston: Houghton Mifflin, 1927).

40. Richard B. Morris, *John Jay, the Nation, and the Court* (Boston: Boston University Press, 1967), chap. 1.

41. See generally Onuf, *Origins.*

42. Henry Steele Commager, ed., *Documents in American History,* 9th ed. (New York: Appleton-Century-Crofts, 1973), no. 76.

43. Ibid., no. 77.

44. Ibid., no. 78.

45. Ibid., no. 82; on colonialism and these territorial ordinances see Henry Steele Commager, *The Empire of Reason: How Europe Conceived and America Realized the Enlightenment* (New York: Doubleday/Anchor, 1977), 195–197; Robert F. Berkhofer, Jr., "Jefferson, the Ordinances of 1784, and the Origins of the American Territorial System," *William and Mary Quarterly,* 3d ser., 29 (1972), 231–262; Jay Amos Barrett, *The Evolution of the Ordinance of 1787* (1891; reprint, New York: Arno Press, 1971); Merrill Jensen, "The Cession of the Old Northwest," *Mississippi Valley Historical Review,* 23 (1936), 27–48; idem, "The Creation of the National Domain, 1781–1784," ibid., 26 (1939), 323–342; Francis Philbrick, *The Rise of the West* (New York: Harper & Row, 1965), chaps. 4 and 5.

46. For a discussion of James Madison's April 1787 memorandum of this title, see Chapter 4 and Irving Brant, *James Madison: The Nationalist, 1780-1787* (Indianapolis: Bobbs-Merrill, 1948). The principal studies of the emergence of a new political generation in the 1770s and 1780s are John P. Roche, "The Founding Fathers: A Reform Caucus in Action," American Political Science Review, 55 (1961), 799–816; and Stanley M. Elkins and Eric L. McKitrick, "The Founding Fathers: Young Men of the Revolution," Political Science Quarterly, 76 (1961), 181–216.

3. An Age of Experiments in Government

1. On this subject see Pauline Maier, *From Resistance to Revolution: Colonial Radicals and the Development of American Opposition to Great Britain, 1765-1776* (New York:

Alfred A. Knopf, 1972); Willi Paul Adams, *The First American Constitutions* (Chapel Hill: University of North Carolina Press, 1980), 27–48. Adams's book is the best study of state constitution-making now available. See also Donald G. Lutz, *Popular Consent and Popular Control: Whig Political Theory and the State Constitutions* (Baton Rouge: Louisiana State University Press, 1980).

2. *Whereas his Britannic Majesty, in conjunction with . . . ,* Broadside (Philadelphia: John Dunlap, 15 May 1776), RB. The best analysis of the resolution is in Adams, *First American Constitutions,* 59–62.

3. Adams, *First American Constitutions,* 61.

4. Ibid., 49–62.

5. Robert J. Taylor et al., eds., *The Papers of John Adams,* 3d ser., 6 vols. to date (Cambridge, Mass.: Harvard University Press, 1977–), IV, 92.

6. On the fever of constitution-making see George Dargo, *Law in the New Republic: Private Law and the Public Estate* (New York: Alfred A. Knopf, 1983), 10; Adams, *First American Constitutions,* 49–98; Allan Nevins, *The American States during and after the Revolution, 1776-1789* (New York: Macmillan, 1924), 117–170. See also Jackson Turner Main, *The Sovereign States, 1775–1783* (New York: New Directions, 1973), a useful supplement to Nevins. The manuscript of the third draft of Jefferson's constitution is in RB; it is reprinted, with annotation and commentary, in Julian P. Boyd, ed., *The Papers of Thomas Jefferson,* 21 vols. to date (Princeton: Princeton University Press, 1950–; cited hereafter as *Jefferson Papers),* I, 356–365, and in Thomas Jefferson, *Notes on the State of Virginia,* ed. William Peden (Chapel Hill: University of North Carolina Press, 1955), 118–129. Jefferson's first two drafts and related documents are published in *Jefferson Papers,* I, 329–386. On the idea of a written constitution see Dargo, *Law in the New Republic,* 13–17; on the colonial heritage of written charters see idem, *Roots of the Republic: A New Perspective on Early American Constitutionalism* (New York: Praeger, 1974), chap. 3.

7. On this pamphlet, the first of Adams's great writings on constitutionalism (other than his pamphlet and newspaper writings on the constitutional controversy with Great Britain), see generally John R. Howe, Jr., *The Changing Political Thought of John Adams* (Princeton: Princeton University Press, 1966), 59–101; Peter Shaw, *The Character of John Adams* (Chapel Hill: University of North Carolina Press, 1976), 92–97; Timothy H. Breen, "John Adams' Fight against Innovation in the New England Constitution: 1776," *New England Quarterly,* 40 (1967), 501–520; Adams, *First American Constitutions,* 121–124. For the most authoritative edition of the text of the pamphlet, excellent annotations and commentary, and all surviving sources concerning its composition, publication, and reception, see Taylor et al., *Papers of John Adams,* IV, 65–93. The first version is John Adams to Richard Henry Lee, 15 November 1775, ibid., III, 307–308. See also L. H. Butterfield, ed., *The Diary and Autobiography of John Adams,* 4 vols. (Cambridge, Mass.: Harvard University Press, 1961), III, 331–332.

8. John Adams to James Warren, 20 April 1776, in Taylor et al., *Papers of John Adams,* IV, 130–132 (quotation at 131).

9. In a prefatory note written in 1811, Adams explained that he had decided to keep his name off the pamphlet because "if [my name] should appear, it would excite a continental clamor among the tories, that I was erecting a battering-ram

to demolish the royal government and render independence indispensable"; Charles Francis Adams, ed., *The Life and Works of John Adams,* 10 vols. (Boston: Little, Brown, 1850-56), IV, 189.

10. The history of *Thoughts on Government* receives most detailed analysis in Taylor et al., *Papers of John Adams,* IV, 65–73.

11. John Adams to James Warren, 20 April 1776, in Taylor et al., *Papers of John Adams,* IV, 132.

12. This paragraph is indebted to Willi Paul Adams's suggestive juxtaposition of *Common Sense* with *Thoughts on Government;* see Adams, *First American Constitutions,* 121–124. The phrase "revolutionary constitutionalism" comes from the short but valuable treatment of the subject in Alfred H. Kelly, Winfred Harbison, and Herman Belz, *The American Constitution: Its Origins and Development,* 6th ed. (New York: W. W. Norton, 1982), 68–85. On separation of powers, see W. B. Gwyn, *The Meaning of the Separation of Powers,* Tulane Studies in Political Science, IX (New Orleans, 1965); M. J. C. Vile, *Constitutionalism and the Separation of Powers* (Oxford: Clarendon Press, 1967); Benjamin F. Wright, "The Origins of the Separation of Powers in America," *Economica,* 13 (1933), 169–185.

13. Alexander Pope, *An Essay on Man,* Epistle III, lines 303–304.

14. *Thoughts on Government,* in Taylor et al., *Papers of John Adams,* IV, 88.

15. Ibid., 90.

16. Ibid.

17. Ibid., 92

18. See the discussion in Taylor et al., *Papers of John Adams,* IV, 69–73.

19. Adams, *First American Constitutions,* 74–76. On the general concept of constituent power see ibid., 63–66.

20. On the Pennsylvania constitution see ibid., 76–80, 179–180, 262–266; J. Paul Selsam, *The Pennsylvania Constitution of 1776: A Study in Revolutionary Democracy* (1936; reprint, New York: Da Capo, 1970).

21. On the "Fort Wilson" riot, see John K. Alexander, "The Fort Wilson Incident of 1779: A Case Study of the Revolutionary Crowd," *William and Mary Quarterly,* 3d ser., 31 (1974), 589–612; Nevins, *American States,* 261–262.

22. See Robert L. Brunhouse, *The Counter-Revolution in Pennsylvania, 1776-1790* (1941; New York: Octagon, 1971).

23. Dumas Malone, *Jefferson the Virginian* (Boston: Little, Brown, 1948), 239; for opposing views see Adams, *First American Constitutions,* 206–207, and works cited there.

24. Malone, *Jefferson the Virginian,* 238, 301–379; Adams, *First American Constitutions,* 267–268.

25. *Notes on the State of Virginia,* Query XIII, 120. See the discussion in Malone, *Jefferson the Virginian,* 380.

26. Robert A. Rutland, ed., *The Papers of George Mason,* 3 vols. (Chapel Hill: University of North Carolina Press, 1970), I, 295–310; idem, *The Birth of the Bill of Rights, 1776-1791* (Chapel Hill: University of North Carolina Press, 1955), chap. 3.

27. See the discussion in Irving Brant, *James Madison: The Virginia Revolutionist, 1751-1780* (Indianapolis: Bobbs-Merrill, 1941), 234–271.

28. Quoted in Malone, *Jefferson the Virginian,* 236–237.

29. See generally William A. Polf, *1777: The Political Revolution and New York's First*

Constitution (Albany: New York State Bicentennial Commission, 1977); Adams, *First American Constitutions*, 83–86; Richard B. Morris, ed., *John Jay: The Making of a Revolutionary. Unpublished Papers 1745-1780* (New York: Harper & Row, 1975), 389–418; Bernard Mason, *The Road to Independence: The Revolutionary Movement in New York, 1773-1777* (Lexington: University of Kentucky Press, 1966), chap. 7.

30. The quotation is from Butterfield, *Diary and Autobiography*, III, 398; the text of the New York constitution of 1777 is reprinted in Polf, *1777*, 43–61.

31. The following paragraphs are based on Adams, *First American Constitutions*, 86–93, 96–97; Robert J. Taylor, ed., *Massachusetts, Colony to Commonwealth: Documents on the Foundation of Its Constitution, 1775-1780* (Chapel Hill: University of North Carolina Press, 1961); Oscar Handlin and Mary Handlin, eds., *The Popular Sources of Political Authority: Documents on the Massachusetts Constitution of 1780* (Cambridge, Mass.: Harvard University Press, 1966); Ronald M. Peters, Jr., *The Massachusetts Constitution of 1780: A Social Compact* (Amherst: University of Massachusetts Press, 1978); Samuel Eliot Morison, "The Struggle over the Adoption of the Constitution of Massachusetts, 1780," *Massachusetts Historical Society Proceedings*, 50 (1916-17), 353–412; and "Symposium: The Massachusetts Constitution of 1780," *Suffolk University Law Review*, 14 (1980), 841–1010.

32. Taylor, *Massachusetts*, 45.

33. Handlin and Handlin, *Popular Sources*, 150.

34. Taylor et al., *Papers of John Adams*, IV, 71.

35. Resolutions of Hampshire Convention, 30 March 1779, Hawley Papers, Box 1, RB.

36. Peters, *Massachusetts Constitution*, 14.

37. Morison, "Struggle," presents this argument.

38. John Adams to Samuel Adams, 23 February 1780, RBBC.

39. John Adams to Samuel Adams, 20 September 1780, RBBC.

40. John Adams to Samuel Adams, 15 June 1782, RBBC.

41. See the discussion in Charles Warren, *Congress, the Constitution, and the Supreme Court*, rev. ed. (Boston: Little, Brown, 1935), 1–40, especially 30–34; Adams, *First American Constitutions*, 4; Dargo, *Law in the New Republic*, 13.

42. Quoted in Correa M. Walsh, *The Political Science of John Adams* (New York: G. P. Putnam's Sons, 1915), 1. See the classic study by Edward S. Corwin, "The Progress of Constitutional Theory between the Declaration of Independence and the Meeting of the Philadelphia Convention," *American Historical Review*, 30 (1925), 511–536.

43. On the Virginia Council of Revision see Malone, *Jefferson the Virginian*, 247–285; Edward Dumbauld, *Thomas Jefferson and the Law* (Norman: University of Oklahoma Press, 1978), 132–143; Alonzo Thomas Dill, *George Wythe: Teacher of Liberty* (Williamsburg: Virginia Independence Bicentennial Commission, 1979), 37–40; David J. Mays, *Edmund Pendleton, 1721-1803: A Biography*, 2 vols. (Cambridge, Mass.: Harvard University Press, 1952), II, 138–143. See also *Jefferson Papers*, II, 325–665, for a compilation of the relevant documents, and the informative headnote at 305–324.

44. Mays, *Edmund Pendleton*, is the definitive study; see also David J. Mays, ed., *The Letters and Papers of Edmund Pendleton, 1734-1803*, 2 vols. (Charlottesville: University Press of Virginia, 1967).

45. George Wythe to Edmund Pendleton, 18 November 1776, RBEC no. 1627, Jefferson wrote an authoritative character sketch of Wythe to accompany his letter of 31 August 1820 to John Saunderson; it has been reprinted in Adrienne Koch and William Peden, eds., *The Life and Selected Writings of Thomas Jefferson* (New York: Modern Library, 1943), 180–183, and in Saul K. Padover, ed., *The Complete Jefferson* (New York: Duell, Sloan and Pierce, 1943), 927–928.

46. On the entail bill see Malone, *Jefferson the Virginian*, 251–257; on entail in the colonies see C. Ray Keim, "Primogeniture and Entail in Colonial Virginia," *William and Mary Quarterly*, 3d ser., 25 (1968), 545–586; Richard B. Morris, *Studies in the History of American Law* (New York: Columbia University Press, 1930), 69–125.

47. Quoted in Malone, *Jefferson the Virginian*, 262.

48. *Report of the Committee of Revisors Appointed by the General Assembly of Virginia in MDCCLXXVI* (Richmond, Va.: Dixon & Holt, Nov. 1784); Malone, *Jefferson the Virginian*, 263.

49. Koch and Peden, *Life and Writings of Jefferson*, 51.

50. On this bill see Malone, *Jefferson the Virginian*, 280–285.

51. Ibid., 269–273 (quotation at 271).

52. The literature on this controversy is enormous. See, for example, Malone, *Jefferson the Virginian*, 274–280; Hamilton J. Eckenrode, *Separation of Church and State in Virginia* (Richmond: Virginia State Library, 1910); Thomas Buckley, *Church and State in Revolutionary Virginia, 1776-1787* (Charlottesville: University Press of Virginia, 1977); Thomas J. Curry, *The First Freedoms: Church and State in America to the Passage of the First Amendment* (New York: Oxford University Press, 1986); Irving N. Brant, *The Bill of Rights: Its Origins and Meaning* (Indianapolis: Bobbs-Merrill, 1965); idem, "Madison: On the Separation of Church and State," *William and Mary Quarterly*, 3d ser., 8 (1951), 3–24; Robert L. Cord, *Separation of Church and State: Historical Fact and Current Fiction* (New York: Lambeth Press, 1982); William Lee Miller, *The First Liberty: Religion and the American Republic* (New York: Alfred A. Knopf, 1986); Irving Brant, *James Madison: The Nationalist, 1780-1787* (Indianapolis: Bobbs-Merrill, 1948); Leonard W. Levy, *Judgments: Essays in American Constitutional History* (Chicago: Quadrangle, 1972), 169–224.

53. The following paragraphs are based on the works cited in note 52 above and are deeply indebted to extensive discussions with Professor John E. Sexton of New York University Law School, who is preparing a major study of the history and doctrinal development of the law of church and state in the United States.

54. See the discussion in Brant, *Madison: Virginia Revolutionist*, 241–250.

55. Curry, *First Freedoms*, 109–192; Levy, *Judgments*, 169–224.

56. Anson P. Stokes and Leo Pfeffer, *Church and State in the United States* (New York: Harper & Row, 1964), 100–103.

57. William E. Nelson, *Americanization of the Common Law: The Impact of Legal Change on Massachusetts Society, 1760-1830* (Cambridge, Mass.: Harvard University Press, 1975), 5. See also Morton J. Horwitz, *The Transformation of American Law, 1780-1860* (Cambridge, Mass.: Harvard University Press, 1977). For an extensive critique of Horwitz's study see John Phillip Reid, "A Plot Too Doctrinaire," *Texas Law Review*, 55 (1977), 1307–21. For a first-rate guide to the best writing on American legal history, see William E. Nelson and John Phillip Reid, *The Literature of American Legal History* (Dobbs Ferry, N.Y.: Oceana, 1985).

58. Lawrence M. Friedman, *A History of American Law*, 2d ed. (New York: Simon & Schuster, 1985), 303; Dargo, *Law in the New Republic*, 8–9.

59. See Hendrik Hartog, ed., *Law in the American Revolution and the Revolution in the Law* (New York: New York University Press, 1981); Jack P. Greene, "From the Perspective of Law: Context and Legitimacy in the Origins of the American Revolution," *South Atlantic Quarterly*, 85 (Winter 1986), 56–77.

60. Wallace Brown, *The King's Friends: The Composition and Motives of the American Loyalist Claimants* (Providence: Brown University Press, 1965), 265, cited in Dargo, *Law in the New Republic*, 7n.

61. Morris, *Studies*, 65–67; Friedman, *History of American Law*, 94–102.

62. Dill, *George Wythe*, 51–77; Friedman, *History of American Law*, 319.

63. John Dickinson to Mathew Carey, 15 January 1789, RBEC no. 3129; on Jefferson's notes of cases see Malone, *Jefferson the Virginian*, 121–122.

64. Friedman, *History of American Law*, 327–328.

65. [Benjamin Austin,] *Observations on the Pernicious Practice of the Law, as Published Occasionally in the Independent Chronicle, in the Year 1786 . . . by Honestus* (Boston: Joshua Belcher, 1814). Nelson, *Americanization of the Common Law*, 205 n. 2, reports an earlier compilation published in 1794.

66. Austin, *Pernicious Practice*, 3–4.

67. On the context of this pamphlet see Nelson, *Americanization of the Common Law*, 69–72.

68. This discussion is based on James H. Kettner, *The Development of American Citizenship, 1608-1870* (Chapel Hill: University of North Carolina Press, 1978), 173–209, 222–224; Claude H. Van Tyne, *The Loyalists in the American Revolution* (1902; reprint, Gloucester, Mass.: Peter Smith, 1959), App. B and C (compilation and analysis of anti-Loyalist statutes); Bradley F. Chapin, "Colonial and Revolutionary Origins of the American Law of Treason," *William and Mary Quarterly*, 3d ser., 15 (1958), 56–70; William H. Nelson, *The American Tory* (Boston: Beacon Press, 1961); Robert H. Calhoon, *The Loyalists in Revolutionary America* (New York: Harcourt Brace Jovanovich, 1971); there are many other studies of this subject.

69. Richard B. Morris, *The American Revolution Reconsidered* (New York: Harper & Row, 1967), 11–12.

70. Edward Countryman, *A People in Revolution: The American Revolution and Political Society in New York, 1760-1790* (Baltimore: Johns Hopkins University Press, 1981), 103–160.

71. Richard B. Morris, *The Peacemakers: The Great Powers and American Independence* (New York: Harper & Row, 1965), 364–373, 417–420.

72. Quoted in Mary Beth Norton, *The British-Americans: The Loyalist Exiles in England, 1774-1789* (Boston: Little, Brown, 1972), 60. See also Brown, *King's Friends*; Paul H. Smith, *Loyalists and Redcoats: A Study in British Revolutionary Policy* (Chapel Hill: University of North Carolina Press, 1966). A valuable firsthand account by the former royal lieutenant-governor and chief justice of Massachusetts is John G. Schutz and Douglass G. Adair, eds., *Peter Oliver's "Origins and Progress of the American Rebellion": A Tory View* (1961; reprint, Stanford: Stanford University Press, 1967).

73. Elbridge Gerry to Samuel B. Gerry, 31 July 1783, RBEC no. 508; Merrill Jensen, *The New Nation: A History of the United States during the Confederation, 1781-1789* (New York: Alfred A. Knopf, 1950), 268–281.

74. On *Rutgers v. Waddington* see Richard B. Morris, ed., *Select Cases of the Mayor's Court of New York City, 1674-1784* (1935; reprint, Millwood, N.Y.: Kraus, 1975), 57–59; Julius Goebel, Jr., and Joseph H. Smith, eds., *The Law Practice of Alexander Hamilton*, 5 vols. (New York: Columbia University Press, 1964-80), I, 282–419; Julius Goebel, Jr., *The Oliver Wendell Holmes Devise History of the Supreme Court of the United States, I: Antecedents and Beginnings to 1801* (New York: Macmillan, 1971), 131–138; Richard B. Morris, *Seven Who Shaped Our Destiny: The Founding Fathers as Revolutionaries* (New York: Harper & Row, 1973), 235–237; idem, *Witnesses at the Creation: Hamilton, Madison, Jay, and the Constitution* (New York: Holt, Rinehart & Winston, 1985), 72–77.

75. For the text of the *Phocion* letters see Harold C. Syrett, ed., *The Papers of Alexander Hamilton*, 26 vols. (New York: Columbia University Press, 1961-79), III, 489–497, 530–558 (quotation at 556–557). On Hamilton's choice of the pseudonym see Trevor Colbourn, ed., *Fame and the Founding Fathers: Essays of Douglass Adair* (New York: W. W. Norton, 1974), 274–275.

4. The Confederation in Quandary

1. John Adams to Samuel Adams, 1 May 1784, Samuel Adams Papers, RBBC.

2. This chapter draws on the growing body of scholarship concerning the history of the United States under the Articles of Confederation. Older works include Merrill Jensen, *The New Nation: A History of the United States during the Confederation, 1781–1789* (New York: Alfred A. Knopf, 1950); Allan Nevins, *The American States during and after the Revolution, 1776–1789* (New York: Macmillan, 1924); Charles Warren, *The Making of the Constitution* (Boston: Little, Brown, 1926 and later editions), Part 1; Andrew C. McLaughlin, *The Confederation and the Constitution, 1781–1789* (1902; reprint, New York: Collier-Macmillan, 1962); and Irving Brant, *James Madison: The Nationalist, 1780–1787* (Indianapolis: Bobbs-Merrill, 1948). More recent works include Jack N. Rakove, *The Beginnings of National Politics: An Interpretive History of the Continental Congress* (New York: Alfred A. Knopf, 1979); Peter S. Onuf, *The Origins of the Federal Republic: Jurisdictional Controversies in the United States, 1776–1787* (Philadelphia: University of Pennsylvania Press, 1983); H. James Henderson, *Party Politics in the Continental Congress* (New York: McGraw-Hill, 1974); Frederick W. Marks III, *Independence on Trial: Foreign Affairs and the Making of the Constitution* (Baton Rouge: Louisiana State University Press, 1973); Joseph L. Davis, *Sectionalism in American Politics, 1774–1787* (Madison: University of Wisconsin Press, 1977); Linda Grant De Pauw, *The Eleventh Pillar: New York State and the Constitution* (Ithaca: Cornell University Press, 1966); and Irwin H. Polishook, *Rhode Island and the Union, 1774–1791* (Evanston: Northwestern University Press, 1969). This list only begins to scratch the surface of the available scholarly literature, yet more work is clearly needed—for example, studies for every state of the depth and quality of the De Pauw and Polishook volumes and new, comprehensive biographies of key figures such as James Wilson.

This chapter—and indeed this entire book—also draws on extensive discussions with Professor Richard B. Morris, whose forthcoming book in the New American Nation series, *The Forging of the Union, 1781–1789* (New York: Harper

& Row), will be the definitive study of its subject for at least a generation. Professor Morris's book will provide references to a wide variety of primary and secondary sources. His other books, *The American Revolution Reconsidered* (New York: Harper & Row, 1967); *Seven Who Shaped Our Destiny: The Founding Fathers as Revolutionaries* (New York: Harper & Row, 1973); and *Witnesses at the Creation: Hamilton, Madison, Jay, and the Constitution* (New York: Holt, Rinehart & Winston, 1985), have also been of great help, as has his volume of documents, *Basic Documents on the Confederation and Constitution* (1970; reprint, Malabar, Fla.: Robert Krieger, 1985). See also J. R. Pole, ed., *The Revolution in America, 1754–1788* (London: Macmillan, 1970).

Indispensable primary materials on this subject are given in the new, scholarly editions of the papers of James Madison, Thomas Jefferson, George Mason, and Alexander Hamilton, as well as the ongoing project directed by Paul H. Smith of the Library of Congress, which will replace Edmund Burnett's edition of the letters of the delegates of the Continental Congress; soon we will also have the third volume of Richard B. Morris's edition of *The Papers of John Jay*, covering the years 1784–1789, when Jay was the Confederation's secretary for foreign affairs. For the papers of John Adams, Benjamin Franklin, Rufus King, John Dickinson, and James Monroe, the historian must use the older editions published at the turn of the century, either because (as for Dickinson, Monroe, and King) no new scholarly edition is under way or (as for Franklin and John Adams) because the new editions will not reach the 1780s for several years at least. There is no edition, old or new, of the papers of James Wilson.

3. The discussion in the text draws on "The Origins of the Constitutional Convention," a lecture by Gordon S. Wood delivered at "A Meeting among Friends," a conference on the bicentennial of the Federal Convention sponsored by the Friends of Independence National Historical Park in Philadelphia, 8–9 February 1985.

4. The most persuasive and detailed presentation of this view is Jensen, *The New Nation*. See also Rakove, *Beginnings*, 333–334.

5. On the important point that politics may not have been central to the lives of most Americans in this period, see Rakove, *Beginnings*, 334.

6. Marks, *Independence on Trial*, 5–11, 55–60, 80–83, 98–105; and see generally Charles R. Ritcheson, *Aftermath of Revolution: British Policy toward the United States, 1783–1795* (Dallas: Southern Methodist University Press, 1969). Extracts from the 1784 edition of Sheffield's *Observations* appear in Morris, *Basic Documents*, 16–19. For a contemporary American view of the matter, see Committee of Merchants [of Philadelphia] to Committee of Merchants, Traders, etc., of Boston, 19 May 1785, RBEC no. 9328.

7. On Spain see Marks, *Independence on Trial*, 21–32, 105–106. See also, on the Jay-Gardoqui talks, Morris, *Witnesses*, 152–159; Davis, *Sectionalism*, 109–126; Rakove, *Beginnings*, 349–350; Jensen, *The New Nation*, 170–173. Two authoritative but contrasting studies of Spanish-American diplomacy in this period are Samuel Flagg Bemis, *Pinckney's Treaty: America's Advantage from Europe's Distress, 1783–1800*, rev. ed. (New Haven: Yale University Press, 1960), and Arthur P. Whitaker, *The Spanish-American Frontier: 1783–1795* (Boston: Houghton Mifflin, 1927).

8. On France see Marks, *Independence on Trial*, 106–111.

9. Felix Gilbert, *To the Farewell Address* (Princeton: Princeton University Press, 1961), 16–18, 43, 51, 56–57, 63, 69–72, 88–89; see also Marks, *Independence on Trial*, 109 n. 23 for Gilbert's views, and passim for emphasis on such foreign policy concerns as a major contributing factor to the movement to revise or replace the Articles of Confederation.

10. For Jay's views on foreign policy issues as a threat to the Confederation, see *Federalist* Nos. 2–5 and 64; Morris, *Witnesses*, 48–52, 143–160; and Richard B. Morris, *John Jay, the Nation, and the Court* (Boston: Boston University Press, 1967).

11. George Washington to James Madison, 30 November 1785, in William M. Hutchinson, William M. E. Rachal, and Robert A. Rutland, eds., *The Papers of James Madison*, 15 vols. to date (vols. 1–9, Chicago: Univerity of Chicago Press, 1962–75; vols. 10–, Charlottesville: University Press of Virginia, 1977–; cited hereafter as *Papers of James Madison*), VIII, 429.

12. Rufus King to [Samuel] Holten, 21 November 1785, RBEC no. 525.

13. Daniel of St. Thomas Jenifer to Gov. [Thomas Sim] Lee, 5 June 1780, RBEC no. 9495.

14. On the Vermont controversy and its theoretical and constitutional implications see Onuf, *Origins*, 103–145. Specialized works dealing with the Vermont controversy include Matt Hudson Jones, *Vermont in the Making, 1750–1775* (Cambridge, Mass.: Harvard University Press, 1939); Chilton Williamson, *Vermont in Quandary, 1763–1825* (Montpelier: Vermont Historical Society, 1949); and Charles Miner Thompson, *Independent Vermont* (Boston: Houghton Mifflin, 1942). Conversations with Marilee B. Huntoon of Bellows Falls and West Rutland, Vermont, provided additional valuable insights into Vermont history, society, and culture.

15. The best study of these issues is Onuf, *Origins*. See also Thomas P. Abernethy, *Western Lands and the American Revolution* (1938; reprint, New York: Russell & Russell, 1958); George A. Alden, "The State of Franklin," *American Historical Review*, 8 (1903), 271–289.

16. See, for example, Robert Morris to Governor [George] Clinton, 16 July 1781, RBEC no. 3949.

17. Supreme Executive Council of Pennsylvania to Governor George Clinton, 16 February 1784, RBEC no. 4209.

18. Committee of Merchants [of Philadelphia] to Committee of Merchants, Traders, etc., of Boston, 19 May 1785, RBEC no. 9328.

19. Henderson, *Party Politics*, 325–338; Polishook, *Rhode Island and the Union*, 53–102; Jensen, *The New Nation*, 63–67, 407–417; Rakove, *Beginnings*, 313–316, 337–342.

20. This account is based on Polishook, *Rhode Island and the Union*, 119–162. See also Peter J. Coleman, "The Insolvent Debtor in Rhode Island, 1745–1828," *William and Mary Quarterly*, 3d ser., 22 (1965), 413–434.

21. The most recent and authoritative study is David Szatmary, *Shays' Rebellion: The Making of an Agrarian Insurrection* (Amherst: University of Massachusetts Press, 1980). An older account, readable but superficial, is Marion Starkey, *A Little Rebellion* (New York: Alfred A. Knopf, 1955). See also Richard B. Morris, "Insurrection in Massachusetts," in Daniel J. Aaron, ed., *America in Crisis* (New York: Alfred A. Knopf, 1952), 21–49; and Robert A. East, "Massachusetts Conservatives in the Critical Period," in Richard B. Morris, ed., *The Era of the American Revolution* (New York: Columbia University Press, 1939), 349–395. A good basic

guide to the other scholarly literature is Szatmary, *Shays' Rebellion*, 135–137 nn. 1–17.

22. Szatmary, *Shays' Rebellion*, 29.

23. Ibid., 37–55; compare Peter Shaw, *American Patriots and the Rituals of Revolution* (Cambridge, Mass.: Harvard University Press, 1981).

24. Szatmary, *Shays' Rebellion*, 57, quoting George Brock of Attleboro, Massachusetts.

25. Ibid., 56–69; for documents describing the uprisings in New Hampshire and Vermont see Morris, *Basic Documents*, 148–158.

26. On the role played by Shays see Szatmary, *Shays' Rebellion*, 99.

27. Levi Lincoln to James Bowdoin, 28 December 1786, RBEC no. 527.

28. Szatmary, *Shays' Rebellion*, 81–82.

29. Ibid., 115–116; Polishook, *Rhode Island and the Union*, 177–178.

30. On the end of the rebellion see generally Szatmary, *Shays' Rebellion*, 114–119.

31. On the influence of Shays's Rebellion on the movement for reform of the Articles of Confederation, see generally ibid., chap. 7; Morris, *Witnesses*, 169–178; Morris, *The American Revolution Reconsidered*, 137, 154. For example, Rufus King at first opposed attempts to revise the Articles but later became one of the junior architects and strongest supporters of the new Constitution; see Massachusetts Delegates in Congress [Elbridge Gerry, Rufus King, and Samuel Holten] to Governor James Bowdoin, 3 September 1785, RBEC no. 9523.

In opposition to the views most recently expressed by Szatmary, Robert Feer, "Shays' Rebellion and the Constitution: A Study in Causation," *New England Quarterly*, 42 (1969), 388–410, argues that the Constitution and the controversy surrounding it would have been pretty much the same had the rebellion never occurred. Marks, *Independence on Trial*, xiii, 95 n. 89, acknowledges Feer's arguments but treats them with caution.

32. On the Mount Vernon Conference see Richard B. Morris, "The Mount Vernon Conference: First Step toward Philadelphia," *This Constitution*, no. 6 (spring 1985), 38–40; Morris, *Witnesses*, 161–162; *Papers of James Madison*, VIII; Robert A. Rutland, ed., *The Papers of George Mason*, 3 vols. (Chapel Hill: University of North Carolina Press, 1970), II, 812–821.

33. *Papers of James Madison*, VIII, 209–210 n. 1.

34. James Madison to Thomas Jefferson, 27 April 1785, in ibid., 268. For George Mason's report to Madison on the conference, see Mason to Madison, 9 August 1785, ibid., 337–339. The "Compact between Maryland and Virginia Relating to the Jurisdiction and Navigation of the Potomac and Pokomoke Rivers," dated 28 March 1785, appears in Rutland, *Papers of George Mason*, II, 816–821.

35. This summary draws extensively on Morris, "Mount Vernon Conference," 39. The bill drafted by Madison for enactment by the Virginia legislature appears in *Papers of James Madison*, VIII, 457–461, under the date 24–26 December 1785.

36. Quoted in Pole, *The Revolution in America*, 159.

37. Massachusetts Delegates in Congress [Elbridge Gerry, Rufus King, and Samuel Holten] to Governor James Bowdoin, 3 September 1785, RBEC no. 9523.

38. Rakove, *Beginnings*, 370–372.

39. "Notes on Ancient and Modern Confederacies," in *Papers of James Madison*, IX, 3–22.

40. On the Annapolis Convention see Henderson, *Party Politics*, 397–400; Rakove,

Beginnings, 368–370, 372–375; idem, "The Gamble at Annapolis," *This Constitution*, no. 12 (Fall 1986), 4–10; Davis, *Sectionalism*, 130–147; Morris, *Witnesses*, 163–168; Marks, *Independence on Trial*, 91–95; *Papers of James Madison*, IX.

41. James Madison to Ambrose Madison, 8 September 1786, James Madison Papers, RB, reprinted in *Papers of James Madison*, IX, 120–121.

42. Jabez Bowen to John Sullivan, 18 August 1786, RBEC no. 9339.

43. [Alexander Hamilton,] "Address to the Legislatures of Virginia, Delaware, Pennsylvania, New Jersey, and New York," 14 September 1786, RBEC no. 9402. This report has been frequently reprinted; the text used here is that given in Pole, *Revolution in America*, 160–163 (quotation at 161). Benson's rough minutes of the Annapolis Convention are RBEC nos. 9398–99.

44. [Hamilton,] "Address . . . ," quoted in Pole, *Revolution in America*, 161–163.

45. Rufus King to Governor [James] Bowdoin, 17 September 1786, RBEC no. 9446.

46. "An Act for appointing Deputies from this Commonwealth to a Convention . . ." [Richmond?, 1786?], RBEC no. 9570; reprinted in Pole, *Revolution in America*, 163–165.

47. Confederation Congress, Resolutions recommending a convention of delegates . . . , New York, 21 February 1787 (extract from the minutes of Congress), RBEC no. 9433; reprinted in Pole, *Revolution in America*, 165–166.

48. George Washington to James Madison, 31 March 1787, GWP; reprinted in *Papers of James Madison*, IX, 342–345.

49. James Madison to George Washington, 16 April 1787, in ibid., 382–387.

50. James Madison, "Vices of the Political System of the U[nited] States," in ibid., 345–358. Joel Barlow's transcript of Madison's memorandum, prepared during a visit to Monticello in September 1808, is in the James Madison Papers, RB.

51. See the discussion in Chapters 5 and 7.

52. Morris, *The American Revolution Reconsidered*, 149–162.

5. The Great Confluence

1. See generally Quentin Skinner, *The Foundations of Modern Political Thought*, 2 vols. (Cambridge, Cambridge University Press, 1978); J. G. A. Pocock, *Politics, Language and Time* (New York: Atheneum, 1971).

2. I have borrowed this term from Daniel Walker Howe, *The Political Culture of the American Whigs* (Chicago: University of Chicago Press, 1979). Howe in turn cites his debt to Pocock, *Politics, Language and Time*.

3. For example, Bernard Bailyn, *The Ideological Origins of the American Revolution* (Cambridge, Mass.: Harvard University Press, 1967) and *The Origins of American Politics* (New York: Alfred A. Knopf, 1968); Gordon S. Wood, *The Creation of the American Republic, 1776–1787* (Chapel Hill: University of North Carolina Press, 1969); Douglass G. Adair, "The Intellectual Origins of Jeffersonian Democracy" (Ph.D. diss., Yale University, 1943); Trevor Colbourn, ed., *Fame and the Founding Fathers: Essays of Douglass Adair* (New York: W. W. Norton, 1974) and *The Lamp of Experience* (Chapel Hill: University of North Carolina Press, 1965); Willi Paul Adams, *The First American Constitutions* (Chapel Hill: University of North Carolina Press, 1980); Linda K. Kerber, *Women of the Republic: Intellect and Ideology in Revolutionary America* (Chapel Hill: University of North Carolina Press, 1980);

Herbert J. Storing, *What the Anti-Federalists Were For* (Chicago: University of Chicago Press, 1981); Clinton L. Rossiter, *Seedtime of the Republic* (New York: Harcourt, Brace, 1955); and the third series of the *William and Mary Quarterly,* the journal of the Institute of Early American History and Culture.

4. Compare, for example, Wood, *Creation,* with Forrest McDonald, *Novus Ordo Seclorum* (Lawrence: University of Kansas Press, 1985).

5. See John Patrick Diggins, *The Lost Soul of American Politics* (New York: Basic Books, 1984).

6. Henry Steele Commager, *The Empire of Reason: How Europe Conceived and America Realized the Enlightenment* (New York: Doubleday/Anchor, 1977). The argument of this chapter is deeply indebted to this remarkable book.

7. Michael Kraus, *The Atlantic Civilization* (Ithaca: Cornell University Press, 1949).

8. On all this see generally Commager, *Empire of Reason;* see also Henry Steele Commager, *Jefferson, Nationalism, and the Enlightenment* (New York: George Braziller, 1975); Henry May, *The Enlightenment in America* (New York: Oxford University Press, 1976); Peter Gay, *The Enlightenment: An Interpretation,* 2 vols. (New York: Alfred A. Knopf, 1965, 1969); R. R. Palmer, *The Age of the Democratic Revolution,* 2 vols. (Princeton: Princeton University Press, 1959, 1964); Ernst Cassirer, *The Philosophy of the Enlightenment* (Princeton: Princeton University Press, 1951).

9. Commager, *Empire of Reason,* 236–245.

10. See the discussion in Chapter 2; see also Colbourn, *Lamp of Experience;* Caroline Robbins, *The Eighteenth-Century Commonwealthman* (Cambridge, Mass.: Harvard University Press, 1959).

11. Quoted in Commager, *Empire of Reason,* 129–130.

12. Commager, *Empire of Reason,* is best on the Americans' eclecticism. See also Wood, *Creation,* 7.

13. The manuscript of the Skipwith list is in the Thomas Jefferson Papers, RB; it is reprinted in Julian Boyd, ed., *The Papers of Thomas Jefferson,* 20 vols. to date (Princeton: Princeton University Press, 1950–; hereafter cited as *Jefferson Papers*), I, 78–81.

14. Thomas Jefferson to Robert Skipwith, 3 August 1771, in *Jefferson Papers,* I, 76–78.

15. On Blackstone and his influence see Daniel J. Boorstin, *The Mysterious Science of the Law* (1941; reprint, Boston: Beacon Press, 1958); on Jefferson's view of Blackstone see Edward Dumbauld, *Thomas Jefferson and the Law* (Norman: University of Oklahoma Press, 1978), 8–11.

16. Quoted in Colbourn, *Fame and the Founding Fathers,* 111.

17. Compare Adams, *Defence,* as quoted in Colbourn, *Fame and the Founding Fathers,* 108.

18. See generally Colbourn, *Lamp of Experience;* Robbins, *Commonwealthman;* Bailyn, *Ideological Origins.*

19. On Catherine Macaulay, see Colbourn, *Lamp of Experience,* 43–45, 153–154; Kerber, *Women of the Republic,* 28–30, 82; Lucille Donnelly, "The Celebrated Mrs. Macaulay," *William and Mary Quarterly,* 3d ser., 6 (1949), 173–207.

20. Meyer Reinhold, *Classica Americana* (Detroit: Wayne State University Press, 1984), is the most comprehensive account of classical influences on Americans in the Revolutionary era. See also Commager, *Jefferson, Nationalism, and the*

Enlightenment, 125–139; idem, *Empire of Reason,* 60–63; Colbourn, *Fame and the Founding Fathers,* 107–124, 272–285; Gilbert Chinard, "Polybius and the American Constitution," *Journal of the History of Ideas,* 1 (1940), 38–58; William Gribbin, "Rollin's Histories and American Republicanism," *William and Mary Quarterly,* 3d ser., 29 (1972), 611–622.

21. The battle over the meanings of republicanism has produced an immense body of literature. See, for example, Bailyn, *Ideological Origins;* J. G. A. Pocock, *The Machiavellian Moment* (Princeton: Princeton University Press, 1975); Wood, *Creation,* 46–90; McDonald, *Novus Ordo Seclorum,* 66–87. See generally Robert E. Shalhope, "Toward a Republican Synthesis: The Emergence of an Understanding of Republicanism in American Historiography," *William and Mary Quarterly,* 3d ser., 29 (1972), 49–80; idem, "Republicanism and Early American Historiography," ibid., 39 (1982), 334–356. A good recent symposium is Lance Banning, "Jeffersonian Ideology Revisited: Liberal and Classical Ideas in the New American Republic," *William and Mary Quarterly,* 3d ser., 43 (1986), 3–19; Joyce Appleby, "Republicanism in Old and New Contexts," ibid., 20–34. See also J. G. A. Pocock, *Virtue, Commerce, and History* (Cambridge: Cambridge University Press, 1985).

22. Frank E. Manuel and Fritzie P. Manuel, *Utopian Thought in the Western World* (Cambridge, Mass.: The Belknap Press of Harvard University Press, 1979), 361–366.

23. A good modern selection is David L. Jacobson, ed., *The English Libertarian Heritage* (Indianapolis: Bobbs-Merrill, 1965).

24. Paul F. Spurlin, *Montesquieu in America* (Baton Rouge: Louisiana State University Press, 1940); Commager, *Empire of Reason,* 110–111, 119–120, 209.

25. Charles, baron de Montesquieu, *The Spirit of the Laws,* trans. Thomas Nugent, 2 vols. (New York: Hafner, 1949), Book VIII, chap. 20, 122.

26. Douglass G. Adair, "'That Politics May Be Reduced to a Science': Hume, Madison, and the Tenth *Federalist,*" in Colbourn, *Fame and the Founding Fathers,* 93–106; for a first-rate modern edition of Hume's essays see David Hume, *Essays: Moral, Political, and Literary,* ed. Eugene F. Miller (Indianapolis: Liberty Press/Liberty Classics, 1985).

27. Donald J. D'Elia, *Benjamin Rush: Philosopher of the American Revolution* (Philadelphia: American Philosophical Society, 1974), 12 n. 31, 76, 80; Reinhold, *Classica Americana,* 128–133, 135–136.

28. See generally Colbourn, *Fame and the Founding Fathers,* 107–123; Robert W. Shoemaker, "'Democracy' and 'Republic' as Understood in Late Eighteenth-Century America," *American Speech,* 41 (1966), 83–95; Reinhold, *Classica Americana,* 94–115.

29. Garry Wills, *Cincinnatus: George Washington and the Enlightenment* (New York: Doubleday, 1984).

30. Minor Myers, Jr., *Liberty without Anarchy: A History of the Society of the Cincinnati* (Charlottesville: University Press of Virginia, 1983).

31. Winthrop D. Jordan, *White over Black* (Chapel Hill: University of North Carolina Press, 1968), is definitive.

32. See generally Kerber, *Women of the Republic,* for the best treatment of this subject.

33. Montesquieu, *The Spirit of the Laws,* Book VII, 207–208, quoted in Kerber, *Women of the Republic,* 20.

34. John Adams to Thomas Jefferson, 13 November 1815, in Lester J. Cappon, ed., *The Adams-Jefferson Letters,* 2 vols. (Chapel Hill: University of North Carolina Press, 1959), II, 458.

35. On this point see generally Commager, *Empire of Reason.*

36. Quoted in Henry Steele Commager and Elmo Giordanetti, *Was America a Mistake? An Eighteenth-Century Controversy* (New York: Harper & Row, 1967), 183.

37. See generally Commager and Giordanetti, *Was America a Mistake?,* and the exhaustive and learned volume by Antonello Gerbi, *The Dispute of the New World,* trans. Jeremy Moyle (Pittsburgh: University of Pittsburgh Press, 1973).

38. On this point see Gerbi, *Dispute;* Clarence Glacken, *Traces on the Rhodian Shore* (Berkeley: University of California Press, 1967).

39. On Franklin's role in this dispute, see Gerbi, *Dispute,* 240–243.

40. L. H. Butterfield, ed., *The Diary and Autobiography of John Adams,* 4 vols. (Cambridge, Mass.: Harvard University Press, 1961), II, 307, cited in P. M. Zall, *Benjamin Franklin Laughing* (Berkeley: University of California Press, 1980), 116; see also Commager, *Empire of Reason,* 21.

41. See the illuminating introduction in Zall, *Benjamin Franklin Laughing,* 1–7.

42. William Carmichael to Thomas Jefferson, 15 October 1787, in *Jefferson Papers,* XII, 240–241; an alternative version given by Jefferson in 1817 is quoted in Zall, *Benjamin Franklin Laughing,* 138.

43. On Jefferson's role in this controversy see Gerbi, *Dispute,* 252–268.

44. On the writings of *Notes on the State of Virginia,* see Gerbi, *Dispute,* 252–254; Dumas Malone, *Jefferson and the Rights of Man* (Boston: Little, Brown, 1951), 93–106; Robert A. Ferguson, *Law and Letters in American Culture* (Cambridge, Mass.: Harvard University Press, 1984), 34–58; Dorothy Medlin, "Thomas Jefferson, André Morellet, and the French Version of *Notes on the State of Virginia,*" *William and Mary Quarterly,* 3d ser., 35 (1978), 85–99; and especially William Peden's learned introduction to the best edition, *Notes on the State of Virginia* (Chapel Hill: University of North Carolina Press, 1955).

45. Peden, *Notes on the State of Virginia,* Query VI, 47.

46. Ibid.

47. Ibid., 63–64.

48. Ibid., 64.

49. Ibid., 65.

50. Ibid.

51. Malone, *Jefferson and the Rights of Man,* 99–100; John C. Greene, *American Science in the Age of Jefferson* (Ames: Iowa State University Press, 1984), 27–36.

52. William Carmichael to Thomas Jefferson, 15 October 1787, in *Jefferson Papers,* XII, 241.

53. J. Hector St. John de Crèvecoeur, *Letters from an American Farmer and Sketches of Eighteenth-Century America,* ed. Albert J. Stone (New York: Penguin, 1981); Johann David Schoepf, *Travels in the Confederation,* trans. Alfred J. Morrison, 2 vols. (Philadelphia: W. J. Campbell, 1911); Durand Echeverria, *Mirage in the West* (Princeton: Princeton University Press, 1957); Howard Mumford Jones, *O Strange New World* (New York: Viking, 1964), 301–307, 329–331.

54. *The Federalist Papers,* ed. Clinton L. Rossiter (New York: Mentor/New American Library, 1961), 90–91.

55. On Hegel's views of America see Gerbi, *Dispute,* 417–441.

56. See Palmer, *Age of the Democratic Revolution*, I, 239–284; Gay, *Enlightenment*, II, 555–568; Commager, *Empire of Reason*, 162–235; Horst Dippel, *Germany and the American Revolution, 1770–1800* (Chapel Hill: University of North Carolina Press, 1977); Durand Echeverria, "French Publications of the Declaration of Independence and the American Constitutions, 1776–1783," *Papers of the Bibliographical Society of America*, 47 (1953), 313–338; Dalphy I. Fagerstrom, "Scottish Opinion and the American Revolution," *William and Mary Quarterly*, 3d ser., 11 (1954), 252–275.

57. Quoted in Adams, *First American Constitutions*, 3.

58. See J. W. Schulte Nordholdt, *The Dutch Republic and American Independence* (Chapel Hill: University of North Carolina Press, 1982), passim; idem, *Till I Knew John Adams* (Amsterdam: Exxon, 1981); Simon Schama, *Patriots and Liberators: Revolution in the Netherlands, 1780–1813* (New York: Alfred A. Knopf, 1977), 58–63.

59. On Turgot see Zoltan Haraszti, *John Adams and the Prophets of Progress* (Cambridge, Mass.: Harvard University Press, 1952), 139–141.

60. On Richard Price see Bernard Peach and D. O. Thomas, eds., *Richard Price and the Ethical Foundations of the American Revolution* (Durham, N.C.: Duke University Press, 1979), 9–14; Carl B. Cone, "Richard Price and the Constitution of the United States," *American Historical Review*, 53 (1948), 726–747.

61. Richard Price to Noah Webster, 29 August 1785, Noah Webster Papers, Box 2, RB.

62. This pamphlet is reprinted, with extensive annotations, in Peach and Thomas, *Richard Price*, 177–224.

63. Haraszti, *John Adams and the Prophets of Progress*, 139–154; Haraszti's volume contains perhaps the best account of Adams's controversy with Turgot. See also Peter Shaw, *The Character of John Adams* (Chapel Hill: University of North Carolina Press, 1976), 206; John R. Howe, Jr., *The Changing Political Thought of John Adams* (Princeton: Princeton University Press, 1966), 133–148, 166–174; Edward Handler, *America and Europe in the Political Thought of John Adams* (Cambridge, Mass.: Harvard University Press, 1964); John Paul Selsam and Joseph G. Rayback, "French Comment on the Pennsylvania Constitution of 1776," *Pennsylvania Magazine of History and Biography*, 76 (1952), 311–325. Correa M. Walsh, *The Political Science of John Adams* (New York: Putnam, 1915), is outdated and mechanical.

64. Peach and Thomas, *Richard Price*, 215–224 (quotations at 218–219, 222).

65. Quoted in Haraszti, *John Adams and the Prophets of Progress*, 145–146.

66. Quoted in ibid., 143.

67. On the writing of the *Defence* see Haraszti, *John Adams and the Prophets of Progress*, 155–164; Shaw, *Character of John Adams*, 207–224.

68. John Adams, *A Defence of the Constitutions*, 3 vols. (1787–88; Philadelphia: Budd & Bartram, 1797), I, vii.

69. John Adams to Richard Price, 4 February 1787, in Peach and Thomas, *Richard Price*, 339.

70. Wood, *Creation*, 567.

71. Ibid., 567–592. See also Daniel Bell, "The End of American Exceptionalism," in *The Winding Passage* (1981; New York: Harper & Row, 1982), 245–271.

6. An Assembly of Demigods?

1. Of the many books dealing with the Federal Convention of 1787, the best are Max Farrand, *The Framing of the Constitution of the United States* (New Haven: Yale University Press, 1913); Charles Warren, *The Making of the Constitution* (Boston: Little, Brown, 1926 and later editions); Conyers Read, ed., *The Constitution Reconsidered* (1938; rev. ed. by Richard B. Morris, New York: Harper & Row, 1968); Walton H. Hamilton and Douglass G. Adair, *The Power to Govern* (New York: W. W. Norton, 1937); Irving N. Brant, *Storm over the Constitution* (Indianapolis: Bobbs-Merrill, 1937); and Clinton L. Rossiter, *1787: The Grand Convention* (New York: Macmillan, 1966). Other general works on this subject include Carl Van Doren, *The Grand Rehearsal* (New York: Viking, 1946); Catherine Drinker Bowen, *Miracle at Philadelphia* (Boston: Atlantic–Little, Brown, 1966); and Christopher Collier and James Lincoln Collier, *Decision in Philadelphia: The Constitutional Convention of 1787* (New York: Random House/Reader's Digest Press, 1986). A superb introduction to American constitutional history and law is John Sexton and Nat Brandt, *How Free Are We? What the Constitution Says We Can and Cannot Do* (New York: M. Evans, 1986).

2. Thomas Jefferson to John Adams, 30 August 1787, in Lester J. Cappon, ed., *The Adams-Jefferson Letters*, 2 vols. (Chapel Hill: University of North Carolina Press, 1959), I, 196.

3. Rossiter, *1787*, gives the best survey of the delegates' lives and achievements.

4. George Washington to James Madison, 31 March 1787, GWP.

5. See generally on this subject Garry Wills, *Cincinnatus: George Washington and the Enlightenment* (New York: Doubleday, 1984).

6. See Carl Van Doren, *Benjamin Franklin* (New York: Viking, 1938), 742–755; Esmond Wright, *Franklin of Philadelphia* (Cambridge, Mass.: Harvard University Press, 1986), 340–343.

7. Arguably Madison was the most important figure at the Convention. Fellow delegate William Pierce of Georgia observed: "Every Person seems to acknowledge his greatness. He blends together the most profound politician, with the Scholar . . . The affairs of the United States, he perhaps, has the most correct knowledge of, of any Man in the Union"; William Pierce, "Character Sketches of Delegates to the Federal Convention," in Max Farrand, ed., *The Records of the Federal Convention of 1787*, rev. ed., 4 vols. (New Haven: Yale University Press, 1937; 2d rev. ed. of vol. 4, edited by James H. Hutson, forthcoming), III, 87–97 (quotation at 94).

   The best account of Madison's role in the Convention is Irving Brant, *James Madison: Father of the Constitution, 1787–1800* (Indianapolis: Bobbs-Merrill, 1950). See also the illuminating brief essay by Harold Schultz, "James Madison: Father of the Constitution?" *Quarterly Journal of the Library of Congress*, 37 (1980), 215–222. On Madison, see also Edward McNail Burns, *James Madison: Philosopher of the Constitution* (New Brunswick, N.J.: Rutgers University Press, 1938); Abbot Emerson Smith, *James Madison: Builder* (New York: Wilson-Erickson, 1937); Harold S. Schultz, *James Madison* (New York: Twayne, 1970); Neal Riemer, *James Madison* (New York: Washington Square Press, 1968); Adrienne Koch, *Madison's "Advice to My Country"* (Princeton: Princeton University Press, 1966); Marvin

Meyers, ed., *The Mind of the Founder: Sources of the Political Thought of James Madison* (1967; rev. ed., Hanover, N.H.: University Press of New England, 1981); and Ralph Ketcham, *James Madison* (New York: Macmillan, 1971). There are two reliable editions of Madison's *Notes of Debates in the Federal Convention of 1787*: that in Farrand, *Records*; and that in Charles C. Tansill, ed., *Documents Illustrative of the Formation of the Union of the American States* (Washington, D.C.: Government Printing Office, 1927). The Tansill text of Madison's *Notes* has been reprinted separately (Athens: Ohio University Press, 1969; with revised index, 1985) with an introduction by Adrienne Koch. All references to the records of the Convention are to Madison's *Notes* in Farrand, *Records*, unless otherwise indicated.

8. Farrand, *Records*, I, 4 (25 May).

9. "Rules for conducting Business in the United States in Congress Assembled," Manuscript in the hand of Elias Boudinot, RBEC no. 441.

10. On this topic see J. R. Pole, *The Gift of Government* (Athens: University of Georgia Press, 1983).

11. See Rossiter, *1787*, 167–169, 415 n. 7.

12. Ralph V. Harlow, *The History of Legislative Methods in the Period before 1825* (New Haven: Yale University Press, 1918), 94–103.

13. Rossiter, *1787*, 251.

14. For example, Caleb Strong to Alexander Hodgdon, 30 July 1787, RBEC no. 545.

15. George Wythe to Edmund Randolph, 16 June 1787, RBEC no. 9542.

16. On the concept of fame in the eighteenth century see the now classic essay "Fame and the Founding Fathers," in Trevor Colbourn, ed., *Fame and the Founding Fathers: Essays of Douglass Adair* (New York: W. W. Norton, 1974), 3–26.

17. On the first day of actual business Pinckney presented his own plan for a new frame of government; Farrand, *Records*, I, 23 (29 May) and III, 595–609 (Appendix D, "The Pinckney Plan"). This plan was generally ignored, although the committee that prepared the first draft of the Constitution found it useful for turns of phrase. But in 1818, when Secretary of State John Quincy Adams asked the elderly Pinckney for the text of this plan, Pinckney sent him what was actually a variant of the first draft of the Constitution reported to the Convention on 6 August. Despite some extravagant claims for Pinckney as the true "father of the Constitution," the detective work of J. Franklin Jameson and Andrew C. McLaughlin has established that, at best, Pinckney made an outlandish mistake that has obscured his many real and valuable contributions to the framing of the Constitution. See J. Franklin Jameson, "Portions of Charles Pinckney's Plan for a Constitution, 1787," *American Historical Review*, 8 (1903), 509–511; Andrew C. McLaughlin, "Sketch of Pinckney's Plan for a Constitution, 1787," *American Historical Review*, 9 (1904), 735–747.

18. Charles A. Beard, *An Economic Interpretation of the Constitution of the United States*, rev. ed. (New York: Macmillan, 1935).

19. Forrest McDonald, *We the People* (Chicago: University of Chicago Press, 1958); Robert E. Brown, *Charles Beard and the Constitution* (Princeton: Princeton University Press, 1955); Richard Hofstadter, *The Progressive Historians: Turner, Beard, Parrington* (New York: Alfred A. Knopf, 1968), 207–284; Henry Steele Commager, "The Economic Interpretation of the Constitution Reconsidered," in *The*

Search for a Usable Past and Other Essays (New York: Alfred A. Knopf, 1966), 56–73.

20. Farrand, *Records*, I, 18–23 (29 May).
21. Ibid., 33–35 (30 May).
22. Ibid., 4 (25 May); III, 574–575 (text of Delaware instructions).
23. Ibid., I, 235–237 (13 June); George Read's manuscript copy of the 13 June report is RBEC no. 9482.
24. Farrand, *Records*, I, 240 (14 June). The best study of Paterson is John E. O'Connor, *William Paterson, Lawyer and Statesman, 1745–1806* (New Brunswick, N.J.: Rutgers University Press, 1979).
25. Ibid., 242–245 (15 June).
26. Forrest McDonald, *E Pluribus Unum: The Formation of the American Republic, 1776–1790)* (1965; reprint, Indianapolis: Liberty Press, 1979), 276.
27. Farrand, *Records*, I, 245.
28. Ibid., 248–333 (16–19 June).
29. Ibid., 450–452 (28 June).
30. Ibid., 492 (30 June).
31. Ibid., 531 (5 July).
32. Ibid., II, 15–16 (16 July).
33. Ibid., 17–18.
34. Ibid., 18.
35. Ibid., 19.
36. Ibid., 19–20.
37. Ibid., I, 87 (2 June).
38. Milton Flower, *John Dickinson, Conservative Revolutionary* (Charlottesville: University Press of Virginia, 1983); James H. Hutson, "John Dickinson at the Federal Constitutional Convention," *William and Mary Quarterly*, 3d ser., 40 (1983), 256–282 (esp. 262).
39. Farrand, *Records*, I, 469 (29 June).
40. Rossiter, *1787*, 191.
41. Farrand, *Records*, I, 33, 235.
42. Ibid., 335–336 (20 June).
43. On this distinction see Gordon S. Wood, *The Creation of the American Republic, 1776–1787* (Chapel Hill: University of North Carolina Press, 1969), 545–547; Rossiter, *1787*, 170–171, 183, 193–194, 246, 264–265; Forrest McDonald, *Novus Ordo Seclorum* (Lawrence: University of Kansas Press, 1985), 225–260.
44. Wood, *Creation*, 347–389; McDonald, *Novus Ordo Seclorum*, 145.
45. Alexander Hamilton, James Madison, and John Jay, *The Federalist Papers*, ed. Clinton L. Rossiter (New York: Mentor/New American Library, 1961), No. 39 (Madison), 240–246. All references to *The Federalist* are to this edition.
46. Charles F. Hobson, "The Negative on State Laws: James Madison, the Constitution, and the Crisis of Republican Government," *William and Mary Quarterly*, 3d ser., 36 (1979), 215–235.
47. Farrand, *Records*, I, 165 (18 June).
48. Andrew C. McLaughlin, *Foundations of American Constitutionalism* (1932; reprint, Gloucester, Mass.: Peter Smith, 1972), 142–143, 145–146.
49. Farrand, *Records*, I, 64–69, 96–97; Charles C. Thach, *The Creation of the Presidency, 1775–1789* (Baltimore: Johns Hopkins University Press, 1922). See also

Thomas E. Cronin, "The Origins of the American Presidency, *This Constitution*, no. 12 (Fall 1986), 11–18.

50. Judith Best, *The Case against Direct Election of the President* (Ithaca: Cornell University Press, 1975).

51. On James Wilson see Charles Page Smith, *James Wilson: Founding Father, 1742–1798* (Chapel Hill: University of North Carolina Press, 1956); Robert G. McCloskey, ed., *The Works of James Wilson*, 2 vols., (Cambridge, Mass.: Harvard University Press, 1967); Geoffrey Seed, *James Wilson* (Millwood, N. Y.: KTO Press, 1979).

52. McCloskey, Introduction, *Works of James Wilson*, I, 1–52.

53. Julius Goebel, Jr., *The Oliver Wendell Holmes Devise History of the Supreme Court of the United States, I: Antecedents and Beginnings to 1801* (New York: Macmillan, 1971), 196–250.

54. See, for example, James Bradley Thayer, "The Original Scope of the American Doctrine of Constitutional Law," *Harvard Law Review*, 7 (1893), 127–156; Charles A. Beard, *The Supreme Court and the Constitution* (New York: Macmillan, 1912); Charles Warren, *Congress, the Constitution, and the Supreme Court*, rev. ed. (Boston: Little, Brown, 1937); idem, *The Supreme Court in U. S. History*, rev. ed., 2 vols. (Boston: Little, Brown, 1926); Louis B. Boudin, *Government by Judiciary* (New York: Tudor Publishing, 1932); Charles G. Haines, *The American Doctrine of Judicial Supremacy*, 2d ed., (New York: Macmillan, 1932); Henry Steele Commager, *Majority Rule and Minority Rights* (1943; reprint, Gloucester, Mass.: Peter Smith, 1968); Raoul Berger, *Congress versus the Supreme Court* (Cambridge, Mass.: Harvard University Press, 1969); Goebel, *Antecedents*, 196–250; Paul M. Bator, Paul J. Mishkin, David L. Shapiro, and Herbert Wechsler, *Hart and Wechsler's The Federal Courts and the Federal System*, rev. ed. (Brooklyn: Foundation Press, 1973) (original edition by Henry M. Hart, Jr. and Herbert Wechsler, 1958); Laurence H. Tribe, *American Constitutional Law* (Brooklyn, N.Y.: Foundation Press, 1978); idem, *Constitutional Choices* (Cambridge, Mass.: Harvard University Press, 1985); John Hart Ely, *Democracy and Distrust: A Theory of Judicial Review* (Cambridge, Mass.: Harvard University Press, 1980); Jesse H. Choper, *Judicial Review and the National Political Process* (Chicago: University of Chicago Press, 1980); and Michael Perry, *The Constitution, the Courts, and Human Rights* (New Haven: Yale University Press, 1982). This list is only a small sample; each of these books contains extensive references to the hundreds of other publications on this issue. *Federalist* No. 78 (Hamilton), 464–472, is one of the basic documents of the controversy.

55. See the discussion in Chapter 8.

56. See generally Donald L. Robinson, *Slavery in the Structure of American Politics, 1765–1820* (New York: Harcourt Brace Jovanovich, 1971).

57. Staughton Lynd, *Slavery, Class Conflict, and the Constitution: Ten Essays* (Indianapolis: Bobbs-Merrill, 1967), 135–213; Collier and Collier, *Decision in Philadelphia*, uncritically accept Lynd's suggestion.

58. See, for example, Farrand, *Records*, II, 449–450 (24 August).

59. See the discussion of the Northwest Ordinance in Chapter 2 above and in Robinson, *Slavery*, 228–229, 378–386.

60. The best analysis is Robinson, *Slavery*, 168–247.

61. See Philip S. Paludan, *A Covenant with Death* (Urbana: University of Illinois Press,

1976); Harold M. Hyman and William M. Wiecek, *Equal Justice Under Law: Constitutional Development. 1835–1875* (New York: Harper & Row, 1982), 86–202; William E. Nelson, "The Impact of the Antislavery Movement upon Styles of Judicial Reasoning in Nineteenth Century America," *Harvard Law Review*, 87 (1974), 513–555; William M. Wiecek, *The Sources of Antislavery Constitutionalism in America, 1760–1848* (Ithaca: Cornell University Press, 1977); Robert M. Cover, *Justice Accused: Antislavery and the Judicial Process* (New Haven: Yale University Press, 1975).

62. See, for example, Farrand, *Records*, II, 371–372 (22 August).

63. Ibid., 372.

64. Collier and Collier, *Decision in Philadelphia*, 139.

65. *Federalist* No. 84 (Hamilton), 510–520.

66. Robert Allen Rutland, *George Mason: Reluctant Statesman* (Williamsburg, Va.: Colonial Williamsburg, 1961); Helen H. Miller, *George Mason: Gentleman Revolutionary* (Chapel Hill: University of North Carolina Press, 1975); Robert A. Rutland, ed., *The Papers of George Mason*, 3 vols. (Chapel Hill: University of North Carolina Press, 1970).

67. George Athan Billias, *Elbridge Gerry* (New York: McGraw-Hill, ·1976).

68. Farrand, *Records*, II, 587–588 (12 September).

69. See Hamilton's defense of the Convention, *Federalist* No. 78, 513–514.

70. Farrand, *Records*, II, 177–189.

71. James Madison to Jared Sparks, 8 April 1831, in ibid., III, 498–500 (quotation at 499).

72. Max M. Mintz, *Gouverneur Morris and the American Revolution* (Norman: University of Oklahoma Press, 1970).

73. Farrand, *Records*, II, 622–33 (15 September).

74. John C. Fitzpatrick, "The Man Who Engrossed the Constitution," in U.S. Constitution Sesquicentennial Commission, *History of the Formation of the Union under the Constitution* (Washington, D.C.: U.S. Government Printing Office, 1941), 761–769.

75. Farrand, *Records*, II, 641–643 (17 September).

76. For example, when Elbridge Gerry recommended that the new charter set a limit on the size of the American army, Washington allegedly suggested that the delegates also include a provision setting the same limit on the size of any future invading army. Collier and Collier, *Decision in Philadelphia*, 242.

77. Farrand, *Records*, II, 647 (17 September).

78. Ibid., 648.

79. We are indebted to Leonard Rapport for drawing our attention to his article "Printing the Constitution: The Convention and Newspaper Imprints, August–November 1787," *Prologue*, 2 (1970), 63–90.

80. See generally Linda Grant De Pauw, *The Eleventh Pillar: New York State and the Federal Constitution* (Ithaca: Cornell University Press, 1966); Stephen Schechter, ed., *The Reluctant Pillar* (Albany, N.Y.: Russell Sage College, 1985).

81. De Pauw, *Eleventh Pillar*, 56–57.

82. Robert Yates to Abraham Yates, Jr., 1 June 1787, RBAYP.

83. Yates's notes are reprinted in Farrand, *Records*, and in Tansill, *Documents*. Lansing's notes were edited by Joseph Strayer and published as *The Delegate from New York* (1939; reprint, Port Washington, N.Y.: Kennikat, 1967).

84. Farrand, *Records,* I, 249–450 (16 June).

85. Ibid., 281–311 (all available accounts); see also Harold C. Syrett, ed., *The Papers of Alexander Hamilton,* 26 vols. (New York: Columbia University Press, 1961–79), IV, 178–211.

86. Farrand, *Records,* I, 301 (18 June) (Yates's notes).

87. Ibid., 288, 289, 292, 291 (18 June) (Madison). See Bower Aly, *The Rhetoric of Alexander Hamilton* (New York: Columbia University Press, 1941), 87–89; also De Pauw, *Eleventh Pillar,* 60–62. On the role of the dissenting appellate judge, see Alan Barth, *Prophets with Honor* (New York: Alfred A. Knopf, 1973), chap. 1.

88. John C. Miller, *Alexander Hamilton: Portrait in Paradox* (New York: Harper, 1959), 159–174; Forrest McDonald, *Alexander Hamilton: A Biography* (New York: W. W. Norton, 1979), 99–105; Aly, *Rhetoric of Hamilton,* 87–89. The best study of Hamilton's political thought is Gerald Stourzh, *Alexander Hamilton and the Idea of Republican Government* (Stanford: Stanford University Press, 1970). See also Cecelia M. Kenyon, "Alexander Hamilton: Rousseau of the Right," *Political Science Quarterly,* 73 (1958), 161–178.

89. Irving Brant, Memorandum, 7 July 1948, filed with "Plan of a constitution for America," Alexander Hamilton Papers, RB.

90. Abraham G. Lansing to Abraham Yates, Jr., 26 August 1787, RBAYP.

91. Farrand, *Records,* I, 288 (18 June).

92. Ibid., II, 646 (17 September).

7. The Struggle for Ratification

1. Robert Allen Rutland, *The Ordeal of the Constitution* (Norman, Okla.: University of Oklahoma Press, 1966); Jackson Turner Main, *The Antifederalists: Critics of the Constitution, 1781–1788* (Chapel Hill: University of North Carolina Press, 1961); Cecelia M. Kenyon, ed., *The Antifederalists* (Indianapolis: Bobbs-Merrill, 1967); Herbert J. Storing, ed., *The Complete Anti-Federalist,* 7 vols. (Chicago: University of Chicago Press, 1981), especially vol. 1, *What the Anti-Federalists Were For.*

2. On this point see Storing, *Complete Anti-Federalist,* I, 3–6, 79–80 n. 6. Compare Main, *Antifederalists,* and idem, *Political Parties before the Constitution* (Chapel Hill: University of North Carolina Press, 1973).

3. Rutland, *Ordeal,* 25, 50–51; Robert L. Brunhouse, *The Counter-Revolution in Pennsylvania, 1776–1790* (1942; reprint, New York: Octagon Books, 1971).

4. See, for example, Kenneth R. Bowling, "Politics in the First Congress, 1789–1791" (Ph.D. diss., University of Wisconsin, 1968).

5. Rutland, *Ordeal,* 17–20; see also the letters from Richard Henry Lee and Nathan Dane to Samuel Adams, October 1787, Samuel Adams Papers, Box 7, RBBC.

6. Rutland, *Ordeal,* 50–51; Brunhouse, *Counter-Revolution in Pennsylvania,* 200–202.

7. These charges appear, for example, in the Lee-Adams correspondence of October 1787. On the conventions themselves, see Charles W. Roll, "'We, Some of the People': Apportionment in the Thirteen State Conventions Ratifying the Constitution," *Journal of American History,* 56 (1969), 21–40, supplementing and correcting Orin G. Libby, *The Geographical Distribution of the Vote of the Thirteen States on the Federal Constitution,* University of Wisconsin Bulletin—Economics, Political Science and History Series, vol. I, no. 1 (Madison, 1894).

8. This paragraph draws generally on Rutland, *Ordeal,* especially 17–36; this book is the single best account of the ratification controversy.

9. See Kenneth Coleman, *The American Revolution in Georgia 1763–1789* (Athens: University of Georgia Press, 1958), 267–275; Rutland, *Ordeal,* 87–88.

10. Quoted in Rutland, *Ordeal,* 73 ("Argus" of Rehoboth, Rhode Island).

11. See generally Linda Grant De Pauw, "The Anticlimax of Antifederalism: The Abortive Second Convention Movement, 1788–89," *Prologue,* 2 (1970), 98–114.

12. See, for example, Richard Henry Lee to Samuel Adams, 22 October 1787, Samuel Adams Papers, Box 7, RBBC.

13. Melancton Smith to Abraham Yates, Jr., 28 January 1788, RBAYP.

14. James Wilson to Samuel Wallis, 22 January 1788, RBEC no. 9444.

15. See Rutland, *Ordeal,* 66–82, 89–114; Samuel B. Harding, *The Contest over the Ratification of the Federal Constitution in Massachusetts* (1896; reprint, New York: Da Capo, 1970).

16. Rutland, *Ordeal,* 116–124.

17. Robert Yates to George Mason, 21 June 1788, RBEC no. 9528.

18. See generally Joseph B. Walker, *A History of the New Hampshire Convention* (Boston: Cupples and Hurd, 1888).

19. This account is based on Rutland, *Ordeal,* 169–198, 218–234, 245–253; Irving Brant, *James Madison: Father of the Constitution, 1787–1800* (Indianapolis: Bobbs-Merrill, 1950), 185–228; and Robert Allen Rutland, Conover Jones, and Kym S. Rice, *James Madison and the Search for Nationhood* (Washington, D.C.: Library of Congress, 1981), 64, 67.

20. Quoted in Rutland, *Ordeal,* 248.

21. See generally Linda Grant De Pauw, *The Eleventh Pillar: New York State and the Constitution* (Ithaca: Cornell University Press, 1966); Stephen L. Schechter, ed., *The Reluctant Pillar* (Troy, N.Y.: Russell Sage College, 1985); Rutland, *Ordeal,* 139–141, 199–209, 235–244, 255–265.

22. On preconvention strategy in New York, see De Pauw, *Eleventh Pillar,* 121–179; Schechter, *Reluctant Pillar,* 65–99.

23. For many examples of Anti-Federalist confidence, see the correspondence for the period October 1787–June 1788 in RBAYP.

24. See Richard B. Morris, "John Jay and the Adoption of the Federal Constitution in New York: A New Reading of Persons and Events," *New York History,* 63 (1982), 132–164; Robin Brooks, "Alexander Hamilton, Melancton Smith, and the Ratification of the Constitution in New York," *William and Mary Quarterly,* 3d ser., 24 (1967), 339–358.

25. Rutland, *Ordeal,* 282–300; De Pauw, "Anticlimax"; Steven A. Boyd, *The Politics of Opposition: Antifederalists and the Acceptance of the Constitution* (Millwood, N.Y.: KTO Press, 1979), 121–167.

26. Irwin H. Polishook, *Rhode Island and the Union, 1774–1795* (Evanston: Northwestern University Press, 1969); Hillman Metcalf Bishop, "Why Rhode Island Opposed the Federal Constitution," *Rhode Island History,* 8 (1949), 1–10, 33–44, 85–95, 115–126 (reprinted privately in Providence, 1950).

27. Louise Irby Trenholme, *The Ratification of the Federal Constitution in North Carolina* (1932; reprint, New York: AMS Press, 1970); Rutland, *Ordeal,* 268–278, 282, 283.

28. Whitfield J. Bell, Jr., "The Federal Processions of 1788," *New-York Historical Society Quarterly,* 46 (1962), 5–39; Schechter, *Reluctant Pillar,* 112–113.

29. The Anti-Federalists' case against the Constitution has been resurrected and reexamined by Main, *Antifederalists*; Kenyon, *Antifederalists*; and Storing, *Complete Anti-Federalist*, especially vol. 1. See also James H. Hutson, "Country, Court, and Constitution: Antifederalism and the Historians," *William and Mary Quarterly*, 3d ser., 38 (1981), 73–96.

30. Storing, *Complete Anti-Federalist*, I, 6.

31. Thomas Fitzsimons to Noah Webster, 15 September 1787, Noah Webster Papers, Box 2, RB.

32. Trevor Colbourn, ed., *Fame and the Founding Fathers: Essays of Douglass Adair* (New York: W. W. Norton, 1974), 272–273; Albert Furtwangler, *The Authority of Publius: A Reading of the Federalist Papers* (Ithaca: Cornell University Press, 1984), 17–44.

33. Colbourn, *Fame and the Founding Fathers*, 272–273.

34. See Storing, *Complete Anti-Federalist*, vols. 2–6; Paul L. Ford, ed., *Pamphlets on the Constitution of the United States* (Brooklyn: privately printed, 1888); idem, ed., *Essays on the Constitution of the United States* (Brooklyn: privately printed, 1892); and Kenyon, *The Antifederalists*.

35. Storing, *Complete Anti-Federalist*, II, 222, n. 6.

36. Ford, *Pamphlets* and *Essays*. During the centennial of the making of the Constitution, Paul L. Ford and Worthington C. Ford published these two volumes of pamphlets and newspaper essays drawn from the "pamphlet wars" of 1787–88. In his notes to these editions, Paul L. Ford sought to identify the authors of the republished essays. He tended to assume that major pamphlets for or against the Constitution were written by major politicians on one side or the other. More recent scholarship has disproved many of Ford's attributions.

37. Charles Warren, "Elbridge Gerry, James Warren, Mercy Warren, and the Ratification of the Federal Constitution in Massachusetts," *Massachusetts Historical Society Proceedings*, 64 (1932), 143–164. On Lee see Storing, *Complete Anti-Federalist*, II, 214–223; Gordon S. Wood, "The Authorship of the *Letters from the Federal Farmer*," *William and Mary Quarterly*, 3d ser., 31 (1974), 299–308. On Caesar and Cato see Jacob E. Cooke, "Alexander Hamilton's Authorship of the 'Caesar' Letters," ibid., 17 (1960), 78–85; De Pauw, *Eleventh Pillar*, 283–292; and Storing, *Complete Anti-Federalist*, II, 101–103.

38. Storing, *Complete Anti-Federalist*, II, 216.

39. [Oliver Ellsworth,] Letters of a Landholder, [Hartford,] *Connecticut Courant*, November 1787–March 1788, reprinted in Ford, *Essays*, 139–202.

40. See Storing, *Complete Anti-Federalist*, passim; Merrill Jensen, Gaspare Saladino, and John P. Kaminski, eds., *The Documentary History of the Ratification of the Constitution and the Bill of Rights*, 17 vols. projected (Madison: State Historical Society of Wisconsin, 1976–).

41. The *Address* is reprinted in H. P. Johnston, ed., *The Correspondence and Public Papers of John Jay*, 4 vols. (New York: G.P. Putnam's Sons, 1893), III, 294–319; Ford, *Pamphlets*, 67–86. The *Address* is referred to in *Federalist* No. 85 (Hamilton).

42. Johnston, *Correspondence of Jay*, III, 318–319; Ford, *Pamphlets*, 86.

43. *The Letters from a Federal Farmer* are reprinted in Storing, *Complete Anti-Federalist*, II; the other modern edition, with full annotations and an excellent introduction and index, is Walter P. Bennett, ed., *The Letters from the Federal Farmer to the Republican* (University: University of Alabama Press, 1978).

44. See Bennett, *Federal Farmer*, xxiv, xxviii–xxx, xxxii–xxxiii, xxxv; see for example, *Federalist* No. 68 (Hamilton), in Clinton L. Rossiter's edition of *The Federalist Papers* (New York: Mentor/New American Library, 1961), 411; all citations are to this edition.

45. Edmund Pendleton to Richard Henry Lee, 14 June 1788, RBEC no. 1551; Storing, *Complete Anti-Federalist*, I, 64–70.

46. *The Objection of the Hon. George Mason to the Proposed Federal Constitution, Addressed to the People of Virginia*, Broadside (Richmond, 1788), reprinted in Storing, *Complete Anti-Federalist*, II, 11–13 (quotation at 11).

47. Luther Martin, *The Genuine Information . . .*, reprinted in Max Farrand, ed., *The Records of the Federal Convention of 1787*, rev. ed., 4 vols. (New Haven: Yale University Press, 1937; 2d rev. ed. of vol. 4, ed. James H. Hutson, forthcoming), III, 172–232, and in Storing, *Complete Anti-Federalist*, II, 24–79.

48. [Mercy Otis Warren,] *Observations on the New Constitution . . . by a Columbian Patriot*, reprinted in Storing, *Complete Anti-Federalist*, IV, 271–286 (quotation at 275). Mrs. Warren's reference is to James Wilson's speech in the Pennsylvania ratifying convention, 26 Nov. 1787, reprinted in Robert G. McCloskey, *The Works of James Wilson*, 2 vols. (Cambridge, Mass.: Harvard University Press, 1967), II, 759–774.

49. Linda K. Kerber, *Women of the Republic: Intellect and Ideology in Revolutionary America* (Chapel Hill: University of North Carolina Press, 1980), 80–84, 227, 240, 246, 250–252, 256–258; Mercy Otis Warren, *History of the Rise, Progress and Termination of the American Revolution* (1805; reprint, New York: AMS Press, 1971); extracts appear in Storing, *Complete Anti-Federalist*, VI, 197–248. See also Maud M. Hutcheson, "Mercy Warren, 1728–1814," *William and Mary Quarterly*, 3d ser., 10 (1953), 378–402; Lester H. Cohen, "Explaining the Revolution: Ideology and Ethics in Mercy Otis Warren's Historical Theory," ibid., 37 (1980), 200–218.

50. Mason, *"Objections,"* in Storing, *Complete Anti-Federalist*, II, 12.

51. Melancton Smith to Abraham Yates, Jr., 17 January 1788, RBAYP.

52. [Benjamin Austin,] *Observations on the Pernicious Practice of the Law . . .* (Boston: Joshua Belcher, 1814). See the discussion in Chapter 3.

53. [Melancton Smith?] *An Address to the People of the State of New-York . . . by a Plebeian*, in Storing, *Complete Anti-Federalist*, VI, 129–146. Storing questions the traditional attribution of this pamphlet to Smith, ibid., 128.

54. Mason, *Objections*, in ibid., II, 13.

55. [Warren,] *Observations . . . by a Columbian Patriot*, in ibid., IV, 286.

56. On the genesis of *The Federalist* see Richard B. Morris, *Witnesses at the Creation: Hamilton, Madison, Jay, and the Constitution* (New York: Holt, Rinehart & Winston, 1985); Furtwangler, *Authority of Publius*, 45–79; Colbourn, *Fame and the Founding Fathers*, 55–65; De Pauw, *Eleventh Pillar*, 106–117; John C. Miller, *Alexander Hamilton: Portrait in Paradox* (New York: Harper, 1959), 184–205; Brant, *Madison: Father of the Constitution*, 172–184; Frank Monaghan, *John Jay: Defender of Liberty* (Indianapolis: Bobbs-Merrill, 1935), 288–291; Gottfried Dietze, *The Federalist: A Classic on Federalism and Free Government* (Baltimore: Johns Hopkins University Press, 1961); and the introductions to the several editions of *The Federalist*: Benjamin F. Wright (Cambridge, Mass.: Belknap Press of Harvard University Press, 1961); Clinton L. Rossiter (New York: Mentor/New American

Library, 1961); Roy P. Fairfield (1961; 2d ed., Baltimore: Johns Hopkins University Press, 1981); and especially Jacob E. Cooke (Middletown, Conn.: Wesleyan University Press, 1961).

57. On the newspaper war in the summer and fall of 1787, see De Pauw, *Eleventh Pillar,* 69–83, 91–105; Schechter, *Reluctant Pillar,* 65–72.

58. The Caesar letters are reprinted in Ford, *Essays,* 283–291; the Cato letters are reprinted in Storing, *Compete Anti-Federalist,* II, 104–125. Although these letters were long thought to be the work of Alexander Hamilton and Governor George Clinton, respectively, Jacob E. Cooke ("Alexander Hamilton's Authorship of 'Caesar'") and Linda Grant De Pauw (*Eleventh Pillar,* 283–292) have refuted these attributions.

59. Born in Italy, Ceracchi came to the United States in 1791 to demonstrate his admiration for the Americans and to persuade Congress to commission him to create a monument to Liberty. While in Philadelphia, he modeled busts of many of the major political figures of his day; he later sculpted marble busts from these models and presented the busts to his subjects as gifts. He also made plaster casts and terracotta copies of these portraits, which he planned to produce in large quantities to sell all over Europe. His plans miscarried, and he returned to Italy, where he spent his remaining years campaigning for the restoration of republican government there. In 1795 and 1796, when he was in grave financial distress, Ceracchi sent bills to each of his "American Heroes" for the marble busts that he had presented them as gifts. Hamilton paid the money but noted in his Cash Book, "this sum through *delicacy* [was] paid upon cherachi's draft for making my bust on his own importunity & as a favor to me"; Harold C. Syrett, ed., *The Papers of Alexander Hamilton,* 26 vols. (New York: Columbia University Press, 1961–79), XVIII, 504 n. 6. Ceracchi died on the guillotine in 1801, condemned by Napoleon I for participating in a plot to assassinate the emperor. See generally Ulysse Desportes, "Guiseppe Ceracchi in America and His Busts of George Washington," *Art Quarterly,* 26 (1963), 140–179.

60. Morris, *Witnesses,* 7–23; Brant, *Madison: Father of the Constitution,* 172–184; Edmund Randolph to James Madison, 3 January 1788, RBEC no. 9537.

61. The best source for the publishing history of *The Federalist* is Cooke's edition.

62. Quoted in De Pauw, *Eleventh Pillar,* 110–111; Furtwangler, *Authority of Publius,* 21.

63. De Pauw, *Eleventh Pillar,* 113–117.

64. We are indebted to Professor Gaspare J. Saladino, coeditor of *The Documentary History of the Ratification of the Constitution,* for information on this point.

65. Elizabeth Fleet, ed., "Madison's 'Detached Memoranda,'" *William and Mary Quarterly,* 3d ser., 3 (1946), 534–568, especially "The Federalist," 564–568 (quotation at 565–566).

66. Jay's draft of No. 2 disappeared in the late 1800s, the drafts of Nos. 3 and 4 are in private hands, the draft of No. 5 is part of the Papers of John Jay at Columbia University, and the draft of No. 64, shown in the text in Figure 7.20, is now in the collections of the New-York Historical Society.

67. Colbourn, *Fame and the Founding Fathers,* 52.

68. The best discussion of the authorship controversy is by Douglass Adair. See Colbourn, *Fame and the Founding Fathers,* 27–74. In these essays Adair established the links between the prevailing views of the authorship controversy in nine-

teenth- and twentieth-century American historiography and the prevailing views of constitutional interpretation at those times.

69. Edward G. Bourne, "The Authorship of The Federalist," *American Historical Review,* 2 (1896–97), 444–460.

70. Frederick Mosteller and David Wallace, *Inference and Disputed Authorship: The Federalist* (Reading, Mass.: Addison-Wesley, 1964).

71. *Federalist* No. 1 (Hamilton), 36.

72. On *Federalist* No. 10 see, for example, Charles A. Beard, *An Economic Interpretation of the Constitution of the United States,* rev. ed. (New York: Macmillan, 1935), 152–188, especially 156–158; Colbourn, *Fame and the Founding Fathers,* 75–106; Garry Wills, *Explaining America: The Federalist* (Garden City, N.Y.: Doubleday, 1981); Theodore Draper, "Hume and Madison: The Secrets of Federalist Paper No. 10," *Encounter,* 58 (February 1982), 34–47; Furtwangler, *Authority of Publius,* 112–146; John Patrick Diggins, *The Lost Soul of American Politics* (New York: Basic Books, 1985); and David F. Epstein, *The Political Theory of The Federalist* (Chicago: University of Chicago Press, 1984). Furtwangler, *Authority of Publius,* 112–146, cites other examples of this literature.

73. *Federalist* No. 51 (Madison), 321–322.

74. Colbourn, *Fame and the Founding Fathers,* 93–106; Garry Wills sought to extend Adair's argument in *Explaining America.*

75. Gordon S. Wood, *The Creation of the American Republic, 1776–1787* (Chapel Hill: University of North Carolina Press, 1969), 519–564, 593–615; Epstein, *Political Theory of The Federalist;* Colbourn, *Fame and the Founding Fathers,* 93–106; Martin Diamond, "Democracy and *The Federalist:* A Reconsideration of the Framers' Intent," *American Political Science Review,* 53 (1959), 52–68.

76. Rossiter, Introduction to *The Federalist Papers,* xiii–xv.

77. *Federalist* No. 85 (Hamilton), 527.

78. See, for example, John Fiske, *The Critical Period in American History* (Boston: Little, Brown, 1888), 342.

79. Colbourn, *Fame and the Founding Fathers,* 28–30, 49–50, 58; Furtwangler, *Authority of Publius,* 19–23, 81–84; De Pauw, *Eleventh Pillar,* 113–117.

80. The most comprehensive bibliography of editions of *The Federalist* is found in Roy P. Fairfield's edition.

81. George Washington to Alexander Hamilton, 28 August 1788, in John C. Fitzpatrick, ed., *The Writings of George Washington,* 39 vols. (Washington, D.C.: U.S. Government Printing Office, 1931–44), XXX, 66.

8. Under the Constitution

1. On Washington's inauguration see Donald M. Matteson, *The Organization of the Government under the Constitution* (1941; reprint, New York: Da Capo, 1970), 118–139; James Thomas Flexner, *George Washington and the New Nation, 1783–1793* (Boston: Little, Brown, 1969), 182–191; Irving Brant, *James Madison: Father of the Constitution, 1787–1800* (Indianapolis: Bobbs-Merrill, 1950), 255–258; John C. Miller, *The Federalist Era, 1789–1801* (New York: Harper & Row, 1960), 17.

2. George Washington to Joseph Jones, 14 May 1789, GWP.

3. See Ralph L. Ketcham, *Presidents above Party: The First American Presidency, 1789–1829* (Chapel Hill: University of North Carolina Press, 1984); James Hart, *The American Presidency in Action: 1789* (New York: Macmillan, 1948); Leonard D. White, *The Federalists: A Study in Administrative History* (New York: Macmillan, 1948).

4. George Washington to Joseph Jones, 14 May 1789, GWP.

5. This discussion of Congress is based on Richard B. Bernstein's work in progress tentatively entitled "'Conven'd in Firm Debate': The Development of the House of Representatives as an Institution of Republican Government, 1789–1812." See also Kenneth R. Bowling, "Politics in the First Congress, 1789–1791" (Ph.D. diss., University of Wisconsin, 1968); Ralph V. Harlow, *The History of Legislative Methods in the Period before 1825* (New Haven: Yale University Press, 1917); Joseph Cooper, "The Origins of Standing Committees and the Development of the Modern House," *Rice University Studies,* 56 (Summer 1970); White, *The Federalists,* 17–25, 67–87. An indispensable primary source is Linda Grant De Pauw and Charlene Bickford, eds., *The Documentary History of the First Federal Congress,* 5 vols. to date (Baltimore: Johns Hopkins University Press, 1972–). See also the only extensive account of the Senate's proceedings in this period, Edgar S. Maclay, ed., *The Journal of William Maclay, 1789–1791* (1890; reprint, New York: Ungar, 1966). Bickford is planning a new edition of Maclay's *Journal.*

6. For useful analyses of these debates see Hart, *American Presidency,* 155–218; White, *The Federalists,* 17–25; Bowling, "Politics in the First Congress," 82–120.

7. Bowling, "Politics in the First Congress," 91–95.

8. See generally E. James Ferguson, *The Power of the Purse: A History of American Public Finance, 1776–1790* (Chapel Hill: University of North Carolina Press, 1961).

9. Bowling, "Politics in the First Congress," 90. See the enlightening discussion in Forrest McDonald, *Alexander Hamilton: A Biography* (New York: W. W. Norton, 1979), 132, 138–142.

10. McDonald, *Alexander Hamilton,* provides a lucid and accessible account of Hamilton's fiscal policies and conduct as the first secretary of the Treasury. See also James Willard Hurst, "Alexander Hamilton: Law Maker," *Columbia Law Review,* 78 (1978), 483–547. On Hamilton's relationship to Washington see Flexner, *George Washington and the New Nation,* 160–161, 195–196, 213–214; McDonald, *Alexander Hamilton,* 14–15, 23–24, 124–129; Richard B. Morris, "Washington and Hamilton: A Great Collaboration," *Proceedings of the American Philosophical Society,* 102 (1958), 107–116; Joseph Charles, *Origins of the American Party System: Three Essays* (Williamsburg, Va.: Institute of Early American History and Culture, 1956), 3–53; White, *The Federalists,* 27–59. On the Treasury Department as an institution see ibid., 117–126.

11. The following discussion is based on McDonald, *Alexander Hamilton,* 143–161.

12. On Hamilton's intellectual preparation for assuming the office of secretary and on the roots of Hamilton's policies, see ibid., 127–142, 160–161. See generally Gerald Stourzh, *Alexander Hamilton and the Idea of Republican Government* (Stanford: Stanford University Press, 1970). A good compilation of Hamilton's reports is Jacob E. Cooke, ed., *The Reports of Alexander Hamilton* (New York: Harper & Row, 1964).

13. On the controversy generated by this report, see McDonald, *Alexander Hamilton,*

164–188; Bowling, "Politics in the First Congress," 202–205; Brant, *Madison: Father of the Constitution,* 290–305; and Miller, *Federalist Era,* 39–54.

14. On this point see Douglass G. Adair, "The Intellectual Origins of Jeffersonian Democracy" (Ph.D. diss., Yale University, 1943); Lance Banning, *The Jeffersonian Persuasion: Evolution of a Party Ideology* (Ithaca: Cornell University Press, 1978); and Drew R. McCoy, *The Elusive Republic: Political Economy in Jeffersonian America* (Chapel Hill: University of North Carolina Press, 1980). But see Joyce Appleby, *Capitalism and a New Social Order: The Republican Vision of the 1790s* (New York: New York University Press, 1984).

15. On Madison's emergence as the leader of the opposition, see Brant, *Madison: Father of the Constitution,* 290–318, 327–370; Robert Allen Rutland, Conover Jones, and Kym S. Rice, *James Madison and the Search for Nationhood* (Washington, D.C.: Library of Congress, 1981), 65–73; Bowling, "Politics in the First Congress," 262–263; and McDonald, *Alexander Hamilton,* 128–133, 140–141, 216–217 (though McDonald's assessments of Madison's motives should be viewed with caution). For primary documentation, volumes 13–15 of William M. Hutchinson, William M. E. Rachal, and Robert A. Rutland, eds., *The Papers of James Madison,* 15 vols. to date (vols 1–10, Chicago: University of Chicago Press, 1962–5; vols. 11–, Charlottesville: University Press of Virginia, 1977–) are indispensable.

16. See Bowling, "Politics in the First Congress," for an insightful linking of these issues; see also McDonald, *Alexander Hamilton,* 170–176.

17. Jacob E. Cooke, "The Compromise of 1790," *William and Mary Quarterly,* 3d ser., 27 (1970), 523–545; Kenneth R. Bowling, "Dinner at Jefferson's: A Note on Jacob E. Cooke's 'The Compromise of 1790,'" ibid., 28 (1971), 629–640; McDonald, *Alexander Hamilton,* 179–187; Dumas Malone, *Jefferson and the Rights of Man* (Boston: Little, Brown, 1951), 299–306; Brant, *Madison: Father of the Constitution,* 312–318; Ferguson, *Power of the Purse,* 319–320.

18. On the first Bank of the United States see McDonald, *Alexander Hamilton,* 189–210; Bray Hammond, *Banks and Politics in America from the Revolution to the Civil War* (Princeton: Princeton University Press, 1957), 89–114.

19. For the opinions on the constitutionality of the Bank see Julian Boyd, ed., *The Papers of Thomas Jefferson,* 21 vols. to date (Princeton: Princeton University Press, 1950–; cited hereafter as *Jefferson Papers*), XIX, 275–280; and Harold C. Syrett, ed., *The Papers of Alexander Hamilton,* 26 vols. (New York: Columbia University Press, 1961–79; cited hereafter as *Hamilton Papers*), VIII, 98–134. See also the brief but informative discussions in McDonald, *Alexander Hamilton,* 202–210, and in Alfred H. Kelly, Winfred Harbison, and Herman Belz, *The America Constitution: Its Origins and Development,* 6th ed. (New York: W. W. Norton, 1983), 130–131.

20. *Federalist* No. 44 (Madison), in Clinton L. Rossiter, ed., *The Federalist Papers* (New York: Mentor/New American Library, 1961), 283–288; all citations are to this edition.

21. *Annals of Congress,* II, 1899 (1st Cong., 3d sess., H.R., 3 Feb. 1791) (remarks of Madison).

22. *Jefferson Papers,* XIX, 275–280.

23. *Hamilton Papers,* VIII, 98–134; Cooke, *Reports,* 83–114.

24. *Hamilton Papers,* VIII, 107; Cooke, *Reports,* 91.

25. See McDonald, *Alexander Hamilton*, 209–210.

26. Banning, *Jeffersonian Persuasion*, chaps. 2 and 3; Brant, *Madison: Father of the Constitution*, 348–350; Noble E. Cunningham, Jr., *The Jeffersonian Republicans, 1789–1801: The Formation of Party Organization* (Chapel Hill: University of North Carolina Press, 1957), 3–88; Charles, *Origins*, 12–13; Miller, *Federalist Era*, 63–69. See generally Richard Hofstadter, *The Idea of a Party System* (Berkeley: University of California Press, 1969).

27. Richard B. Morris, quoted on back cover of Cooke, *Reports*.

28. McDonald, *Alexander Hamilton*, 230–236. The *Report* is reprinted in Cooke, *Reports*, 115–205.

29. See generally Julius Goebel, Jr., *The Oliver Wendell Holmes Devise History of the Supreme Court of the United States, I: Antecedents and Beginnings to 1801* (New York: Macmillan, 1971); Dwight F. Henderson, *Courts for a New Nation* (Washington, D.C.: Public Affairs Press, 1971); Charles Warren, *The Supreme Court in U.S. History*, 2 vols., rev. ed. (Boston: Little, Brown, 1926), I, 1–123; idem, "New Light on the History of the Federal Judiciary Act of 1789," *Harvard Law Review*, 37 (1923), 49–132.

30. Goebel, *Antecedents*, 457–551; Warren, "New Light"; idem, *Supreme Court*, I, 1–30.

31. See Goebel, *Antecedents*, 552–554; Maeva Marcus, ed., *The Documentary History of the U.S. Supreme Court*, 2 vols. to date (New York: Columbia University Press, 1985); Richard B. Morris, *John Jay, the Nation, and the Court* (Boston: Boston University Press, 1967); and Warren, *Supreme Court*, I, 31–57.

32. Warren, *Supreme Court*, I, 31–57.

33. Mary K. Bonsteel Tachau, *Federal Courts in the Early Republic: Kentucky, 1789–1816* (Princeton: Princeton University Press, 1978), is a first-rate case study of the workings of a lower federal court in one jurisdiction. See also Goebel, *Antecedents*, 552–661; Morris, *John Jay*, chaps. 2 and 3; and Warren, *Supreme Court*, I, 57–61.

34. Warren, *Supreme Court*, I, 62–90; Morris, *John Jay*, chaps. 2 and 3. For the documents of the Connecticut and Rhode Island cases, together with commentary and analysis, see Richard B. Morris and Ene Sirvet, eds., *John Jay: Chief Justice and Federalist Statesman, 1789–1829* (New York: Harper & Row, forthcoming).

35. *Federalist* No. 78 (Hamilton), 464–472; Warren, *Supreme Court*, I, 65–69; Goebel, *Antecedents*, 589–592.

36. Linda Grant De Pauw, "The Anticlimax of Antifederalism: The Abortive Second Convention Movement, 1788–89," *Prologue*, 2 (1970), 98–114; Steven Boyd, *The Politics of Opposition: Antifederalists and the Acceptance of the Constitution* (Millwood, N.Y.: KTO Press, 1979).

37. Application of the Assembly of the State of New York, 5 February 1789, RBEC no. 9584.

38. Robert Allen Rutland, *The Birth of the Bill of Rights, 1776–1791* (Chapel Hill: University of North Carolina Press, 1955), 197, 199, 201–204; Bernard Schwartz, *The Great Rights of Mankind* (New York: Oxford University Press, 1977), 162–163.

39. Rutland, *Birth*, 192–196, 198–208; Rutland, Jones, and Rice, *James Madison*, 86–88; Schwartz, *Great Rights*, 160–186; Brant, *Madison: Father of the Constitution*, 264–275.

40. Jefferson raised this issue with Madison several times in his letters. See, for example, Jefferson to Madison, 20 December 1787, in William M. Hutchinson, William M. E. Rachal, and Robert A. Rutland, eds., *The Papers of James Madison*, 15 volumes to date (vols. 1–10, Chicago: University of Chicago Press, 1962–1975; vols. 11–, Charlottesville: University Press of Virginia, 1977–; hereafter cited as *Papers of James Madison*), X, 335–339; Jefferson to Madison, 6 February 1788, in ibid., 473–475; Jefferson to Madison, 31 July 1788, ibid., XI, 210–214 (esp. 212–213); Jefferson to Madison, 18 November 1788, ibid., 353–355; Jefferson to Madison, 15 March 1789, ibid., XII, 13–16. Madison's replies are contained in Madison to Jefferson, 17 October 1788, ibid., XI, 295–300 (esp. 297–300); Madison to Jefferson, 8 December 1788, ibid., 381–384 (esp. 382–383); Madison to Jefferson, 27 May 1789, ibid., XII, 185–186. Madison reported his introduction of amendments on the floor of the House to Jefferson, Madison to Jefferson, 14 June 1789, ibid., 217–218, and Madison to Jefferson, 30 June 1789, ibid., 267–272 (esp. 272). Jefferson's reaction is in Jefferson to Madison, 28 August 1789, ibid., 360–365 (esp. 363–364).

41. John C. Fitzpatrick, ed., *The Writings of George Washington*, 39 vols. (Washington, D.C.: U.S. Government Printing Office, 1931–44), XXX, 295.

42. *Annals of Congress*, I, 248–251 (1st Cong., 1st sess. H.R., 5 May 1789).

43. Ibid., 442–459 (1st Cong., 1st sess., H.R., 8 June 1789) (remarks of Madison). See also *Papers of James Madison*, XII, 193–209.

44. Rutland, *Birth*, 210–212; Bowling, "Politics in the First Congress," 143, 146–147, 150–151. Because Senator William Maclay of Pennsylvania was ill on the days when the Senate debated the House proposals for amendments, his journal—the fullest extant source for the views of the Senate in the first Congress—has little useful information on the Senator's views on the Bill of Rights.

45. Rutland, *Birth*, 213–215; Bowling, "Politics in the First Congress," 146–147.

46. Rutland, *Birth*, 216–218; Robert A. Rutland, *The Ordeal of the Constitution* (Norman: University of Oklahoma Press, 1966), 301–305; Matteson, *Organization of Government*, 175–177.

47. Matteson, *Organization of Government*, 185–188.

48. On the problem of the "wayward sisters," see Matteson, *Organization of Government*, 328–359; Louise Irby Trenholme, *The Ratification of the Federal Constitution by North Carolina* (1932; reprint, New York: AMS Press, 1970), 192–232; Irwin H. Polishook, *Rhode Island and the Union, 1774–1795* (Evanston: Northwestern University Press, 1969), 163–206; Rutland, *Birth*, 215–217; Rutland, *Ordeal*, 301–305.

49. Trenholme, *Ratification by North Carolina*, 233–249; Rutland, *Birth*, 216; Rutland, *Ordeal*, 303; Matteson, *Organization of Government*, 338–340.

50. Polishook, *Rhode Island and the Union*, 181–206, is by far the best account.

51. George Washington to Jabez Bowen, 27 December 1789, GWP.

52. Polishook, *Rhode Island and the Union*, 207–230; Matteson, *Organization of Government*, 342–358.

53. Matteson, *Organization of Government*, 179–185; Rutland, *Birth*, 217; Rutland, *Ordeal*, 305–306.

54. On the Constitution's impact on American culture, see the magisterial work by Michael Kammen, *A Machine That Would Go of Itself: The Constitution in American Culture* (New York: Alfred A. Knopf, 1986).

LIST OF ILLUSTRATIONS

Color Plates

XV. John Wesley Jarvis. Portrait of William Samuel Johnson. Oil on canvas, ca. 1814. Courtesy of the National Portrait Gallery, Smithsonian Institution, Washington, D.C.

XVI. William Russell Birch and Thomas Birch. *Bank of Pennsylvania, South Second Street Philadelphia.* Colored engraving, 1799–1800. AP.

XVII. David Grim. *Federal Banquet Pavilion built in New York City.* Watercolor, ca. 1800. Courtesy of The New-York Historical Society, New York.

XVIII. Giuseppe Ceracchi. Bust of Alexander Hamilton. Marble, 1794. AP; gift of Alexander Hamilton II.

XIX. John Joseph Holland. *A View of Broad Street, Wall Street and the City Hall New York.* Watercolor with pencil, 1797. APSC.

Black and White Illustrations

1.1. Artist unknown. *View upon the Road from New-Windsor, towards Morris Town Jersey.* Line engraving, 1789. Courtesy of The Library of Congress, Washington, D.C.

1.2. James Peake after Paul Sandby after Governor Thomas Pownall. *A Design to represent the beginning and completion of an American Settlement or Farm.* Line engraving, 1768. Courtesy of The Library of Congress, Washington, D.C.

1.3. Attributed to Philip Dawe. *A Society of Patriotic Ladies, at Edenton in North Carolina.* Mezzotint, 1775. Courtesy of The Library of Congress, Washington, D.C.

1.4. Artist unknown. A bankruptcy scene. Mezzotint, ca. 1750–1800. AP.

2.1. Benjamin Franklin and others. "Short hints towards a Scheme for a General Union of the British Colonies on the Continent." Copy in the hand of Meshech Weare, 1754. RB.

2.2. [John Dickinson.] Olive Branch Petition. 5 July 1775. RB.

2.3. Charles Willson Peale. *His Excellency George Washington Esquire, Commander in Chief of the Federal Army.* Mezzotint, 1780. APMC.

2.4. Attributed to Edward Savage after Robert Edge Pine. Congress Voting Independence. Stipple engraving, ca. 1798 (plate). AP.

2.5. Thomas Jefferson. Declaration of Independence. Fair copy, ca. 1790. RBEC no. 1524.

2.6. *Articles of Confederation and Perpetual Union between the States of New-Hampshire, Massachusetts-Bay, Rhode-Island . . .* (Lancaster [Pa.]: Francis Bailey, 1777). RB.

2.7. James Trenchard after Charles Willson Peale. *A N.W. View of the State House in Philadelphia.* Line engraving, 1787. AP.

2.8. "According to the order of the Day . . . " Copy in the hand of John Adams, 1 March 1781. RBEC no. 4151.

2.9. Nicolas Ponce. *Précis du Traité de Paix . . .* Etching, ca. 1784. BC.

2.10. Letter from General Nathanael Greene to Governor John Rutledge, Head Quarters, 21 January 1782. RBMC.

2.11. Letter from John Adams to Samuel Adams, Passy, 7 December 1778. RBEC no. 1551.

2.12. *Authentic Copies of the Preliminary Articles of Peace . . .* (London: J. Debrett, 1783). RB.

2.13. M. Smith. *The Blessings of Peace.* Etching and engraving, 1783. AP.

2.14. George III. *A Proclamation . . .* Broadside (New York: James Rivington, 1783). RBBC.

2.15. Thomas Kitchen after John Mitchell. *A Map of the British and French Dominions of North America* (detail). Colored engraving, 1755. MD.

2.16. *The Committee to whom was recommitted the Report of a Plan for a temporary Government of the Western Territory . . .* Broadside (Annapolis: John Dunlap, 1784). RB.

3.1. *In Congress, May 15, 1776.* Broadside (Philadelphia: John Dunlap, 1776). RB.

3.2. Thomas Jefferson. Proposed constitution for Virginia. Third draft, before 13 June 1776. RB.

3.3. [John Adams.] *Thoughts on Government . . .* (Philadelphia: John Dunlap, 1776; reprint, Boston: John Gill, 1776). RB.

3.4. *The Constitution of the Common-wealth of Pennsylvania . . .* (Philadelphia: John Dunlap, 1776). RB.

3.5. *Ordinances Passed at a General Convention . . .* (Williamsburg: Alexander Purdie, 1776). RB.

3.6. Artist unknown. Public buildings of Williamsburg. Engraving, ca. 1740 (modern restrike). APSC.

3.7. Abraham Yates. Minutes of the New York Constitutional Convention. Draft (fragment), 1777. RBAYP.

3.8. *The Constitution of the State of New-York* (Fishkill: Samuel Loudon, 1777). RB.

3.9. Samuel Hill. *A S.W. View of the State House, in Boston.* Etching, July 1793. APSC.

3.10. *A Constitution or Frame of Government . . .* (Boston: Benjamin Edes & Sons, 1780). RB.

3.11. Artist unknown. Portrait of George Wythe. Pencil and ink on paper, 25 April 1791. Courtesy of Art and Picture Department, The Free Library of Philadelphia.

3.12. *Report of the Committee of Revisors . . .* (Richmond: Dixon & Holt, 1784). RB.

3.13. William Hogarth. *Hudibras and the Lawyer.* Engraving, 1726. AP.

3.14. [Benjamin Austin.] *Observations on the Pernicious Practice of the Law . . . by Honestus* (Boston: Joshua Belcher, 1814). RB.

3.15. Artist unknown. *SHELB-NS SACRIFICE or the recommended Loyalists, a faithful representation of a Tragedy shortly to be performed on the Continent of America. Invented by Cruelty. Engraved by Dishonor.* Line engraving, 1783. AP.

3.16. Board of Agents for American Loyalists. *The Summary Case of the American Loyalists* (1785). RB.

3.17. [Alexander Hamilton.] *A Letter from Phocion . . .* (New York: Samuel Loudon, 1784). RB.

4.1. Circular letter from Robert Morris to Governor George Clinton, Philadelphia, 16 July 1781. RBEC no. 3949.

4.2. United States fifty-dollar certificate. Engraving, 26 September 1778. RBEC no. 14027.

4.3. Artist unknown. *Gen. Daniel Shays, Col. Job Shattuck.* Woodcut, 1787. Courtesy of the National Portrait Gallery, Smithsonian Institution, Washington, D.C.

4.4. Governor George Clinton. *A Proclamation.* Broadside (New York: S. & J. Loudon, 24 February 1787). RB.

4.5. Samuel Smith after Thomas Leitch. *A View of Charles-Town, the Capital of South Carolina.* Etching and engraving, 1776. AP.

4.6. Bénoit Louis Prévost after Pierre Eugène Du Simitière. Portrait of John Dickinson. Engraving, 1781. APEC.

4.7. John Vanderlyn after Gilbert Stuart. Portrait of Egbert Benson. Oil on canvas, 1794–95. Courtesy of The Metropolitan Museum of Art, New York; bequest of Alphonso T. Clearwater, 1933.

4.8. [Egbert Benson.] Minutes of the proceedings of the Annapolis Convention. Draft, 11 September 1786. RBEC nos. 9398–99.

4.9. John Trumbull. Portrait of Alexander Hamilton. Oil on canvas, ca. 1804–1808. Courtesy of The Metropolitan Museum of Art, New York; gift of Henry G. Marquand, 1881.

4.10. [Alexander Hamilton for the Annapolis Convention.] "Address to the legislatures of Virginia, Delaware, Pennsylvania, New Jersey and New York." 14 September 1786. RBEC no. 9402.

4.11. *An Act for Appointing Deputies from This Commonwealth . . .* (23 November 1786). RB.

4.12. James Madison. "Vices of the Political System of the U. States." Fair copy, April–June 1787. Transcript prepared by Joel Barlow. RB.

5.1. Artist unknown. *A Plan of the City of Syracuse Besieged by the Athenians.* Engraving in Charles Rollin, *The Ancient History of the Egyptians, Carthaginians, Assyrians . . . ,* vol. III (London: J. and F. Rivington, 1774). GRD.

5.2. Thomas Jefferson. A list of books for a private library (detail), contained in a letter to Robert Skipwith, 3 August 1771. RB.

5.3. Jean Louis de Lolme. *The Constitution of England . . .* (London: G. Kearsley and J. Ridley, 1777). GRD.

5.4. William Faithorne. Portrait of Oliver Cromwell. Engraving, 1656. AP.

5.5. Sir William Blackstone. *Commentaries on the Laws of England,* vol. I (Philadelphia: Robert Bell, 1771). RB.

5.6. Robert Scott. Portrait of David Hume. Line engraving, ca. 1797. AP.

5.7. Catherine Sawbridge Macaulay. *The History of England from the Accession of James I . . .* (London: I. Nourse, 1766). GRD.

5.8. Giovanni Battista Piranesi. Column of Trajan (detail). Engraving, ca. 1770. AP.

5.9. *Plutarch's Lives,* translated by Sir Thomas North (London: George Sawbridge and Thomas Lee, 1676). RB.

5.10. Peter C. Verger after John Francis Renault. *Triumph of Liberty.* Engraving, 1796. AP.

5.11. Artist unknown. *America trampling on Oppression.* Etching, 1789. RB.

5.12. Thomas Jefferson. *Notes on the State of Virginia* (Paris, 1782 [1785]). RB.

5.13. Unknown artist after H. D. Pursell. *A Map of The United States of N. America.* Engraving in Johann David Schoepf, *Reise Durch Einige Der Mittlern Und Südlichen Vereinigten Nordamerikanischen Staaten,* vol. I (Erlangen: J. J. Palm, 1788). RB.

5.14. *Constitutions des Treize Etats-Unis de l'Amérique,* translated by Louis Alexandre, Duc de La Rochefoucauld d'Enville (Paris: Ph.-D. Pierres and Pissot, 1783). RB.

5.15. Turgot's letter in Richard Price, *Observations on . . . the American Revolution . . .* (London: T. Cadell, 1785). RB.

5.16. John Adams. *A Defence of the Constitutions of Government of the United States of America,* vol. I (London: C. Dilly, 1787). RB.

5.17. [John Stevens, Jr.?] *Examen du Gouvernement d'Angleterre, Comparé aux Constitutions des Etats-Unis* [translated by M. Fabre] (Paris: Froullé, 1789). RB.

5.18. Raphael Morghen after Georg Dillis after A. Bronzino. Portrait of Niccolò Machiavelli. Line engraving, 1795. AP.

6.1. Gilbert Stuart. Portrait of James Madison. Oil on canvas, 1822. Courtesy of the Mead Art Museum, Amherst College; bequest of Herbert L. Pratt.

6.2. James Madison. Notes on the debates in the Federal Convention, 14 July 1787. Courtesy of The Library of Congress, Washington, D.C.

6.3. John Wayles Eppes and John C. Payne. Notes of debates in the Federal Convention of 1787 by a member. Letterpress copy, 1791–1836. RB.

6.4. Attributed to John Norman, *The Grand Convention.* Woodcut, 1787. RB.

6.5. Attributed to Elkanah Tisdale. *Convention at Philadelphia.* Engraving, ca. 1823. GRD.

6.6. Attributed to James Sharples. Portrait of Richard Dobbs Spaight. Pastel on paper, ca. 1796–97. Courtesy of Independence National Historical Park Collection, Philadelphia.

6.7. Letter from George Wythe to Edmund Randolph, Williamsburg, 16 June 1787. RBEC no. 9542.

6.8. James Barton Longacre after Robert Edge Pine. Portrait of George Read. Stipple engraving, ca. 1834. AP.

6.9. The Virginia Plan as reported out of the Committee of the Whole. Working copy, 13 June 1787. RBEC no. 9582.

6.10. Unknown artist after Ralph Earl. Portrait of Roger Sherman. Watercolor on ivory, ca. 1810–1820. Courtesy of Yale University Art Gallery, Lelia A. and John Hill Morgan Collection.

6.11. William Satchwell Leney after Joseph Wood. Portrait of Rufus King. Stipple engraving, 1815. AP.

6.12. Letter from James Madison to Ambrose Madison, Philadelphia, 18 July 1787. RB.

6.13. James Barton Longacre after Jean Pierre Henri Elouis. Portrait of James Wilson. Watercolor on artist board, ca. 1825. Courtesy of the National Portrait Gallery, Smithsonian Institution, Washington, D.C.

6.14. James Peale. Portrait of John Rutledge. Oil on ivory, 1780–1790. Courtesy of the J. B. Speed Art Museum, Louisville, Kentucky.

6.15. W. Ralph. *Negroes just landed from a Slave Ship.* Line engraving, 1808. AP.

6.16. James Akin after James Earle. *General Pinckney late Envoy Extraordinary to the French Republic.* Stipple engraving, 1799. AP.

6.17. John Vanderlyn. Portrait of Elbridge Gerry. Black chalk on paper, 1798. Courtesy of The Fogg Art Museum, Harvard University; purchase, Louise E. Bettens Fund.

6.18. Attributed to James Sharples. Portrait of Gouverneur Morris. Pastel on paper, ca. 1800. Courtesy of the City of Bristol Museum and Art Gallery, England.

6.19. *The Pennsylvania Packet and Daily Advertiser.* Philadelphia, 19 September 1787. RB.

6.20. Alexander Hamilton. "Plan of a constitution for America." Draft, September 1787. RB.

7.1. Artist unknown. *The Rising Glory of the AMERICAN EMPIRE.* Woodcut, 1788. RB.

7.2. [William Findley?] *To the Citizens of Philadelphia.* Broadside, 1787. RB.

7.3. Artist unknown. *The Federal Pillars.* Woodcut, 1 March 1788. RB.

7.4. Paul Sandby after Governor Thomas Pownall. *A View in Hudson's River of Pakepsey & the Catts-Kill Mountains.* Line engraving, 1761. AP, Eno Collection.

7.5. Charles Balthazar Julien Fevret de Saint-Mémin. *View of Richmond.* Etching with wash, 1804–1807. APSC.

7.6. Lawrence Sully. Portrait of Patrick Henry. Watercolor on ivory, 1795. Courtesy of the Mead Art Museum, Amherst College.

7.7. Charles Balthazar Julien Fevret de Saint-Mémin. Portrait of Governor George Clinton. Black and white crayon on paper with wash, ca. 1797–98. Courtesy of The Metropolitan Museum of Art, New York; anonymous gift.

7.8. Gilbert Livingston. "Notes for a speech," 24 June 1788. RB.

7.9. North Carolina's call for a Declaration of Rights. Broadside, 1788. RBEC no. 9583.

7.10. Artist unknown. *The federal Ship Union.* Woodcut in *American Museum,* vol. IV (Philadelphia: Mathew Carey, 1788). RB.

7.11. Artist unknown. *The Federal Procession in New York, 1788.* Engraving in Martha J. Lamb, *History of the City of New York* (New York: A. S. Barnes & Co., 1877). GRD.

7.12. *In Honour of American Beer and Cyder.* In *American Museum,* vol. IV (Philadelphia: Mathew Carey, 1788). RB.

7.13. [Noah Webster.] *A Examination into the Leading Principles of the Federal Constitution . . .* (Philadelphia: Prichard & Hall, 1787). RB.

7.14. *A Letter of His Excellency Edmund Randolph, Esquire, on the Federal Constitution* (Richmond: A. Davis, 1787). RB.

7.15. [John Jay.] *An Address to the People of the State of New-York, On the Subject of the Constitution . . .* (New York: Samuel and John Loudon, 1788). RB.

7.16. *Observations Leading to a Fair Examination of the System of Government . . . in a number of Letters from the Federal Farmer to the Republican* ([New York: Thomas Greenleaf,] 1787). RB.

7.17. Luther Martin. *The Genuine Information . . . Relative to the Proceedings of the General Convention, Lately Held at Philadelphia* (Philadelphia: Eleazer Oswald, 1788). RB.

7.18. [Mercy Otis Warren.] *Observations on the New Constitution, and on the Federal and State Conventions* (New York, reprint, 1788). RB.

7.19. Cornelius Tiebout after Gilbert Stuart. Portrait of John Jay. Stipple engraving, 1795. APEC.

7.20. [John Jay.] *The Federalist* No. 64. Draft, 1787–88. Courtesy of The New-York Historical Society, New York.

7.21. [Alexander Hamilton, James Madison, and John Jay.] *The Federalist: A Collection of Essays Written in Favour of the New Constitution . . . ,* vol. I (New York: J. & A. M'Lean, 1788). RB.

7.22. [John Jay.] *The Federalist* No. 2 (fragment) [Richmond: John Dixon, 1787?]. RB.

7.23. [James Madison.] *The Federalist* No. 10 (detail), in *The New-York Packet,* 23 November 1787. RB.

7.24. Alexander Hamilton, James Madison, and John Jay. *Le Fédéraliste . . . ,* vol. I (Paris: Buisson, 1792). RB.

8.1. James Trenchard after Charles Willson Peale. *An East View of Gray's Ferry, near Philadelphia, with the Triumphal Arches, &c. erected for the Reception of General Washington, April 20th 1789.* Line engraving, 1789. Courtesy of The Library of Congress, Washington, D.C.

8.2. Amos Doolittle after Peter LaCour. *Federal Hall The Seat of Congress.* Line engraving, 1790. APSC.

8.3. Artist unknown. *Washington Giving the Laws to America.* Etching and engraving, ca. 1800. APMC.

8.4. *Reports of Alexander Hamilton, Esq. . . .* (London: J. Debrett, 1795). RB.

8.5. Artist unknown. *Cong[re]ss Embark'd on board the Ship Constitution of America . . .* Engraving, 1790. Courtesy of The Library of Congress, Washington, D.C.

8.6. *A Bill to Establish the Judicial Courts of the United States* (New York: Thomas Greenleaf, 1789). RB.

8.7. Resolution by the New York Assembly to apply to Congress for a convention to amend the Constitution. Albany, 5 February 1789. RBEC 9584.

8.8. The Bill of Rights. Engrossed copy, September 1789. RBEC unnumbered.

8.9. *The Picture Exhibition.* Broadside (Albany: Charles R. and George Webster, 1790). RB.

8.10. Samuel Hill after Jonathan Edes. *View of the triumphal Arch and Colonnade, erected in Boston.* Line engraving with wash, 1790. AP.

8.11. Letter from George Washington to Jabez Bowen, New York, 27 December 1789. GWP.

8.12. *Ratification of the Constitution of the United States by the Convention of the State of Rhode-Island and Providence-Plantations* (Newport, 1790). RBEC 9586.

ACKNOWLEDGMENTS

THIS BOOK is an integral part of The New York Public Library's project to commemorate the bicentennial of the Constitution of the United States. The Bicentennial Project's central feature is a major historical exhibition embodying the arguments presented in these pages and drawn primarily from the Library's extensive collections of original manuscript, printed, and pictorial sources for the history and culture of the eighteenth-century United States.

The Bicentennial Project originated with Vartan Gregorian, President and Chief Executive Office of the Library, and Richard B. Morris, Gouverneur Morris Professor of History Emeritus at Columbia University, editor of *The Papers of John Jay,* and Co-Chairman of Project '87.

A remarkable community of scholars, administrators, curators, government officials, and enthusiasts provided help of all kinds. A twenty-three-member National Advisory Committee offered stimulating and invaluable advice: Bernard Bailyn, Adams University Professor, Harvard University; Derrick A. Bell, Jr., Harvard Law School; Charles L. Black, Jr., Columbia University Law School; Patricia U. Bonomi, Department of History, New York University; William T. Coleman, Jr., Esq., O'Melveny and Myers, Washington, D.C.; Henry Steele Commager, Simpson Lecturer in History, Amherst College; Hon. Wilfred Feinberg, Chief Judge, U.S. Court of Appeals for the Second Circuit; John Hope Franklin, James B. Duke University Professor, Duke University; Hon. Ruth Bader Ginsburg, Circuit Judge, U.S. Court of Appeals for the District of Columbia Circuit; Gerald Gunther, William N. Cromwell Professor of Law, Stanford Law School; George L. Haskins, Biddle Professor of Law, University of Pennsylvania Law School; Hon. A. Leon Higginbotham, Jr., Circuit Judge, U.S. Court of Appeals for the Third Circuit; Stanley N. Katz, President, American Council of Learned Societies; Linda K. Kerber, Department of History, University of Iowa; Paul J. Mishkin, Heller Professor of Law, School of Law, University of California at Berkeley; William E. Nelson, New York University Law School; Hon. Louis H. Pollak, U.S. District Judge, U.S. District Court for the Eastern District of Pennsylvania; Robert A. Rutland, Department of History, University of Virginia; Simon Schama, Department of History, Harvard University; Benno C. Schmidt, Jr., President, Yale University; Cyrus Vance, Esq., Simpson, Thacher & Bartlett, New York City; Hon. Patricia M. Wald, Chief Judge, U.S. Court of Appeals for the District of Columbia Circuit; Bernard Wolfman, Fessenden Professor of Law, Harvard Law School. Special thanks are also due to Professor Gaspare J. Saladino of the University of Wisconsin-Madison, coeditor of the *Documentary History of the Ratification of the Constitution and the Bill of Rights,* for his good advice and willingness to share his project's research with us.

We also wish to thank the many lending institutions for their co-operation: Professor Frank Trapp and the staff of the Mead Art Museum, Amherst College; André Miquel of the Bibliothèque Nationale, Paris; Karen Holtzman and Richard Dowd of The Catalogue of American Portraits, the Smithsonian Institution; Francis Greenacre of the City of Bristol Museum and Art Gallery; Professor Henry S. Martin, III, Librarian and Professor of Law, Harvard Law School; Bernice Loss, Harvard Law School Art Collection; Ada Bortoluzzi, Harvard University Art Museums; Louise Todd Ambler, Harvard University Portrait Collection; Hobart C. Cawood, Robert K. Sutton, David Kimball, John C. Milley, and Shirley A. Mays, Independence National Historical Park; Daniel J. Boorstin, John C. Broderick, James H. Hutson, Ingrid Maar, John Sellers, and Donna Elliot of the Library of Congress; Colta Ives, Suzanne Boorsch, and John K. Howat of the Metropolitan Museum of Art; Jane Hankins and Patricia Loiko of the Museum of Fine Arts, Boston; Beverly J. Cox and Suzanne Jenkins of the National Portrait Gallery; Dr. James B. Bell, Paul Cohen, Jean Ashton, Mary Alice MacKay, and Katherine C. Naylor of The New-York Historical Society; Melanie Prejean of the J. B. Speed Art Museum; Clement E. Conger and Kathryn A. McCutchen of the Diplomatic Reception Rooms, U.S. Department of State; Charles F. Hummel of The Henry Francis Du Pont Winterthur Museum; and Michael Komanecky and William Cuffe of the Yale University Art Gallery.

At every level members of the Central Research Library of The New York Public Library contributed their enthusiasm and support. Foremost among them are the staff of the Exhibition Program Office: Diantha D. Schull, Manager of Exhibitions; Richard Newman; Susan Saidenberg; Albina De Meio; Joseph Arkins; Lou Storey; Myriam de Arteni; Edward Rime; Rich Rubin; Barbara Bergeron; Jeanne Bornstein; Jill Entis; and Lauren Stringer. Lawrence P. Murphy of the Exhibition Program Office organized the task of photographing items from the Library's collections for inclusion in this book, and Robert D. Rubic took the photographs. We also wish to thank Donald Anderle, Associate Director for Special Collections; Bernard McTigue, Curator of the Arents Collections; Susan Davis, John D. Stinson, Anastacio Teodoro III, and Melanie Yolles of the Manuscript and Archives Section, Rare Books and Manuscripts Division; Francis O. Mattson, John Rathe, Miriam Mandelbaum, and Dan Tierney of the Rare Books Section, Rare Books and Manuscripts Division; Roberta Waddell and Robert Rainwater of the Art, Prints and Photographs Division; Alice Hudson of the Map Division; Howard Dodson, Robert C. Morris, Julia Hotton, and Deborah Willis-Ryan of the Schomburg Center; Rodney Phillips of the General Research Division; Lola Szladits of the Berg Collection; Gregory Long, Harold Snedcof, Susan Rautenberg, Trudy Hayden, Jay Golan, and Anne Asdahl of the Development Office; David Cronin, Nicole Aron, Nina Morais, and Christopher Packard of the Public Education Program; Betsy Pinover and Shellie Goldberg of the Public Relations Office; Marilan Lund of the Graphics Office; Marie Sexton, Paul Goren, Susan Linder, and Myrna Martin of the Public Affairs and Development Office; and Louis Mintz and the legion of pages and assistants who work in the stacks of the Central Research Library. All these people demonstrate each day why The New York Public Library is one of the world's great research institutions.

We are also grateful to J. Carter Bacot and Allis Wolfe of The Bank of New York; Tom Phelps and Malcolm Richardson of the National Endowment for the Humanities; Professor Vernon F. Snow of Syracuse University, Trustee of The John Ben Snow Memorial Trust; and Peggy Barber, Associate Executive Director for Communications of the American Library Association.

Many other people contributed to this book and the Project: The New York University School of Law's Legal History Colloquium, Professors Norman F. Cantor and Darline G. Levy of New York University's Department of History, and Professor John Phillip Reid of New York University School of Law provided additional suggestions and ideas.

Dennis G. Combs and Ed Rime read the entire manuscript, and Maureen K. Phillips, Joseph Newpol, Marilee B. Huntoon, Thomas C. Mackey, Veronica Bailey, and Mary P. Commager read large parts of it—a testimony of friendship that needs no elaboration. Ene Sirvet, associate editor of *The Papers of John Jay*, offered many ideas and useful criticisms. Barbara W. Kern, Mark Rice, Steve Faber, Lucy Ann Craig, Edward D. Young III, Gina Tillman-Young, Tim and Terry Hanford, Ken Forbus, Marian D. LeBlanc, Tamara Jacobs Bell, Kevin Griffin, Susan Stein, Chris Miles, Michael G. Psareas, Andrew Paul Rubenfeld. Joel Solomon, Jane Hatterer, Frederick Mandler, and Allen P. Grunes provided friendship and moral support. K. C. McDaniel of the New York Bar gave trenchant criticisms. Donald F. X. Finn of Natchez, Mississippi, a faithful friend of both the Constitution and the Bicentennial, shared his vast knowledge of both subjects with us, as did Leonard Rapport of the National Archives. We also wish to thank Sheilah Mann and Cynthia Harrison of Project '87, Wilcomb E. Washburn of the Smithsonian Institution, Professor Stephen L. Schechter of Russell Sage College, and photographer Enid M. France. Because new books cannot be written without a steady supply of old books, we also thank Marsha Shapiro of the Argosy Book Shop, Tom Weatherly of the Strand Book Store, Jack Biblo of Biblo Books, Alan Marks, and the staff of the Isaac Mendoza Book Company.

Aida Donald, Elizabeth Suttell, Marianne Perlak, and especially Ann Hawthorne of Harvard University Press turned our manuscripts and photographs into a real book, preserving good humor and a steady commitment.

The work and personal examples of Professors Henry Steele Commager, Richard B. Morris, and William E. Nelson have inspired this book. We cannot thank them adequately for their friendship and concern. The same is true of Professor John Sexton of New York University School of Law, who provided intellectual encouragement and unstinting friendship, and in many other ways made the completion of this book possible.

Jed Sexton and Dave Cavalier heard early versions of the arguments presented here; their incisive questions and growing fascination with the subject made this book much better. Kathleen Spencer and Nathan Spencer time and again administered healing doses of sanity, humor, and perspective; they, too, listened patiently but criticially and set things straight more than once. Someday Christa, Adam, and Noah Tillman-Young will read this book; while it was being written, they all were living reminders that there is more to life than a word-processor screen and a stack of unrevised manuscripts.

Errors of fact and viewpoint that slipped by these friendly critics are our fault alone.

Richard B. Bernstein
Kym S. Rice

INDEX

Franklin, Benjamin (*cont.*)
    writings, 14, 24, 137; as a diplomat, 33,
    34, 132, 138, 144; and Federal Conven-
    tion, 152, 166–167, 171, 184, 185, 186;
    and U.S. Constitution, 202, 223
French and Indian War (1755–1763), 17
Fugitive slave clause (U.S. Constitution), 177

Gallatin, Albert, 128
Galloway, James, 17
Gardoqui, Don Diego de, 84–85
Garnerey, François (1755–1837), Pl. VIII
General Court (Massachusetts). *See* Massa-
    chusetts, legislature
George III, 20, 24
Georgia, 103; colony, 13; ratification of U.S.
    Constitution, 203, 206; laws, 260; and Bill
    of Rights, 271
Gerry, Elbridge, 76; and Federal Conven-
    tion, 100, 157, 158, 179–181, 184, 185,
    186, 197; and U.S. Constitution, 207, 218,
    221, 225
Gideon, Jacob, 237
Gilman, Nicholas, 157
Goethe, Johann Wolfgang von, 129
Gordon, Thomas, 118–119, 123
Gorham, Nathaniel, Pl. XIII; and Federal
    Convention, 156, 181, 185, 186
Government, 106, 123; created by Articles
    of Confederation, 12, 24–28; proposed by
    Albany Plan of Union, 14–15; proposed
    by Paine, 49–50; proposed by J. Adams,
    49–52; created by U.S. Constitution, 170–
    175, 229; proposed by Hamilton, 194,
    196. *See also* Aristocracy; Monarchy; Re-
    publican government; Self-government;
    State governments
Government powers, 16, 120, 164, 167, 180;
    in Articles of Confederation, 12, 24, 82;
    in U.S. Constitution, 168, 170, 177, 201,
    203, 223, 228, 243–244, 256, 261, 271.
    See also Balance of power; Executive
    power; Judicial power; Legislative power;
    Separation of powers
Governors, state, 55, 56, 59, 61
Great Britain: relations with colonies, 11,
    12–13, 15–17, 19–22, 43, 44, 47, 48; rela-
    tions with United States, 2, 83–84, 86–87,
    95. *See also* American Revolution; Consti-
    tution, English; Loyalists; Treaty of Paris
    (1783)
Great Compromise, 167–170, 177
Great Lakes, access to, 84
Green, General Nathanael, 31
Greenleaf, Thomas, 223, 232, 235
Grim, David (1737–1826), Pl. XVII

Hamilton, Alexander, 4, 30, 36, 76–80; eco-

nomic thinking, 90–91, 257; writings, 103,
105, 179; and Federal Convention, 157,
172, 182, 186, 191, 192, 193–196, 197–
198; and U.S. Constitution, 205, 211, 213,
221, 230–232, 235, 237, 240, 242; as sec-
retary of the Treasury, 240–253, 254–
259, Pl. XVIII
Hancock, John, 95, 207
Harrison, Robert Hanson, 260
Harvard University, 63
Hegel, G. W. F., 136
Henderson, Archibald, 97–98
Henry, Patrick, 20, 97; and religious free-
    dom, 67–68; and U.S. Constitution, 183,
    210, 211; and Bill of Rights, 261, 271
Hesselius, John (1728–1778), Pl. IV
Hill, Samuel (active, Boston, 1789–1803),
    60, 268
Histoire Naturelle (Buffon), 113, 130, 132–
    133, 134–136
History, influence on political thought, 117–
    118, 123, 124, 129, 144
History of England (C. Macaulay), 120
History of the Two Indies (Raynal), 129–130,
    136
Hogarth, William (1697–1764), 71
Holland, John Joseph (ca.1776–1820), Pl.
    XIX
Holton, Samuel, 100
Honestus (pseudonym), 71. *See also* Austin,
    Benjamin
Hooper, William, 48
Hopkins, Stephen, 14
House of Representatives (U.S.), 223, 246,
    247, 248–249, 250, 264, 267
Human nature, 239
Hume, David, 119, 120, 121, 124, 239
Hutchinson, Thomas, 14, 16

Impeachment, 56, 160, 249
Implied powers, 256
Indentured servants, 5, 8
Independence Hall, 149
Indians, 4, 59; relations with colonies, 4–5,
    13–15, 130; opinion about, 111, 127, 134;
    relations with federal government, 249
Individual rights, 115, 179, 181, 201, 209,
    217, 221, 229, 239, 242, 264, 267, 271–
    272. *See also* Bill of Rights
Industry and state, 257
Intellectual life, 112–124, 127–136, 137
International law, 77, 78
Interstate rivalries, 11–12, 26, 82, 88, 97–
    98, 100. *See also* Boundaries, interstate ri-
    valries over
Interstate trade, 82, 88, 90, 98, 101, 105,
    191
Iredell, James, 259, 260
Iroquois Confederation, 13

Republicanism (*cont.*)
147–148, 194, 248
Revenue, 74, 164; under Articles of Confederation, 39, 82, 88, 90, 191; under U.S. Constitution, 167, 243, 248, 250, 252. *See also* Taxation
Rhode Island, 95, 97, 103; fiscal problems, 9, 82, 91–92; colony, 12, 13; and Articles of Confederation, 90–91; legislature, 91–92; and Federal Convention, 191; ratification of U.S. Constitution, 213, 271; laws, 260; and Bill of Rights, 267, 268, 271
Rittenhouse, David, 135
Rollin, Charles, 113, 119
Rule of mutability (Federal Convention), 155–156
Rule of secrecy (Federal Convention), 154–155, 157, 166, 168, 186
Rush, Benjamin, 52, 124; and slavery, 5, 127, 128
Russia, 34
Rutgers v. Weddington, 77–78
Rutledge, John, 31, 175, 260; and Federal Convention, 168, 174, 177, 181

Saint-Memin, Charles Balthazar Julien Fevret de (1770–1852), 209, 212
Sandby, Paul, 4, 208
Savage, Edward (1761–1817), 22
Schuyler, Philip, 211
Scott, Robert (active, Philadelphia, 1793–1820), 121
Sectionalism, 4, 9–10, 157, 169
Sedgwick, Theodore, 248
Self-government, 1, 81, 83, 111, 129, 138; in colonies, 13, 17, 48
Senate (U.S.), 231, 246–247, 259, 260, 267
Separation of church and state, 67–69, 89, 138, 267
Separation of powers, 43, 49, 51, 109, 140, 264; in Articles of Confederation, 26, 27–28, 160; in state constitutions, 55, 61, 112, 141; in U.S. Constitution, 160
Separatist movements, 40, 74, 82, 271
Sergeant, Jonathan Dickinson, 49
Shallus, Jacob, 184
Sharples, James (ca. 1751–1811), 156, 182, Pl. V
Shattuck, Job, 93, 94
Shays, Daniel, 93, 94, 95, 97, 158
Shays's Rebellion, 73, 82, 91, 92–97, 144, 180
Sheffield, Lord, 83
Shelburne, Sir William Petty, Marquis of Lansdowne, 75, 83
Sherman, Roger, 165; and Federal Convention, 164, 167, 171, 180–181
Shippen, Edward, 70
Shirley, William, 13, 14, 16

"Short Hints" (Franklin), 14
"Short Hints towards a Scheme for a General Union of the British Colonies on the Continent" (Weare), 14
Simitière, Pierre Eugène du (ca. 1736–1784), 101
Size, of United States, 1, 34, 223
Skipwith, Robert, 117
Slavery, 67, 181; attitudes toward, 5–6, 127–128, 177–178; in territories, 40
Slaves, 3; and representation, 26–27, 162, 167, 177–178
Slave trade, 177, 178
Smith, Adam, 120, 257
Smith, Melancton, 206, 213, 228–229
Smith, Meriwether, 99
Smith, Samuel (ca. 1745–ca. 1808), 99
Smith, William, 74
Smith, William Loughton, 248
Society for Encouraging Useful Manufactures, 257
Society of the Cincinnati, 33, 109, 127
South Carolina, 6, 103; colony, 13; legislature, 44; and Federal Convention, 168, 175, 177–178, 186; ratification of U.S. Constitution, 208; laws, 260
Southern states, 4, 5–6, 84–85, 101, 253–254; on representation, 26–27, 162, 169, 177–178; and financing government, 27, 253; and Federal Convention, 162, 169, 175, 177–178
Sovereignty: of colonies, 14; of national government, 109–110, 170, 171, 174
Sovereignty of states, 12, 170, 171, 194, 201, 261; under Articles of Confederation, 24, 27–28, 81–82, 90–91, 109
Spaight, Richard Dobbs, 155, 156
Spain: relations with United States, 33–34, 84–85; colonies of, 130
Spirit of the Laws, The (Montesquieu), 123, 128, 134
Stamp Act Congress (1765), 17
State constitutions, 21, 47, 51–52, 111–112, 137–138, 140–146, 237; bills of rights, 55–56, 59, 61, 69, 92, 180–181. *See also under individual states, e.g.,* Virginia, constitution
State conventions, to ratify U.S. Constitution, 201, 205–213
State courts, 59, 91–92, 93, 100, 174, 228
State governments, 44, 47–48, 85–86, 124, 158, 160. *See also* Sovereignty of states
State interests, 81, 157, 168, 169, 178, 191
State laws, 110, 162, 164–165, 171, 174, 260. *See also under individual states, e.g.,* New Hampshire, laws
State legislatures, 24, 129, 161, 203. *See also under individual states, e.g.,* Massachusetts, legislature
States' rights. *See* Sovereignty of states

Wythe, George (*cont.*)
 constitution, 49–50, 64, 67; and U.S. Constitution, 210, 211

Yale University, 140
Yates, Abraham, Jr., 56, 57, 192, 196–197
Yates, Robert, 56; and Federal Convention, 157, 192–194, 196–198; and U.S. Constitution, 208–209, 218, 228, 230, 231